SEVENTY YEARS OF
LIFE AND LABOR

BY THE SAME AUTHOR

LABOR MOVEMENTS AND PROBLEMS IN AMERICA. In 2 vols.

I. LABOR AND THE COMMON WELFARE

II. LABOR AND THE EMPLOYER

With William English Walling

"OUT OF THEIR OWN MOUTHS"
A Revelation and an Indictment of Sovietism.

E. P. DUTTON & COMPANY

SAMUEL GOMPERS AT 65

SEVENTY YEARS OF LIFE AND LABOR

An Autobiography

BY

SAMUEL GOMPERS

VOLUME TWO

NEW YORK
E. P. DUTTON & COMPANY
681 FIFTH AVENUE

CONTENTS

VOLUME TWO

BOOK III (*Cont'd*)

BOOK IV

BOOK V

ANALYTICAL CONTENTS

VOLUME II

LIST OF ILLUSTRATIONS

BOOK II

SEVENTY YEARS OF
LIFE AND LABOR

SEVENTY YEARS OF LIFE AND LABOR

CHAPTER XXVI

MY ECONOMIC PHILOSOPHY

THE first economic theory that came under my eyes was not calculated to make me think highly of economists. My mind intuitively rejected the iron law of wages, the immutable law of supply and demand, and similar so-called "natural laws." As a matter of fact the laws had no connection with nature or economic forces, nor were they laws but merely theories which sought to justify existing practices. Everywhere those directing industries were seeking to bring about a control that served their purposes. Those who did not participate in determination of policies were treated as industrial spoils. It was revolting to me that human beings should be used without regard to their needs or their aspirations as individuals. I love men and a sort of passion surges in me when I see them treated unjustly or forced to forego freedom in their own lives. As the control built up by holders of capital rested upon strategic economic advantage, I saw no reason why it was not just as practical for employes to mobilize and control their economic power as a counter-move. The force of such economic organization would interpose a protecting barrier against arbitrary employers who failed to understand that those who supplied human labor for industries were human beings, and thus make possible the development of constructive methods.

Organization of wage-earners brought together economic power that could force recognition of human interests. If the employer refused to recognize the needs of the workers, the result was conflict of forces. Until there is acceptance of mutual rights, the labor movement is of necessity a militant movement, and as I have often quoted, "Eternal vigilance is the price of freedom." Knowing how much depended upon the virility and the sustained efficiency of our organized economic force, I have vigilantly guarded against moves to curb or restrict economic action.

In my conception, the spirit of militancy expresses sustained consecration to a high purpose. My counsel has consistently been against assuming responsibilities that would introduce any intimation that the purposes of labor were not solely humanitarian. There were many efforts, good in themselves, which labor could help, but I have been jealous that the American labor movement should retain the character of a crusade for human justice. I know men and I love them and I also know that the effort to secure justice for the under-man must be a fight. I also keep myself in fighting trim—mentally and spiritually. My enemies say that I take blows as well as I give them. I never ask quarter nor do I hesitate to attack anyone making proposals subversive of the freedom of workers. I have fought many a fight in support of the principles of voluntary institutions.

My unfailing support of voluntary principles reflects my aversion to any theory of economic fatalism. Through years of study, observation, and work has grown my conviction that economic organization must be based upon an understanding of all factors concerned in production—materials, power, and human workers, and that research holds the key to additional scientific information. Experience has disclosed to me the potency of information and intelligence in directing economic development. I have seen this intelligence in the making.

My span of life includes a series of industrial periods marked by panics, business depression, and wide-spread unemployment followed by a period of recuperation leading gradually to a return of "prosperity," better wages, and general employment. The period of depression was often called a period of so-called overproduction, which was really a period of underconsumption for the people I knew, a period of hard times. When I came to the United States in 1863, war-time high prices were developing. I was too young and too new to the country to get much of the meaning of things. But when the crash of 1873 came, I could see the whole industrial structure stagger, shattered by the forces of contraction. The puny trade unions of that day were ground to powder by some national force that seemed above control. Our wages kept on going down until 1877 when we undertook drastic action to stabilize conditions. A period of slow upbuilding followed. Then came the panic of 1893 followed by that of 1907 and the depression of 1921 and 1922.

In a country as big and as fertile as ours, with so many willing workers seeking the chance to give service, the periods of unemployment accompanying depression in the business cycle have seemed to me an unnecessary blot upon American institutions, presenting a challenge to all our claims to progress, humanity, and civilization. Unemployment means irrecoverable waste of forces and materials— human as well as economic—not only of production but of all civilization.

When the panic of 1893 crashed down upon us, I was holding a responsible labor position and consequently was in touch with attempts to meet resulting problems. In New York, distress from unemployment was acute.

When late in the summer of 1893 abnormal conditions of unemployment became alarming, I wrote Governor Roswell P. Flower, urging him to call a special session of the Legislature to consider the unemployment and to determine upon relief measures. But the Governor—who was a banker—did not decide favorably upon the suggestion and the great industrial state of New York devised no constructive policy with which to meet the emergency.

I suggested to the labor organizations of New York that we arrange an unemployment demonstration to be held in Madison Square Garden. This place was chosen to typify the size of the problem. The meeting was held and an immense crowd gathered. When the speaking began another problem was manifest. Henry Weismann was the first speaker. Weismann was splendidly developed physically, and had a stentorian voice which never modulated whether speaking of human freedom or the death of a fly. He made a brilliant beginning, but only lasted a few minutes. Then Dr. Felix Adler spoke, but not a word was heard. Others had the same fate. The audience waited patiently perhaps because they had no employment elsewhere. When my time came, no one expected to hear me, but without an effort every word of mine rang through the immense building. It reminded me of a mass meeting years before called by the cigarmakers. The Socialists had organized a concerted effort to prevent any speaker from being heard. One man tried to speak, but couldn't be heard. I was standing by him and knowing the impatience of the crowd, I said to him, "Talk or——." "I can't be heard," he replied. "Get away then and let me talk," I rejoined and sweeping him aside I earnestly discussed the issues. It was not ruthlessness or lack of consideration on my part. I was simply too much engrossed with the cause to consider anyone or anything. That Madison Square speech was one of the few in which passion dominated my judgment. I was seething against injustice done to human beings. I deeply resented the conditions of life which permitted children of tender years to be employed in trades and callings, and exemplified in my own life when I was permitted to go to work at a trade when I was a little more than ten years of age. When put to work at that age, I had no understanding of the wrong done to childhood, but the inhumanity of it I have felt more keenly with every year of my life. This realization accounts for the intensity of feeling in all my activities to safeguard the child life of my country and of all the countries of the world.

Next to the intensity of my desire to protect child life was my resentment of unemployment, particularly unemployment in the United States. In such a country with all its resources, richness of its soil, almost boundless areas of its territory, with all the achievements of past ages, utilized in the high development of modern production, that millions of men and women, willing to work, to produce and to give service not only for their own maintenance and those dependent upon them but service to the whole country and to the people of the entire world, were denied the opportunity to give that work and service, was a blight upon our boasted intelligence and civilization.

The factory and mines were there, tools and machinery were at hand, raw materials were waiting to be converted into articles of service, human workers were clamoring for work and opportunity to earn a living, but some blighting power halted industry, and men, women, and children must suffer want. It was brutally stupid.

The whole situation had forced upon me a feeling of outrage. If a blight came as an act of nature or what is termed an act of God, there could be no just cause for criticism or complaint or protest. But in a country such as ours, rich as a nation could be, when large masses of our citizenship were forced to endure hunger because unemployed, my protest knew no bounds.

Such was my state of agonized feeling in my early manhood I would not have hesitated in entering into any undertaking that would bring about a radical change and make amends for a state so horrid in a country of intelligence and civilization.

At that great mass meeting of the unemployed I indulged myself in an attack upon the conditions, misery, and poverty by which we were surrounded and of which I was at times one of the victims. In the bitterness of my soul, in the course of my speech I rendered with the most dramatic inflections I could command the following lines:

Oh, that a poor man's son as has been said,
Became a convict to earn his bread,
That a poor man's daughter to earn a crust
Became a victim of some rich man's lust.
Oh, angels shut thine eyes,
Let conflagration illumine the outraged skies!
Let red Nemesis burn the hellish clan
And chaos end the slavery of man!

The state of mind of the audience, nearly half of whom were unemployed, was such that at the conclusion of my address I doubt if there was one person who was not on his feet, cheering and shouting his approval. It was a wild scene, there was not one among them but was in an ugly frame of mind. I could not imagine the lengths to which, under the influence due to their own misery and my harangue, they might have gone. The responsibility of my utterance haunted me not only that night but for many a day after.

When I now contemplate the exploitations of child life to satiate greed of exploiters, when I think of the unemployment of millions of willing workers, there is no abatement of my feeling of resentment, but I realize that relief of such conditions will not come by burning the "hellish clan" but by constructive effort and gradual upbuilding. I have tried to impress upon my fellow-workers to organize for self-protection and promotion of their rights and interests and to make these organizations strong and effective.

The same deep sentiment and resentment which the exploitation of child life and imposition of idleness upon millions of people rouse in me I feel too in respect to the demands which have so frequently been made to impose compulsory labor in any form upon the people. As an eleven-year old boy in a factory in England, I heard from my elder shopmates the denunciation of slavery in America. I had learned the anti-slavery songs and sang them in resonant tones. When I was brought with my parents and brothers to the United States July 29, 1863, the spirit for the abolition of slavery had already found its lodgment within me. I prepared as a boy to use whatever influence I had that slavery not only be abolished in the

United States but never re-established—at least, not without my most emphatic protest no matter where that protest might lead.

During the fall and winter of 1893, there was widespread unemployment such as I had never seen before.

When the convention of the Federation met in Chicago in the fall of 1893, we held our sessions in the old City Hall. When the session of the convention ended for the day, there were hundreds of homeless, workless men seeking refuge in the corridors. When we held evening sessions, as the elevators did not run at night, we had to walk down the stairs very carefully for we had to pick our way over men who were lying on the steps and on the floor with only newspapers for protection. It was a scene that burned into my mind. But the labor unions weathered the storm and industrial standards were not completely overthrown. The unemployment was terrible, but the idea that panics were the result of uncontrollable and unknowable forces was passing.

When the session of the New York Legislature began the winter of 1893, I watched its deliberations carefully. Thomas C. Platt, president of the United States Express Company, was then a member of the Senate and controlled the Republican state party machine. When adjournment was approaching, there was no evidence of any constructive thought upon the unemployment problem. Even the appropriation bills carrying funds for public works were unpassed. Now I had no love for Platt and knew he had none for labor—but regardless of this, if Platt could do anything for the unemployed I was willing to use him as an instrumentality. I wrote him, asking that he consider the advisability of enacting legislation to appropriate money for public work, for I reminded him it would be bad policy to add to unemployment by failure to act upon the measure.

As I considered these facts, they seemed to me to indicate the necessity for a sustained policy of wage-increases in order that consumption levels should be maintained commensurate with the increases in production levels, and that credit control should be based upon production needs rather than upon speculative gain.

General stagnation of business which followed the financial storm was terrific, and was manifest in industry, construction, and all employing concerns, which slowed down if they did not stop. Family bread-earners walked the streets. There was an appalling amount of destitution and suffering. All kinds of people were without work. There was a curious money scarcity. There seemed to be plenty of everything but money and confidence or credit. Those of us who had no Wall Street connections were somewhat blindly sure there was a money trust somewhere and that we were its victims. Our whole economic structure was paralyzed. Workingmen all over the country found themselves without work or money. They were helpless in the clutches of some invisible power.

In the West where there had been rapid building of railroads, numbers of men from the East suddenly found themselves adrift. There was nothing to do anywhere, so the men determined to come East. Men traveling the road without money naturally fell into step together. They shared the benefits of their ingenuity as well as their common misfortune. Outwardly, they were bands of homeless vagabonds roaming the country. There was a picturesque element in the situation that lent itself to publicity. The newspapers gave it much space. Someone conceived the idea of utilizing the eastward movement of the unemployed as a national demonstration to focus attention on the need for relief measures.

By some mysterious folk-agreement in all parts of the country, there was a general determination to take the problem to Congress—to present a "petition in boots". Men wanted work and a financial system that would function. They had faith in the power of Congress. Some one of the bands called itself the Army of the Unemployed. The idea caught popular favor. Each group of marchers was called an army and leaders appeared. There were Frey of California, Kelly from the Northwest, Coxey from Ohio. The men who rallied to these standards were not all fanatics, vagrants, or professional hoboes. The men were for the most part earnest, thoughtful men, skilled workmen, and only the minority belonged to the migratory element. There were expert machinists, miners, and practically every kind of craftsman.

As the armies went eastward through the country, their approach was heralded days in advance of their appearance. In some localities they were treated kindly, fed, and given other hospitality. In other places, they were not permitted to enter towns, but were hastened onward by police. The "powers that be" were watching anxiously. If the armies ever broke through the ludicrous interpretation which the press fastened upon them, there were present some of the elements of which revolutions are made.

General Coxey of Ohio who had a specific plan for good roads and the inauguration of a system of long-needed public works, became the central figure of the movement. He had a fine stock farm at Massillon, Ohio. Associated with him was Carl Brown from the Pacific Coast who had

married the daughter of General Coxey. I had met Brown
in California. He was a man of parts, a big-hearted lover
of men, a dreamer and an idealist. Early in the spring,
Coxey and Brown were in Indianapolis where headquarters
had been established at the Circle House. A mass meeting
in Indianapolis was addressed by Debs and Howard of the
American Railway Union. The provisional committee had
planned for a march of all bands to Washington and a
National Labor Congress in that city on July 4, 1894.
They were soliciting the co-operation of all labor organizations in that Congress. I had several letters from both
Brown and Frey asking me to endorse the plan and seeking
to show that the Chicago Convention of the A. F. of
L. had endorsed the Coxey good-roads plan. I never
officially endorsed their program, but I went to Washington to consult with General Coxey and to help him get
a hearing. On behalf of his good-roads project I went
personally to many Representatives and Senators and urged
the right of petition. I held that the unemployed had come
to Washington to exercise the rights of free citizens, to
present their grievances and ask for redress, and that they
had the right to a hearing. I spoke to several divisions of
the army camped outside of Washington. At one time
when I was speaking to the army, a collection was gathered
to relieve the urgent physical needs of the unemployed. I
emptied my pockets without a thought as to my own needs.
I had to walk back to town and go to my son's house.
Then I got supper, stayed all night, and borrowed enough
money to take me back to New York. An arrangement was
made for a parade and a great open air meeting to be held
in the Capitol grounds where Coxey spoke from the steps.
A little later a few of the "soldiers" of the unemployed

stepped on the grass and were arrested and the army began to melt away. This was the only answer the government gave to an urgent problem which lay at the very foundation of national progress.

Coxey returned to his stock farm. Brown went to Sacramento where he huddled in a shack, working over a flying machine he was perfecting. I met him there during one of my trips and he told me all about his invention. After it was completed he brought it to Washington for a demonstration in order to realize on his work. On that long protracted mission Brown became a well-known figure in the halls of the Capitol and on the streets of Washington where he was a frequent speaker in open-air meetings. The organized labor movement kept on working to alleviate unemployment and to better conditions of employment.

Wage-earners had to bear the consequences of the mismanagement and wrong-doings of others. Though I felt that industry was responsible, there was not at the time sufficient data to establish the case—unemployment attending the period of depression was then considered unavoidable. The theory was repeatedly advanced, that the cause of the situation was to be found in the money question, but I felt sure there was some more fundamental cause. I felt that there was some maladjustment in industry that was responsible. In 1897 I wrote for the *Forum*:

During the industrial stagnation of the past four years, the organizations of labor have performed a service to the people of our country for which they have never received recognition, and for which, perhaps, they will never receive the gratitude to which they are justly entitled. One of the great causes of this stagnation —if not the greatest cause—was undoubtedly the fact that the productive power of the workers progressed at a greater ratio than their ability—or rather their opportunity—to consume. In other words, there exists in our economic system the evil sometimes called "overproduction" but which might be more correctly termed "under-consumption." For, were the consumptive power of the workers to keep better pace with their productive ability, the anomalies of a people going a-hungered with ever-recurring industrial, commercial, and financial panics, crises, and stagnation—in the midst of plenty —would be unknown.

In 1903 I noted indications of a recurring period of depression and in my report to the Boston Convention declared it the height of economic unwisdom to curtail the consuming power of the masses, because no industry or country could become great if founded upon poverty. Based upon my conception that wage rates can be used as a stabilizing force, I recommended that the working people should resist any attempt to reduce their wages or increase their hours of work, and embodied that slogan in the parody:

> It is better to resist and lose
> Than not to resist at all.

A short time after the convention the annual meeting of the National Civil Federation was held. Somehow I felt that that meeting was especially called so that I might have the opportunity of revising the thought which I had recommended to the Boston Convention, and that the hope was entertained that through the influence of my surroundings I would modify my declarations or the declaration of the convention.

With that feeling strong within me, and in resentment of that assumption, in the most emphatic terms I repeated the declaration that labor would resist reductions in wages, let the consequences be what they may. During my talk the scenes that I witnessed in several places and particularly in Chicago came to me vividly and I portrayed them as best I could: the thousands upon thousands of unemployed, hungry workmen, protesting, demanding work instead of charity or the soup houses, and all that damnable situation which brought millions of our people into a state of unemployment, without homes and hungry. To finish I said something like this: "And by the gods, such a condition of affairs shall never be repeated in the United States if I can help in any way to prevent it." With the finishing of this sentence Bishop Potter, who was in the meeting, picked up his hat and hurriedly walked out with a very much flushed face. I learned that he understood that I had blasphemed and taken the name of the Lord in vain.

When the business crisis came in 1907, I was prepared to make good use of my experiences. One of the functions of the annual meetings of the National Civic Federation is a dinner which is attended by important employers, big financiers, trade unionists, and many people well known nationally. The dinner furnished an extraordinarily advantageous stage from which to make a declaration for which I wanted national consideration. There were fully four hundred there talking conventionalities, men and women in evening clothes, the women gorgeous in gleaming jewels. Never have I felt more peculiarly alone. I was conscious that I was the spokesman of the "working class" and I didn't care how I startled or shocked the millionaires if I protected my fellows. I was ruthless in what I intended to do. The fire of the revolutionary was burning through me as I rose to make labor's reply to the careful, smug suggestions of retrenchment and wage reductions as the way out of the industrial stagnation. I fairly flung defiance at the buccaneers of industry as I declared, "Labor will not submit to any wage reductions."

That dinner party gasped. On the days that followed Wall Street considered. Wage-earners throughout the country heard the rallying call, and stiffened their backbones. Up and down the country went the slogan, "No wage reductions," like a fiery cross. A stabilizing element was injected into cumulative forces that like witches were stirring the cauldron of panic.

The Carriage and Wagon Drivers of New York were out on strike at that time. Marcus M. Marks was chairman of the Committee on Conciliation of the National Civic Federation and he called the employers and the drivers into conference. I knew of this conference, but I could not participate in it because of my other activities. Mr. Marks was a fairly liberal employer and was always helpful in conciliating and adjusting disputes between employers and unions of workmen, but he was seldom helpful in his own industry.

In the dispute to which I have referred, the union of the drivers had been suspended from the Brotherhood of Teamsters and Stablemen and it was therefore not in direct or indirect affiliation to the A. F. of L. Mr. Marks came to me one evening just at the close of the meeting of the day and said, "Mr. Gompers, I have some interesting information to give you. You know of the conferences which have been held for the purpose of adjusting the differences between the drivers and their employers. Notwithstanding the fact that they are not part of your Federation, with the opening of the proceedings the spokesman for the union announced: 'We will arbitrate everything except wages. Our chief, President Gompers, has declared that we are forbidden to accept any reduction in wages.' "

The dispute between the union and their employers

was adjusted by Mr. Marks without any change in the wages of the men.

The result of the 1907 experience convinced me that panics and business depression can be controlled, perhaps avoided, if we know contributing causes. I felt there must be certain fundamental principles of industrial order to which we could cling at such times. But I had to wait many years before I saw a comprehensive effort launched to study periods of depression and to determine principles of intelligent control. That came with the World War aftermath. Again labor opposed wage reductions and was fairly successful in holding normal increases. By this time management had begun to appreciate that maintaining wage levels means maintaining a stable purchasing demand and hence is a stabilizing force. Wage reductions by decreasing demand adds impetus to the trend toward business depression. On the other hand, gradual wage increases tend to absorb increases in production. It is my opinion based upon six decades of experience that the future will bring progressively high wage levels with gradual price decreases. Our financial problems during the transition from war to peace organization were handled by the Federal Reserve Board in such a way as to avoid any financial crash, but the period was ushered in by wide-spread depression and unemployment. In the Unemployment Conference that was called under the leadership of Herbert C. Hoover, Secretary of Commerce, attention was turned to the problem of major consideration—how to organize industry so as to achieve stability of employment.

I went into the conference hopeful that something could be done to promote that spirit of co-operation necessary for working out the problems of industry. The representatives of reaction predominated in the conference and they opposed every suggestion I made with a systematic if not intelligent consistency, characteristic of the "open-shop" movement, then at its height. In the Committee on Manufactures on which I served, I introduced three resolutions which could not be designated as destructively revolutionary. The resolutions advocated: first, uniform system of cost accounting so there might be available comparable bases of production information; second, that all parties accept the challenge implied in the report on the Elimination of Waste in Industry by the Federated American Engineering Societies and join in the practical work of eliminating causes of high production costs in industry; and third, the compilation of unemployment statistics by government agencies.

The employer members of my committee as a unit opposed my proposals. When I saw their attitude, I determined to test them to the limit and I resorted to every rule of parliamentary tactics to try their metal. They defeated my resolutions, but they did not contribute credit to their own cause. They made it impossible for the conference to make recommendation embodying the most enlightened thought on industrial problems. When I contrast industrial conditions of the ten years following the war between the states and the conditions now, I am convinced that tendencies can be controlled in accord with principles developed through experience and study. As our knowledge widens, we shall be able to establish a stable industrial order in which organizations of wage-earners will be an integral part.

At no time in my life have I worked out definitely

articulated economic theory. As there has been need for
practical action in various fields, I have always squared
proposals upon the few fundamental principles that determine all my judgments. I am very frankly a partisan—
a union man—not a half-hearted advocate who may be
swayed either to the one side or the other. I repeat and
emphasize the statement, that in so far as the organization
of labor in trade unions is concerned, the general policy
they pursue, their purposes and aspirations, I am unalterably with them, yea, even to the extent of their errors, their
mistakes. If I cannot advocate or defend publicly an
error or mistake made, I shall try to find an excuse and
apologize for it. I have criticized and will criticize and
attack a union to the union itself; endeavor to influence it
to avoid error, to rectify a mistake, to undo a wrong, without regard whether they were aimed at a fellow-unionist,
a non-member, or an employer. But to the other world,
the large world, the world of selfish antagonism to the de-
fenders and protectors of the workmen's rights and interests, the trade unions, I am a union man, and one who even
under most adverse conditions will defend the trade union
movement.

My experience has extended over periods in economic
development in which the whole nature and organization
of industry have been transformed. Within my span of
life have come inventions that have been revolutionizing
in effect. Electricity both for lighting and power, the telephone, the wireless, the submarine cable, the radio, the
transcontinental railroad, aeroplane, electric street cars, internal combustion engine, cold storage, are a few of the
changes that I have seen come. Methods of work, methods
and agencies of communication, and facilities for travel

have brought society so close together that merging of economic interests and activities has been an inevitable result.
The consolidation came so gradually that many did not see
the trend of development until some of the new trusts were
exercising their newly found and rapacious powers. The
spring of 1884 gave to New York an inkling of the nature
of a packers' trust. Up until that time the meat for the
New York market had been prepared either in New York
State or New Jersey and there were a number of butcher
workmen in New York City. New York had killed weekly
from ten to thirteen thousand head of cattle and Chicago
only one thousand, but with changes in transportation and
in other economic factors the Chicago packers were able
to put meat into New York markets at a lower price. The
immediate result was the development of the Chicago Packing Trust. New York butcher workmen did not understand the economic meaning of their enforced unemployment and they launched a campaign against the importa-
tion of foreign meat. They held a big mass meeting in
Cooper Union and asked their fellow-workers to join in
boycotting Chicago meat. But the butcher workmen were
fighting industrial forces too powerful to be checked by
their protest. The economies of the Chicago packing houses
and the power of their economic organization soon wiped
out small independent firms. On the other hand, the corporation is a method of group ownership accompanying
quantity production which in turn necessitates the dividing
of work into operations so that groups performed what was
formerly the work of an individual. The change brought
danger to the individual workers until they learned to protect their individual rights and opportunities through organized activity in groups. The trust was a part of this gen-

eral movement to associated effort that is a distinctive feature of our present economic organization. The trade union movement is labor's constructive contribution to democratic regulation of large scale production. I believe that industry can devise and operate economic principles of administration that will result in constructive control and continuous progress. So I hold that trusts should not be suppressed, but regulated and helped to develop constructive control. The trust movement came with the development of quantity production. In their infancy these Gargantuan creatures were conscious only of their power and were unrestrained by ethics or experiences. They developed with ruthless disregard of competitors and without understanding or care for the human agents that were necessary in developing the network of creative force necessary to make the economic structure a going machine. The trusts and the large-scale industries generally made the mistake of thinking they could treat employes as impersonally as they did material things. The corporation form of ownership had replaced the system of individual ownership and personal management. Expansion of credit revolutionized methods of financing. The early trust seemed only a devouring monster for those without practical industrial experience.

American spirit rebelled against it as a new form of tyranny and the trust problem became a foremost issue in public discussion. The reformers in state Legislatures and Congress began to discuss legislation to protect the people. Most of the politicians seemed to think that by making a law they could prohibit trusts.

From the first I mistrusted the proposal to take the trust problem into the political field. It seemed to me we could not safely trust policies of repression, and furthermore, the economic field was competent to deal with policies of regulation. Just what the procedure would be I did not attempt to foretell, but I considered organization of all factors concerned an essential prerequisite to orderly development. Organization would assure opportunity for co-operation in working through the problems that concerned all.

Regardless of anti-trust agitation, consolidation remained the trend. Quite contrary to the prevailing economic dogma that free competition was the necessary basis to industrial progress, the economies and efficiency of consolidation presaged tremendous strides.

When both in transportation and industrial organization there came pooling or merging of interests, the problem of financing the combines made the older financial game seem like child's play. Only central banks were competent to finance the large-scale undertakings, so the control of industry gravitated into the hands of Wall Street. The development seemed to me natural. I believed absolutely that the organized labor movement was the efficient way to protect and to promote the interests of wage-earners. It seemed to me perfectly logical that employers should recognize the relation between organization and orderly development in their business. I did not condone the evil practices which marked the evolution of the trust system (on the contrary I severely condemned them) but I believed the cure for those evils would develop most effectively through voluntary recognition that better practices bring more permanent and more satisfactory progress. I hold that good practices must be self-justifying.

The trust was a phase of the new industrial organization where groups replaced individual effort. Our problem was not to try to prevent a normal development but to find the principles and technique for utilizing group action and group production in furtherance of general welfare. It is a problem to whose solution the groups concerned should jointly contribute. The organization of management, finance, and producing workmen is the way to develop discipline and information within those groups. The next step, to my mind, is co-operation of all the groups with the pooling of information to determine control of the industry. The industry would thus become self-regulated and disciplined while checks interposed by organized consumers would deter non-social tendencies. As my contribution to this development, I have promoted the organization of workers and opposed attempts of politicians to bungle the economic development.

Organization was response to economic forces, and therefore I did not believe that arbitrary limitations especially by law could prevail against it. When the Sherman Anti-Trust Law was proposed, I did not believe it would be effective in curbing trusts, but fearing that attempts would be made to use the law against collective action by wage-earners, I went to several members of Congress and told them my fears. The bill originally introduced by Senator Sherman considered in the debates of 1890 was an anti-monopoly bill intended to restore full and free competition. I was very apprehensive that such a law would be used against labor organizations and I presented this point of view to a number of Senators. Senators Teller, Morgan and Stewart expressed the same point of view in a debate in the Senate. Senator Sherman did not share their apprehension, but in order to avoid confusion accepted a proposal made by Senator George which specifically excluded arrangements, agreements, and combinations between laborers made with a view of lessening the number of hours or increasing their wages. Similar exemptions were provided for persons engaged in horticultural or agricultural pursuits who were seeking to increase the prices of agricultural or horticultural products. The Sherman Anti-Monopoly proposal with the exemption proviso was referred back to the Committee on the Judiciary with instructions to report within twenty days. When the bill was reported at the end of that time, it had been changed from an anti-monopoly to an anti-combination bill. In view of this change the Senators did not believe it necessary to include the labor exemption proviso. Senators George, Hoar and Stewart were sympathetic with the position that there was a fundamental difference between labor organizations and organizations for profit. However, Senator Hoar had so clearly defined in his own mind the fundamental difference between these two organizations that he failed to appreciate the confusion that might be in the minds of others and the measure was finally reported from his committee without the George proviso.

Events soon demonstrated that the law was to be applied to labor unions and that it was not effective in curbing trusts. After the Sherman Anti-Trust Law had been in effect about nine years, a four-day conference on trusts was held in Chicago for the purpose of assembling opinion and information upon the results of the law. In my statement in the conference I declared that the state is not capable of preventing the development or the natural concentration of industry and that all propositions to accomplish that purpose react for the greater injury to wage-earners than to trusts. At another time in expressing myself upon the issue I declared, "I am not going to join the howl against trusts; all I ask is to give us the freedom we want to work out our own salvation and to give industry the same opportunity." Economic law and necessity are stronger than legislation or police power. To my mind only development based on voluntary institutions holds promise of permanent progress, for such development is responsive to developing technology and cultural advance of individuals and group activity.

In addition to proscription of trusts, our government began to develop a system of state regulation of privately owned and operated enterprises—such as railways. To this effort I gave my hearty support and co-operation, but I have resisted unswervingly all proposals to inaugurate government ownership and operation for two reasons: first, because I believe our main dependence lay in individual initiative; and secondly, because I believe the economic field is essentially different from the political and the legal.

I reached this conclusion gradually after discarding proposals to which I temporarily subscribed. Some which I have discarded have not infrequently been suggested again by "progressives" who dub me "conservative" or even reactionary. My method of evolving my philosophy has been intuitive.

The principles of political freedom worked out in our Republic have been based upon political equality. If the rights of any individual are infringed, he has the right of counsel. But where political conditions touch a man's daily life once, economic conditions will affect it fifty times. To insure economic justice, therefore, I hold that the principle of the right of counsel maintains. By economic coun-

sel I mean an agent expert upon the matters in question
selected with the approval of the individual.   Thus the
economic organization of the workers is basic.   This economic organization, in addition to its defensive service,
is free to develop constructive functions as soon as it is
accepted by the management and its spokesmen admitted
to conferences considering various problems in which their
work is concerned.   This procedure provides a way to utilize the experience and the information of workmen which
in turn can be collected and systematized only through organization.

The next step is organization of the shop, thus creating
a trade council in which all factors in the industry have
representation, and then organization of the whole industry
along the same lines.   This is a natural development which
we see now in the making.   Ultimately perhaps, those
things which concern all industry may be determined by a
national economic body, truly representative, competent to
make decisions and to secure compliance, or political regulation must develop a new technique and more competent
personnel.

The methods and the agencies for progress in the economic world must be evolved out of economic experience
and life.   It is a serious mistake to confuse the two fields
or to carry the problems of one into the other.

The evident decline of the Legislature in recent years
confirms my belief that the economic world must work out
its own procedure and principles of order.   Trade unions
or voluntary associations of wage-earners constitute one of
the essential agencies for establishing procedure of control.
The development of large-scale production, the increasing
authority of science in determining processes, and the more

recent investigations of management for the purpose of making it truly scientific, together with the marked tendency toward trade associations, are to me a most gratifying exemplification of my thought that discernment of the essential difference between the economic and the political clarifies the problem of progress.

I have often allowed myself to dream of the possibilities of production if all were free to work unretarded by the existing restraints. The tremendous increase in output, together with sustained advancement in quality or workmanship, would transform standards of material welfare for the whole world. But more important than the material results would be the satisfaction of the higher qualities of men and women.

Several times the plain question has been put to me by members of the Senate Committee on Judiciary: "Mr. Gompers, what can we do to allay the causes of strikes that bring discomfort and financial suffering to all alike?" I have had to answer, "Nothing." My answer has been interpreted as advocating a policy of drift. Quite the contrary to my real thought. Foremost in my mind is to tell the politicians to keep their hands off and thus to preserve voluntary institutions and opportunity for individual and group initiative and leave the way open to deal with problems as the experience and facts of industry shall indicate. I have, with equal emphasis, opposed submitting determination of industrial policies to courts. But it is difficult for lawyers to understand that the most important human justice comes through other agencies than the political. Economic justice will come through the organization of economic agencies, the increasing adjustment of economic relationships in accord with principles evolved by experience, the formulation of material scientific standards, and development of the principles and co-ordinating functions of management, based upon understanding of human welfare. Just where this sort of endeavor will carry us—who can say? But of this I am certain, it means progress toward a better day. Though frequently impatient with existing wrongs, I am not impatient with what sometimes seems the slow progress of the labor movement.

My patience has rested upon realization of facts, not upon lack of idealism or sentiment. I realized that since the labor movement is a living, sentient thing, growth comes from life within. It can be aided, directed, but not forced. Just as a plant may be cultivated and pruned, cared for in every way, still it cannot be compelled to grow or flower, so the labor movement cannot be handled or computed as material quantities. The degree or extent of organization is a relative term. There is a potential or temporary organization which may become permanent as soon as two men come together and discuss organization. Latent possibilities are quickened and one of the stages that leads to permanent organization exists. So, when a great mass of workers ceases to be indifferent to organization, that is the first indication of organization viewed as evolutionary process. These facts I knew intuitively and have turned them about in my mind during the decades I have been in the movement, but it is an understanding that those outside of the movement rarely grasp.

This shifting and indeterminate line of demarcation between labor and organized labor I have also used for another purpose. Whenever an achievement has been accomplished, I claim it for organized labor. Anything for the benefit of the workers I may claim by emphasizing organized labor. Wherever there is doubt, I let all labor share the responsibility.

I have worked a lifetime for the labor movement and I feel that I know it as few others do. Out of that knowledge is born faith in its destiny and its high service.

CHAPTER XXVII

My knowledge of men and affairs in foreign countries
is based upon two general avenues of information: that
gained through contacts with foreigners within the United
States and through foreign travels. Since I left England
in 1863 I have made five trips to Europe, in 1895, 1909,
1918, and two in 1919. The occasion of my first trip I
have already related and that of the trips in war-time will
be told later.

My second trip to Europe came about as a result of
several invitations to be present at gatherings of representative labor movements. One invitation was from the
Parliamentary Committee of the British Trade Union Congress to attend the annual meeting to take place in Ipswich.
A second was from the International Secretariat to be present at its biennial congress in Paris in August. Others
were from central organizations in the leading countries
of continental Europe. The evident purpose of these
invitations was to bring about closer relations between the
labor movements of Europe and America. In accepting
the invitations I saw an opportunity of bringing to the attention of European labor the purposes, methods, and spirit
of American trade unionism. I hoped also to gain much
from observing European labor conditions and talking with

29

those interested in industrial and social problems. I asked
to accompany me on this trip James W. Sullivan, a union
painter, who had been a friend for many years, who would
be able to help me not only in making the trip but in
accumulating the information I desired. Between us we
were able to pursue our investigations in six languages.
I spoke German and Holland Dutch; he spoke French and
had a ready translation knowledge of Italian and German.

On the American continent those parts which are outside the boundaries of the United States which I have
visited are Porto Rico twice, Cuba three times, Mexico once,
Canada many times—her workers belong to our Federation.

During the six decades in which I have been identified
with the organized labor movement, I have met the labor
leaders of practically every country of the world. Though
I was very young when we left London to join the immigrants in the New World, I was strongly imbued with the
spirit of internationalism which the English factory workers of that day, at the cost of personal privations, were
making the basis of the policies of their labor movement.
Without understanding why, I accepted the principle that
human freedom is a world-wide struggle.

Later years gave me the reasons for the interdependence
of all nations. In fact, all of the forces in my life have
facilitated my acceptance of the internationalization of the
great agencies in human development. This has made it
natural for me to think through many problems, without
narrowing conceptions to national limitations. This natural inclination has been strengthened by constant contacts with friends, and fellow-workers of foreign countries.
Yet on the other hand, as the years have passed, I have
become increasingly American although I never fully

plumbed the depth of my feeling for America until the World War came; but it never occurred to me in all the years that I have lived in this country to question that I am an American. The spirit of America took possession of me so completely that I have never felt alien and I used the term "foreign" as a native American would use it. So, many among those whom I regard as my foreign friends are those who were born in the land of my birth.

My earliest foreign friends were men in the labor movement in New York City but whose vital interests were still in the land of their birth. For the most part, each of these was still in correspondence with fellow-workers "back home." From these sources I got information of labor movements in various countries and some knowledge of individual leaders. In some cases, my friends would write about me to the others back home and thus a mutual acquaintance developed, and not infrequently, in later years, brought personal meetings and real friendships. There was probably greater relative intercourse in the early days than now. Absence of money was counterbalanced by migratory habits of workmen and their indifference to inconveniences. The labor movements in many European countries were identified with efforts to overthrow the government; thus, many in New York were refugees, not a few of whom continued from that sanctuary to help the revolutionary group back home. These efforts always appealed to me, for I could never think of human freedom dispassionately.

The movement of this type with which I was longest associated was that for Irish freedom. New York was headquarters for the Irish Land League and a succession of efforts of a similar nature. The early organization was identified with the paper, *The Irish World and Labor Agi-*

tator, the office of which was the Irish headquarters.
Patrick Ford, the editor of the paper, was a very warm
friend of mine as was O'Donovan Rossa who wrote for
the paper and served as the direct connection with the agitation work in Great Britain and Ireland. When J. P.
McDonald sought refuge in this country, I, of course, met
him both at that office and in labor circles. Through this
group I became actively identified with the movement for
Irish Home Rule and I came to know all of the Irish patriots and through them the Irish labor leaders.

When Michael Davitt came to New York, I was on
the committee which arranged for his reception. I talked
over with him the Irish situation very frequently, so that
I felt that I understood conditions thoroughly. Later, I
was on the reception committee at the time of the first
visit of Charles Stewart Parnell. Our committee arranged
for a huge meeting in Cooper Union which Parnell addressed. In 1887 I was a member of the Mayor's Committee on Relief for Famine in Ireland.

When John Redmond's brother came in later years, I
had repeated conferences with him. I knew T. P. O'Connor
very well. Each time that I went to Europe before the
War, I made it a special point to go to Ireland and visit
Dublin and Cork and such readily accessible places as I
could reach in my limited time; so between meeting them
in New York, Ireland, and the House of Commons in
London, I have known practically all of the men prominent
in Irish agitation.

I met De Valera through P. H. McCarthy and Andrew
Gallegher while in San Francisco in 1920. An arrangement was made by which we spent an entire evening together, talking over the Irish situation. At the next con-

vention of the A. F. of L. held in Denver, the Irish question was one of the pivotal issues. The Federation went the limit in support of "Free Ireland," but as the Irish cause approached its goal it fell into the hands of those who were not so unselfishly dedicated to the cause as the old leaders, and achievement was handicapped by professional Irishmen in America.

As the German labor movement was numerically the strongest of all countries, it had much to do with shaping the international labor thought. The Socialist movement developed in Germany before the trade union movement. The conception of relationship between these two movements that existed in Germany was reflected in the international movement. In the early days, I had no special fight with Socialism. I maintained an open mind and was willing to learn from Socialists and to adopt any thought of theirs in which I could see constructive possibilities.

Through my German friends and many German publications I had a fairly good knowledge of the German situation. I was eager to meet German leaders, Socialists or trade unionists. I was seeking better understanding wherever offered. As I have related elsewhere, it was solely because of the tactics of Socialists that it became necessary for the American labor movement to protect trade unionism against the invasions of Socialism.

Among my friends who were in contact with German Socialists were Dr. Wishnewetzki and his wife well known as Florence Kelly. I knew them both well and when they made a trip to Europe in the 'eighties I was glad of an opportunity to share the information they collected.

In 1888 I received a letter from William Liebknecht asking me to allow the use of my name in the call for the

International Congress of Workingmen to be held in Switzerland. Much as I regretted the necessity, I felt that both individually and officially I was bound by the decision of the Federation to concentrate upon the development of our economic organization before attempting to participate in international movements. So I wrote to Liebknecht that I found it impossible to differentiate between personal and official relations and I was constrained by my sense of duty to decline the honor. When Liebknecht came to this country, I had the pleasure of meeting him.

My first contact with Carl Legien came through my friend A. von Elm, who left New York and returned to Hamburg, Germany, in the early 'eighties after working at his trade in New York twelve years. Von Elm did everything within his power to promote understanding and friendship between the German labor movement and labor in the United States.

Legien, for many years as president of the German Federation of Trade Unions, had his office at Hamburg. That organization was developed along lines similar to the American Federation of Labor. He was editor of the *Korrespondenzblatt*, the official organ of the German Federation. After his return from the United States, von Elm became an outstanding figure in the German trade union movement. He was an officer in the Cigarmakers' Union, one of the largest in Germany. He was elected to the Reichstag. He led the group that regarded economic power as the basic agency of the labor movement. It was my custom to send von Elm copies of the *American Federationist* and other A. F. of L. literature. Soon after I began editing the *Federationist*, I published two editorials on "Cheap-John Unionism" in which I made a plea for high dues, business stability for the union, and trade union benefits. These von Elm translated into German and gave to Legien who published them in the *Korrespondenzblatt*. They were later called to the attention of those who were organizing the German workers in railroad transportation and the policy became a part of their practices. I met Legien first when I was in Hamburg in 1895 and again when I was in Europe in 1909. In 1911 he wrote me of his plans to come to the United States. He was anxious to know something of our country and our labor movement. He indicated his financial difficulties in making the trip. I at once offered to arrange a lecture tour under trade union auspices.

Like most German workingmen, Legien was a Socialist and a member of the party. The Socialist Party made an offer similar to mine. It so came about that I arranged with the trade unions a lecture tour for Legien across the country, and a return trip was arranged under Socialist Party auspices. I went to New York to meet Legien when he arrived. He came to Washington accompanied by his secretary, Mr. Baumeister, who also acted as his interpreter, as he did not speak English. With characteristic German efficiency, Legien had prepared in advance the speeches he intended to make on this lecture tour and translations also were in manuscript ready for use. Baumeister, was without doubt one of the cleverest linguists with whom I have ever come in contact. He was a waiter, and had traveled in nearly every European country remaining in each of them long enough and visiting them frequently enough to learn their languages. I have heard him within an hour interpret extemporaneous speeches in English, German, French, Italian, Spanish, Bohemian, Russian, Yiddish, and

several other languages which he spoke with equal fluency
and in the languages which I understood he spoke with
splendid fluency and accuracy and without any accent that
would betray any foreign enunciation or pronunciation. As
Legien was a member of the Reichstag, I arranged with W.
B. Wilson to secure for him the courtesy of addressing
the House of Representatives, a courtesy usually extended
to a member of a foreign Parliament. Mr. Wilson introduced the necessary resolution, which Victor Berger, the
only Socialist member of the House, nearly ruined. He
made his usual *faux pas*. He made a number of wild,
radical statements. It required unanimous consent for the
privilege. On account of Berger's "eloquence and logic,"
objections were raised by two members of the House who,
upon Representative Wilson's appeal, withdrew them.
Legien submitted his address to me before it was delivered
and made several revisions upon my suggestion. It was
interpreted in English to the House by Baumeister. After
the delivery of the address, Legien, Berger, Baumeister,
and I met in Berger's office and had quite a "pow-wow,"
at which I took opportunity to demonstrate the misrepre-
sentations that Berger had uttered in regard to the American
Federation of Labor during his then recent visit to Germany. From that time I could never see Mr. Berger and
he never wanted to see me. I called Mr. Legien's attention
to the unjustified statement of Mr. Berger in his speech at
Berlin, as reported by the Socialist official paper, the
Berlin Vorwaertz, and later printed in Berger's paper, the
Milwaukee Leader. In that article, Berger stated that
the officers of the A. F. of L. were able to perpetuate themselves in power through the unfair practice of denying to
state federations and city central bodies more than one vote

in the conventions of the A. F. of L. regardless of their membership. Berger illustrated this "corruption," as he termed it, by declaring that International unions had one vote for every hundred members and that state and city bodies, sometimes representing as many as one hundred thousand or more, were entitled to only one delegate and one vote. Under this arrangement he declared that twenty-five or thirty international unions in the convention of the Federation could outvote all other delegates. Berger acknowledged that this was virtually the statement that he had made. I explained to Legien that, as a matter of fact, it is the national trade unions which are represented by their delegates and the vote cast is in accordance with the membership; that the unions in the city central bodies were already represented by the delegates from their respective international unions, and that one delegate and one vote for central bodies affords participation in the discussion without much influence in the casting of votes. To allow the same voting power to delegates from central bodies as is given to the delegates from national trade unions would be a duplication, and with state federations, a triplication of the same membership. Mr. Legien said: "Why, that is the system in the conventions of the German Federation of Labor. In addition to this fact, German central bodies of any kind are not entitled to a delegate or to a vote."

We then discussed another proposition urged by the Socialist Party of the United States, the election of the officers of the American Federation of Labor by the system of the initiative and referendum. Mr. Legien said that such a system did not obtain in Germany nor in any other general federation of trade unions in the whole civilized world, that such a proposition was impractical, impossible, and ridiculous. Berger's discomfiture was so manifest that he left our little company abruptly.

This illustration is typical of the sort of propaganda Socialists conducted to discredit the American trade union movement in the minds of European wage-earners. The effect of the propaganda runs through European literature and comes back to us in the prejudices of our immigrant workers and our "intellectuals" who sit at the feet of European Socialists.

We arranged a luncheon for Mr. Legien so that the representative labor men might have an opportunity to meet him. Legien was a very able man and seemed to be making a serious endeavor to understand American labor. However, upon his return to Germany he published a report of his trip through the United States which I thought in many respects very unfair. Baumeister carried a kodak on the journey and made a number of pictures. From these Legien selected a few pictures of workingmen's homes to illustrate his report. Some were shacks in outlying districts as homes for workingmen in the packing house district of Chicago. The workingmen who lived in those houses were immigrants who had not yet become Americanized and did not conform to American standards of living. The impression created through these pictures and certain portions of Legien's report were not calculated to do credit to the American labor movement. However, I think they were the natural mistake of a traveler who could stay only a few weeks in our immense country and who did not speak English. Because of my knowledge of Legien's great ability and my confidence in his integrity, I never doubted his purpose. He was German from the tip of his toes to the last hair of his head and assumed a general attitude of German superiority.

One of the first French workingmen I met was Victor Delahaye, through whom I came to know many others. Delahaye had had a most vivid career. He was a short, robust-looking man with a flowing beard and beautiful hands. He belonged to the machinists' organization and had been active in the French Commune for which he was exiled for a time and lived in London with the Marx group. In 1886 he was sent to New York to inspect the modern machinery for cottons and woolens. The Machinists' Union of Paris had begun manufacturing on a co-operative basis, and had asked the government for a loan. Practically all European countries at that time bought their textile machinery in England or Belgium. But the French government thought all sources ought to be inspected and sent Delahaye and his group to the United States. As soon as I learned of their mission, I got in touch with them and offered them every assistance within the power of American labor. I saw that they met American workingmen and arranged meetings for them. Delahaye himself I liked very much and frequently took him home with me where he was soon on the best of terms with my whole family, especially with my son Sam. I was glad to add to my acquaintance with men in foreign labor movements. Delahaye gave me much valuable information about the French workers. The labor movement there was a secret, revolutionary movement from 1794 when workingmen's clubs were prohibited until 1884 when labor unions were legalized. When they were legalized, they were taken under the patronage of the government and thus in a considerable degree were restricted from becoming vital industrial agencies.

In 1893 two official French missions came to the World's Fair, one representing the municipal government of Paris and the other the national government. There were labor men on both missions. Delahaye was in the first group, accompanied by Le Grand, a Parisian actor, who had organized the actors of France. He was a congenial companion with a very clever mind. When we met again two years later, he was foremost in arranging opportunities for me to have contact with men and affairs of his country. Delahaye also had a wide circle of friends and acquaintances, for he was a man of considerable information and standing. He and Keufer had much in common. To my regret, August Keufer was away from Paris attending the annual meeting of his trade. Through correspondence I had come to regard him very highly as a trade unionist. He had made a lasting favorable impression upon my mind. For many years Keufer served as the executive officer and secretary of the French Typographical Federation. He was a Positivist in addition to his being a devotee to trade unionism. My meetings with him in the United States on two occasions and abroad revealed his intrepid character, great ability, and his faithfulness to carry on the work in the interests of the wage-earners in the printing industry. His endeavor to exert a constructive influence upon the rash and indiscreet leaders of the general labor movement of France had been to his great credit. During my last stay in Paris he invited me to the headquarters of the Typographical Union where a reception and brief talk took place at the conclusion of which he presented to me, in the name of his organization, two bronze medals—one of them depicting the succor given by America to the suffering Belgians during the early stages of the War; another was an embossed medallion with a portrait of President Wilson.

I was the unofficial delegate from the A. F. of L. to the International Conference of the International Secretariat in Paris in 1909. This somewhat irregular capacity was due to the fact that the A. F. of L. had not at that time decided the question of affiliation with the International Secretariat, but had such action under consideration. After some discussion I was received as a delegate with the right to participate in discussion but not to vote. Because I did not then and there commit the A. F. of L. to the affiliation, the Austrian representative, Heuber, ferociously attacked me charging that I had the power to commit our Federation to the Secretariat. I answered that such autocracy and power may be vested in the head of the labor movement of Austria, but it does not conform to the principles of the A. F. of L.

This was my initiation into the active work of organized international labor. I saw there men whom I had known by name only and I got in a new way the spirit and the method of international labor, thereby making me better able to cope with problems of the following years. The presidency of the International Secretariat was under the leadership of the French Confédération Générale du Travail, and Yvetot and Jouhaux presided alternately. Yvetot was a syndicalist who had written a book on sabotage. Jouhaux was a trade unionist with close Socialist affiliations. They were of entirely different temperaments. Yvetot was a soft-voiced, persuasive speaker, and yet his philosophy and activity landed him in jail for longer periods than he enjoyed in freedom. On the other hand, Jouhaux was an "orator," who orated frequently and with equal force upon a fundamental principle or a point of procedure. After a few years of activity, I learned during my last visit to France in the War, that Yvetot had taken up some commercial proposition and dropped out of any participation in the labor movement in any of its phases. Jouhaux has continued his services and has continued strongly against the policies of Longuet, Karl Marx's son-in-law, and Cashen to prevent the labor movement of France, such as it is, from being absorbed into the Soviet or Bolshevik ranks at Moscow. In this work he has rendered valiant service.

My friendship with Paul Deschanel extended over many years. I met him in New York by introduction of Charles A. Dana of the New York *Sun*. M. Deschanel, upon his first visit to this country, was engaged in an investigation of industrial problems in the United States. We spent many an hour together in discussion of these subjects and I went with him to many industrial establishments in New York and vicinity. Some years later he paid another visit to the United States. In the meantime, a correspondence was kept up between us at infrequent intervals.

When in Paris at any time, he would always seek me and some interesting evenings were passed between us. I visited the Chamber of Deputies, in 1909. M. Deschanel was Speaker of the Chamber. He left the chair, came up to my seat in the gallery, and we were engaged in conversation but a few minutes, when he placed me in the invited visitor's box. When he was elected President of the French

Republic, I took occasion to send him a cablegram of one word, "Congratulations," to which he did me the courtesy of a cordial reply.

During that same time of my being in Paris, a messenger called upon me and stated that M. Briand desired to have a conference with me. Briand at that time was not in great favor. I called upon him at his office or apartment—which, I cannot recall—and with a friend who spoke English and French, and through the interpreter, he stated his point of view of the political and international situation in which France and the continental countries were so engrossed. I remember vividly an incident connected with his becoming Premier of France in 1909. At the time that I was in Paris, I had been interviewed by newspaper men and I recall that when M. Briand assumed the Premiership he had made a conciliatory and constructive pronouncement as to the policy which he would pursue and in a statement to the press later declared that on labor he was in entire accord with the principles which I had laid down. This statement was published in the Paris newspapers and cabled to America. The next time I saw M. Briand was at the Washington Conference for the Limitation of Armaments in 1921, where I had several interesting conversations with him.

During my visit to France in 1909, I called to pay my respects to René Viviani who was then Minister of Labor of the government. We had fully two hours' conference. In my book, *Labor in Europe and America*, I devoted a chapter of more or less interest to the conference. I met him, too, at the Washington Arms Conference. I found him a very much different man than I had known twelve years before. He was no longer the urbane, genial personality that I had known, but rather assumed an austerity which brooked no difference of opinion.

One of the reasons why my feeling toward the French was always most kindly was due to Perreard's Restaurant and Hotel—an old Washington institution. It was housed in a three-story brick house and managed by Perreard and his wife. There one had the best of French cooking and cosmopolitan society, and the "count" and Madame dispensed hospitality as though presiding over a salon. In truth it was a rare intellectual center to which came official and unofficial Frenchmen, reporters, those in the diplomatic service of all countries, sometimes Ambassadors, and free spirits of the world.

When I could not go home to dinner but had to return to my office in the evening, I would go to Perreard's. I was always welcomed and, of course, introduced by the "count" to everyone who happened to be there at the time, as "citizen Gompers." The "count," with neatly waxed mustache, was usually in shirt-sleeves. "Countess" Perreard, his wife, was Swiss-French. Both she and the "count" had remarkable voices and sometimes when asked and at other times without the slightest provocation would burst into song. Immediately after July 4, Independence Day, invitations would be received by the habitués of the café called the "reptiles" to participate in the ceremonies of the "Fall of the Bastille" on July 14, to a dinner and a bottle of "red ink" for two dollars. With the exception of the year I was in Paris, 1909, until the death of the Perreards, I never failed to be in attendance on that celebration. In 1909 I sent a cablegram of felicitation to the other "reptiles."

My interest in conditions in Russia was first aroused

by Russian immigrants who came to New York in the early 'eighties. Those wretched, hunted people seemed for a while just as likely to be exploited in the New World as in the Old. Their exploiters were largely their own fellow-countrymen. The danger to the Russians was also a menace to working standards in some of the trades in which they worked and thereby to American standards of life for all the workers in those trades. It was the labor movement of New York that first undertook the practical problem of Americanizing the immigrant workers. We set about Americanizing the Russians. The most effective agency to that end was the trade union. I worked both with the Baron Hirsch Fund and with the Hebrew labor organizations. I did not approve of organization along racial lines, but we all realized that to organize Hebrew trade unions was the first step in getting those immigrants into the American labor movement. Three men who were prominently identified with this work over a long period of years and with whom I became intimately acquainted through our work were Gregory Weinstein, Joseph Barondess, and Abram Cahan. Weinstein and Cahan were employed in a form of unskilled labor in the Stachelberg factory where I was working at my trade. They had but recently come from Russia to the United States. Cahan has rendered as great service to the Russians of this country as any other one individual. That relationship has been more or less similar to that of the old Jewish patriarch. He has been father, counselor, and spiritual advisor. Through his work as editor of the *Jewish Forward*, he has exerted a tremendous influence in New York City and in the Jewish labor movement of our country. We have not always been in harmony on policies, but of late years there has been no stancher defender of the American trade union than Abe Cahan.

Through the New York Russian centers we heard of constantly recurring pogroms in Russia and the exile of active revolutionaries to Siberia. Many who were working for freedom in Russia managed to escape and find their way to the New World. The fight for religious and political freedom roused the emotion that is strongest in me. When the Czar's government sought to make our government sign an extradition treaty under which we would relinquish to the imperial government the poor wretches who found refuge in this country, I led an urgent protest against the making of such a treaty. I issued an official circular to the American labor movement acquainting them with the outrage against our institutions which the Senate was trying to perpetrate. In response to my warning, an urgent protest was made against the treaty. J. P. McDonnell arranged a mass protest meeting in Newark at which Thaddeus B. Wakeman, J. H. Edelmann, Alexander Jonas, Henry Weissman, Dr. Solotaroff, and I spoke. Seldom have I made a speech into which I poured more unreservedly my passion for human freedom. It embodied the fire of youth.

Bloody Sunday in Russian history (January 25, 1905) shocked the world, but it drove the Russian people to revolt. The friends of Russia in the New World rejoiced when Russia's workmen struck and demanded the right to present a petition to the Czar. Organized rebellion against oppression called a halt to Russian tyranny and in the fall of that year the Duma was called and Count Witte put in charge of establishing a constitutional government. Recognizing the significance of the helping hand which America had extended to the Russian struggle for freedom, Witte sent a mission to the American people asking co-operation. I sent a cable to Count Witte in behalf of American labor expressing our joy in the great achievements of the Russian workmen, urging that religious persecution be stopped and our hope that the new liberty would be permanent.

Sometime afterward during a gathering in Washington I was introduced to Baron Rosen, the Russian Ambassador, and at his invitation visited him later at the Russian Embassy. We went over a large field of subjects and among them the denial of rights to the Russian people under the Czar. I shared fully the view and the feeling of Americans against the autocracy of the czardom and the brutality imposed upon the people. Siberia was in itself a term of horror and terror. I did not fail to emphasize my feelings to him upon these subjects.

On a few later occasions I met him informally and a number of questions were covered in our conversations which sometimes lasted more than an hour. As the Czar's Ambassador he had all the dignity and reservations of the continental diplomat; as a man, I found him most cordial, full of sympathy, and in almost entire agreement with my views. When James Duncan went to Russia with the Root Commission, appointed by President Wilson, he met Baron Rosen and in conversation with him (so Duncan on returning informed me) the Baron expressed his appreciation of me and the course I had pursued, and wanted to be remembered to "Sam."

Alexis Aladyn and Nicholas W. Tchykovsky, official representatives of the movement for the freedom of Russian workingmen, came to my office in Washington. I arranged with them to meet with the Executive Council and explain to us fully the Russian situation and the assistance which they desired from organized labor of America. I prepared a resolution which was adopted by our Council, commending the Russian patriots to American workingmen and asking their support and co-operation.

When the Czar of Russia issued his call for a World Peace Congress, he shocked many. There were those who ridiculed the idea because the Czar was the instrumentality. But to my mind it was not a question whether he was the Czar or President; the important fact was that he had some prestige and a conception that might prove a great boon to the human race. It was not the first time when king and the lowly made common cause against industrial and agricultural free-booters and made for progress. Alliances of the character to which I have referred have frequently occurred; only, after the accomplishment of the immediate purpose each alliance was dissolved and each assumed a mutually antagonistic attitude.

In view of the fact that there was at that time no apparent power to overthrow czardom and establish a progressive constitutional republic in Russia, it seemed to me though far away from the scene of action that it would have been an advantageous move to be willing to accept that which the Czar offered without any permanent alliance. It would place the peasantry and the workers in industry in Russia in the more advantageous position from which they could better prosecute their work of organization, education, agitation.

In 1908 the chairman of the Executive Committee of the Pouren Defense Conference of New York City brought to my attention the case of Jan Pouren, a political refugee of Russia of Lettish descent whose extradition was asked for by the Russian government under the charges of having committed a penal offense in his native country during the revolutionary upheaval in 1905–6. Pouren was a peasant and stood for the interests of his class against the oppression of Baltic barons who were in sympathy with the Russian Czar. He succeeded in escaping from Russia after the defeat of the revolution. He came to America where he endeavored to earn an honest living.

Russian spies discovered his whereabouts and representatives of the Russian government induced the Federal authorities to have him arrested on charges of crimes committed in the Baltic provinces, requesting that the prisoner be turned over to Russian authorities. Pouren had been in prison for months waiting the outcome of the proceedings.

Commissioner Shields finally decided in favor of the Russian government. I was invited to act as vice-president of a mass protest meeting held in Cooper Institute, September 11. The Executive Council authorized me to request President Roosevelt to intervene in behalf of Jan Pouren. He was extradited despite our efforts.

When the overthrow of the Czar's government came in the great World War, I felt that if little more were accomplished human freedom had gained a tremendous opportunity and I hastened to express my great joy. This story is told in pages following.

There were many Englishmen who took a prominent part in the American labor movement and through them and through my reading I was early familiar with the leaders of the British labor movement. The Dockers' strike

in London attracted world-wide attention. It developed
a number of new men, among them John Burns, Ben
Tillett, James Sexton, and Tom Mann, and as a result I
immediately began correspondence with them and received
replies of a most fraternal character. That movement
had done much to raise the standards of the Dock Laborers. One of the results of this correspondence was that in
1894 there was established between the Federation and
the British Trade Union Congress, the custom of exchanging fraternal delegates annually which constituted a
powerful influence making for better understanding and
friendliness between the labor movements of the two most
important English-speaking countries. As I have stated
elsewhere in these memoirs, David Holmes and John
Burns were the first fraternal delegates from the British
Trade Union Congress to our Denver convention in 1894.
David Holmes was a sturdy, intelligent trade unionist, and
a most congenial companion, and made many friends;
John Burns, able, alert, assumed an air of superiority and
the latter caused somewhat of a coldness between him and
some of our men. He was hypercritical of everything he
saw in the United States except the Library of Congress
in Washington.

A curious incident happened a day or two after the
arrival of David Holmes and John Burns. The Lexow Committee, a committee of investigation into the corruption of
the police force of New York City, was meeting, and Burns
being a member of the London County Council, I was
sure that the investigation in progress would interest him.
We went to the Council Chamber where the hearing was
on and I introduced Mr. Burns to the chairman of the
committee, Mr. Lexow, who invited both of us to a

seat on either side of him. After Judge Goff, who was conducting the investigation for the committee, severely cross-examined several witnesses and brought out some startlingly corrupt transactions, we left the chamber and, standing in the corridor, engaged in conversation with one or two newspaper men and one plain-clothes man who was assigned by Commissioner of Police Voorhees, to see that no harm came to Burns, Holmes, and me. In a few moments Burns became engaged in conversation with some person whom I seemed hazily to recognize, but I did not attempt to interfere. The plain-clothes man drew me aside and informed me that the stranger was a bunco-steerer and would surely wheedle some money out of Mr. Burns unless he was protected. He had no authority to interfere with the man because he could not press the charge against him. I turned rather abruptly and saw Mr. Burns in the act of handing two golden sovereigns and a ten dollar bill to this stranger. Quick as a flash I put my hand over the outstretched hand of the bunco man, got the money, held it in my hand for a moment, much to the consternation of the bunco-man and John Burns. I threatened the man that unless he quit at once I would have him arrested on the charge of fraud. I said that by my side was an officer of the police department to take him into custody upon my charge at once. He fled as if he were already pursued. Then I turned to Mr. Burns and handed the money to him, informing him of the character of the man and that he would have been swindled had I not interposed. Much to my surprise Mr. Burns was not at all pleased; indeed, he manifested anger at my intervention and later said that he would rather have been swindled out of the money than to be humiliated in his own estimation.

I have also recorded in these pages the fact that it was at the Denver Convention that I failed of re-election to the presidency of the American Federation of Labor, and together with P. J. McGuire I was elected as the first fraternal delegates to the British Trades Union Congress in 1895. We both seemed to make good impressions upon the Congress and I made many acquaintances and new friends. David Holmes was chairman and Henry Broadhurst the secretary. John Burns had a bitter controversy with Broadhurst upon the subject of the representation of local central bodies in future congresses. Since then for twenty-eight years, every year two different delegates from the British Trade Union Congress have attended the conventions of the American Federation of Labor and through them old friendships were renewed and new ones made. I was fraternal delegate to the congress of the British Trades Union in 1909.

On my first as well as my second trip to Europe, I spent a longer time in England than in any other country. On each trip I went back to the little house at 2 Fort Street where I had lived when a boy and greeted those of our old neighbors who were still living in that spot.

On a second trip to England I took more time to visit labor offices and to study the tendencies of the labor movement than at any other time. I met a number or practically all of the prominent British labor men. Some, of course, I learned to know better than others. Among these were Ben Tillett, Tom Mann, C. W. Bowerman, Will Thorne, Havelock Wilson, James Seddon, W. A. Appleton, Harry Gosling, Ben Cooper, J. B. Williams, J. R. Clynes, Keir Hardie, David Shackelton.

Ben Tillett was one of the leading spirits in the great

Longshoremen's strike in England, the strike which brought about the organization of this class of workers which had hitherto been considered unorganizable. In order to make the English strike effective, it was desirable to secure the co-operation of the seamen and longshoremen of the world. Tillett wrote to me, asking me to bring the matter to the attention of the seamen's and longshoremen's organizations of this country. However, the American seamen had not received very gracious treatment at the international meeting of seamen and did not respond to the British appeal. While no special action was taken, the work we were able to do in disseminating information of the British situation was helpful. I met both Ben Tillett and Tom Mann many times during the 'nineties. I was very fond of Ben Tillett. He suffered greatly from asthma and often moved around to get temporary relief from changes of climate. He made a long tour through Australia and New Zealand and came back by way of the United States, paying his expenses by the lectures he was able to deliver *en route*. I was able to help him in this work. He was a very delightful companion, with a good tenor voice and fond of music. He could impersonate the typical London cockney in a very clever way and his rendition of the old costermonger songs was the best I have ever heard—and I have heard Albert Chevalier. Ben Cooper was another dear personal friend of mine. He was a cigarmaker, and for years secretary of the Cigarmakers' Society of England. He took a very active part in labor affairs and public affairs of England and was a member of the London County Council, member of the Parliamentary Committee of the British Trade Union Congress for years. He came over to the United States two or three times. Keir Hardie I met on my trips to England. I got to know him well during his trip to the United States. He stayed several days in Washington and during that time the labor men here gave a dinner in his honor at Fritz Reuter's. Our talks and his observations did much to remove misunderstandings of our labor movement, which Socialists had been deliberately fostering.

My personal acquaintance with George Barnes began on his first trip. Mr. Barnes was then secretary of the Amalgamated Society of Engineers (now the Amalgamated Engineering Union). The members of that organization in the United States constituted a rival or dual body to the International Association of Machinists. More and more as time went on it became evident that the trade union movement of America would develop its own entity and character and under conditions and circumstances particularly affecting America and the diverse character of her population.

The Amalgamated Society of Engineers which had been formed in England had its main offices in London and its branches in nearly every large city in the world. The Brotherhood of Blacksmiths and several other metal unions were formed under various names. The members of the American branch of the Amalgamated Society of Engineers were unable to maintain anything like a permanent existence. In the year 1888 the International Association of Machinists was formed at Atlanta, Georgia. It was regarded as a southern organization and only after some years of its existence did it establish organizations in the eastern and northern parts of the country. With the election of James O'Connell as its president, new energy was injected, and after a few years I convinced O'Connell of the advantages of affiliation to our Federation. He had no difficulty in having the convention of the organization adopt the proposal and make application. The situation as it existed in the English and the American organizations of machinists was duplicated in the Amalgamated Society of Carpenters and the formation later of the United Brotherhood of Carpenters and Joiners of America, with this exception—that the Brotherhood of Carpenters was one of the organizations which formed the American Federation of Labor. In the full swing of rivalry between the American and English organizations, feeling became very bitter and it fell to my lot to conduct much correspondence with the officers of the Amalgamated Society of Engineers and the Amalgamated Society of Carpenters and Joiners to bring about a recognition of the principle that the American trade union movement must have the exclusive right and jurisdiction over wage-earners of the trades in America. I had conferences with the officers of both the American organizations and the officers of the organizations in London and Manchester, and arrangements of jurisdiction and amity were established. In this work the officers of the two organizations of the Building Trades and Metal Trades Associations materially aided. Similarly, without the slightest prejudice to England or Englishmen, I know that I carried that thought from the experience of my young manhood into the labor movement to which I have referred when with Alonzo B. Caldwell, I started the Independent Order of Foresters with authority vested in officers elected by citizens of America and with the American administrators for the functions of the fraternity.

Many of my Italian friends I met in work growing out of immigration problems. One of the most constructive movements for dealing with the immigration question was that inaugurated by the Italian government. As I have elsewhere said, the Italians in this country were robbed by padrones, bankers, and immigration officials. Through the efforts of Italian workingmen the Italian government appointed a commission to visit the principal countries to which Italians had emigrated and then called a conference in Rome to recommend protective policies. That conference suggested that emigrants be encouraged to settle away from industrial and congested districts. The Italian government developed a policy of extending supervisory care over its citizens within any foreign countries and established the Italian Emigration Commission to have charge of the administration of the policy. The commission protected the emigrant in his rights and obtained for him all possible comforts of the steerage transportation. It organized hostelries which afforded lodging accommodations for emigrants and supplied them with authentic information. It assumed supervision over the business of shipping companies and prevented their inducing emigration or misrepresentation of conditions in the New World. The commission provided facilities for emigrants to exchange Italian money into American or for buying postal orders. Sanitary facilities were also provided at the Italian ports. The supervision was continued by Italian consuls and representatives of the Emigration Commission in the United States.

The Italian government made the proposal to the American Federation of Labor that we take Italian immigrants under our protection and assist them in finding employment. It was with regret that I found myself unable to comply with the suggestion, but we did not have the facilities for rendering that service even to American trade unionists and the United States government had not established employment agencies. However, I did work very closely with those representatives of the Italian Emigration Commission in this country and I helped them secure co-operation of labor organizations to which Italians belonged. One of our trade unionists who rendered most valuable service in carrying out this constructive Italian emigration policy was Dominic D'Alessandro. The Italian government conferred upon him the title of Chevalier in recognition of his service. In the course of this work there was held an Italian-American Congress in which I authorized a representative of the Federation to participate. The congress provided for the organization of Italians within the United States to facilitate the naturalization of Italians and to consider the distribution of Italian immigrants with regard to labor demands, both agricultural and industrial. The congress urged Italians to take part in local politics, and called upon Italy to abandon its custom of impressing into military service Italians born in foreign lands or naturalized citizens of other countries. It called upon all Italian laborers to join the labor unions in their industries and by allying themselves with the American labor movement to refute the accusation that Italian immigrants were being used as strike breakers to degrade the standards of American workingmen.

Shortly before I left on my second European trip in 1909 I had conferences with the Italian Ambassador at Washington. While in Italy I was almost continually in conference with either Italian workingmen or Italian government officials interested in the immigration problem.

When in Rome in 1909, Ernest Nathan, then Mayor of Rome, called upon me to extend a welcome on behalf of the municipal government. He was a profoundly able man whom I found a congenial, interesting companion. He gave a dinner in my honor which was attended by important public and private citizens of Rome and proved an excellent opportunity for me to learn Italian conditions. On September 22 I was invited to speak in the celebration held in honor of the taking of Rome by the Garibaldian forces and the resulting unification of Italy. This great mass meeting was held at that point in the wall through which the army had entered.

In Rome I met my old friend David Lubin. The International Institute of Agriculture was then formally established and doing good work. I was glad to find Mr. Lubin happy in the success of his undertaking.

I was asked to confer with groups representing all governmental and industrial agencies co-operating under the Italian emigration policy. A conference was arranged by Professor Montemartini, director of the National Labor Bureau. There were represented agencies as widely diverse as the National Provident Bank and the National Federation of Labor, the Association of Manufacturers, and the National Federation of Agricultural Laborers. Participating in the conference were Francesco Nitti, Mayor Ernest Nathan, Luigi Rossi, an emigration official who had lived a number of years in the United States.

The secretary of the Italian labor organization was Rinaldo Rigola whom I found a most delightful companion. Although blind, he had a buoyant enthusiasm in his work. I met him both in Turin and in Paris at the International meeting. In 1918 I went to see him in his office.

When I returned to the United States, I continued my co-operation, especially with Signor di Palma Castiglione, in aiding Italian immigrants. This old-time friend of mine I met some years later in war-time when he was designated by the Italian government to be my military escort from Paris to Modane, the border town between Italy and France. A year later we worked together in the International Labor Commission.

In the 'nineties I met Fusataro Takano who was then a student at Columbia University. He became very much interested in the labor movement and came down to my office to ask me for information on our trade union movement which would be helpful to Japanese workers. After several conferences with him I was convinced of his ability and his sincerity. Takano was called home for service in the Japanese-Chinese war. When he was ready to return to Japan, I helped him to establish relationships with various labor papers that would enable him to sell an occasional letter containing Japanese labor news. During a number of years I kept in touch with Takano and supplied him with information of developments in the American labor movement. He spread among his fellow-workers information of trade unionism and helped to kindle a spirit that afterwards found expression when there was opportunity for Japanese workers to organize. From conversations with Suzuki and other Japanese there is no question in my mind but that the seeds sown by Fusataro Takano in his country found fruition in the organization of the Laborers Friendly Society in Japan.

Japan was over-populated and everywhere her people were coming in increasing numbers to the western coast of this country and were taking possession of whole localities in California. In addition to the differences in standards of life, there was a racial issue which made the situation critical. Organized labor of California determined to protect American workers. They united with other indignant Californians in demanding that the Legislature of California pass a law denying Japanese the right to own land in California. This agitation reached its height shortly after the World War had begun. In accord with the Anglo-Japanese Alliance, Japan became an active belligerent against Germany. The proposal of California to enact legislation that would precipitate difficulties between the United States and the government of Japan made the situation very acute. The Wilson administration was extremely anxious. The Secretary of State, William J. Bryan, went to California in person to effect a compromise. During this critical time it was necessary for me to see the President. When I called up Mr. Tumulty to make an appointment, he told me that there was an urgent matter which he would like to discuss with me and it was arranged that I should go to the White House in advance of my appointment with the President in order to have a talk with his secretary. Mr. Tumulty told me of the international implications of the California situation and asked me whether I would not request the California State Federation of Labor to withhold for the time being its demand for the enactment of anti-Japanese land laws. I told him I would do the best I could and drafted a telegram to Paul Scharrenberg which I showed to him. Mr. Tumulty took the telegram in to show to the President and returned with the statement that in his opinion it would be materially helpful.

Shortly afterwards, Dr. Gulick, who had been in Japan for thirty years, came to urge my co-operation in promoting a more friendly attitude toward the Japanese. He thought that considerable of the feeling against the Japanese was due to a hostile press. Dr. Gulick as he was preparing to return asked me if I had any advice to send to the working people of Japan. I dictated for him the philosophy underlying the labor movement organized upon principles of voluntary co-operation. The wisdom to use freedom and power must develop through experience was the keynote of the message I sent to Japanese workers.

In my later conferences with representative business men, newspaper men, statesmen, publicists, and representatives of labor of Japan as well as of China, without hesitancy I have given them as my reply the same principles and policies as were outlined in this communication to the Japanese.

In 1916 there came to my office in Washington Bunji Suzuki who had organized the Laborers' Friendly Society of Japan. Suzuki presented credentials as evidence of his good faith and dependability. I supplied him with information about the American labor movement and how to proceed to organize wage-earners. I found him a most thoughtful and sincere individual, actuated by the highest motives and purposes. He spoke beautiful English. He attended the convention of the Federation the following year. He extended on behalf of the workers of Japan a most cordial invitation for me to visit that country and help them with their labor movement.

The news of the invitation to visit Japan having spread

to the Far East, invitations began pouring in upon me from different cities in the Philippines, China, as well as Hawaii. Indeed, preparations were under way in each of these countries for my reception, entertainment, and opportunities for addresses. In the case of Japan, an invitation was also extended on behalf of the government in a semi-official way. However, the entrance of America into the World War precluded my acceptance of the invitation. Although it would have given me genuine pleasure to have gone to Japan and to have helped in their constructive work, I felt it to be my first duty to give my services to my own country and its labor movement and to do what I could to help encourage and steady the workers in Europe and in America so that nothing might be left undone to bring victory to our common cause.

After the close of the War, during the International Labor Conference and the International Conference on the Limitation of Armaments held in Washington, I met a great number of the Japanese delegates to those conferences, both representatives of wage-earners and other groups of national life. I met them in conference bodies, and the majority asked for appointments with me in my office. The delegates to the 1919 Washington Labor Conference, who represented labor and their delegates' advisors, presented me with a sword of the Ancient Knighthood of Japan. It is a work of great artistic merit. The Laborers' Friendly Society of Japan had adopted the knighthood sword as its emblem of fidelity, chivalry, and justice. They informed me that the sword was the expression of appreciation and confidence of the Japanese organized workers and added that the sword was over a thousand years old and that it took one man three years to make it. The sword is not a military sword, but had been used in the days of knighthood and chivalry in Japan. When a man failed to live up to the standards of chivalry, honor, and knighthood, he used it to take his own life; and this sword had been used three different times for that purpose. The spokesman for the party had been for twenty years a factory worker in Japan, although he was but thirty-three years old. During that time he had never seen daylight outside of the factory because the workers in Japan go to work at daylight and work until dark.

I became acquainted with the revolutionary movement in Cuba in much the same way. There had long been Cuban cigarmakers in New York City and some of these were identified with the Cuban junta. At the solicitation of some of these workers who were shopmen of mine, I at first attended their meetings. As I became more interested I went more frequently. It was there in that work that I met Charles A. Dana whom I came to know very well. As I had long admired Dana's editorial work, I counted it a privilege to be associated with him in the movement to free Cuba from Spanish tyranny. He had a wonderful ability to attract people to his leadership and a sustained virility and incisiveness of expression that made the numerous Dana stories so delightful. One became almost a legend— Dana's office cat. This vigorous, well-nourished animal Dana declared lived on manuscript. The cat was especially fond of inferior articles, but if such were not available its appetite could be appeased on various degrees of mediocrity. That cat was accredited with consuming editorials and articles that would otherwise have lowered the standards of the New York *Sun* and many an anxious inquiry from persons who had submitted articles met the urbane reply, "We are very sorry but our office cat was beyond control and your manuscript was the only one available." No goat in all the world ever had so rapacious an appetite as *The Sun's* office cat.

Through Mr. Dana I met José Marti, a writer and a member of the Cuban Junta. Then I met Estrada de Palma, the first President of free Cuba, and many others prominent in the long struggle.

The Cubans with whom I worked in the factory were usually skilled workmen and belonged to our union. Cuba, which was the chief foreign market from which the United States imported tobacco and finished cigars, was of special interest to cigarmakers. In order to evade high tariff on cigars, Cuban cigar factories not infrequently opened shops in New York. Cuban workmen followed these shops. It was important for us that not only Cuban cigarmakers in New York should be organized but that we should spread the gospel of unionism in Cuba. But a labor movement was practically impossible under Spanish rule which was at variance with the idea that the poor have rights. Because they found me very sympathetic, Cuban cigarmakers arranged that I should meet many of the Cuban revolutionary leaders at their headquarters in 48 Broad Street. As the years went by, I think I was able to render service, as was true in the case of many Latin-American countries. The Cuban revolutionary movement found the free masonic lodges effective agencies through which to work. I had not at that time joined the masonic movement, but this experience was one of the chief reasons which influenced that action.

When the Spanish-American War began in 1898, I was

glad of aid for the Cuban revolutionaries, but I was very apprehensive lest the United States inaugurate a régime of imperialism.

About a year after the close of the war with Spain, I visited Cuba in company with Gabriel Edmonston of Washington, the first president of the Brotherhood of Carpenters and at one time treasurer of our Federation. Upon the second anniversary of the sinking of the *Maine*, I accepted an invitation to participate in the ceremonies, which were most interesting—chiefly addresses and songs. While all were in high spirits a rain and thunder storm suddenly arose and placed almost everyone in jeopardy. But a few moments after we returned to the shore, the storm was over and the sun beautiful and clear.

I had many conferences with labor men while in Cuba and delivered several addresses which were interpreted in Spanish. I visited several cigar factories, particularly the Bock Factory. Mr. Bock was a German, born in Hamburg, who migrated to the United States and then went to Cuba. At that time he had lived in Havana more than forty years. He spoke both Spanish and English. He was very courteous and showed me all the interesting cigar factories in Cuba. This relationship served a good purpose a few years later when I again visited Cuba in 1904.

I had been suffering intensely during that winter with neuralgia of the face and as I could get no relief the doctor recommended a warmer climate. When finally it was possible for me to go, I sailed, in the hopes of getting relief, but I found that change of climate was not sufficient. However, there was in Havana an eminent American dentist who found the origin of my suffering in teeth. During the first few days of my stay on the Island, I wore about my face a silk handkerchief which was the cause of an amusing story, I was afterwards told.

Ralph Easley had accompanied me on the trip, but could not stay in Havana longer than four days. When I went to the steamer with him to see him off, he requested me to send a cablegram to his wife, letting her know when he would arrive in New York. While in the cable office I met Thomas Alward, the Cuban correspondent of the *New York Herald*, who stopped at the same hotel in which I stopped and whom I had known for a number of years in New York. We greeted each other heartily and then he said, "Mr. Gompers, I have got a good one on you." "You have, what is it?" He said, "I can't tell you now, but when I get a chance to tell you, you will agree that it is a good one." I said, "You have me on the anxious bench, I want to know." He indicated that in the presence of the Cubans he did not want to repeat the story. After we had gone outside he said, "I have just come from the Governor's palace and he told me this story. The Chief of Police had come into his office that morning, his eyes protruding and his hair standing on ends, and said in the most excited tones, 'Governor, I have unearthed a plot for the destruction of our government. There is an American here who goes from hotel to hotel. He meets people in these hotels and talks to them; others come to him; he has had conferences in his room—one of them lasting until three o'clock in the morning. They come and they go and there is a hurrying and scurrying about his place that is mysterious. He came here under an assumed name. I have him under surveillance now. I can arrest him at any moment. When he goes about in the streets his face is masked with a large brown silk handkerchief so as to hide his identity.' "

I had met the Governor on the day after my arrival when I called to see him and presented the compliments of the United States, President Roosevelt having asked me to convey his New Year's and personal respects in my interview with the Governor. During that interview I was in such suffering that I had to ask the Governor for the privilege of keeping my hat on and the handkerchief about my face. When the Chief of Police mentioned the fact that his suspect was walking the streets with a brown silk handkerchief over his face, the Governor immediately suspected that it was I and asked the Chief of Police, "Do you know the man's real name?" The Chief answered in a whisper, "Gompers." The Governor threw his hands up and said: "Well, I think you would better not interfere with that man nor molest him. I know him very well. He came here with a message from the President of the United States to me and called on me the day after his arrival."

The day before I left Cuba I called upon the Governor to bid him good-by and we had an hour's conversation. He prolonged the interview longer than I had expected because he wanted me to give him my views as to conditions and situations that I had observed. Just before leaving I said, "Well, Governor, you had a pretty good joke on me." He laughed and said, "I never enjoyed anything more in my life, particularly when he described your going about with your face muffled in that silk handkerchief."

Some years later when I was again in Cuba, the cigar-makers had been on strike for several months. They sent a committee to me, asking me to meet them in their headquarters. I had conferences with them, inquiring into the situation and learned that from the time the strike occurred until then, there had been no communication either by letter or conference respecting the strike and no suggestion for its adjustment. I informed them (some of them I knew personally) of the meeting that I had had on my previous visit to Cuba, with Mr. Bock. I asked them if they would consent to my visiting Mr. Bock and discussing the strike situation and conditions with him and to ascertain whether there would be any fair basis of settlement. Of course, I assured them that I would say and do nothing that would commit them to any acceptance of any suggestion which either he or I might make until the men had an opportunity of determining circumstances. To this they agreed, and the following day I asked a friend of mine whom I had known for some years in New York to inquire whether I could have a conference with Mr. Bock. The response came that I would be welcome at any time— immediately if I so wished. I went over to see Mr. Bock at his factory. He greeted me very cordially and then he discussed with me and my friend matters of current interest, not mentioning the thing which was uppermost in my mind—the strike. The factories had all been closed for a long period and there was no way of getting cigar-makers into Cuba to take the places of the strikers and the men themselves were hard pressed by their unemployment.

Finally, I broached the subject of the strike. Only in part were wages a matter of dispute. The principal point was that the manufacturers were charged with giving Spaniards and Spaniards' sons the preference in the work and discriminating against the Cubans and intending to reduce wages. Mr. Bock said that neither charge was true. I asked him whether he would be willing to say so publicly or to me. He at once declared that he would. I asked him whether he would write a letter to the cigarmakers to that effect to which he emphatically answered in the negative and said, "Since they have not come to me to lay the complaint I am not going to address them." I asked him whether he had any objection to addressing such a letter to me to which he responded in the negative at once. He said: "Here is my stenographer. You write this letter yourself and I will sign it." I availed myself of the offer, dictated the letter, addressed and written to me on Mr. Bock's letterhead in which he denied that he or his fellow-manufacturers contemplated any wage reduction or that they had discriminated against Cubans in favor of Spaniards or others and gave the assurance that no such practice would be used in the future. Mr. Bock, after reading the letter, readily signed it, and I lost no time in formalities. I thanked him, went directly to the union meeting of the strikers and presented the letter to them, and the strike came to an end the following day.

In 1900, during the convention of the A. F. of L. meeting in Louisville, I received a communication from Santiago Iglesias who was at that time in New York. Iglesias, Spanish by birth, had been living a number of years in Porto Rico and had been active in the revolutionary movement. He was a carpenter by trade and his understanding of the labor movement was based upon the Spanish school. He was then working in Brooklyn at his trade. In his usual resourceful way he got in touch with what were known as the radical centers in New York. He met Theodore F. Cuno who was at the time working on the *New Yorker Volkszeitung* and told him about labor conditions in Porto Rico. Cuno although a "radical" by profession thoroughly understood that the only agency that could help develop the labor movement in Porto Rico was the American trade union movement. He advised Iglesias to get in touch with me, and as the convention was then in session, some official action might be secured in regard to Porto Rico.

The convention directed that the labor movement declare for the right of fair trial, freedom of assembly, speech, and press for the workers of Porto Rico. Under this pledge of assistance Iglesias returned to Porto Rico where he was met at the docks by a government representative with a warrant for his arrest. He and other workmen were sentenced to terms of imprisonment on the ground that they had attempted to increase wages and better working conditions. Iglesias cabled to me the outcome of his return to Porto Rico. I wrote to the President of the United States, urging that the Porto Ricans be recognized as American citizens and that the Porto Rican workingmen be accorded the rights of free workers. Under authorization of the A. F. of L., I went to Porto Rico in 1904 where I made a thorough investigation of conditions on the Island. Under the Spanish régime, labor unions had been illegal and were disbanded. With the coming of the American flag, Porto Ricans had expected the rights and opportunities for which our flag stands.

Before our coming into possession of the Island of Porto Rico, Porto Ricans had the right to a proportionate number of representatives in the "lower" and the "upper" branches of the Spanish Cortes. All commercial or trade regulations were referred by the Cortes to the Porto Rican delegation for consideration and recommendation, and when the recommendation did not conflict with the international relations of Spain to other countries, it was usually adopted and became law. During our war with Spain, the Porto Rican people, believing in the justice and democracy of our Republic, hailed with delight and enthusiasm the opportunity of aiding our army of occupation in Porto Rico, Iglesias acting as a guide and interpreter for General Brooks. When Porto Rico became a possession of the United States, her people had neither the right of citizenship nor of representation in either house of Congress of the United States. Its international trade relations and regulations in so far as tariff was concerned were determined by the United States. They were bound by the same conditions as prevailed in any part of the United States. This reacted to the disadvantage of the people of Porto Rico both industrially and commercially.

As I had covered practically the whole Island and under the direction of men who knew the working people of the country, I saw existing conditions of work and life. They were horrible. I undertook to present these facts to our government and to the American people. This step I felt sure would materially assist in bringing better government for Porto Rico and facilitating the introduction of American practices and standards in place of the prevailing Spanish methods. Upon my return to the United States I made a series of public talks in which I presented the situation as I had found it.

About two weeks after my return from Porto Rico to our mainland (my criticism of conditions in Porto Rico had been published in our newspapers), I received a letter from Iglesias, informing me that there had been two representatives of the Department of Commerce and Labor who had undertaken an investigation in Porto Rico, that neither one of the American "investigators" had come into contact with any representative of the working people of the Island, that these investigators had been wined and dined and had been in frequent conferences with the sugar *centrales*. On receiving this information, I hied myself to the Department and sought an interview with Secretary Cortelyou. He was out of town and I had a conference then with Mr. Hanger, his assistant. I gave him the information of the course which the Department's investigators had pursued and I declared that if these men made a report which in the slightest manner undertook to discredit the statements that I had made I would inaugurate a campaign of publicity, exposing in all its nakedness the falsity of such a report, how and for what purpose it was concocted, and then take my chances with the American people for them to decide as between the veracity of the Department's investigators and me. He informed me that the two men had almost completed their report and that he would undertake to learn its nature, bring it to the attention of Secretary Cortelyou, and see what could be done. He assured me that I would be consulted in respect to the decision reached. The report was finished, but it was never made public and if it is in the archives of the office it has never reached the light of day.

I later suggested to Secretary Cortelyou—and he acted upon it—that he send a representative to Porto Rico, a fair, unbiased man, a man with an open mind, who could not be cajoled or influenced by one group or another. All I asked was that an opportunity be given to have someone accompany the Department's representative to help him to see phases of Porto Rican conditions. The Department appointed Meyer Bloomfield of Boston. Santiago Iglesias and a representative of the sugar *centrales* and tobacco planters aided Bloomfield. Bloomfield made a thorough and complete investigation and his report to the Department corroborated in every respect the situation as I had declared it to be.

I have been personally acquainted with each of the Governors of Porto Rico. With some the relations were of cordial friendship and co-operation. Governor Hunt presented me with the pen with which he signed the eight-hour law of the Island. The tributes which most of the Governors of the Island paid to the loyalty of the organized labor movement of Porto Rico to the United States were well deserved, for it was that movement as encouraged by our Federation which undertook to spread the gospel of Americanism among the people of the Island.

Governor Yager was an exception. The last time I was on the Island the workers struck against the awful conditions of life and work. Governor Yager wanted them to return to work and submit their grievances to the "kindly" interest of organized employers in a trust-controlled industry. In an interview with him in San Juan, I advised him that I might be able to come to a conclusion upon the wisdom of such a course after I made an investigation in several centers of the Island. I came in contact with the representatives of the interests and the workers, and the night before my sailing from the Island I addressed a mass meeting and advised the men not to comply with the Governor's request, for when they were thoroughly hungry they could accept that situation at any time, but while there was an opportunity to resist and secure some better result they need not capitulate. The men held out and in the course of a week real negotiations began and a settlement was reached which brought somewhat better conditions to the workers.

My Mexican friendships are related in following chapters.

CHAPTER XXVIII

ONLY once have I ever been a member of a political party. When I became of age I joined the Republican organization in the district in which I lived. To me it was an organization which still had a great purpose to fulfill. Lincoln typified that purpose in my mind. I received citizenship papers October 4, 1872, and have always tried to live up to the serious obligations of citizenship. My first vote was for Grant for President.

When I left the Republican Party I joined no other. In view of the fact that I have been charged with belonging first to one party and then to another, it may be of some interest to have the names of those for whom I have cast my ballot for president. As I have stated, my first vote after naturalization was cast for Grant; in 1876 I voted for Peter Cooper; in 1880 for James B. Weaver whom I knew personally and with whom I was on terms of good friendship. James Weaver had been influential in throwing open the Territory of Oklahoma and I aided him in his effort. A number of years later he held up the House for three days, filibustering in behalf of his plan and finally succeeded in having the Territory of Oklahoma made a state. I helped him in this movement. In the convention which formulated the Oklahoma constitution, held later, several friends of mine were members and through them I was in a position to render considerable aid. At the conclusion of the convention a resolution of thanks to me was adopted. The pen with which the proposed constitution was signed was presented to me by unanimous vote of the convention. That pen with a letter of transmission is now framed and hanging in our Federation building.

In 1884 I voted for Ben Butler; in 1888, for some cause which I do not now remember, I did not vote; in 1892 for General Weaver; in 1896 for William J. Bryan; 1900 for Bryan; 1904, Judge Alton B. Parker; 1908, Bryan; 1912, Woodrow Wilson; 1916, Woodrow Wilson; 1920, James B. Cox.

It will be observed that in recent years, I have voted for the presidential candidate on the Democratic ticket, and this has been interpreted by many to mean that I am a member of the Democratic Party. This relationship has been charged against me by Republican Party leaders and yet never claimed by Democratic Party leaders, for they know better. The Republicans used it with the hope of weakening my influence in the political field.

As I have already stated, in the first four years of my citizenship I was a member of the Republican Party. For years after in presidential elections I cast a protesting vote. I believed that the Republican Party had fulfilled its mission, growing out of the Civil War, and so far as the Democratic Party was concerned, it had no concept of the political and industrial problems of the times.

Any one who will doubt the sincerity of the non-partisan policy which I have endeavored to pursue may compare the platform declarations of the Democratic and Republican Parties and judge for himself whether I was not justified as a labor man and I hope I may say, as a forward-looking citizen, in casting my vote for a candidate nominated upon the Democratic platform. In the elections for Senators and Representatives, there is better opportunity to exercise the non-partisan policy, for I have supported or opposed the election of men aspiring to those offices with absolute impartiality, basing my course upon the pledges, attitude, and records of those candidates. That in recent years more Democratic candidates have been favorably disposed toward the cause of labor and freedom than have Republicans, is not the fault of my associates or myself.

In addition to our interests which we as citizens have in the outcome of elections and legislation, we have a primary interest in the protection and promotion of the rights, interests, and welfare of the toiling masses of our country.

I have always sought to use political situations for labor's advantage. My first acquaintance with politics came in New York in the halcyon days of Tammany Hall when John Kelly was chief. There was nothing in that sort of politics that interested me, for I was concerned for good government. In the days when I was working at my trade, before the Australian ballot system was adopted, it was hard for a workingman to maintain his right to independent use of his ballot.

No one will for a moment deny that even to the present day employers, particularly in big business, exercise altogether too much power and influence over the votes of their employes, but that does not indicate to any degree the former power and coercion of employers to control the votes of their workmen. It was not an uncommon practice in establishments employing a large number of men that the workers, under the leadership of some overseer or foreman, were marched to their various voting precincts to cast their votes under immediate surveillance.

In New York City and Brooklyn and in many other cities of the country, the only way by which men could find employment on the street railways was through the endorsement of the alderman or the other ward politicians. These held their places at the will or the whim not only of the company but of the ward politicians who, of course, controlled the votes of workmen so employed. This practice was supplemented by the influence of the saloon-keeper over the workmen, particularly workmen who were employed in and around the street car service and the river fronts. It was due to these conditions that organized labor initiated a movement to bring about secret voting, then known as the "Australian Ballot."

I did not want to be under party dictation; neither was I willing to submit to coercion from any other source. When I was working for Stachelberg, such an effort against the independence of my shopmates and myself was attempted. General Ben Butler had been nominated by the Greenback Party for the presidency. I believed in General Butler. Mr. Stachelberg took an active interest in the campaign of Grover Cleveland. He talked politics with many of the cigarmakers, of course urging his views. At one time standing behind me as I worked he said, "I understand Mr. Gompers, you are a Butler man." I was entirely taken by surprise, but turned to him and said: "You are mistaken, Mr. Stachelberg, I am not a Butler man. I am no man's man. Butler is my man."

A few days afterwards while we were at work, Mr.

Stachelberg asked for attention and told us he wished to address us on subjects involved in the campaign. The incident aroused considerable commotion and was generally discussed by the employes on leaving work. A number of us determined we would not cease work to listen to Mr. Stachelberg. We were piece-workers and would lose our own time and, in any event, we did not believe we should contribute to establishing a precedent of being compelled to listen to a political address by the employer in the factory.

About four-thirty in the afternoon Mr. Stachelberg appeared with a written manuscript, took a position midway on the stairs leading to an upper floor overlooking the factory and asked all employes to gather and listen to him. There were about two hundred and fifty of us, of whom over two hundred gathered around. The remainder of us continued at our work.

The address lasted about thirty minutes, during which time my nerves were so wrought up that I did not do more than five minutes' work. At the conclusion of his address Mr. Stachelberg said if anyone desired to ask questions he would undertake to answer. He repeated the statement, and from his changed position, I could hear and almost feel that his challenge was directed at me. He again repeated his statement and I looked up and saw that he was addressing me. I said:

"Mr. Stachelberg, I regard your proposition as entirely unfair. I may ask you a question occupying less than a minute which you could completely lose in the time of your reply. Some of the statements you have made in your address are entirely untenable, and with equal opportunity to discuss them with you I would be perfectly satisfied to take issue, but I must be excused from asking you a question."

He descended the stairs, came by my side, and we discussed the matter over half an hour. A number of the employes had already left. On reaching the street, there was much excitement among the men. In a few minutes one of the office help came into the street and stated that I was wanted in the office. I was fully under the belief that I would be told my services were no longer required. Stachelberg's partner said to me, "Mr. Gompers, I wanted to ask you whether you believe my partner exceeded his rights when he addressed the men on the political issues of the campaign?" I answered, "Most decidedly." He asked me my reasons. I answered, "Mr. Stachelberg is an employer. We come here to work to support our families, not to listen to political addresses, no matter whether they have merit or not, and he has no right to take advantage of his position as an employer to impose his political opinions upon his workmen." Stachelberg interposed and said, "You do that very thing yourself. You talk politics to the men." I answered, "Yes, that may be so, but if any of the men do not care to listen to me, they can tell me to go to hell. They can not tell you that. If you want to talk politics, if you desire to deliver an address, you can do so anywhere you please outside of the factory, and invite any and all to go, and it will rest upon any one to choose for himself whether he cares to go; but in the factory the time should be devoted to work and to supervision, not taking advantage of your position as an employer, to impose your political opinions upon your employes."

Stachelberg said, "Well, that is only your opinion." I said, "Yes, that is only my opinion." He stated, "I venture to say others will not agree with you." I answered, "Perhaps that may be true." He called one of the workmen in and he asked the same question which he put to me. The workman answered, "Well yes, it is your own shop, you can do just as you please in it." I said, "Yes, I have frequently found workmen who never have an opinion contrary to their employers."

He called a second and a third who agreed with the position I took, but scarcely with as much emphasis. There was much excitement and nervous strain during the entire incident, but it passed and a cordial good night was exchanged. I returned to work the following day and continued at employment for the firm for considerable time, being treated with respect and only leaving there on the occasion of a trade dispute. But Mr. Stachelberg never repeated the attempt to address his workmen upon politics.

The first congressional campaign in which I actively participated was that of Henry W. Blair, Senator from New Hampshire. The investigation of the Senate Committee on Education and Labor resulted in Senators Blair of New Hampshire and George of Mississippi being converted to the cause of labor and strongly impressed with the necessity for the thorough organization of the working people into trade unions. As Senator George was from an agricultural state, his position was not questioned by his constituents. There were none of them who would be materially affected by the investigation, but he, despite that fact, was very strongly sympathetic and became the supporter of organized labor as evidenced later by his amendment introduced in the making of the Sherman Anti-Trust law. Senator Blair was not only from an industrial but a railroad corporation-ridden state. The Boston and Maine, the New York, New Haven and Hartford Railroads

and the corporations operating in his state made an effort
to defeat him. Gabriel Edmonston, Frank K. Foster, and
I went to New Hampshire and helped in the re-election of
Senator Blair. He unreservedly gave the credit of his re-
election to the help of the organized labor movement.

The first time I actively participated in a political party
contest was in the Henry George campaign. Going in under
the direction of the trade union movement, I gave the best
service of which I was capable.

In 1893 occurred the preliminaries to the New York
Constitutional Convention which was held the following
year. That convention offered an opportunity to wage-
earners to prohibit practices through which the judiciary
was usurping authority to outlaw union activity. In order
to get constitutional changes, it was necessary for labor to
see to it that men who understood were elected to the
convention. For that purpose the New York trade unions
formed the Trades and Labor Conference. I was in Milwaukee attending the Cigarmakers' Convention at the time.
When in Chicago on my return trip, I learned the conference had been requested to submit names of two union men
to be placed on the Democratic ticket and that my name
had been used for this purpose, I sent a telegram to them
and to the Police Commissioners of the city of New York
(who were in charge of the administration of the elections)
declining the nomination and asking that my name be
omitted from the ballot. When I reached New York, I
learned that telegraphic communication did not constitute
legal notification and as it was too late for other methods,
my name appeared on the ballot.

This campaign occurred at the time of the municipal
reform movement. An organization to promote good

municipal government, which met twice a month in the
Amity Building, was composed of the liberals of New York
City. Dr. Parkhurst was the leader of the group. I went
to their meetings frequently and took part in their pro-
grams. This relationship helped me to get a hearing for
labor before a yet wider circle.

During this campaign in the interest of better government, the Federation was urging the initiative and referendum as a means which would enable the non-office-hold-
ing masses to protect their rights. James W. Sullivan,
father of the initiative and referendum movement in this
country, had made a study of direct legislation in Switzerland. The Federation later employed him as a lecturer
to speak on the principles and the operations of the initiative and referendum. We had but little money to spend,
but contributed what we could to better government.

I took little or no interest in the campaign for my own
election to the convention. The expense account I filed
totaled $49.65. I preferred to have the opportunity
to address the committees having these specific labor matters
in charge. When the constitutional convention met, labor
representatives P. W. Springweiler and H. F. Treffer
applied to me for detailed information on injunction and
anti-conspiracy cases in order to present these matters to
the convention. The chairman of the Convention Committee on Industrial Interests consulted me in regard to
several measures referred to his committee. As the work
progressed, a public hearing was arranged which I attended,
accompanied by representative labor men. When the draft
of the constitution was completed by the convention, the
only clause in which we were particularly interested as
wage-earners was the provision forbidding the products of

the labor of convicts coming in competition with the products of free wage-earners.

In 1914 I was again nominated for membership in the state constitutional convention and defeated. That convention under the chairmanship of Elihu Root prepared proposals that would have been harmful to the welfare of wage-earners. I entered into the campaign in which the constitution was an issue and did my best to point out its defects. It was defeated by half a million majority.

In 1889 I was nominated for the New York Senate by the Republican Party. The largest faction of the Democratic Party also nominated me. Election was practically assured. Desirous of following my own inclination as well as the pledge which I with others made to devote my activities entirely within the ranks of labor and for the trade union movement, I consulted Henry Emerick, George Block, George McKay, Henry O. Cole, and several others whose names I cannot recall and laid before them my point of view. They agreed with me that I could give no better service in the situation than to decline the nomination of both parties. However, realizing the fact that an active group leaned more toward partisan political activity of the workers, we concluded to have the opinion of one of their leading representatives, S. E. Schevitch, the Sunday Editor of the *New Yorker Volkszeitung*. If we could bridge over differences which existed between the economic movement and the political partisan movement, some unity of action could be secured for the immediate future. The five of us took the street car and ferry over to Hoboken where Schevitch lived and reached there at two o'clock in the morning, arousing him from his bed. We talked the matter over freely and fully and he agreed with our position. We felt that something had been accomplished so that co-operation between the purely political and the real labor movement would result. But in this I must candidly admit we were mistaken. At any rate, I declined the nomination of both parties in courteous but emphatic manner, giving my reasons for the declination.

In 1894 the Republican organization in the congressional district determined to offer me the nomination for Congress, but before taking formal and final action, a committee headed by Mr. Brockway, who was the proprietor of the Ashland Hotel, called upon me, gave me the assurance of my nomination by the District Convention, but wanted to know in advance whether, if nominated, I would accept. Of course, I appreciated the compliment, but I declined.

Following the industrial depression and financial panic of 1893, the money problem became the paramount issue in the presidential campaign of 1896. The monetary system of our country had, from its formation, been the free coinage of silver at a ratio of sixteen to one. The Republican Convention which nominated Mr. McKinley for President declared for the gold standard. The Democratic Convention nominated Mr. Bryan upon the silver platform. It is not necessary for me to discuss the wisdom of either declaration. However, a large mass of our people were "greenbackers" and a much larger portion of them had been swept upon an enthusiastic wave for the free coinage of silver.

The 1893 convention of the A. F. of L. had declared in favor of free coinage of silver. This position was reaffirmed in 1894 when the issue still had no partisan bearings. There was a greater tenseness of feeling accompanying the presidential campaign of 1896 than any other within my experience except that of 1916. Free silver meant to the masses who were not capitalists, liberation from the gold-bugs of Wall Street who seemed to have a strangle hold on the nation. Feeling was so intense as to play havoc with party regularity and to make dispassioned judgments impossible.

It happened that I went to the Upper Peninsula of Michigan on official business and on my return trip to Indianapolis I stopped over in Chicago where the Demo-cratic Convention was being held. The Federation offices were in Indianapolis. The Iron Miners in the Michigan Upper Peninsula were struggling hard for some betterment and the latter part of June when a strike was on I went through their mining towns, conferring with them and ad-dressing mass meetings. The situation was deeply gratify-ing and the organization was in good shape. My return trip took me through Chicago where I had engagements with a number of labor men. It was coincidence and not pre-arrangement that I was in Chicago at that time.

The convention was held in the Coliseum and I had opportunity to attend the sessions. The temper of the con-vention reflected the shifting of ordinary alignments. The old-fashioned Democrat, David B. Hill, was rejected for temporary chairman and the revolt broke through party control. The tumult in the building defied speakers. Ben Tillman and Hill both tried in vain to be heard. Then a practically unknown speaker with a remarkable, mellow, resilient voice tried for a hearing. His voice penetrated every corner of the building and forced attention. The "crown of thorns speech" became history and Bryan had leaped out of obscurity because of the carrying power of his voice. Bryan spoke the language of humanity and he appeared as the proclaimed savior of the common people who would break the power of the gold standard scepter of Wall Street.

While I was on that trip a dispatch was sent from Indianapolis to Baria Wilkins over my name endorsing John R. McLean for the presidency. When I saw the telegram in the papers, I issued a public statement declaring the telegram a clumsy forgery. I had no desire to exert influence either for or against Mr. McLean. Later in the campaign it was necessary to take up matters pertaining to the iron miners' strike with Mark Hanna. It was a delicate matter to hold the conference and prevent the newspapers from making political capital out of it.

I was active in that campaign as was necessary in order to carry out the mandate of the Federation in favor of free silver. The Federation found itself in danger of being drawn into partisan politics. I had been directed to issue a bulletin relating labor's position on silver coinage. This produced a storm from the Bryanites because it failed to endorse the Democratic Party and a protest from the Republicans who interpreted it as favorable to Bryan.

During that summer I made a number of speeches. I was for free silver, not the Democratic Party. If the Democratic Party favored free silver, well and good, for legislation is altogether too frequently enacted by partisan sponsorship.

I had come to know Colonel Wetmore of St. Louis very well in the course of negotiations in an effort to adjust the difficulties of striking tobacco workers against the Liggett and Myers Tobacco Company, of which the Colonel was president. Colonel Wetmore was one of Bryan's closest

personal friends and frequently entertained him at his home
or his camp.   The Colonel was a genial man who always
had a crowd of good fellows in his rooms.   I occasionally
went there on his pressing invitation, for I found it helpful
to get information from the group.   They always asked me
to sit in their card games, but their stakes were too high
for me.

Mr. Bryan sent a number of messages that he was anxious to meet me to which I made no reply, though I met
him once or twice without prearrangement.   One of these
meetings was in Chicago.   I had been delivering the Labor
Day address at Danville, Illinois, in Uncle Joe Cannon's
district and in the evening went to Chicago where a dinner
was arranged in King's Restaurant.   Among the guests was
Mr. Bryan.   In his address he announced that if he were
elected to the presidency he would appoint me as a member
of his Cabinet.   Of course, speeches were made by all and
during my remarks I publicly announced that though I
urged and hoped for the election of Mr. Bryan, under no
circumstances, if he were elected, would I accept any office
either in his Cabinet or in any other capacity.   To this Mr.
Bryan expressed great regret and hoped that I would change
my mind.   I then repeated with emphasis that I could accept no political office and that I knew of no circumstances
which could induce me to change my position on this subject.

Throughout the campaign I refused to let the labor
movement be annexed by a political party and I refused to
lead them into a policy from which it would take decades
to recover.   I was attacked by the silver people, but I
refused to yield my responsibility to the American labor
movement.   In Colorado feeling was intense.   Every effort

was made to force me from my non-partisan stand. My reply to W. H. Milburn of the *Denver Evening Post*, who protested against my attitude may be of interest as it expresses a life-time principle:

"You say that if I value my position as 'leader' of the common people I should lead them now. This betrays what a poor conception you have of the fundamental principles of our labor movement. Your idea seems to be that an executive officer of an organization should be their 'leader.' You do not seem to understand that a leader implies followers, and that where there are leaders and followers, there are dupers and duped. You do not know that our movement is based upon the recognition of the sovereignty of the workers; that when they declare for a purpose, they're presumed to mean what they say, and to act in accordance with it; that they require their executive officer, not to lead them, but to execute their will."

The ramifications of politics are wide, including the executive and judicial as well as the legislative branches of the government. Despite the pretensions of civil service regulations, civil service employes formerly had no redress from arbitrary decisions of politicians. I have often been called upon to intercede to prevent injustice. This often happened on behalf of the employes of the Bureau of Engraving and Printing of which the director was a political appointee. The plate printers were well organized and were thereby able to protect themselves and lend a helping hand to others. Often they brought their troubles to me.

When Claude M. Johnson of Kentucky was appointed Director of the Bureau, he soon manifested hostility not only to the plate printers' union but also to the women and girls. A committee called upon the Director with a view to having him increase the wages of the female employes. We desired to have their wages increased from $1.75 to $2 per day. Director Johnson replied that he could get girls from Kentucky, his own home state, for $5 per week and therefore would not accede to our request. Of course, I felt disappointed at his refusal to increase wages and resented his statement that he could, and by implication would, either reduce the girls' wages or import girls to take their places.

I was informed through good authority that Mr. Johnson was interested in the development of a water-power machine at Atlantic City and that some of the employes of the department had been assigned by him to that project on government time. I made complaint to the Secretary of the Treasury, Lyman Gage, and he appointed a committee consisting of Assistant Secretary of the Treasury, Frank Vanderlip; Solicitor General of the Treasury, George O'Connell, and another whose name I cannot recall. The committee had a session in the morning which I attended and presented evidence and witnesses whom I called to testify. The committee took a luncheon recess. During that time I learned over the telephone from an official of the Bureau that during the recess plate printers, whom I had asked to appear as witnesses, were taken into the Director's room and appealed to and admonished as to the testimony that they should give.

At the afternoon session I called these men as witnesses and questioned them as to their conference in Mr. Johnson's room. They confirmed my information. The committee reported, however, that there was no substantial evidence of wrong-doing on the part of Mr. Johnson.

A few days after that report was made and accepted, two plate printers came to my office and stated that they had been called into the Director's room and commissioned to come to me to say that I could have anything within the power of the Director to give if I would cease my opposition to his retention of the office. Of course, I was astonished, but said to them that I had no doubt that they conveyed the Director's proposal; yet he might change his mind and if, therefore, he was in earnest in making the offer he might write it to me. They returned to Mr. Johnson and within an hour came to me with a written promise to do anything which I desired if I would discontinue my efforts to have him removed.

I made an engagement over the telephone with Secretary Gage and went over to see him that Saturday afternoon. In brief I related the misdoings of Director Johnson as set forth by the proof which I had furnished to the committee. I then submitted the letter of Director Johnson. During the conversation I made the following remark to Secretary Gage to which he afterwards frequently referred with amusement. "I am not vindictive, but I do want that man's scalp." Within twenty minutes Director Johnson was called to the office of Secretary Gage and his letter to me was shown to him. Inasmuch as it bore his signature and was written on the letterhead of the Bureau, he could not and did not deny it. The Secretary told him that he would accept his resignation if immediately tendered. It was tendered.

One of the few attempts to get me to make a corrupt bargain occurred in connection with the Ship Subsidy Bill of 1899. A great movement was on foot by the people of New York to improve the waterways of the state and particularly the Erie Canal. In addition to increasing the carrying trade by water the intention was to create keener competition with the railways, and so a comprehensive project for the improvement of the Erie Canal and other waterways was submitted to a referendum for the raising and expenditure of several millions of dollars to carry out the project. During that campaign I traveled through the state, delivering labor addresses and holding conferences. In my talks I would refer to this project and urge co-operation and votes for the proposal. A Mr. Alexander Smith was at the head of a committee of shippers who visited my office in New York several times to furnish me data upon the subject. A few years after when under the leadership of the shipping interests a ship subsidy for the United States was proposed, Smith, because of the relations which I had with him and presuming that I would go to any lengths, first endeavored to argue and cajole me into co-operation to press the Ship Subsidy Bill.

It was being pushed by a group of lobbyists at Washington who were so bold in their methods that they approached me and offered to pay me any sum that I might mention if I would help promote the Ship Subsidy bill to subsidize a Merchant Marine and to have the government absorb the losses attendant upon a new venture. They also offered me a specific sum of ten thousand dollars for a list of the names of the delegates to the next convention together with their addresses. I knew that these lobbyists would be in Detroit with practically unlimited funds to accomplish their purpose. I was making my plans to be in Detroit among the first arrivals.

A short time before the date set for the convention, I returned to Washington to keep an engagement with President McKinley. I took a midnight train from New York and went to my home before going down to the office. That was in the time of the popularity of the bicycle and I used one in going about town. After seeing the family a few minutes, I mounted my wheel in front of the house and had gone about ten yards when some way or other (I never understood how) a passing street car caught the guard of my bicycle and threw me into the air with such force that I landed about twenty feet beyond where the collision took place, and one wheel was completely smashed. I fell upon one of the steel spokes which pierced through my clothing into my right lung. Undoubtedly, I was an unpleasant-looking object when I was picked up unconscious and carried back into the house with my head cut open and blood gushing out of my mouth. Doctors were summoned at once and three of them worked over me. My ribs were badly crushed in, ligaments were torn from both knees, the puncture through my lung made it impossible for me to breathe or speak without intense agony. The doctors bound up one side so tightly that I could not breathe through that lung. At the end of a few days it was possible to make further examination and determine the extent of the internal injury. Fortunately, there were no complications of that sort; but uncomfortable as my body was, I was still more uneasy in mind. The opening of the Detroit Convention was at hand.

During the preceding year a number of new organizations had become identified with the Federation and these would for the first time send delegates. New men were coming from old organizations. This meant that a number of delegates to the 1899 Convention would be men who were less experienced with the policies of the Federation and the principles that had thus far made for constructive progress.

P. J. McGuire was then first vice-president and I felt every confidence that he would be able to handle the situation, for he knew of the Ship Subsidy schemers. I sent him a message through Harry Szegedy and received from him a return message which did more than anything else to quiet my mind, promising that he would be on guard. Immediately after I heard that McGuire had become indisposed. News came to me also from Detroit that the ship subsidy lobbyists were diligently at work.

I think it was the second or third day of the convention that my friend John Morrison wired me asking if there was anything he could do for me. I dictated the following reply to my secretary: "You are too far away." The next day John Morrison and Mrs. Morrison were in Washington. I told him the situation and stated: "You asked if there was any way in which you could help me. There is. I am going to Detroit." Morrison protested. I was lying in bed flat on my back and had been told by the doctors not to move. I replied to his protests: "It is of no use, I am going to Detroit. You asked me if there was any way in which you could be of service. There is. I do not think it safe for me to go to Detroit alone. I want you to go with me. If you will not help me, then I will go alone." Morrison protested again and asked me to see my physician. I consented, saying that I would be glad if the physician decided yes, but anyway I was going. The physician forbade my going, but I proceeded with my preparations. It was impossible for me to wear shoes so I secured some arctics and on crutches, with the assistance of Morrison, went to Detroit and appeared in the convention. When the ship subsidy proposal came up for consideration, I told the story. It was very difficult for me to speak, but slowly and deliberately I

related the attempt to bribe me and I said. "The men on
that ship subsidy lobby are now in this hall. I could, if I
wished, point to them where they sit. I am morally certain
that they have made proposals to delegates to this convention." When I had finished my statement, the vote on the
resolution was taken and the result was that with only one
dissenting vote endorsement of the Ship Subsidy Bill was rejected. The one man who voted for the resolution was
Gilthorpe of the Boilermakers, whom no one believed to be
really dishonest in spite of his vote. There have been but
a few occasions upon which the conventions of the American
Federation of Labor have more whole-heartedly demonstrated confidence in my integrity and appreciation of my
service than after my exposure of the plans of the ship
subsidy gang. As I was hobbling out of the hall, Max
Hayes leaned forward and said to me earnestly, "Good for
you, Sam." I responded with my usual spirit of jocose-
ness: "What have I said or done, Max, to win praise from
you? It must be something awful."

The convention elected me president for the following year by unanimous acclaim. The effort sent me back
to bed in the hotel where I was compelled to remain
for more than a week. My friend John Morrison stayed
with me until I was able to leave.

I have accepted political appointments to which no
salary was attached. One which afforded most genuine
satisfaction was membership on the New York State Factory Investigating Commission.

The needless loss of 145 lives in the Triangle fire in
1911 shocked the public into a realization that something
ought to be done to eliminate the preventable hazards of

industry. The New York Legislature authorized the appointment of a commission to inquire into factory conditions and make recommendations to the Legislature. The following were appointed by the Governor: Senator Robert F. Wagner, Chairman; Assemblyman Alfred E. Smith; Charles M. Hamilton; Edward D. Jackson; Cyrus W. Phillips; Simon Brentano; Robert E. Dowling; Mary E. Dreier, and I. Abram I. Elkus was our chief counsel with Bernard L. Shientag as his assistant; Frank A. Tierney, Secretary.

As I was the only representative of labor, it was necessary for me to be in constant attendance on the meetings of the commission and help in all work. Beginning with its organization in August, 1911, until our report was filed in 1913, I gave intensive service. Deplorable as were the conditions which our investigations disclosed, I found reason for tremendous encouragement when I contrasted the situation with that of thirty years before when we cigarmakers undertook securing the abolition of the tenement house factory system and the beginnings of sanitary legislation. The commission held about thirty public hearings in industrial centers and listened to the testimony of several hundred witnesses. In addition we made personal inspections of factories. We, of course, had an adequate staff of technical experts and tried to mobilize all of the information which science and experience had developed as the basis for our recommendations and report. The deliberations and findings of our commission were an important event in the development of industrial safety, sanitation, and hygiene. We recommended to the Legislature bills to establish the necessary administrative governmental machinery. This involved re-organization of the state De-

SAMUEL GOMPERS AT 50

partment of Labor. Other measures dealt with safety standards, hours of work for women and children, and other measures to conserve human life and health.

The report of our commission was a stimulus for constructive measures in many other states. Humanitarian legislation was urged with renewed vigor and a new authority that resulted in the enactment of much valuable law and the inauguration of constructive work. As Governor Sulzer was committed to humanitarian legislation and the chairman of the commission, Senator Wagner, was leader of the majority of the Senate, and the vice-chairman, Alfred Smith, leader of the majority of the Assembly was elected Speaker, there was an extraordinary legislative situation favorable to the enactment of measures suggested by the commission.

After our report and recommendations had been submitted, February 19, 1913, was designated by the joint committees of the Legislature as the day upon which hearings would be held on bills prepared by our commission and also upon Workmen's Compensation Bills. A hearing was later to be held before Governor Sulzer in the executive chamber. Two special trains were chartered to carry the delegation from New York City to Albany for this special day. One of the trains was for the representatives of the Building Contractors' Association and of the unions of the building trades. The other was for a party of about four hundred social workers appearing in favor of the commission bills. I was on the regular train, the Empire State Express, with about half-dozen representative labor men. The executive chamber was crowded and Governor Sulzer delivered an address, declaring his purpose to aid in having the best laws enacted so as to benefit and protect not only the working people but all of the people of the sovereign state. Miss Margaret Wilson, Mr. Elkus, and I were the official spokesmen for the commission to wait upon the Governor. I engaged the Governor's attention upon a number of subjects and then repeated to him what I had conveyed on a number of occasions both orally and in correspondence, that it would be a serious mistake if he appointed any other than a labor man to the position of Commissioner of Labor whether under existing law or under the proposed re-organization of the Department. The Governor replied, "Well I offered you the position and I offer it to you now." I thanked him and said I could not accept. He replied by saying that he had made up his mind to appoint a big man, one who could measure up to the importance of the position. I mentioned a number of well-known labor men in the state of New York, particularly the name of John Mitchell.

The hearing before the Joint Labor Committees of the Legislature, to which I have already referred, was jammed to the utmost capacity. It was a remarkable sight, between fifteen and seventeen hundred people crowded into the Assembly Chamber. Not only the members of the committees of both the Senate and the Assembly were intensely interested throughout the many hours of the hearing, but there was keen interest shown by the men and women from all walks of life gathered to advocate labor measures, one after another pleading and urging the enactment of legislation to protect and better conditions of men, women, and children of toil. There was little opposition to the commission bills except the one prohibiting thereafter the construction of bakeshops below the street level. The disposition of time was in the hands of Attorney Elkus. He called upon me to be the first speaker of the commission for its bills.

While the hearing on the commission's bills was in progress there was also a hearing on compensation proposals.
Assemblyman Jackson, who had the disposition of time on
the Compensation Bill, sent a message to me, requesting me
to come over to the chamber to make an argument on his
bill which had been drafted at the request of New York
labor. I went over to the Senate Chamber and with some
difficulty got together a group of labor men including
Daniel Harris, Mr. Fitzgerald, and others representing the
state labor body.

The contractors and employers from various sections
of the state who had come up on the special train appeared
in the Senate Chamber in opposition to the bill. Some
made arguments and others simply arose in their seats to
announce their opposition. The opponents had secured the
commissioners from New Jersey, Massachusetts, and Michigan to discuss the principles of compensation law. Each
in turn claimed that the Workmen's Compensation Act of
his respective state was the most perfect of any in existence
and inasmuch as there was such great divergence among the
acts, it afforded me opportunity for facetious comment
upon the peculiar attitude of these commissioners who
claimed the most perfect law within their state yet desired
the legislature to postpone consideration of the bill for
further investigation. Daniel Harris, who left a sick bed
to go to Albany on behalf of the bill, spoke briefly and
emphatically. It was the last public appearance of Dan
Harris.

In 1914 the Legislature passed a Workmen's Compensa-
tion Law to be administered by a commission of three.
When I happened to be in Albany on business, Governor
Glynn told me that he wanted to appoint me as chairman

of that commission, an office which carried a salary of
$10,000. I told him that I did not want the position nor
did I wish to accept any political position with a salary.
He then asked me to suggest a labor man for appointment
and I mentioned John Mitchell. However, a few days
later I received a long distance telephone message from
Frank Tierney, secretary to the Governor, asking for a conference in New York City. I agreed as I was to be in New
York in a few days for a meeting of the International Social
Insurance Organization Committee.

The Governor's secretary again urged me to accept the
office of commissioner, but I refused and again submitted
the name of John Mitchell. Mr. Tierney asked me to put
my statement in the form of a letter to Governor Glynn
which I did. Soon afterwards Mr. Mitchell was appointed
chairman of the commission.

Not only have I followed the practice of not accepting
political appointment to which salaries were attached, but
I have never asked any political favors for any member
of my family or in any way assisted any of them to secure
office or advancement. On the contrary, my relatives have
found that associations attaching to the name of Gompers
through my activities have made it a handicap in the business world.

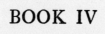

BOOK IV

BOOK IV

CHAPTER XXIX

TWENTIETH CENTURY PROBLEMS

THE coming of the twentieth century found the Federation with well-developed policies and methods. The vicissitudes which had beset our Federation in the early years, the antagonism, the rivalry of the Knights of Labor, the lagging confidence and support of the rank and file of the organized, and the lethargy of the unorganized made it a most difficult task to lay a firm foundation for growth in numbers, effectiveness, and power.

The first step in securing permanent betterment for wage-earners of America was to organize them into bona fide unions of trades or callings, skilled or unskilled, to unite and federate them so that they might exercise influence and power upon the economic field to maintain what they had and to drive on and on for a better day. Wage increases, reductions in the hours of labor, at least one rest day in the week were more potential in the meaning of the life and progress of the workers of our country than the voting for any candidate of any political party. In making these purposes the compass of the labor movement, we had entered a period of stabilization and expansion made possible by the firm foundations we had laid.

By the beginning of the Twentieth Century our Federa-

tion had developed concrete and comprehensive methods
of work. With the period of industrial prosperity which
accompanied the new century, our work of organization
was extended along lines paralleling industrial developments. Our agitation work had to do with problems arising out of sustained and organized opposition which employers began to interpose through their organizations. It
was the period of rapid development of large-scale organization and trusts.   Industrial corporations introduced a
system under which the actual owners had practically nothing to do with management. The corporation substituted
a fictitious person for the oldtime employer who knew each
of his workmen, and thereby dehumanized industrial relations.   There were the beginnings of the technology of
management, the rudiments of so-called efficiency. Like
many another field of activity, the first attempts failed to
find all the fundamentals. It proposed to treat wage-
earners in just the same fashion that it treated the materials
of industry. Against this mechanistic trend the labor movement interposed a demand that the human factor in production be considered and workers treated as men and
women.

We had developed the machinery and the discipline of
the labor movement. Discipline and regularization supplemented other cohesive forces that sustained it. We had
developed self-imposed discipline that enabled us to go
through a period of financial depression with our lines
pretty well intact. We had established the leadership of
the Federation in the labor world and as a national force.

With the Twentieth Century there came a period of extraordinarily rapid growth in the American Federation of
Labor. It was the harvest of the years of organizing work

which were beginning to bear fruits. Increase in numbers took the form of affiliation of national trade organizations and the extension of the principle of organization to workers in what were then called the "unskilled" occupations.

There were many more national trade organizations in those days than now. The structural bases of unions have varied with the development of machinery, new processes and changing materials. Many national trade unions have consolidated, merged unions in allied trades or passed out of existence. It was obvious that the keystone to sustained constructive service by the labor movement was the trade agreement reached through collective bargaining. In a large measure the work of establishing collective bargaining as a part of industrial procedure was educational. To have the support of public opinion was of strategic advantage in arguing for recognition as a normal industrial agency. The growth and expansion of the Twentieth Century multiplied the contacts between the labor movement and outside agencies and directed the activity of the labor movement as a constructive force in society as well as in industry.

Among the pioneer organizations which recognized responsibility for developing national industrial policies was the National Civic Federation. This organization brought together individuals committed to the policy of recognizing the necessity and service of organized labor. It arranged personal contacts between three groups: labor, employers, and the so-called public. It helped to establish the practice of accepting labor unions as an integral social element and logically of including their representatives in groups to discuss policies. I entered the organization with many reservations and with a distinct attitude of alertness if not suspicion. I was not in the habit of meeting employers except for the purposes of avoiding labor troubles or effecting labor agreements and adjustment of labor difficulties.

In N. C. F. conferences, wage-earners were on an equal footing with employers. Such contacts contributed to the making of a new concept of human relations in industry and to laying the foundation for the rule of reason. Such an organization was possible only because of the progress that the labor movement had made. Of course, the N. C. F. was useless without the support of the A. F. of L. The first president was Mark Hanna, an outstanding employer of that day who stood for the principle of collective bargaining before others were ready to accept it.

John Mitchell, Dan Keefe, and I were appointed to wait upon Senator Hanna to ask him to accept the presidency of the N. C. F. Hanna had wide influence in addition to his pride in maintaining good relations with his employes through collective bargaining. It was his attitude which prompted us to believe that his acceptance of the position would help bring a much larger and more influential number of men in the industrial world to become part of the N. C. F. It was at that time when the name of Mark Hanna was upon the lips of many in connection with the nomination for the presidency of the United States. He expressed himself as opposed to any movement to promote his nomination or election to the presidency, and said he would rather work as a private citizen. Knowing that the acceptance of the presidency of the N. C. F. would actually put him out of consideration for the nomination, he said, "I accept your proffer and will do everything within my power to carry out the policies which you have outlined to me." By common consent I was made first vice-president, an office which I have held continuously. In 1904 Senator Hanna died. I was acting president for eight months—that is, until the following annual convention. It was during the period of my acting presidency that I subordinated myself more than at any other period of my connection with that organization. My thought was that if the N. C. F. was to have any influence in the work it had set out itself to perform, no labor man, no matter who he might be, ought to be its president. I was very careful to designate myself either as acting president or vice-president.

I was very closely in touch with the work of the organization through whose general conferences I found innumerable opportunities to present labor's story to employers while we were talking as man to man. The contacts helped me to reach the men who controlled the making of industrial policies. There were representatives of the biggest business interests in America in the N. C. F. and in attendance at its general meetings.

As Hanna was also United States Senator from Ohio, he spent the greater part of his time in Washington. He would often bring together in conferences prominent men including men active in the labor movement. He most frequently included James Duncan, John Mitchell, Daniel J. Keefe, and me. I always found him interested in a constructive suggestion.

One day a strike broke out among the men who were employed in the Hanna Blast Furnaces in Buffalo. Within a very few minutes after the information of the strike came to me, I had a telephone call from Senator Hanna's office stating that the Senator desired me to come over to see him at his office at the Capitol. The message explained that the Senator was suffering from an attack of rheumatism and he could not come to my office. Of course, I went to see the Senator. He complained very strongly about the men striking in the Buffalo Blast Furnaces. He said that if the fires went out it would mean that the molten metal would solidify and then neither the furnaces nor the metal would be of any further use. I called his attention to the causes of the strike—that is, that the superintendents and the foremen were in league with each other and they had required men to pay from ten to fifty dollars for securing employment and that when the men had paid this money either in advance or in installments, within a short time after the payment was made they were discharged and new men employed who were also required to make the identical payments. The scheme had grown to such an extent that the men who were employed and those who had been idle on account of the trick which had been played upon them, struck work in protest against the system. The Senator was astounded and would not accept my statement as true. I answered that if he would have two or three of his superintendents and foremen in his office the following morning I would see to it that a few of the men who were the victims would be there also and my statement would either be refuted or confirmed. I added that if he would carry this plan out I would advise the men by telephone to return to work immediately and I felt confident that they would do as I requested.

I got into telephonic communication with Thomas F. Tracy, one of our most intelligent and active organizers who at the time was located in Buffalo, and conveyed to him the message to get to the men, tell them the situation and urge them to return to work immediately as I felt sure the grievances, if founded on fact, would be remedied. I asked him also to have six or more of the men who were victims and those who had joined the strike, to be in Washington the following morning and the Federation would pay their traveling expenses. The conference was held the following morning in the Senator's office. The Senator was astounded when the true situation was disclosed and at once peremptorily discharged all the men who were responsible for the scheme. It was a sorry lot of superintendents and foremen who left the Senator's office, for the disclosure of their practices not only cost them their positions but the positions of others to whom the message would come in a few hours by telephone or telegraph.

The Senator asked me to stay after all the others had gone and he said, "Sam, I didn't know that any such thing could exist in any plant and much less in a plant which I owned. I am glad you brought it to my attention. If it can be stopped in any way, I will stop it. But," said he, "these men in striking in blast furnaces acted so undiplomatically." I replied, "Yes, that is true, Senator, very undiplomatic, but we don't raise diplomats on thirteen, fourteen, or fifteen cents an hour." My reply changed his entire mood. It hit him just right. He leaned back in his chair and laughed more heartily than I had ever seen him.

The man who was chiefly responsible for the general opinion of Hanna was Homer Davenport, the cartoonist. Davenport came to see me at my office a short time before his death. He discussed with me many things of interest and importance. Among the things he mentioned was regret which he felt for two acts of his professional career as a cartoonist: one his misrepresentation of labor; and the

other, his caricature of Senator Hanna as the man with the
dollar mark, and added, "I placed a suit of clothes with
the dollar mark on the wrong man." He closed that statement by saying he had determined to rectify his error by
paying a tribute to the high character and purpose of Mark
Hanna. When the Senator passed away, Davenport drew
a sketch which was published in the New York *World* as
his testimonial of respect and appreciation.

My duties have been with the workers and with employers and business men not only in the avoidance of an industrial rupture, but when such a situation existed, in the
effort to adjust matters in dispute. With the increasing
importance of labor work came a number of invitations
from employers and important financiers to meet them or
groups of their friends. For years I have been engaged
in a militant movement which inevitably develops strong
partisan feeling. I could not bring myself to accept social
invitations without the assurance of the presence of other
labor men. I knew the rank and file of my movement and
I did not want in any way to arouse suspicion or doubt
in their minds. That I knew would render all of my work
ineffective.

Though I was willing to meet employers frequently on
the common ground of general conference and committee
work, I refused to meet them individually or accept invitations to their homes. A number of such personal invitations
came to me from those who were genuinely interested in
me and my cause and from others who were merely seeking the novelty of entertaining a labor leader. I accepted
only a few of such invitations. One of the first was from
Charles R. Flint who took a great pride in the statement that he was the organizer of the first American

trust. He was much interested in my position and statement upon trusts. In order to understand fully just what was in my mind and perhaps to secure co-operation of the labor unions in defense of economic expansion, Mr. Flint asked me to dine with him at his home. He said that he was inviting a number of big business men at the same time. I told him very frankly that I would not go unless he would invite also one or two labor men whom I would suggest to go with me. I did not intend to go into any such conference without labor men present who would be in a position to confirm by personal knowledge any statement that I might make. Mr. Flint invited Sam Donnelly and Henry White. The dinner was in Mr. Flint's house in New York. I do not now recall the names of any of the business men present except Colonel Colt of the Colt Firearms Company. We discussed economic conditions and tendencies in the United States. I expressed myself freely and frankly, reiterating statements that I had made elsewhere that the trust or centralized control over production was a natural development of industry and that legislation to curb this development was really a limitation on the industrial and commercial development of the United States. I told them that so far as I was concerned I favored greater freedom for employers and business men in the development of economic plans. I told them that labor organizations were also voluntary associations for production and distribution and that whatever restrictive or prohibitive legislation was enacted was always used more drastically against associations of workers than against associations of employers. I recognized that combinations of capital were seriously embarrassed by anti-trust legislatian, and that capital was diverting industrial combinations from industrial functions to control the judicial, the legislative, and the executive functions of government, both Federal and state, in order to pervert the administration of anti-trust law. I declared that if concerns, which were employers of labor and possessors of capital, proposed to continue to ignore or make war upon labor unions it would make no difference to labor what happened to the industrial organizations. If the captains of industry expected any assistance from labor, they must see to it that the same rights of organization were accorded to labor which they demanded for themselves and they must make common cause with us for the full rights to which we as labor unions were entitled; otherwise, what happened to them under the anti-trust laws was of no concern to us.

Although I have gone freely and frequently among meetings of employers and to any sort of a conference that they might invite me, I have gone as the spokesman for labor, and have always felt that I had to be on guard for I have feared the Greeks even when bearing gifts. The way that I have been able to best maintain most complete alertness has been to defer gratification of any physical appetite or pleasure. At this dinner of Charles R. Flint as at many similar dinners and banquets I did not eat the food served. After the dinner Donnelly and White went with me to a restaurant where I got a bite to eat. My practice about eating, however, was never extended to prohibition of smoking, if good cigars were available.

I remember a similar conference years later with Vincent Astor and Ogden Mills. These men became interested in a discussion at one of the meetings of the National Civic Federation, and an appointment was made to continue the conference the next day. I spent considerable time recounting the purposes and methods of the American Federation of Labor. I made a special effort to appeal to their understanding, for their influence as men of wealth gave them a peculiar power to be helpful in the struggle for the betterment of wage-earners. I told them that as a spokesman for those who toil I welcomed their co-operation and if instead of co-operating they opposed trade unionism for my part I was perfectly willing that they should be thrown to the wolves to make way for the progress of the labor movement. Perhaps my statement to them was about the most brutal they had ever listened to, but I did not make it in a spirit of brutality, but in appreciation of the struggle of life in which victory for some might mean destruction for others.

That invitations began to come to me to address organizations representative of big business such as Boards of Trade, Chambers of Commerce, business men's clubs, etc., was evidence that they had begun to realize that there was a labor problem and that it was of national and industrial importance. Of course, I had met a number of these men in adjusting industrial difficulties, in reform gatherings and in civic meetings, but in their hearts they regarded me as an agitator and a more or less dangerous rebel against the existing order. One of the first invitations that came to me from the Brahmins of big business was to speak at the banquet of the New York Board of Trade and Transportation in 1902. Realizing the importance of that address I prepared my statement in advance. I was to respond to "Labor is Always Honorable; To the Laborers Always Honor Is Due." I wrote a simple statement of the meaning of the trade union movement.

In addressing a group usually classed as labor's enemies,

I felt the responsibility of an ambassador to seek to bring about better understanding between two contending forces. An amusing but illuminating sidelight on my new undertaking was a personal problem—should I wear a dress suit? I talked the problem over with my secretary who, like every real secretary, was an emergency institution. Finally, I concluded that non-conformity to conventions would only make me conspicuous and would not help my cause, so I bought my first evening suit.

At another meeting of the National Civic Federation at which George W. Perkins of the International Harvester Company presented his ideas of profit-sharing, again it fell to my share to say unpleasant things. Other representatives of labor made merely polite speeches. I presented an interpretation of the struggle of labor in all of the brutality which attends any struggle for the survival of the fittest.

In all my relationships with the National Civic Federation, I have been on the alert, but in all justice to that organization it should be understood that no position it has taken upon labor has been adopted in which I did not have an influencing vote. If any mistake in policy was made, it was not through a desire to injure labor but because there was not a complete understanding, and such mistakes have been remedied when I have submitted the good reasons why the policies ought to be revised. My association has been conditioned upon the helpfulness of the relationship. Undoubtedly, the forum instituted under the auspices of this organization made possible a wider understanding of labor issues and afforded a rather dramatic background for important statements. Before the Federal Department of Labor was authorized by Congress, the N.

C. F. undoubtedly rendered a constructive service in its corps of conciliators whose services were available in industrial disputes. However, my relationship with the N. C. F. has not been viewed without suspicion by some of those within and without the labor movement.

Objections have come chiefly from those who relied upon declarations on "class consciousness" as a claim to leadership in the labor movement. These self-advertised radicals have time and again tried to force me to withdraw from the N. C. F. Because I knew I was advancing the interests of the labor movement through that relationship I steadfastly refused to withdraw; several times the issue was injected into the conventions of the American Federation of Labor, notably at Atlanta, but after full discussion on the issue my course has uniformly been heartily endorsed. Within my own organization, the Cigarmakers, I have had also to defend my policy. At one time the local union of which I am a member, No. 144, called a special meeting to consider my reply to a challenge to defend my connection with the N. C. F. Morris Brown and others who were opposed to my policy were spokesmen for the opposition. I maintained my position without assistance. Although Brown, through his contacts with the membership of the organization, had a large personal acquaintance, at the close of the debate my course was sustained by the vote an overwhelming majority.

At the convention of the International Cigarmakers' Union, Mahlon Barnes introduced a resolution that no member of the N. C. F. could also be a member of the International Cigarmakers' Union. As I was the only member of the International who also belonged to the Federation, I was the only person affected. At my suggestion the resolution was made a special order. Barnes and Brown and others divided the time of those in favor of the resolution, but I again maintained my own defense. Although there was a considerable portion of the convention hostile to the administration of which I was a member, the proposal was overwhelmingly defeated.

A later chapter came during war-time, when the secretary of my local union, Morris Brown, and other cigarmakers—all Socialists—came to me to arrange a conference for them through the N. C. F. to adjust an industrial dispute. I enjoyed rendering the service.

The changing industrial tendencies of the twentieth century were first manifest in the basic industries. Impersonal management supported by concentrated economic power presented difficult problems to our scattered and comparatively weak unions. The coal industry had been partly organized. Out of the coal strike inaugurated in 1897 came the agreement for collective bargaining in the central competitive field in 1898. On the other hand, union development did not keep pace with rapid consolidation in the steel, textile, and packing industries. Our progress was conditioned by many human factors which determined action by the rank and file as well as leadership.

The second big achievement in coal came through the anthracite strike of 1902, which was an epoch-making event in labor history. Since the 'nineties there had been no trade unions in the anthracite district and the Coal Trust was in control. It was a combination of mines and coal-carrying roads. When I was in the district in 1897 with George Chance and P. J. McGuire, we discovered very definitely that one of the chief conditions by which the operators prevented organization was the power they exercised through company police and detectives.

After the United Mine Workers established collective bargaining in the bituminous field, they undertook to secure a similar agreement in the anthracite region. There followed a battle royal with the anthracite trust. John Mitchell, who had become president of the United Mine Workers in 1898, was then a young man and comparatively inexperienced. As he had been a member of the Executive Council since his election to the presidency of his organization, I met him very frequently and he talked over his problems very frankly with me and sought my advice upon matters of important policy.

Control of the anthracite mines and the coal-carrying roads of Pennsylvania was in the hands of two Wall Street groups unfriendly to each other. J. Pierpont Morgan was at the head of one group. The partner of his firm who was closest to him was George W. Perkins, who was very active in the work of the National Civic Federation. Perkins had a broad human understanding of the problems of industrial relations. The group with which he was associated had submitted a three-year agreement which was receiving attention until the Miners' convention, contrary to the advice of President Mitchell and his Executive Board, declared solidly in favor of a sympathetic strike of the bituminous miners in support of the anthracite union. As the bituminous miners were working under an unexpired contract, the very discussion of a sympathetic strike aroused unfavorable criticism even though it was never approved. The anthracite operators at once seized this action as an opportunity to declare that labor agreements were worthless. Because there has been need for so much militancy in the labor movement it has not always been possible to maintain an even balance of judgment which makes against violation of contracts.

I knew that a strike was inevitable in 1902 unless the operators conceded the Miners' demands. It was improbable that they would concede, so we prepared to gain the utmost of advantage in the way of the support of public opinion. The National Civic Federation had just organized its Division of Conciliation and Mediation. The division was made up of three representative groups. Among those representing the public were ex-President Grover Cleveland, Cornelius N. Bliss, Oscar S. Straus, Charles Francis Adams, Archbishop Ireland, Bishop Potter, Charles W. Elliott, Franklin McVeagh, John J. McCook, John Milburn, Charles J. Bonaparte, and Ralph M. Easley. The representatives of employers were Marcus A. Hanna, Charles M. Schwab, S. R. Callaway, Charles A. Moore, Edward P. Ripley, J. Kruttschnitt, and H. H. Vreeland. Those representing labor were Frank P. Sargent, Theodore J. Shaffer, James Duncan, Daniel J. Keefe, James O'Connell, Martin Fox, James M. Lynch, Edgar E. Clark, John Mitchell, and Samuel Gompers.

I was asked to draft a statement of the purposes of the Division that would be acceptable to labor and I remember performing that particular duty, going downtown to a meeting of the Civic Federation in one of the New York street cars. It was as follows: "To do whatever may seem best to promote industrial peace and prosperity; to be helpful in establishing rightful relations between employers and workers; by its good offices to endeavor to obviate and prevent strikes and lockouts;

to aid in renewing industrial relations where a rupture has occurred." All agreements were to be mutual and no power of compulsion was permitted.

When the anthracite coal situation became acute, it was arranged that this Division should call conferences of the operators and the Miners. Two such conferences were held before the existing agreement expired. Leadership among the operators lay with George F. Baer, W. H. Truesdale, E. B. Thomas, and R. M. Olyphant. The employers were thoroughly organized under the interlocking system by which the mines and the coal-carrying roads were consolidated. The operators felt so sure of their power that they were arrogant in their clear-cut declaration of absolutism. George F. Baer added to industrial autocracy a divine sanction which has become a classic. He proclaimed the trusteeship of the operators, declaring: "The rights and interests of the laboring man will be protected and cared for not by the labor agitator but by the Christian men to whom God in his infinite wisdom has given the control of the public interests of the country."

During the entire anthracite coal strike, no man was more in earnest in his effort to bring about adjustment for improved conditions for the miners than Oscar S. Straus. He was indefatigable. When feeling ran highest during the strike, Mr. Straus found that it was impossible for him even to have conferences with men with whom he had always been upon most intimate terms—friendly, business, and financial. He was rebuffed. Indeed, the generally well-contained, dignified, and diplomatic neutrality of the man gave way to bitter resentment.

On May 12 work was suspended in the mines. All mine workers remained out until October 23. During the summer months, no one worried about the strike.   The American Federation of Labor helped to finance the strikers, for the United Mine Workers did not have big resources. We issued an appeal to all wage-earners.   The anthracite miners showed no signs of weakening, but week after week maintained a solid front.

Coming at a time when the hue and cry against the trusts was at its height, the declarations and course of the anthracite operators made friends for the striking miners. The public felt a sympathetic understanding of the injustices heaped upon the men.   There was a strong public opinion in favor of President Roosevelt's taking over the mines and operating them.   Roosevelt considered this course and asked for legal advice upon it.   Finding no legal authority he began to devise a way to adjust the situation. President Roosevelt made several other proposals which were discussed with me in formative stages, one of which was communicated to me through the Commissioner of the Bureau of Labor Statistics, Carroll D. Wright, proposing the miners return to work and allow three judges of the Federal Court to hear and make award regarding wages and conditions of the miners.   Mr. Mitchell at that time was in Buffalo and I finally got in communication with him over the long distance telephone and submitted my apprehensions of the President's proposal.   After hearing fully he answered that under no circumstances could he agree to such a proposal.   Much to my surprise the newspapers the following morning carried the story accurately, disclosing that there must have been a leak in the telephone service. I entered protest against the company's violation of confidential conversation and business ethics.

About the middle of September, when public interest

in the strike was keenest, occurred the first formal meeting of the Coal Trust under its official name "Temple Iron Company." The group comprising this trust were the anthracite operators and representatives of the coal-carrying roads. The meeting was attended with the kind of publicity that made it an affront to public intelligence. It was deliberate defiance of the Sherman Anti-Trust Act as well as public opinion and welfare. There had been arranged for the evening of that same day a gigantic protest meeting to be held in Madison Square. It was Saturday evening and there was an immense attendance. The meeting denounced the coal barons for refusing to arbitrate the cause of the strike. Mitchell, of course, was the chief speaker. Among the others were Henry George, Jr., Charles Francis Adams, John H. Crosby, O. S. Crosby, and I. After the meeting Arthur Brisbane asked me to come with him to Lüchow's Restaurant on Fourteenth Street as he wanted to say something to me of importance. I asked a couple of my friends to come along with me and there and then Brisbane handed me one thousand dollars in bills which he said Mr. Hearst wanted to present in aid of the striking miners. I asked my friends to accompany me to the Ashland Hotel and I arranged with Mr. Brockway the proprietor to take the thousand dollars and make out a check in that sum payable to me which I presented the following Monday to the Secretary of the United Mine Workers of America and confidentially informed him the name of the donor. Appeals for aid for the miners brought a generous response from all classes of people. A number of lawyers gave not only money but offered to give professional services without fee. Labor men gave generously as likewise did a number of government officials.

The Federation sent an address to all organized workers, suggesting that in each locality the business, professional, and public men form relief committees and solicit
financial and other contributions, that the hour between ten
and eleven each Monday be, during the remainder of the
strike, miners' hour, and the wages earned during that hour
be contributed to the strike.

When it became time for coal consumers to lay in the
winter supply, anxiety developed, but it was significant that
no one questioned the position of the miners.   The politicians became anxious, particularly the two Senators from
Pennsylvania, Quay and Penrose.   On October 1, President Roosevelt sent telegrams to the miners and mine operators asking them to come to Washington for a conference.
Roosevelt was confined to the house at the time following
a minor operation on his limb which was performed in
Indianapolis.   He was at the time living in a house in
Jackson Place while changes were being made in the White
House to separate the executive offices from the house
proper and to add sufficient room accommodation to make
the building more adequate.   The President's request was
complied with.   John Mitchell arrived early the next
morning.   I went down to the Hotel Reuter to confer with
him before he went to the White House.   There were with
him three other miners, Thomas Nichols, Thomas Duffy,
and John Fahey.   The operators' representatives were
there.   Although President Roosevelt put the case bluntly
and insisted that public interest was primarily concerned,
the operators refused absolutely to make any concessions.
President Roosevelt asked the representatives of both sides
to submit the issues in dispute to a commission to be named
by him.   Again the operators refused.   Following this sug-

gestion, John Mitchell made the proposal that the entire controversy be submitted to J. Pierpont Morgan. Morgan was heavily interested in the anthracite situation, but the miners had confidence in his fairness and confidence in the justice of their demands. After the conference Mitchell and I again discussed the situation before he returned to Pennsylvania. In a few days, conferences were called in New York. Morgan was working indirectly to bring about an adjustment. Again the operators rejected all suggestions. Then Mr. Morgan came to Washington.

Before naming the personnel of the anthracite coal commission, Roosevelt had a series of conferences with John Mitchell, Frank Sargent, and me. Mitchell made a strong plea to have a representative of the mine workers on the commission or in any event to have a representative of organized labor. Roosevelt did not feel that he could force the operators to go along in case he made such an appointment. However, when the commission was made public I gave an interview, stating that I thought organized labor ought to be represented on the commission. The commission was not only to make recommendations upon the industrial controversy but was to point out methods by which the industry itself could be better organized in order to avert future industrial ruptures. The work of that commission was one of the pioneer studies of an industry from the approach of scientific organization. In view of the scope of the inquiry which the commission was developing, it advised those interested to appoint counsel to represent them. This suggestion was made in a spirit of intended fairness.

While this commission was working out its procedure, there came to my office one day Henry D. Lloyd, John R.

Commons, and Walter Weyl. They stated to me that they had been in conference with John Mitchell of the Miners and with Carroll D. Wright of the Department of Commerce and Labor, and also a member of the Coal Commission. The commission had that day advised Mr. Mitchell to be represented the following Monday at hearings by counsel. I suggested the names of several lawyers if legal counsel were to be had. Among the names that I suggested was one who I was told had during the day been designated as not desirable. My comment was that in any contention I did not care to have either the court or my opponent determine for me who my counsel should be. I then stated I had the volunteer offer of other eminent lawyers and while they were in a position to contend for the legal phases involved in the control and ownership of railroads and mining companies, yet I doubted whether they were in sympathy with trade union contention on the matter of wages, hours, conditions of employment, and union rules. I knew that the coal companies would have the most eminent and best-known lawyers of the country. If counsel were needed for the miners, it was technical counsel to enable them to present industrial situations more convincingly and accurately. I therefore said it was my firm conviction that Mr. Mitchell ought to insist that he and his colleagues conduct the miners' side before the commission because the introduction of lawyers into the hearing would becloud and befog the investigation and minimize its industrial effectiveness. I believed Mr. Mitchell should insist that so far as the miners were concerned the hearings should be confined to the question of determining wages, hours, and conditions of employment in the mines. Mr.

Lloyd and Mr. Weyl agreed with me. Professor Commons remained silent. We agreed that I should call up Mr. Mitchell over the long-distance telephone which I did, speaking to him at Wilkes-Barre. Although Mr. Mitchell agreed that my position was the right one and would bring the most practical and advantageous results because it would focus the investigation on questions of industry and economics and not of law, he had already been advised of the course of the commission and had agreed in the suggestion to be represented by counsel.

The principal attorney for the coal operators was Wayne McVeagh. The leading attorney for the miners was Clarence Darrow. The day before the final hearing, Darrow and Mitchell both talked to me over long-distance telephone from Scranton. They asked me whether I would not come to Scranton at once to be there the following day and give testimony on behalf of the miners. Of course, I at once answered that I would and left Washington that evening for Philadelphia, changing trains there. When I arrived at Scranton about 1:45 in the afternoon, Darrow and Mitchell were awaiting me at the station. We got into an old-time cab and drove up to the City Hall and there I went upon the stand.

To the questioning of Darrow I made answers and explanations and made point after point in favor of collective bargaining, higher wages, the shorter work-day, the benefit which I knew would accrue to the miners and their families, to operators, to the public generally, and to our country. I was then turned over to Mr. McVeagh for cross-examination. He asked me but one question. Upon the conclusion of my testimony which ended the hearing, Judge

Gray, chairman of the commission, called me over where the commissioners were sitting and publicly in the name of the commission thanked me for my testimony.

Several times I have been asked what in my opinion was the most important single incident in the labor movement of the United States and I have invariably replied: the strike of the anthracite miners in Pennsylvania. The conditions of the miners in the bituminous and anthracite fields were terrible. The 1897 strike formed the beginning of the movement for the regeneration of the miners, and then the anthracite fields were affected, but there were so many varieties of nationalities, of politics, of religious antagonisms that concerted action was practically impossible; neither trusted the other and all lost confidence in themselves. The shacks and huts in which the anthracite miners lived and the "pluck me" stores were in full blast. The miners' families had not only to pay rent to the corporations which owned the shacks but they had to make their purchases of all the necessaries of life, meager as they were, from the company stores at double the prices for which they could be had elsewhere. If the full amount earned had not been purchased, they were haled before some overseer and threatened with eviction and discharge. The tools, gunpowder, and clothes, such as they were, all had to be purchased from the company. There was the company doctor for which the men had to pay, the company graveyard, the company parson or preacher, so that it was a common saying that children were brought into the world by the company doctor, lived in a company house or hut, were nurtured by the company store, baptized by the company parson, buried in a company coffin, and laid away in the company graveyard. Boys of ten, eight, and six years of age were employed at breaker-boys in the mines. The strike of the miners abolished that whole system. They secured the shorter work-day with higher pay, and from then on the miners became not merely human machines to produce coal but men and citizens, taking their place among the fairly well-paid, intelligent men, husbands, fathers, abreast of all the people not only of their communities but of the republic. The strike was evidence of the effectiveness of trade unions even when contending against trusts.

In steel, the second basic industry, the elements in the problem were slightly different from those of coal, and the union policies practically the opposite. In that industry came the culmination of the trust idea, with the formation of what was then regarded as a super-trust, the United States Steel Corporation. Up until that time labor organizations maintained their standing in the steel industry.

In the 'eighties and the early 'nineties the Amalgamated Association of Iron and Steel Workers was the strongest trade union in America. It had been officered by able men. Its membership had been chiefly English, Irish and Welsh. The Amalgamated Association had been accepted by employers as one of the necessary agencies in the industry. The Association united with employers in furtherance of protective tariff. When the flood of new immigration began sweeping into the steel industry, the Amalgamated refused to organize the unskilled workers who were increasing rapidly in numbers. At the time of the Carnegie strike, the Amalgamated controlled eighty per cent of the workers in the industry. When the steel corporation was organized by J. Pierpont Morgan and Company, Shaffer, then president of the Amalgamated, contrary to my advice, made a demand upon Morgan for the establishment of the closed union ship. Morgan resented Shaffer's demand and flatly declared he would oppose him and break him if it took five years. The Steel Corporation adopted a policy of opposing extension of trade union organization. The steel workers called strike after strike, but made no progress. In the much-discussed strike of 1904 I made use of every agency available to me to assist Shaffer by getting conferences for him with the powers of Wall Street and by trying to further mutual understanding.

At one time in a conference with Charles M. Schwab, who was then president of the United States Steel Corporation, we obtained an offer that the mills which were union before the strike occurred would be recognized as union establishments, but in the other mills recognition of the union should not be forced, for, as Schwab stated, "the unionization of those plants must be your job, not mine." This offer I communicated from New York to President Shaffer in Pittsburgh over long-distance telephone. He flatly rejected it, saying that he would rather lose all than to accept any such offer. Though we rendered every assistance within our power, the contest was bitterly fought and finally was brought to a close without the realization of the aims. Under the old policy of that organization, they refused to accept mills as union establishments unless the union scale was put into operation at once. As a compromise they agreed that the Federation should organize these plants and by every means within our power try to secure the scale for the men, but when that was obtained the mill as a union establishment was to be turned over by the Federation to the Amalgamated Association.

Certain phases of this controversy were coming before the New Orleans convention. Mark Hanna, who was then president, was using all of his influence to prevent the full story of the activity of the National Civic Federation from being disclosed in the convention. I vigorously protested against Mr. Hanna interfering in this or any other internal labor affair, and the course was never again attempted.

A few months later Mr. Hanna attempted to get me to intervene in a political controversy in Connecticut in behalf of a labor candidate. I ignored his request. From that time on there has been practically no difficulty in maintaining the practice that internal affairs of the Federation shall be determined entirely by labor men.

Things went on from bad to worse, until in 1909 I made the proposal that we launch a new campaign for organizing the steel workers. My plan was to have a committee of representatives of those organizations immediately concerned and to accompany the work of organization with a demand upon the government to investigate the United States Steel Corporation. I did not believe in the Sherman Anti-Trust Law because I did not believe that legislation would prevent normal, necessary development of industry, but since the law was on the statute books and the practices of the steel corporation were in open and flagrant violation of that law and since the corporation denied to wage-earners the right of collective action which they arrogated to themselves, it seemed to me that the labor movement was in a strategic position to call attention to the situation.

Together with a committee of labor men I presented to President Taft a bill of particulars charging the United States Steel Corporation with violation of Federal law and with practices subversive to human welfare. It was our plan that similar charges and indictments were to be submitted to the Governors of those states in which were the principal plants of the corporation. In Pennsylvania and in Ohio the charges were presented to the Governors by a committee of labor men. In Indiana I accompanied the committee that presented the complaint to Governor Thomas R. Marshall. In all cases we asked for an investigation. President Taft referred the matter to the Department of Justice which reported it was inadvisable to take additional action then because there was pending a decision by the United States Supreme Court which was expected shortly and which would vitally affect procedure by the Department. However, President Taft requested the Department of Labor and Commerce, through Dr. Charles P. Neill, then head of the Federal Bureau of Labor Statistics, to make a study of labor conditions among the steel workers. Dr. Neill performed a very comprehensive and valuable piece of work which caused the officials of the steel corporation to "cuss him" and gnash their teeth.

However, the organization campaign did not succeed. Under its cheap labor policy the steel industry filled its mills with workers from Eastern and Southeastern Europe, creating difficulties of Americanization and unionization. It was not until the European War and stoppage of immigration that another real opportunity arose that made an organization campaign seem feasible.

As this letter indicates, I have been unreservedly opposed to any type of compulsory arbitration. In truth, I have never looked hopefully upon arbitration as a method for achieving satisfactory industrial results. Satisfactory industrial agreements must, it seems to me, be evolved out of a mutual experience and understanding between the parties most concerned. Arbitration injects influences not immediately concerned in production. But disinterestedness should not be confused with equity. Absence of industrial dislocations does not necessarily mean industrial peace. Nor does industrial peace necessarily indicate industrial progress. The suggestion is deceptive because it seems an easy way to accomplish a difficult task. Some trade unionists were deceived by the suggestion. These were chiefly men whose thinking was not directed by a well-grounded economic philosophy, and usually they worked in trades that were not well organized.

The first proposals within my experience for compulsory arbitration were suggested with reference to transportation. Though the proponents had railroads in mind, those employed in water transportation would have come under the provisions submitted. Some of the advocates stated they desired to establish the same status between railway employees and their employers as existed between sailors and ship-owners. The seamen could not quit work even when the boat was in safe harbor. Realizing the bitter consequences of involuntary servitude, under Furuseth's leadership the seamen had begun their long struggle for the rights of free men. Furuseth immediately grasped the danger hidden in the arbitration proposals. But there was no unity in the thought of the labor movement upon that point at that time. The chiefs of the Railroad Brotherhoods favored the proposals and they were representing the workers chiefly concerned. The Brotherhoods were then weak organizations with little promise of their present splendid strength. The situation involved difficulties.

During 1895, the year McBride was president of the Federation, the first Erdman Bill with its compulsory features was introduced in the House. He was in favor of the principle, having written several newspaper articles advocating the adoption of legislation to establish compulsory arbitration. It was said that the first draft of the bill came from Richard Olney who defeated the Pullman strike with Federal injunctions. Furuseth and Strasser were in Washington that year as legislative committeemen for the Federation. They opposed the measure, but concentrated on having the workers in water transportation excluded from its provisions. Furuseth secured from the Denver Convention condemnation of efforts to apply maritime laws to railroad workers with consequent involuntary servitude. McBride's attitude upon compulsory arbitration was a factor that contributed to his defeat.

The New York Convention adopted a resolution drawn up by Furuseth and me, making earnest and emphatic protest against compulsory arbitration of labor disputes—compulsory compliance with award and decision which would make it an offense to quit employment.

Since labor representatives had not been able to reach a unanimous conclusion on the proposal, I arranged for a conference between the Brotherhood chiefs and the Executive Council of the A. F. of L. in Indianapolis as a step toward clarifying thought. The conference directed the Executive Council to secure legal advice upon the effects of the measure. I requested Ralston and Siddons of Washington, D. C., to give me an opinion upon the application of the bill and the compulsory element.

However, the Railroad Brotherhoods made up their minds they wanted the Erdman Act and asked their attorneys for a legal opinion. That opinion, of course, did not find any reason for apprehension as to involuntary servitude, and the brotherhoods officially endorsed the bill. Edward E. Clark of the Brotherhood of Railroad Conductors came to the Cincinnati Convention to explain the position of the Railroad Brotherhoods. The convention appointed a special committee to consider the matter. On the ground that the proposed law contained provisions for enforcing the award, the committee reported against endorsing the bill. In order not to prejudice the case of the Brotherhoods, the convention referred the report to the Executive Council, directing the Council to secure legal opinion upon the bill. When the offices of the Federation were removed to Washington, it was possible for me to give much more sustained attention to legislative happenings. I was able to keep in touch with legislative development and to talk over proposals with congressmen. The four Brotherhood chiefs authorized Dolphin of the Railway Telegraphers to submit the measure to an attorney for an opinion. I could not get Dolphin to accept any other attorney but J. J. Darlington, and I finally yielded to his selection against my own judgment of his lack of understanding of the theory and the fundamental principles involved. On a given day Dolphin and I appeared before Mr. Darlington and argued our respective sides, and Mr. Darlington, as I expected, gave his opinion that the proposed bill did not involve compulsion for laborers to work against their will. By strange coincidence, or perhaps perfectly logical sequence—J. J.

Darlington was associated with Daniel Davenport in the Buck's Stove and Range Company in the proceedings against John Mitchell, Frank Morrison, and me.

When the bill was introduced in the next Congress by General Grovenour of Ohio, P. J. McGuire, Furuseth, and I went before the House Committee on Labor in opposition.

In the Senate, Senators Allen, Turner, Spooner contended against the principle of jurisprudence embodied in the bill. The Railroad Brotherhoods were seeking the passage of the bill. As the members of the railroad unions would be most affected by the measure, I could not well maintain my opposition to the bill. My effort was turned toward excluding other groups of transportation workers from the scope of the legislation and toward preventing further acceptance of the principle of compulsion.

E. A. Moseley, secretary of the Interstate Commerce Commission, was one of the most active workers for the Erdman Act. He was recognized as the Administration's spokesman. He called upon me in May, 1898, to find out whether I had any additional objections to the arbitration bill as it had passed the Senate. Frank Morrison and George Chance were present during that interview which was reported stenographically as a protection for the Federation's course. Mr. Moseley interpreted the law not to permit imprisonment for failure to carry out an agreement, and that there would be no interference with due process of the law. He declared the measure would not institute compulsion.

The Erdman Act, approved June 1, 1898, provided for mediation, conciliation, and arbitration in case of industrial disputes affecting railroad employes engaging in the operation of trains in interstate commerce. Contrary to expectations, it was the mediation and conciliation service that proved to be important and effective. Voluntary adjustment prevented for a number of years any railroad strike of considerable importance.

I saw in the proposal to establish arbitration carrying any degree of compulsion a blow at the fundamentals of voluntary institutions which to my thinking are the heart of freedom. I felt we had to keep open opportunities for freedom and initiative. All worth-while achievement is based upon progress of individuals. My idea of voluntary institutions has been my most dependable measuring stick in many perplexing problems which the years have brought. Many have thought me over-insistent upon this point because they failed to grasp the directing vision. My insistence has made me not a little obnoxious to some within the labor movement and others without who have advocated short cuts to desirable objectives.

My resistance to the entering wedge of compulsion in industrial relations in America probably was a deterrent to efforts to bring the railroad organizations into the Federation. A proposal to affiliate had been discussed with Frank Sargent, the Grand Chief of the Order of Railroad Firemen, and W. S. Carter, who succeeded Eugene Debs as editor of the official journal of the Firemen. Upon their urgent request I went to Galveston in 1896 to address their convention. James O'Connell of the machinists was there at the same time. I felt sure that if the Firemen decided to affiliate, the other Brotherhoods would follow as a natural result. The chief difficulty was to get somebody to make the break. Though my address was received cordially, the desired action did not follow. It had and has been one of my fondest ambitions that the Federation should gather into the fold all national labor organizations, but I have never been willing to sacrifice fundamental principles for mere growth. Again and again in cases of emergency the Railroad Brotherhoods have come to the Federation for help. My advice and counsel have always been in favor of the Federation's co-operating with the Brotherhoods even though they did not assume the duty of affiliation. Not a few protests have been made against my course, but I have always held that we ought to protect the workers even though they themselves had not done their full part.

During my entire course I have never attempted to compel anyone to yield to my judgment, much less to my conclusions. There is inherent in every man a resentment against being compelled to do anything. In every contingency or circumstance in which I have had to deal with men, I have found that when a course was presented to them, giving reasons for that position and I appealed to their better judgment to accept that which I advocated, they have voluntarily and gladly accepted my position. I record this not merely for the purpose of indicating my own experience and the results achieved but because I am firmly persuaded that the principle applies practically to every human being. In the New Orleans Convention of the American Federation of Labor, November, 1902, the Brewery Workers had a matter of controversy with the Engineers and the Firemen. I was fully on the side of the latter organizations in the matter of the controversy. In haste and wholly unexpectedly a delegate, D. D. Driscoll of Boston proposed a substitute for the report of the Executive Council and the report of the Committee upon the Executive Council's report in which occurred this statement—*"The Brewery Workers must comply."* I opposed that substitute because it implied compulsory methods to enforce the general opinion of the delegates and with which I was in entire accord. I felt that the adoption of that substitute would be a departure by the American Federation of Labor from its voluntary course to a compulsory character and I did not hesitate to write an editorial upon the subject in the January, 1903, issue of the *American Federationist* in which I criticized and declared that inasmuch as the action of the convention in respect to this matter went outside the scope of the organization as defined by our constitution, I felt it my duty to administer the office of the Federation in accord with its principles and declarations.

It was some time after the Erdman Act discussion that Hugh Lusk came to this country from New Zealand, scattering enthusiastic accounts of compulsory arbitration in his home country. He spoke to many public audiences. I was in Chicago at the time of a meeting which Mr. Lusk addressed. After he had finished his address I said, "I want to ask you a question, Mr. Lusk: Does your New Zealand Compulsory Arbitration Law provide that employers against whom an award is made and who fail, or declare that they cannot meet the award and continue to conduct their business—is that not really confiscation of property?" He said, "no." I then asked him, "Does the New Zealand Compulsory Arbritration Law provide that in the event of an award being made against the workers they must work against their will?" He hesitated and evaded the question, but I finally got him to admit it. I asked him whether that did not involve compulsory labor and that if the men still persisted in refusing to accept the award and work, that they could be arrested and imprisoned. He answered in the negative. I asked him then whether they

would not be fined and he answered that they would be
fined. I asked him then if they could not pay the fine or
refused to pay it, whether they would be put in jail. He
then admitted that that would follow. As a matter of
fact, up to the time Mr. Lusk came to the United States,
the decisions of the courts and boards were against the employers and in favor of the workers and, therefore, no
worker had been fined or imprisoned at that time; but later
when the decisions of the Boards and Courts of New Zealand were against the workers, men were not only fined
and imprisoned but brutally treated.

Discussion of compulsory arbitration paralleled the development of the idea that the public has an interest in
industrial disputes. Compulsory arbitration enforced by
the government sounded well to the intellectual groups to
which Lusk talked. One of his hearers, Henry D. Lloyd,
went over to New Zealand and got the materials for his
book, *A Land Without Strikes*. Compulsory arbitration
was launched as the panacea for industrial ills. It fell to
my lot to tell the other side of the story. New Zealand was
far away and it wasn't easy to get the facts about the effectiveness of the law at first. But there were at hand incidents
enough in our own labor movement to make plain to wage-
earners and employers why the proposal was fundamentally
unsound. It was a matter of no small gratification to me
that when Hugh Lusk returned to this country after a number of years he publicly declared that he had been mistaken as to the efficacy of the compulsory arbitration law
and that he could not recommend it to the American people.

There was in this period a widening in men's thoughts
—the liberals were beginning to find the labor movement.
In Bishop Potter's church there was organized the Church

Association for the Advancement of the Interest of Labor, or the C. A. I. L. Active in this organization were Seth Low, Josephine Shaw Lowell, Edward King, and John M. Bogart. Edward King, in his usual kindly, friendly way, was helping to lead the religious world to knowledge of the labor problem. He was a man of such broad information that he was at home in any circle. The C. A. I. L. established a Council of Mediation and Conciliation inspired by the experience of the English Cotton Spinners' Association. This movement was founded upon the thought that labor problems are susceptible to intellectual methods. Of course this method of discussion and the development of mutual agreement are impossible without proper organization of both management and wage-earners. This little church experiment helped to turn the attention of the Church toward the important ethical problems in the everyday business world as well as it helped to establish voluntary mediation and conciliation agencies as permanent social agencies.

I confess I had little faith in the Church's interest in the labor problem. The labor issue was studiously ignored in most pulpits. It was practically impossible for any preacher to identify himself with labor's side of any controversy. The kind of work initiated by the C. A. I. L. was extended and developed under the National Civic Federation.

As both the Grand Chiefs of the Brotherhoods and representatives of the Federation were identified with the N. C. F., the organization was in a position to render real service. However, I was always on the alert to avert a mistake similar to that of the Social Reform Club in attempting to dictate labor policies. I never had much occasion for anxiety.

In 1913 while I was in the hospital a few days after an operation for mastoiditis, Ralph Easley called on me and incidentally mentioned that the principal purpose of his visit to Washington was to secure an amendment to the Erdman Act to conform to the wishes of the representatives of the Railroad Brotherhoods and railroad managers. The desired change would have increased the number of arbiters to be selected in the event of a dispute between companies and employes. Neither side was willing to submit an issue to arbitration by the Board of three as constituted under the Erdman Act. He wished my approval of the amendment. My answer was substantially that any amendment which the Railroad Brotherhoods' representatives regarded as satisfactory to them would be entirely so to me except that I would object to the extension of the act to apply to any group of workmen who might object thereto. I further stipulated that no essential feature of the act should be changed without further consideration. At the time the Railroad Brotherhoods were taking a strike vote upon a demand for an increase in wages, the situation appeared to be critical as neither side was willing to submit to the existing arbitration board provided in the Erdman Act. In the Senate, Senator Newlands presented a bill containing the proposed changes which passed the Senate and was introduced by Representative Clayton of Alabama in the House.

I was less concerned about these considerations than the feature that separated the arbitration of labor cases from the Department of Labor. The fact that this field was made independent of the Department was really a reflection upon it and a desire to handicap the Department. As soon as I was able to go to my office for a short while I asked Secretary Wilson to meet me there. He very will-

ingly deferred to my incapacity and came to my office for
a conference with Secretary Morrison and me and the members of the Legislative Committee.   In that conference I
learned for the first time that the Newlands Bill proposed
other provisions than the one I have mentioned and practically nullified the feature of the Erdman Bill which stopped
the courts from the enforcement of compulsory service.   I
was considerably disturbed by the situation.   My physician
had ordered me to Atlantic City and I had to go.   I directed
my secretary to write to Mr. Easley, asking him to meet
me in Atlantic City before the Washington conference with
the President which I knew was to take place shortly.   I
wanted to urge upon Mr. Easley my protest against the
Newlands Bill before that conference.   However, this plan
miscarried.

I was considerably perturbed until my peace of mind
was restored by a telephone message from Mr. Easley who
told me how effectively Secretary Wilson had presented in
the conference the very arguments that I wished urged
against the bill.   I was glad, not only for the sake of the
principle, but because, if the situation had not developed
as it did, I should have felt it necessary to have severed my
connection with the N. C. F.

When next the issue of compulsory arbitration arose, it
was in the shadow of the World War.   Its forerunner was
a recommendation in the Engineer's award handed down in
the winter of 1912.   The railroad men in the operating
service, the four Brotherhoods acting together for the first
time demanded the eight-hour day in 1916.   The railroad
executives tried to force them to submit the eight-hour day
and all other issues to arbitration.   The refusal of the
Brotherhoods brought the country face to face with a na-

tion-wide railroad strike as a declaration of war was impending. Fortunately, there was a real man in the White House. He asked the 640 railroad representatives to come to the White House to confer with him. The President met first the railroad managers and the presidents; then he talked with the Brotherhood Chiefs. Then Mr. Wilson declared that the eight-hour day had been accepted by society and was not properly an issue to be arbitrated. He announced as part of the governmental program: To add to present agencies of mediation, conciliation, and arbitration full public investigation of disputes before a strike or lockout may lawfully be attempted.

The eight-hour law for private employment and compulsory arbitration were at variance with the policies of the labor movement. It was an embarrassing situation. Labor did not wish to jeopardize the nation at a time when foreign difficulties were imminent nor did it wish to seem unappreciative of the magnificent endorsement of the eight-hour day which the President had expressed. The Brotherhood Chiefs asked for a conference with me and my colleagues. This was the first conference held in the new A. F. of L. Building. They asked me to appear with them before the Senate Committee on Interstate Commerce. This I readily agreed to do. In that hearing I dealt only with the principles of compulsory arbitration as I could not give my approval to regulating by law hours of work in private industry. The Adamson Eight-Hour Law was approved just prior to the date designated for a strike to attain that purpose, but the compulsory arbitration measure was not enacted.

The Brotherhoods at this time were not advocating compulsion. They had had experience with that principle in

Canada under the Lemieux Act, and the labor movement was united in opposition to compulsion.

The story of the defeat of the Compulsory Investigation Bill is not generally known. It was in December, 1916, Frank Feeney of the Elevator Constructors came to my office and told me that he thought Senator Penrose was desirous of helping in labor legislation before Congress. Feeney arranged with the Senator for an interview. In that interview Senator Penrose declared himself unalterably opposed to the enactment of any law that would in the least interfere with the right of workmen to quit their work either collectively or singly. He remarked that it was a great pity the Adamson Law had been passed, for he believed that even though a strike had occurred for eight hours a proper and better adjustment would have finally been reached without any law complicating the situation. He said that no one contemplates a strike without regret, but sometimes a strike stirs the blood of people and revives their activities and finally brings good results.

As I was discussing the whole situation with him, I found myself substantially in agreement with his position. I recounted to him the position of the American Federation of Labor as well as my own personal understanding. His comment was significant: "Once you get the government to do things with men, you never know what the end is going to be." This was in exact coincidence with my own point of view.

As he was so strong an advocate of voluntary institutions and because of his great political influence, I then set forth to him the political situation and suggested to him that it certainly would not injure the cause of the Republican Party to aid labor in defeating the Compulsory Investigation legislation. This could be done, I pointed out, by simply co-operating with a group of Democratic Senators who were unwilling to assist in forcing compulsion upon American wage-earners. Senator Penrose asked me to let him have various materials dealing with labor's position on voluntary institutions. Of course, I complied. The legislation was blocked. It was one of the very few proposals that President Wilson submitted to Congress during his first term, upon which he did not secure favorable action.

The Adamson Law was for a basic eight-hour day to become effective January 1, 1917. The railroad executives secured an injunction, preventing the law from becoming operative and challenged its constitutionality. In March the four Brotherhoods declared that if the law did not go into operation on the evening of March 17 they would declare a strike. The strike threat came just at a time when we were daily expecting a declaration of war on Germany. I felt that the Railroad Brotherhoods had made a mistake in not striking on January 1, the date when the law was to become operative, but I did what I could to help present that case. At the time, I was a member of the Advisory Commission of the Council of National Defense. For months I had been giving daily service to this important work as well as straining all my energy to protect and direct the labor movement in the crisis which I knew was sure to come. It happened that on March 16 I had gone to Atlantic City for the week end to break the strain. In order to insure temporary relief, I did not give my Atlantic City address to my secretary. I purposely avoided meeting press representatives. On March 16, Mr. Baker, then Secretary of War and Chairman of the Council of National Defense, wrote that the Council had appointed Secretary Lane, Secretary Wilson, Mr. Daniel Willard, and me as a commission to bring about an adjustment of differences in the railway situation. Of course, the commission was made public. As my office could give no information about me, the newspapers carried the story that I was hiding and trying to avoid serving on the commission. I was unaware of my appointment until a message from my secretary succeeded in reaching me on long-distance telephone the following afternoon. I hurriedly packed and left for New York where I got in touch with my associates early the next morning. The four Brotherhood Chiefs were present and Elisha Lee, representing all the railroads, authorized by them to make a settlement in order not to interfere with necessary war-time activity. It was a hard, long session lasting all through the night until early dawn. As we watched the light breaking in the east, W. S. Carter remarked it was the breaking point for which he had long waited, the dawn of the eight-hour day for railroad men.

As William G. McAdoo, railroad administrator, endeavored to base all his policies on equity to railroad men, the next few years moved forward with good will and co-operation for national service. When the railroads were about to be returned by the Federal Rail Administration to private control, the thought was uppermost in many minds how to retain improvements in management that had been worked out in war-time. The railroad workers understood that their welfare was dependent on better management that made possible concentration on production and service problems. As a result of this desire a plan was suggested under which those in railroad work could control all decisions. With this purpose were associated government ownership and kindred suggestions that were at variance with industrial experience. While I was in attendance at the Peace Conference in Paris, this new railroad proposal was launched. The proposal which unfortunately was labeled the "Plumb Plan" was heralded in such a way as to create a sensation. The "intellectuals" filled the highbrow organs with praise, "Labor to operate the railroads!" The hard-headed and practical saw the old frame of government ownership in a new dress. Again it was my unpleasant task to point out the pitfalls lurking under appealing phrases. The Montreal Convention followed quickly and the Federation at the request of the railroad unions endorsed government ownership of railroads. So when the Esch-Cummins Law was in the making, these unions were not in the most strategic position to oppose compulsory measures or the substitution of governmental agencies for voluntary methods. However, there was nothing to curb my expression of opinion and I forcefully opposed compulsory arbitration and government boards. As the legal mind dominates Congress, it is hard to make a congressional committee understand that there is no way that Congress can create industrial good will by law. We succeeded in preventing the incorporation of compulsory measures. The Labor Board authorized was a colorless agency which would either accomplish nothing or repeatedly demand "more power." My counsel was to let the board remain exclusively a governmental experiment and for labor to refuse to assume responsibility by submitting nominations for labor representatives. With the given make-up of the board it was inevitable that its findings should be prejudicial to labor's interests. The unions would have to fight the Railroad Labor Board sooner or later. However, the policy prevailed that by going along with the experiment and appointing representatives, labor would be in a better position to influence findings or at any rate would be in a position to have information. After giving the plan a trial, the railroad men are asking for the abolition of the Railway Labor Board.

Under our Federal system, the power of legal precedent is tremendous. An idea that gains a hearing in any legislative circle may travel the whole circuit. The compulsory arbitration doctrine developed many of the aspects of a legislative fad. Little groups formed to promote the cause. Almost unnoted the state of Kansas passed a law authorizing a court of industrial relations and Henry J. Allen, who happened to be Governor, constituted himself the champion of the idea. Every effort was made to develop an industrial cult out of compulsory arbitration.

When proposals were made to establish similar institutions in New York and New Jersey—the very heart of industrial life—I appeared before joint sessions of the Legislature in those states in opposition to the bills. I regard no public service of mine of greater importance than my efforts extending over forty years to prevent the enactment of legislation of this character. I have tried to help others to understand that this type of legislation would only complicate industrial problems by introducing outside control. There is now practical unanimity among all labor men against all forms of compulsory arbitration, and employers and the general public have come to the same conclusion.

On the other hand, voluntary industrial institutions must come through the development of organization, the utilization of the intelligence of all concerned within the industry and the accumulation of industrial records.

The causes of strikes can largely be eliminated by the

organization of working people into bona fide trade unions and by the organization of the employers, followed by provisions for chosen representatives to sit around the table and there discuss and determine the problems of industry, transportation, of standards of life and work and service. It is something not yet understood, that industrial agreements reached by negotiations between the organized workers and organized employers are a real product of industry, developed through experience and experimentation, unrestricted and competent to adjust themselves to the growth of the industry out of which they have developed.

CHAPTER XXXI

IMMIGRATION

In my boyhood home in London, emigration to the New World was regarded as a very special opportunity for those who were able to make the journey. We heard that there was land in plenty for everyone, work in manifold abundance for everybody. The song of the day, "To the West, To the West," represents the sort of vision that we had of the vastness of the United States. When I reached the New World, never for a moment did I think of myself as an alien. I spoke the same language as the citizens of the United States though around about our little home in Attorney Street were to be heard many more different languages than could have been found in East Side London. Instinctively, I thought of those speaking other languages as the foreigners. As for myself, I felt identified with the people of my new home and it was without a question that I accepted American customs and American institutions and the American life. To my mind the foreigner was the one who did not identify himself with American life and purposes.

So when I went to work in David Hirsch's shop, I found myself surrounded by fellow-workers who spoke little but German. However, I never thought of them as foreigners because they had identified themselves with the effort to work out the problems of our industry and participated in the common life of the city. But when the Bohemians began to come to New York in large numbers and allowed themselves to be used by the employers to build up the tenement-house factory system which threatened to submerge standards of life and work that we had established, I felt that those tenement workers were foreigners. The first step in Americanizing them was to bring them to conform to American standards of work, which was a stepping stone to American standards of life.

The next big industrial problem in immigration with which I came in contact resulted from the enormous influx of Jewish workers into New York in the 'eighties. As the volume of these workers increased, they could no longer be absorbed into existing industrial opportunities without disturbing the balances in industrial forces.

I became interested in the racial problem in organization. Beginning in the early 'eighties, the number of Jewish workers from Russia and other Eastern European countries greatly increased. Very few of the Jews who came had industrial training. Those who did were handicapped by not speaking English. Consequently, those immigrants crowded into any available employment where training and language offered the fewest obstacles. They were strangers in a new land. They had to provide subsistence for tomorrow in whatever opportunity it could be found. They crowded into unskilled callings and worked at starvation wages. They undermined standards and labor organizations, but they were under the urge of dire necessity. They were the products of decades of persecution. Even trades that had previously not been organized, under the need of protection against foreign workers began to struggle to establish an agency to maintain definite standards.

We found it practically impossible to organize these Jewish workers in unions with other nationalities and, in fact, very hard to get a language by which we could give them an understanding of unionism. It was through an extraordinary little group which included Abraham Cahan that Yiddish became the medium of propaganda. Joseph Barondess, Gregory Weinstein, Henry Miller were among those most active in this organization work. Despite many difficulties, we organized several Hebrew trade unions. There was a racial emotionalism and aspiration that both helped and hindered unionism. The Jews were fairly ravenous for education and eager for personal advancement, so that all industrial work was merely a stepping-stone to professional or managerial positions. We formed unions of cap makers, chorus singers, cutters, cloak makers and others. Individual unions fluctuated sharply, but the union movement grew steadily. I gave a great deal of time to this work and finally assisted in organizing the United Hebrew Trades—a policy that was theoretically bad but practically necessary and has eminently justified itself.

By the beginning of the 'nineties, the racial problem in the labor movement was beginning to assume serious proportions. Our problem was part of the larger national problem, for the majority of immigrants no longer came from Western Europe where language, customs, and industrial organization were similar to those of the United States but from the countries of Eastern Europe where lower standards of life and work prevailed. As these immigrants flooded basic industries, they threatened to destroy our standards.

I approached the immigration problem with the somewhat mixed feelings of one who had been an immigrant himself. Grateful that no barriers prevented my coming to this new country, I have always felt that restricting opportunities for others is a grave responsibility; yet as the number of immigrants rapidly increased and the admixture of various races was too rapid for assimilation, I could not escape the conclusion that some way must be found to safeguard America. America is the product of the daring, the genius, the idealism of those who left homes and kindred to settle in the new land. It is an ideal typifying a haven and an opportunity. In the early days, boundless and undeveloped resources made possible and expedient a policy of stimulating immigration. It was not until industrialism developed and there were evidences that the newer immigration was not being assimilated that as a nation we began to consider policies of regulation. The labor movement was among the first organizations to urge such policies. Our first proposal was the contract labor measure under which we hoped to prevent employers from importing strike breakers or workers to lower the standards by overcrowding what was termed the labor market.

As New York was the port of entry for a great majority of immigrants, it was there that we felt most keenly the seriousness of developing constructive immigration policies. It was my custom to keep in close touch with the affairs of the Immigration Bureau of New York City. I was able to give them information which it would have been difficult if not impossible for them to have secured otherwise. Workers in various industries had first-hand knowledge of immigrants inducted into shops, factories, mines, etc.

The work of the Immigration Bureau involved knowledge of labor problems. This explains why so many labor men were appointed to this Bureau. A long line of labor men pass across my memory as I think of the Immigration Bureau of New York—among them Robert Blatchford, Ed. A. McSweeney, M. M. Garland.

The steel industry was among the first to inaugurate deliberately the practice of importing cheap labor in order to maintain low wages and thereby assuring a surplus of workers to replace those who became Americanized. In the coke makers' strike in Pennsylvania of 1891, the Federation tried to call a halt to the violations of the Foran contract labor law. The coke makers, who themselves had been immigrant strike breakers of a decade before, went on strike against the arbitrary action of employers. The plant of H. C. Frick was involved and the same labor policy was responsible for the more serious happenings in the Homestead strike of the following year. In both strikes it was known that steamship companies were bringing immigrants for use as strike breakers. I arranged to have union pickets at Castle Garden to collect evidence of violation of law. The same arrangement was made in Philadelphia, and by prompt co-operation at these ports of entrance we were able to defeat company tactics.

When I was in Pittsburgh at the headquarters of the Amalgamated Steel Association during a strike in the 'nineties, I met a young Italian, Saverio Merlino, unusually intelligent and alert and interested in the welfare of his fellow-countrymen. I talked over the immigration situation with him and pointed out the necessity for safeguarding the welfare of American as well as Italian workers.

In addition to the difficulties which confronted all immigrants, the Italians had to combat a system under which they were exploited by their own fellow-countrymen. Italians with some knowledge of American conditions and with some influence and financial backing would offer to secure for Italian immigrants employment under paternalistic supervision. These men were called padrones. They made contracts with employers in this country to supply labor. The padrone was to collect and pay wages to his group of workers and, of course, took his fee before distributing compensation to the immigrants. Vicious exploitation and the worst sort of graft resulted. As the majority of the Italian immigrants were illiterate, the padrones' grip was very strong.

My personal knowledge of the padrone system came in the early 'eighties, during the big dock strike in New York. For several weeks the railroads and shipping were completely stopped by a most effective protest against low wages and bad working conditions. The first break in the strike came when the employers secured strike breakers from Castle Garden, chiefly Italians and Russian Jews. Dock workers at that time were considered unskilled and unorganizable. This was some years previous to the famous Dockers' strike and the organization campaign of Ben Tillett and Tom Mann in England. The oppression that developed under the padrones finally became so great as to check immigration from Italy and thus brought the situation to the attention of the government. As Italy was over-populated for its industrial development, the government felt it necessary to find an outlet. It had the co-operation of Italian labor. Saverio Merlino wrote me from Naples that Italian labor leaders realized that the welfare of Italy's workers and the solution of the immigration problem depended upon organization in Italy as well as in the United States. I put into my reply to Merlino some of the conclusions that I had reached as a result of my study of the immigration problem. I told him that the labor organizations of the world were not sufficiently developed to deal with the immigration problem, desirable as that method would be, although I realized that the American people in their generosity wished to maintain the United States as an open, free asylum to the oppressed of the whole world yet we realized also that the United States could not solve all the problems of the world and that the struggle for human freedom and advancement would largely have to be worked out by each country for itself.

Since each country had its distinctive part in the establishment of institutions of world freedom, there was need for those devoted to the cause to remain within their own countries and help in national struggles. So I did not feel that restrictions necessary to the well-being of our nation would work an unfair hardship upon the citizens of other countries. At that time when monarchical institutions prevailed in practically all of the European countries, it seemed that about as much could be accomplished for the human cause by preventing the perpetuation of these institutions as through unrestricted opportunity for all individuals in the New World. I was not at the time an advocate of rigorous restrictions on immigration.

The steady development of industrial interests in this country made demands for increased number of wage-earners more rapidly than could be supplied by the normal increase in population. Stimulated immigration resulted. Immigrants to this country are the raw materials out of which the labor movement has to develop an organized disciplined industrial machine. We immediately realized that immigration is in its fundamental aspects a labor problem. However, the earliest immigration proposals of the

Federation were concerned only with honest administration of immigration bureaus and contract labor legislation which was intended to prevent the use of immigrants to disrupt the trade union movement.

The number of immigrants coming into this country had been growing steadily. Not only were the numbers increasing, but the character of immigration was changing. They were largely undisciplined in trade union policies and practices in their own country. This flood of immigrant workers drifted to so-called "unskilled" work. Practically, all of the basic industries were revising their production methods to substitute machine work in the place of previously indispensable craft skill.

In the early years of this period of transition the idea prevailed that the workman should be only a machine tender and hence an unskilled workman. For this sort of work the immigrants were considered desirable. In mining, steel making, and the garment industry, the new immigration was in the majority.

The labor movement approached the problem of immigration restriction reluctantly. Because of my familiarity with Castle Garden and those sections of New York which had become practically foreign colonies, I appreciated the seriousness of the immigration problem in advance of many of the other trade unionists.

Immigration bureaus had been repeatedly used as supply stations for strike breakers. Time and time again I had asked for state and Federal investigation of the New York Immigration Bureau and had helped to produce the evidence disclosing the bad industrial situation resulting from the practices of the Bureau. With the assistance of David B. Hill, the Senator from New York, I was able to get a good deal of this information before the Senate Committee on Immigration.

The organized labor movement went about the development of a constructive immigration policy with deliberation and careful consideration of the important factors concerned in the problem.

To the 1896 Cincinnati Convention I reported that several immigration bills were then pending before Congress and that it had become necessary for the Federation to determine whether it would approve restriction of immigration, and if so, what methods should be endorsed. I did not recommend specific action, but I pointed out that we could no longer remain without a positive policy. The convention authorized the appointment of a special committee on immigration which I appointed. The committee recommended that the Executive Council employ a lawyer to draw up a Federation bill and pending such action, that the Lodge-Corliss bill be endorsed. The following five suggestions were to eliminate existing evils:

1. Stricter enforcement of the present measures to guard against criminal and pauper elements, through a greater efficiency of our foreign consular service and immigration department.
2. Punishment for violation of the Alien Contract Labor Law by imprisonment, as the wealthy violators of this law can easily afford to pay the price of detection.
3. Steamship companies to be held responsible for a term of years for the character and nature of their passengers.
4. Stricter civil and educational qualifications for naturalization.
5. Every immigrant landing on our shores shall declare his or her intention to become a citizen of the United States within one year after arrival. We recommend that a copy of these resolutions be sent to each representative in the United States Congress and Senate.

As the delegates could not agree to these recommendations, they referred the matter to the Executive Council to investigate and report within six months. A circular letter was sent to all Nationals and Internationals, asking for an expression of opinion upon immigration restriction. The vote was sharply divided. The Nashville Convention to which report was made adopted the report of its committee recommending that inasmuch as the majority of organizations favored restriction, the convention declare itself in favor of reasonable restriction, such as the educational test contained in the Lodge-Corliss measure. The discussion on this report was spirited. The convention declared in favor of a policy of restriction with educational tests. Upon no other proposal did we encounter more persistent or better organized opposition. The big employing interests of the country were determined to maintain a huge reserve of common labor which in their language meant low-waged labor. They were willing to flood the country with persons whose standards of living were low and who could not but exert a retarding influence upon national progress. These propagandists for "big business" were abetted by idealists and sentimentalists who believed in the "open door" policy. That was a day before there was general understanding of the principle that maintenance of the nation depended upon the maintenance of racial purity and strength.

I realized that continual progress in organizing the wage-earners of the country involved the education and Americanization of the hordes of immigrants coming through our ports of entry. I did not believe that our national interests would be furthered by granting to the trusts unrestricted right to import cheap labor that could not be Americanized and could not be taught to render the same intelligent efficient service as was supplied by American workers. I did not believe that cheap labor contributed to national welfare and development. I gave much time and thought to immigration problems and to efforts to secure constructive immigration policies and the enforcement of the law excluding Chinese. My efforts brought me in touch with the many governmental executives of successive administrations as well as constructive members of Congress.

Among the great economic and social problems which gripped me was Chinese coolie immigration to the United States. When Charles Bergman, with such clarity and force, laid the whole Pacific Coast situation before the Federation Convention at Pittsburgh in 1881, the convention declared without a dissenting vote the necessity for restricting Chinese coolie immigration and for their exclusion from the United States. Later, when Dennis Kearney came to New York, I had several conferences with him and with Hermann Gudstadt. I fully aligned myself with the California movement for exclusion and at every opportunity aided in safeguarding the people of America from the dangers which confronted us.

In advance it is my desire to state emphatically that I have no prejudice against the Chinese people. On the contrary, having some understanding of their history and the philosophy of their early sages, I have profound respect for the Chinese nation.

I have always opposed Chinese immigration not only because of the effect of Chinese standards of life and work but because of the racial problem created when Chinese and white workers were brought into the close contact of living and working side by side. After the Chinese Exclusion Law was reaffirmed in 1902, there appeared frequent notices in newspapers that Chinese were being arrested in the

United States charged with being here in violation of the law. From various sources I learned that a small number of Federal officers were in league with others who were engaged in this illegal traffic. It was my opinion that Chinese merchants, who were in this country lawfully, were in league with the smugglers and encouraged the emigration of Chinese from their home country to the United States. When, or soon after, this information was given me, I had a conference with President Roosevelt at Sagamore Hill. James Duncan and John Mitchell accompanied me. After we had discussed some other matters with the President, I called his attention to the increased immigration of Chinese laborers. The President declared emphatically that under no circumstances must Chinese workmen be permitted to enter the United States whether they were skilled or unskilled. I called the President's attention to the discontent of the people of the United States, particularly on the Western coast, with immigration of Japanese and Koreans. The President said he realized the grave danger from these people as well as the grave problem brought about by Asiatic immigration. He told me he had given the situation serious consideration and had taken official action to safeguard the rights of American workers. Roosevelt remarked that we must approach the question of Japanese immigration in an entirely different manner from the method used in regard to the Chinese. The Japanese had shown themselves to be great fighters and sailors, and if they were angry the United States would find itself in a serious situation as we were not prepared for aggressive warfare and also would find it necessary to protect the Philippines and Hawaiian Islands.

The National Civic Federation made this Chinese question one of its studies and arranged a big conference which was held in Madison Square Garden. A general discussion ensued in which I took part, and the tendency seemed toward a declaration for relaxation of stringent Chinese exclusion. After a very heated discussion, the subject was referred to a committee of which Dr. Albert Shaw was chairman and I a member. That committee met in the afternoon and continued in session throughout the evening and late or early in the wee sma' hours of the morning. I could not understand the position which Dr. Shaw took in the committee meeting. Somehow it impressed me that he was representing others rather than speaking out of his own soul. The fight was on. Though I was the only labor representative in that meeting, no agreement was reached and a report was made. I submitted a minority report to the conference where a battle royal ensued. A Chinese government official made a vicious attack upon me. I made apparently an effective reply, in consequence of which both majority and my minority reports were laid upon the table and the conference made no declaration upon the whole question; but the position of the American labor movement stood as the expression of the American people upon this most important subject.

It was about 1905 when I met a man who had long been connected with affairs in financial circles of five governmental offices. In these various relationships he learned the inside facts of a band of men engaged in systematic Chinese smuggling throughout the country in illegal collusion with corrupt district attorneys and interpreters. He assured me that the Chinese merchants of this country were opposed to this smuggling and desired to see the law rigidly enforced because they themselves were constant victims of

the schemes of smugglers who embarrassed their business
and were constantly challenging their right to dwell in the
United States.   Not only their peace of mind but their
lives would have been endangered had it been known that
they were giving any assistance to the effort to interfere with
the plans of the smugglers.   Some of the Federal officials
who were responsible for this smuggling were so high up
in administrative circles that they were able to prevent
enforcement of the Chinese Exclusion Law.   When T. V.
Powderly attempted, as Commissioner of Labor, to enforce
the law he was plainly told to cease his activity.

After a little investigation I was convinced of the accuracy of this report, although positive proof, of course, was
impossible.   When Frank Sargent was made Commissioner
General of Immigration, he started with the very highest
purpose of enforcing all law and particularly that part that
applied to Chinese exclusion.   He immediately came into
conflict with the shipping and railroad interests and felt
the power of the band of smugglers and the influence that
they had in the Department of Commerce and Labor.   I
had several conferences with him in which he related to
me incidents of his attempts to enforce the law, all of which
verified the information given me from other sources.   It
was because he was so disappointed and crestfallen as well
as uncomfortable in his office that he sought re-election to
the presidency of the Brotherhood of Locomotive Firemen,
the position which he had resigned to become Commissioner
of Immigration.

Sargent was not a man of large means, and an assured
income was necessary to enable him to support his family.
When his effort to return to his official position in the
Brotherhood proved ineffectual, he did not feel that he

could resign his governmental office because the salary, he felt, was necessary to him. If ever a man died of a broken heart it was he, because he found himself in a position which he deemed it necessary to retain and yet was unable to carry out his ideals of public service and righteous conduct.

Soon after the presidential election of 1908, President Roosevelt appointed Daniel J. Keefe Commissioner of Immigration. Keefe also tried to carry out the law and he too ran against the snag of the Department of Commerce and Labor.

The state of California undertook to deal with the Japanese immigration problem within its own borders. The great majority of Japanese immigrants settled in localities close to the point of entrance until the proportion of Japanese began to grow in an alarming fashion. The white citizens objected to indiscriminate mingling of the two races in schools. When E. E. Schmitz became Mayor of San Francisco, the labor people naturally expected him to take action as Schmitz was a labor candidate and elected on a labor platform. Schmitz did not evade the issue, but with his School Board began the work of segregating Japanese children from the white children in the public schools. This was done under the Enabling Act of California.

Since many of the Japanese were not American citizens, it was necessary to take up with the Federal government such phases of the problem as were complicated by rights insured under foreign treaties. Mayor Schmitz kept me confidentially advised of all developments of the problem and I was able to be helpful in conducting the necessary negotiations with President Roosevelt.

Roosevelt, as I have said, was of the opinion that the Japanese could not be summarily dealt with by legislative enactment as the Chinese were. I had several other conferences with him. In one of these conferences the President stated that he would emphatically censure California's treatment of the Japanese and hoped thereby to placate the Japanese government and to create the groundwork for the negotiations of the treaty between the two govrnements for the mutual exclusion from both countries of the laborers of each country.

Secretary of Labor and Commerce Metcalf called upon me at my home to submit confidentially the report prepared for the President upon the segregation of Japanese children from the whites in the schools of San Francisco. Mr. Metcalf told me he wanted my help and counsel and that he had already conferred with Mr. Furuseth and the other delegates from the Seamen's Convention, some of whom were returning to San Francisco where they expected to hold a meeting of representative labor men to consider the subject.

I wrote to Olaf Tveitmoe, laying before him the whole situation in order that he might take it up with his fellow-unionists and friends who constituted the Chinese, Japanese, and Korean exclusion movement. Mr. Tveitmoe wrote me the problem was temporarily solved when Mayor Schmitz and the School Board of San Francisco worked out a plan of segregation so far as the schools were concerned.

In the 59th Congress an attempt was made to pass a law to permit the employment of Chinese coolies in the construction of the Panama Canal. The canal was the largest individual undertaking of the United States up to that time and labor was particularly concerned that the best standards of work should prevail on that construction job. When it seemed probable that the bill would pass peacefully by the House, I began vigorous and persistent effort to bring out the meaning of this attack on the Chinese Exclusion provision. It was common understanding that President Roosevelt was intensely interested in the whole canal project and that he approved the proposal to use Chinese labor in digging the ditch. However, when labor made its protest, he did not interpose further insistence.

In the 59th Congress immigration legislation was given unusual prominence. Senator Lodge and Representative Gardner were co-operating to have incorporated in the law a literacy test. Uncle Joe Cannon was opposing this feature of the bill with most diligent persistence. When the Japanese school issue originating in San Francisco focused attention on the Japanese phases of the immigration question and made it necessary for the Administration to consider treaty rights of the Japanese, there developed an opportunity of getting action on immigration. With the help of the interest evoked, the bill was passed in the Senate. The bill was reported to the House with the literacy test intact.

We were able to get through Congress that year a measure which placed control of Japanese and Korean immigration in the hands of the President. The law also provided for an immigration commission consisting of three members from the Senate, three from the House, and three to be appointed from the citizens of the country by the President. This commission was to report findings to Congress.

In February, 1909, a conference was held in Mr. Keefe's office over which Secretary Straus presided. The object of the conference was to discuss administration of labor laws that came under the purview of the Department of Commerce and Labor as well as to consider a foundation for the promotion of industrial peace to which President Roosevelt intended to devote the Nobel Peace Prize given him. When in the course of the conference discussion occurred on the enforcement of immigration law and the duties of the Division of Information I made the charge that the division had been used simply as a strike-breaking agency. In making that charge I submitted data showing the percentage of unemployed and indicating how immigrants were referred to positions where strikes existed without giving them information of that fact. I had just been in conference with the National Farmers' Union which represented two million people and submitted from that organization resolutions protesting against the existing administration of the Division of Information and asking for its abolition.

My charges were substantiated by other labor men participating in the conference. Both Secretary Straus and Mr. Powderly attempted to make a defense for the government bureau, but I continued my insistent presentation of charges and submitted additional evidence. I called attention to the very crude chart on unemployment which I was publishing in the *American Federationist* and submitted a proposal that I had first made to a Senate committee in 1883—namely, that the government inaugurate a daily bulletin on the condition of industry similar to the service furnished under the Weather Bureau. Such bulletin based on systematic data secured by telegraph would advise of industrial trends. There is as much need of that service today as when I made the suggestion forty years ago.

In the next Administration Charles P. Nagle of St. Louis succeeded Mr. Straus. Mr. Nagle quickly put an end to Keefe's attempt to enforce the Immigration Law and to prevent the agency from being used for strike-breaking purposes.

Shortly after Congress created a commission for the purpose of investigating the subject of immigration the man who had furnished me with information rendered valuable assistance to this commission. He worked under the greatest difficulties as his mail was tampered with, his salary remittances intercepted, and he was constantly under a system of espionage. However, he could secure more valuable information than any other investigator because he had been made a freemason in a Chinese lodge in China and under this fraternal relationship he secured the full confidence of the Chinese merchants of the United States who are largely members of the Chinese lodge of the masonic fraternity. He never betrayed a confidence.

Early in 1912 my friend came to Washington and submitted a report of official corruption and the evidences of constantly increasing numbers of Chinese smuggled into the United States. I concluded it was time the whole situation should be exposed by official investigation. With the investigator and several representatives of the Federation we called upon Speaker Clark. After we had told the Speaker some of the important facts of the situation, he sent for John L. Burnett, chairman of the House Committee on Immigration, and asked him to come to his room. We then discussed the practical difficulties of an investigation. A number of investigations had already been held by the Democratic Party which in itself was the occasion for considerable criticism. It was concluded that if a special commission were appointed or even the House Committee on Immigration should undertake this investigation it would be impossible to keep the real purpose from the public and thus an opportunity would be given the smugglers and their allies to get under cover. This would result in the suppression or the destruction of the evidence which we desired to get.

Both Mr. Clark and Mr. Burnett felt that Congress ought to have the latest information and that it would be best to have my confidential informant collect the information. It would be impossible, however, to use government funds or make an appropriation for this preliminary investigation. I consulted with a number of friends and each of us contributed to the fund for such an investigation, my friend agreeing to give his services for little more than his actual expenses. He visited several states, going as far as the Pacific Coast, and returned to Washington with a written report giving details and proving conclusively the constant increase in Chinese smuggling.

To consider this report, another conference was held with Speaker Clark and Mr. Burnett. Since the session was drawing near an end it was extremely doubtful whether an appropriation could be secured. It was then suggested that inasmuch as the House had already passed a bill for the creation of a commission to investigate industrial conditions it would be better to have a Senate amendment incorporating a provision authorizing the commission to make an investigation of Chinese smuggling. Mr. Burnett and I then drew up the necessary amendment which we took over to the Senate wing where we had a conference with Senator Borah. He agreed to sponsor the amendment and later offered it when the bill was under consideration by the Senate. Senator Borah's resolution was adopted and became part of the bill as signed by President Taft, August 23, 1912.

Public opinion moved just as slowly to accept the proposals for restricting immigration as did the organized labor movement. Throughout the intervening years I continued my effort to secure an Immigration Restriction Law for the United States. The literacy test remained the accepted method for setting up the restrictive standards. The two members of Congress who became distinctively identified with the literacy test were Senator Henry Cabot Lodge and his son-in-law, Augustus P. Gardner.

So far as I remember, this is the only issue upon which I have ever found myself in accord with Senator Lodge. I made a number of trips to the Capitol and the White House. On the "Hill" we encountered the same organized opposition which blocked the way of our injunction regulation proposals. It came, of course, from organized employers, such as the National Association of Manufacturers which inaugurated a campaign of hostility.

Speaker Cannon was particularly determined in his hostile opposition to immigration legislation. At one time when there was a possibility of our bill passing the House, Mr. Cannon left his seat on the Speaker's stand and went down to direct opposition from the floor. When a vote had been called and members were passing between the tellers and it became evident that the majority were voting for the bill, Mr. Cannon carried his activity to such an extent that he ordered the members of his party on the floor to vote from the smoking-rooms and even pulled one man up by his collar and ordered him to pass between the tellers. But that activity was one of the final straws that broke the camel's back and hastened the revolt against "Cannonism."

Perhaps no measure has been more hotly contested than the various phases of the Immigration Bill. The opposition came from both sentimental and from financial motives, and the combination for a long time proved effective in blocking the enactment of the measure. It was in 1912 that I had accumulated sufficient evidence against the German American Steamship Companies to denounce them as the instigators of the opposition to the Immigration Bill and to submit evidence against them. This exposé proved so convincing as to result in the approval of the bill by Congress. However, this progress was only to be checked by the President's veto. Three times immigration laws have been passed by Congress and three times vetoed by the President.

When President Wilson had under consideration the Burnett Immigration Bill to establish a literacy test, the last week in December, 1914, he called a public conference in the White House for those most actively interested in the formulation of the legislation. About three hundred attended including both those who were opposed to the bill and those who favored it. Shortly after President Wilson vetoed the bill and returned it to Congress with his objections. As I had been unable to participate in the conference in the White House, I wrote a letter to John Burnett, in which I set forth reasons why the President's various objections ought not to deter Congress from repassing the measure. I called attention to the character of the opposition to immigration limitation and submitted documents which disclosed that the opposition was not disinterested. I showed that the officers of the National Liberal Immigration League were financed by big business; the Hamburg-American Steamship Company, the Campagnie Générale Transatlantique, and the Steamship Companies and industries generally that found a financial profit in employing cheap immigrant workers. The dangers etched on a background of war had been sufficiently conclusive to convince a two-thirds majority of both houses in Congress that it was necessary to conserve American institutions.

The bill passed the Senate by a two-thirds majority, but failed to pass in the House. It was introduced again at the next session of Congress and passed both Houses by over two-thirds majority. Again vetoed by President Wilson, it passed both houses over the President's veto.

CHAPTER XXXII

VIOLENCE

SINCE I have been associated with the labor movement, it has been my duty to direct policies during crises when violence brought discredit upon the movement. Personally, I have an abhorrence of violence. Physical suffering is something that I cannot contemplate without personal pain, yet I never feel that I have a right to constitute myself the judge of those responsible for acts of violence. Long years of work in industry and the labor movement have brought to me understanding of the motives and the incentives that lead men to commit acts of violence. Situations that have been followed by acts of violence indicate that the major responsibility rests not upon wage-earners but upon those who have control over the determination of industrial and social policies. Be that as it may, it is invariably the labor movement that suffers most from connection with violence and yet as against all other organized groups in society the labor movement owes it to its members to stand by them in time of need and to insist and see to it that opportunity for justice and a fair trial is accorded.

The labor movement, like all institutions whose purpose is to promote a revolutionizing ideal, has had to resist tendencies to violence. The difficulty in this country has not been lessened by that indefinable something in the

spirit of America that finds expression in direct action.
Sometimes we praise direct action as personal initiative and
sometimes we condemn it as violence.   The underlying
philosophy—anarchism—has its roots in a concept of human freedom in which there is absence of repression.

Some of the gentlest, most spiritual men I have known
were men who called themselves philosophical anarchists.
Such a man was Joe Labardie, a poet-printer of Detroit.
He loved human freedom and, like Benjamin Tucker of
Boston, was one of the most amicable and inoffensive of
men.

At a gathering in Cooper Union, New York, where Joe
Labardie delivered a lecture on anarchism, someone in the
audience asked him whether he proposed the physical
overthrow by force of the present system of government.
He answered at once in the negative, saying that any such
violent overthrow would bring its reaction and that unless
the spirit of freedom and the concept of individualism were
held by the people generally, anarchy was impossible.   His
questioner said, "You are a hell of an anarchist."   He
replied, "Yes, that's the kind of an anarchist I am."

Benjamin Tucker of Boston was one of the leaders of
the philosophical anarchists. I knew him but slightly, but
heard much of him through Gus McCraith who was as fond
of him as it was possible for McCraith to be of anybody.

Dyer Lum was one of the most important of the New
York anarchists who was actively identified with the labor
movement.   Lum was a good friend of David Kronburg
and we met frequently.   He had an understanding of economic power that enabled him to render valuable service to
the labor movement.

The arrival of Johann Most in New York put new

impetus in the activity. Those who gathered around Most advocated propaganda by deed. I rarely went to any of their meetings, but I met various anarchists from time to time in such places as workingmen would meet—usually saloons, such as Justus Schwab's place. The saloon was the only club the workingmen had then. For a few cents we could buy a glass of beer and hours of congenial society. Talk in these meeting places had a peculiar freedom from formality that engendered good-fellowship and exchange of genuine intimacies. The saloon rendered a variety of industrial services. Frequently, wages were paid there— in checks which the saloon-keeper cashed. Of course, it was embarrassing to accept that service without spending money with him. All too frequently the saloon-keeper also served as an employment agent. But on the other hand the saloon-keeper was often a friend in time of strikes and the free lunch he served was a boon to many a hungry striker. Nearly every saloon had a room or a hall back of it or over it that could be rented for a nominal sum. Of course, the saloon was counting on increased receipts due to gatherings held in the hall. These rooms were practically the only meeting places available to unions which were poor and small in numbers. I seldom went to Schwab's place. Sometimes I went with Louis Berliner who never outgrew his yearning for revolutionary eloquence. Most was there frequently and under his influence the talk became increasingly irrational and explosive, often wildly declamatory.

It was upon one of these occasions in Schwab's place that the discussion became quite heated between Most, Schwab, and me on one side and Berliner on the other. I listened intently, but when Most accused the trade unionists of England of having the gold of the capitalist class jingling in their pockets, I resented it both orally and physically as I have recorded elsewhere.

Most represented in a rather spectacular fashion the prevailing world-wide current toward the philosophy of anarchism. He talked violence, but he practiced prudence. After one of his meetings had been dismissed by the police, Most was seen to emerge cautiously from the heavy red curtains of the stage.

But the serious phase of Most's influence was that there were those who took seriously the loose talk of violence and dynamiting. In Chicago the situation was more serious than in New York. A Chicago group formed a Central Labor Union in opposition to the existing trade union assembly and under the leadership of Spies, Parsons, and Griffin, dynamite became a familiar thought. Those of us who were trying to develop a constructive trade union movement were exceedingly apprehensive of the reckless swing toward force. We knew that nothing permanent could be based on force and that the only way to counteract the destructive tendency was to develop the constructive trade union which would inevitably by its growth crowd out the barnacles that sought to restrict development.

The anarchist propaganda moved along without serious results until the Chicago catastrophe which demolished the eight-hour movement and struck at the foundations of the organized labor movement. The trade union movement was in no way responsible for the teachings or the deeds of the anarchists, and yet for years we suffered through their unwisdom. Nor could we leave them to the mercy of persecution in the name of justice. We stood for a fair trial for the under-dog whether called anarchist or any other name.

The Chicago anarchists were charged with murder on the ground that advocacy of force makes the advocate responsible for actual violence that may develop, and were denied even the semblance of fair trial. Some of those charged with murder declared they did not even attend the meeting in Haymarket Square where the explosion took place. Reports of proceedings in the anarchists' trials before Judge Gary came through the daily press and other avenues and it was a shocking story of official prejudice and clumsily disguised effort to punish men for identification with anarchy. The labor movement has ever had its radical wing of those who despair of practical constructive methods or who have become embittered by injustice. Though the more evenly balanced rank and file does not approve of the radical wing, yet they cannot safely abandon the radicals to the vengeance of the common enemy. As the Haymarket bomb in Chicago destroyed our eight-hour movement, we trade unionists had no reason to sympathize with the cause of the anarchists as such. However, labor must do its best to maintain justice for the radicals or find itself denied the rights of free men.

Because there was no direct evidence showing that these men were guilty of throwing the bombs, there were numbers of men who believed that clemency should be exercised by commutation of sentence from death to imprisonment. I opposed capital punishment, not only because I thought that the execution of these men was unwise and unjust, but I have always been, as I now am, opposed to the taking of life whether by an individual, a group, or the aggregation of individuals as expressed by the state. About the seventh or eighth of November, 1887, I was sitting in my small office back of Union No. 144 when Ed King and James Lynch (of the Carpenters) came to me and asked me whether I would not go to Springfield to make a plea before Governor Oglesby for commutation of the sentence. The time had been set for the hearing in the Governor's office and it was either to decide to go at once or else lose the opportunity of making the plea.

They presented to me the idea that because of my being well and favorably known and that I was regarded as a conservative man, my plea would help. Without further ado I closed my office door, and without any belongings other than those which I wore I went directly to the train and with them to Springfield.

The hearing was in the Governor's chamber and was under the leadership of George Schilling of Chicago. Very earnest pleas were made.

There were in the group representatives of trade unionists, farmers, the Legislature, women's organizations, and nearly every social group.

I said in part:

I have differed all my life with the principles and methods of the condemned, but know no reason why I should not ask the Governor to interpose and save condemned men from the gallows. The execution would not be one of justice; not to the interest of the great state of Illinois; not to the interests of the country; nor the workingmen. I come as a representative of the New York Central Labor Union and as president of the American Federation of Labor, organizations opposed to anarchy.

I then reviewed the eight-hour movement of 1885 and 1886 and the strike in McCormick's factory where a man was killed. I called to attention the meeting that was called in Haymarket Square to protest against the killing of that man.

If these men are executed it would simply be an impetus to this so-called revolutionary movement which no other thing on earth can give. These men would, apart from any consideration of mercy or humanity, be looked upon as martyrs. Thousands and thousands of labor men all over the world would consider that these men had been executed because they were standing up for free speech and free press.

We ask you, sir, to interpose your great power to prevent so dire a calamity. If this great country could be great and magnanimous enough to grant amnesty to Jeff Davis, it ought to be great and magnanimous enough to grant clemency to these men.

The workingmen of the country, the people of the country even apart from the workingmen, have their eyes centered upon you. The eyes not only of the people of this country but of the entire world are directed toward Springfield, Ill. We have found that throughout the length and breadth of the civilized world wherever an opportunity exists for the people to manifest their wishes they have protested strongly the execution of the sentence and ask, sir, that the only power that can intervene between these men and death —the hand of Governor Oglesby—be exercised to stand between them. The working people have long begged for justice and very frequently not in vain. They arise now and ask in the name of mercy, in the name of humanity, in the name of progress, not to allow this execution to take place, but, sir, to stand between these men and death, and as I in a letter and dispatch sent to you have said, you will not only be blessed by the country but the unborn thousands that come after us.

I want to say to you, sir, I am not desirous of going into the details of the question. I don't believe I am competent to do so; but I believe that in some measure, however remote, the police of Chicago have been somewhat responsible for this trouble. I ask myself what good can come to the people of the state of Illinois; what good can come to the people of our country; what good can come to the good name of our country and people if these men are executed? Are we not strong enough, and intelligent enough to protect our lives and interests as a people without the execution of these men? I cannot conceive what possible good results the execution of these men will have upon society.

I remember speaking coolly and calmly, and I pleaded as strongly as I could for the exercise of the Governor's clemency, at least to grant a reprieve to the men for a considerable time so that an opportunity might be had to establish their innocence, if they were innocent. At the close of my statement Governor Oglesby arose to greet me, and thanked me and added that my appeal made the strongest impression upon his mind. However, all the appeals were of no avail for the Governor declined to stay the execution. The men were executed on November 11, 1887.

On the evening after the hearing before Governor Oglesby, a group of us took the midnight train to Chicago. We found that a number of women were without reservations and with a few others we surrendered our berths to them and sat up all night in the day coaches. The close experience with the taking of human life and apprehension of the reaction that would come to the labor movement filled me with forebodings. I remember that my old friend Sam Goldwater of Detroit was with me all the time. He was a splendid type of man, intelligent, faithful, and active in the cause of labor, justice, and freedom. He was an Alderman in the City Council and had been a candidate for Mayor of Detroit upon the Progressive Reform ticket. We spent a night of horror together. I have always been an opponent to capital punishment; the idea of taking the lives of these men whether guilty or innocent and the consequences that might follow depressed Sam and me beyond words. Goldwater and I wandered the streets all the following day and twice I was approached by men who urged me to leave the city. I am not sure whether they were friends or detectives—whether their admonition was a warning or an act of friendship or personal regard. Be that as it may, I could not leave and I remained until the evening after the execution, depressed at the tragedy which had occurred.

In 1895, in connection with my trip to Cardiff, Wales, as a Federation fraternal delegate to the British Trades Union, I visited a number of cities on the Continent and in nearly every labor hall there were pictures of Parsons, Spies, Liegg, etc., and with an inscription: "Labor's Martyrs to American Capitalism." During my later visits to the labor offices on the European Continent, I have seen the same pictures still there.

The second crucial experience the Federation had with the results of violence was in connection with the Moyer-Haywood-Pettibone case. The Western Federation of Miners, after it withdrew from the Federation, became the leader in the western secession movement. That group was frankly antagonistic to the trade union movement and emphasized destructive methods in replacement of constructive policies. The spirit of the West is partly the pioneer spirit bred by necessity that individuals depend upon their own initiative in dealing with their problems. When in the Miners' strikes of Colorado and Idaho the Governors had called out the militia, the miners determined to maintain what they considered their rights. They thought it un-American to force them into bull-pens and forbid them the right of free action which belongs to every free man. Those who knew the desperate conditions brought about by the use of the military in the West were not surprised at the use of dynamite against those held responsible. I had no personal knowledge of the activities in the West, but was dependent upon reports made to me. It was my feeling that regardless of whoever might be responsible for the Steunenberg murder the American labor movement could not abandon the labor men helpless to the vengeance of employers who were in control of the machinery of the state. I felt that the accused men ought to be assured fair trial which I knew they could not have without the financial assistance and backing of the labor movement.

As spokesman for the American labor movement, I urged that contributions be made for this defense. The Executive Council of the Federation set an example by appropriating a sum for the defense of the three men. It was soon after this that the Western Federation of Miners applied for reaffiliation with the Federation and thus made it possible for the Federation to have greater influence for constructive policies among the miners. I have always felt that the policy pursued by the Federation during that time of need contributed materially to solidify the labor movement of the country and bring it again under constructive leadership. Since the metal miners rejoined the Federation, there has been a gradual transformation in the policies of the organization which was later expressed in a change of title so that the present policies of the organization might not be handicapped by the traditions of the old name.

But the difficulties of this early episode were as nothing to the trial by fire that came with the McNamara case. For a number of years the National Erectors' Association and the American Bridge Company had been making war on the Bridge and Structural Iron Workers. Among the members of these two organizations were some of the employers most bitterly hostile to organized labor. Their "open-shop" campaign was evidently part of that waged by the National Association of Manufacturers. Walter Gordon Merritt, the legal adviser of the National Erectors, was closely identified with the activities of the Anti-Boycott Association in the litigation by which hostile employers hoped to cripple our movement. It was common knowledge even before the Mulhall exposé before the committees of Congress that those waging this anti-union warfare had in their employ operatives of various detective agencies. Those of us who know labor problems first-hand understood only too well the sort of work these detectives were expected to perform. When the use of dynamite in the strike situation was reported, we knew the chances were that the responsibility lay with operatives in the services of the "open-shop" crowd.

For many years General Harrison Gray Otis, the owner of the *Los Angeles Times*, had been one of the most bitter enemies of organized labor. Our most obviously constructive policies appeared in his eyes as diabolical schemes to undermine the rights of employers. The editorial columns of the *Times* were filled with bitter vituperation and abuse of labor men and labor organizations. The explosion which wrecked the *Times* building and destroyed human life was a terrible happening which I felt as deeply as did any other citizen. I knew of nothing that connected the catastrophe with organized labor.

Without doubt, Otis incurred the resentment of the working people and the overwhelming condemnation of all our people. That such a resentment would ever be manifested in the destruction of the *Times* Building and the death of a number of employes, not only did I not know, but certainly I did not expect or even imagine. When Detective Burns, who had publicly acknowledged the moral depravity of the majority in the employ of detective agencies, made his spectacular arrest of the McNamara brothers,

charging them with blowing up the *Times* Building and
carried these men out of their home state in defiance of the
safeguards which the state had prescribed to guarantee all
citizens a fair hearing, I felt that the whole affair savored
too strongly of jungle tactics to be part of the machinery
of justice of a republic. That Burns kidnapped the Mc-
Namara brothers in order to evade the Extradition Law
of Indiana seemed an admission that his purpose was not
to uphold law. W. G. Merritt was in Indianapolis at
the time the kidnapping took place. Like all other labor
officials, I was appalled and shocked by Burns's methods.
I felt that if he were attempting to bring men to justice he
was following rather strange tactics if he had nothing to
fear.

I never met or knew James McNamara; indeed, I had
never heard of him until after the arrest. I had met J. J.
McNamara only occasionally, but I had been assured of his
intense devotion to organization and the mission of the
trade union movement. Nothing of his habits and conduct
indicated that he could be guilty of a crime. He was a
devoted, practicing Catholic who stood in good repute with
the Church and with all who came in contact with him.

The representatives of labor in Indianapolis formed
what they called a Legal Defense Committee, and both by
telegraph and long-distance telephone insisted up my coming to a conference, with which I promptly complied. There
I was informed of the plans which had been made which
were subject to my review and approval. They informed
me that they, together with Edward Nockles of Chicago,
had tentatively engaged the services of Clarence Darrow
and Job Harriman to defend the accused; that they had

already made a public appeal for funds and wanted me to take over the administration and receipt of the funds and their distribution for defense purposes.

I approved the plan and later submitted it to the Executive Council of our Federation which designated Frank Morrison, Secretary of our Federation, to receive all moneys and to disburse them as directed.

The responses, though in small sums, came from many individuals from all over the country. Here it may be said that every contributor was given a receipt by Mr. Morrison; that the expenditures were made through Darrow and that a final itemized report was printed and sent to every labor organization of the country as well as to every individual contributor; that a copy of this printed report is still extant in the office of the A. F. of L.

Later, when the indictments for conspiracy were under consideration by the grand jury, Secretary Morrison was subpœnæd and ordered to bring to Indianapolis all financial and other books of the Federation concerning his own and the affairs of the officers of the American Federation of Labor. The examination of the books and accounts was made and the books and papers retained for months by the District Attorney and finally returned without the slightest adverse comment.

While labor was marshaling its resources to get before the public an understanding of the underlying forces in the "open-shop" fight, one of the most influential men in the United States, Theodore Roosevelt, published an editorial which was one of the most unfair declarations I had ever seen. The whole tone of that editorial entitled, "Murder is Murder," was an insidious indictment of organized labor for standing by fellow-workers until the courts had had an opportunity to produce evidence. I replied to Colonel Roosevelt most vigorously both through the *American Federationist* (June, 1911), and in my public addresses. In that reply I quoted a statement which J. J. McNamara sent me, which said: "That I am innocent of any infraction of the law in word or deed needs no emphasis from me, for the truth is mighty and will prevail right speedily; and for it I shall be content to wait." Colonel Roosevelt's article, I felt, was on a par with his letter to Senator Knox which was for the purpose of political propaganda. Colonel Roosevelt was such a power in molding opinion in the country that I could not understand why he would write an editorial of that sort without giving a fair interpretation of the motives of organized labor in trying to secure funds to insure a fair trial to the McNamaras. No one was denying that murder was murder, but we were trying to protect the McNamaras from being branded with the ignominy of murder until a fair trial had taken place. I sent a copy of this editorial to Colonel Roosevelt and which he later published in the *Independent*, with a statement modifying his previous attack. But Colonel Roosevelt was too vigorous an actor always to wait for the verdict of mature consideration. Probably, his picturesqueness as a public man was due in considerable measure to his impetuousness. He was essentially an agitator and his "big stick" did much to hasten political thought to a higher and broader plane.

Late in the summer of 1911 it was necessary for me to make a trip to the Pacific Coast. In California I went to see the McNamara brothers in the Los Angeles jail. Both men seemed very much cheered by my visit and when I was leaving John J. took my hand and said, "I want to assure you that we are innocent of the crime with which we are charged." This was the message I carried to the labor movement and upon which reassurance we continued to base our plans to help them.

I believed the McNamara brothers when they told me they were innocent. Had they told me they were guilty I would not have betrayed them, but I would not have engaged in the work of collecting money for their defense, neither would I have urged that course upon the labor movement.

The full story of the facts as we knew them was reported to the Atlanta Convention. The work of collecting the defense fund went forward. When the trial opened, the McNamara brothers pleaded not guilty.

On December 1, I was on my way from Washington to New York, for a meeting of the New York State Factory Investigating Commission. At Manhattan Transfer two newspaper men came on board the train to tell me that the McNamara brothers that afternoon had pleaded guilty. The newspaper men had telephoned to Washington and learned that I was on my way to New York. They kept up a running conversation and questions. They asked me what I then thought of the situation. I answered that the McNamara brothers had insistently informed me of their absolute innocence of any crime or wrong-doing. Now that they had pleaded guilty I had no other alternative or desire than to believe them guilty.

In about fifteen minutes we reached the Pennsylvania Station and there was a gathering of not less than fifty newspaper men and detectives surrounding me, questioning me, to all of whom I gave no other answer than what I had already given to the newspaper men while on the train. There was about three hours between my arrival in New

York and the departure of the New York Central train for Albany—from there I was to go to Troy where the hearing of the New York State Factory Investigating Commission was scheduled. After a while I managed to get out of the crowd, undetermined what course to pursue—that is, whether to go on to Albany and Troy in the performance of my duty as a Commissioner or to return to Washington and there await whatever developments might arise. I used the telephone freely and called upon my brother Lew Gompers of Brooklyn, my friend, John Morrison, and another friend whose name I cannot now recall. They met me in the station and I asked their advice as to what they thought was the course I should pursue. They agreed with me that I ought to proceed to Troy. I had a suitcase and a handbag which they carried for me from the Pennsylvania Station to the New York Central Station. As we walked over, fully a dozen detectives and newspaper men followed me. Every now and then I was accosted by one of them with some question or other pretext to engage me in conversation.

I bought my ticket and berth and my friends went with me to the car. The followers followed. For a while I sat in the smoking-room, then decided to retire. Not fifteen minutes of time elapsed while I was lying in the berth but that one or more of the detectives wakened me or if I was still awake questioned me. As a consequence, I passed a sleepless night.

Reaching Albany in the morning, these followers were still with me. I took the train to Troy and they were still with me.

The commission meeting opened at ten o'clock. Because of the absence of Senator Robert P. Wagner, chairman, and Alfred E. Smith, I, as next ranking member of the commission, presided over the hearing in the City Hall. The hearing lasted until about one o'clock and then adjourned. During the entire session I was at intervals handed a slip of paper containing some question or some reminder of the situation regarding the McNamara brothers' having pleaded guilty and as to what my future course would be. I sometimes wrote my answer, stating that I should determine that when I got back to Washington.

On the train from Troy to Albany and from Albany to New York the same followers were there and they pestered me in every conceivable way. I could not protect myself against them. On arriving in New York I went to the Victoria Hotel, 27th and Broadway, and registered and there some friends met me. The hallway to the room I occupied was filled with the followers. They were relieved by their associates and kept vigil in relays. Some of them had hired near and adjoining rooms to the one I occupied and through the night their loud talking prevented me from getting any sleep or rest.

Sunday this same routine was continued. In the evening my friend John Morrison came to me and suggested my visiting Elks Lodge No. 1. It was a splendid suggestion. I knew the followers could not follow me into the precincts of that lodge. At least for two hours I was free from the insolence and the annoyance of the newspaper men and the detectives, the former acting just as impudently and unfairly as if they were detectives.

At that meeting of the Elks Lodge No. 1 the presiding officer called upon me to deliver an address upon the meaning of the eleven o'clock ceremony obtaining wherever Elkdom is known. I could not recall a minute after what I

had said, but I must have related the incidents which so
oppressed me. After the conclusion of my remarks the
lodge, by a unanimous vote, passed a resolution expressing
confidence in my innocence of any wrong and expressing
respect for my honor and the integrity of my life's work.
It was a great comfort to me and as I left the hall many
men who surrounded me greeted me, shaking hands with me
and manifesting their friendship for me.

I left the hall in company with John Morrison and went
to the hotel, there to find the same followers who kept up
the same vigil and same nuisance all night.

Monday morning came with a repetition of the days
and nights before. On Tuesday I traveled to Washington
and was nearly in a state of collapse. I had been put
through four days of the "third degree."

I went immediately to my office in Washington in the
Ouray Building only to find in the corridor a number of
newspaper men and detectives. A treatment by an osteo-
path afforded me an hour's sleep after which I was much
refreshed, and called for a conference with some of the
representative labor men in Washington. Afterwards, I
had a fairly good night's rest at my home.

W. J. Burns was strangely exultant over the situation.
He did not seem to be particularly gratified because he had
contributed to the doing of justice, but only that he had
been clever in hunting down men. In numerous interviews
he promised new sensations and declared he was going to
get the men higher up. In these declarations my name was
used in such a way as to carry the insinuation that I was
implicated in the dynamiting. Evidences of his methods
were later given by Olaf A. Tveitmoe, secretary of the
Building Trades Council of California. In his annual re-

port to the California Building Trades, Tveitmoe told how the Prosecuting Attorney induced by Burns had promised him immunity if he would implicate me in the dynamite conspiracy. Tveitmoe spurned the offer for, as he assured the convention, informed me by letter, and told me months after in person, he had no evidence of any kind, direct or indirect, to connect me at all with the conspiracy and that to have given evidence against me would have been purely false and untrue.

The purpose of Burns and his detective agency was to fasten some crime upon me. The newspapers of the time will bear evidence of his almost daily denunciation of me and assurance that he was sure "to get the man higher up," always associating my name in some way. He was determined to besmirch and if possible to destroy my work and the cause of labor. In the investigations of the grand jury at Indianapolis, the relations of the American Federation of Labor and the activity of the Bridge and Structural Iron Workers were carefully scrutinized and all books examined and that grand jury completely exonerated the Federation and its officers of any participation in wrong-doing.

But for years Burns continued to endeavor to besmirch my name and character by every means within his power. During the War, Burns wrote me a letter commending me highly for the stand which I had taken in the War and the service which I had rendered, and expressing confidence in my integrity and patriotism. In interviews with Mr. Easley, Burns had expressed the great change in his judgment of me and sought an opportunity to meet me; his letter was filed and his request denied. I had no bitterness in my heart for him or for any other man but I did not feel that I could meet a man who had endeavored to get

me into prison or to the gallows. Burns's conduct in the
land fraud cases in the state of Washington, the letter under
date of May 10, 1912, from Attorney-General Wickersham
to President Taft, charging Burns with jury fixing and
subornation to convict an innocent man, the President's
pardon for the man convicted under such circumstances,
confirmed me in my judgment that I did not wish to meet
Mr. Burns if I could avoid it.

When it was announced that Attorney-General Daugherty proposed to appoint Mr. Burns as the head of the U.
S. Secret Service, I felt it my duty to meet Mr. Daugherty
and lay before him copy of Mr. Wickersham's letter to
President Taft and to protest against the appointment of
such a man to a position of such great responsibility.

In addition, Mr. Burns's detective agency licenses in
New York, in Montreal, and in other parts, had been
revoked.

I felt justified in the belief that no citizen's life or liberty was safe with a man such as Burns in such a responsible position.

CHAPTER XXXIII

INJUNCTIONS I HAVE ENCOUNTERED

ONE of the first injunctions which came under my observation was that issued by a judge in the Cigarmakers' strike at Binghamton, New York, in the early 'eighties. It enjoined the doing of many things, but nothing comparable to the lengths to which injunctions went as time passed.

The second was the injunction issued by a Federal court in New Orleans in connection with the Cotton Screw Workers' strike and the strike of many workers in several trades. That writ, so far as I can recall, was the first issued by a Federal court based upon alleged interference with interstate commerce in violation of the Sherman Anti-Trust Law.

The use of the injunction in industrial disputes by Federal courts made the issue acute. The lower courts had long followed the practice. During the session of the New York Legislature in 1891, I sent Senator Charles T. Saxton a crude amendment to prohibit the use of injunctions in labor disputes and I furnished him with injunction exhibits from Binghamton, Rochester, and elsewhere—one of them I remember forbade the payment of strike benefits as a form of bribery.

The Birmingham (1891) Convention of the Federation cited an injunction issued by a Pennsylvania judge and authorized the Executive Council to challenge this judicial precedent and carry the case to the highest tribunal of the land. Three hundred dollars was appropriated to test conspiracy and equity cases. However, the trial case was not carried through at that time. But we had yet to learn the full meaning of the perversion of the injunctive process which was rapidly being developed by Judges Taft, Ricks, Jenkins, Jackson, Dayton, and others by which the economic freedom of the workers was invaded, their normal activities prohibited, their rights restricted, and they themselves tied to their jobs. Under this system the discretionary power of the judge supplanted government by law and substituted personal government by discretion, or, as I have said elsewhere, that as government by law recedes or is forced back, government by injunction—by discretion —gains ground. Overwhelming realization of the power of this governmental agency came with the American Railway Union strike of 1894. We were appalled. A placard bearing the seal of the U. S. Government made crimes of lawful and normal activities necessary to make the strike effective. The injunction converted the strike of the American Railway Unions against the Pullman Company into a strike against the government. That is the effect sought by practically every injunction used in industrial disputes and labor resents being tricked into such a false position. When the employer tries to sidestep and induce the government to make his fight for him, the working man feels he is the victim of conspiracy.

From that time, injunctions came in rapid succession, from both state and Federal courts. The provisions of these injunctions and all that were issued afterward undertook to forbid workmen from doing the things which in themselves were perfectly lawful and normal. The abuse of this beneficent writ, applied to human beings and not concerned with property or property rights, inhibited freedom of speech, freedom of the press, freedom of assemblage, freedom to persuade and in a lawful, peaceful manner to induce their fellow-citizens to make common cause against the deterioration of the standards of life and work. Under resultant equity proceedings the judge sitting in equity constituted judge, jury, and executioner. The defendents were not to be confronted by a jury of their peers. It was necessary for the defendant to prove his innocence—a reversal of the Anglo-Saxon principle in law, that a man must be assumed to be innocent until he is proven guilty. The whole procedure was based upon the supposition that the employer had a property right in the labor of those who might be willing to accept work.

The great difficulty in testing the injunction cases is, that as a rule those writs are issued during a period when the workers seem to have the most favorable outlook for a successful termination of the dispute with the employers. For a time the injunction itself, instead of overawing the men, gives them a renewed spirit of determination and they hire attorneys; but these attorneys usually take the position of entering a plea of not guilty not only for unlawful but lawful acts of the men and do not raise the fundamental issue involved—the right of the courts to issue injunctions forbidding the doing of lawful and normal acts. The question which the courts consider is one of discretion, and though they may modify the injunctions they make them permanent in essentials and forbid feeding the needy or holding meetings to exchange views and encourage the men in their just stand. When the strike or lockout is ended, either by victory, defeat or compromise, the injunction appeal to higher courts ends; the writs, however, stand as the edict of the courts.

Such injunctions regulating industrial relations I hold to be illegal. Many injunctions have sought to prohibit workers from exercising their constitutional rights. Such injunctions can and ought to have no real authority. I believe that those to whom such injunctions are intended to apply ought to pay no attention to them whatsoever, but should stand upon their constitutional rights and take the consequences whatever they may be. "Resistance to tyranny is obedience to God," and resistance to the tyranny and injustice of injunctions which have been issued by our courts is necessary for a clear understanding by all our people of the principles involved. Men who resist these unwarranted injunctions and exercise their normal and lawful rights despite them, must be ready and willing, as I have tried to be, to assume the responsibility and the consequences of the exercise of these rights.

Such has been my course in dealing with injunctions that have affected me. The first of these was issued against the officers of the United Garment Workers and me as president of the A. F. of L.

The injunction which the Clothing Manufacturers of New York issued against the United Garment Workers of America in 1893 was brought by Sinsheimer and Levinson. The firm went to the cutters in every shop and endeavored to compel them to sign statements to the effect that they were not members of the United Garment Workers of America, and threatened a lockout if this was not done. They finally did lock the cutters out.

The American Federation of Labor was represented by John Goff, former Recorder of New York, and the United

Garment Workers of America by Fromme Brothers. Judge
Bartlett presided. The court decided that the firm of Sinsheimer and Levinson who brought the suit did not come
into court with clean hands because they had preceded the
action by a lockout.

Local Union 4 of the United Garment Workers of
America then brought suit for conspiracy on the part of the
manufacturers. This case was finally adjusted out of court.

I again encountered the injunctive writ in the Miners'
strike in 1897. The miners contended against more repressive conditions of life and work than existed in any other
large industry.

Soon after the 1891 strike, P. J. McGuire, George
Chance, and I went into the anthracite field to organize the
miners. There was not a union to be found, not even a
secret organization. We were seeking a few men in each
locality who would be willing to constitute the nucleus of
a labor union. Miners were thick in that district, but the
kind of men we were seeking were then very rare. But we
found them here and there after a long hunt. The hunt
was not exactly a safe undertaking. There were company
gunmen everywhere, brutal creatures who had no compunc-
tion against giving a blow with a "billy" that would put
a man to sleep, or shooting a hole through him. Though
we took our lives in our hands, we went through, planting
the seeds of unionism.

In 1897 the condition of the miners in the country and
the organization work, was at its lowest possible ebb. I
called a conference at the Monongahela House in Pittsburgh, Pa., at which M. D. Blatchford, the president, John
Pierce, Michael Carrick of the Painters, W. D. Mahon of
the Street Railway Men and who had formerly been a

miner, and I participated. The result of the conference was that a statement was prepared and made public, demanding that the mine operators restore the last reduction of wages (reductions among the miners at that time were enforced in season and out of season) and if the operators refused to make the restoration, calling upon the miners in all bituminous regions of the country to lay down their tools and stop work on July 4, 1897. There was everything to gain and nothing to lose from such a venture. The coal operators, having had complete sway for so many years, did not believe that there would be any response from the miners to the call, and ignored the declaration entirely, only to find that on the day, July 4, more than 50 per cent of the miners had quit work and that within a few days less then five per cent of the bituminous miners of the country were at work.

Mahon and I did more than help to plan this strike. We were in the thick of the fight, going from meeting to meeting, speaking, encouraging, exhorting. Organizers were sent into West Virginia to stop the steady stream of coal which the railroads and the boats on the Ohio were carrying into Pittsburgh. Our organizers soon rallied the miners to the battle standard and therefore drew the ire of Judge Jackson who issued a drastic injunction against them and anyone who might attempt the same work. This injunction denied miners and their sympathizers the right of free speech and assemblage on the public roads of West Virginia. Even the non-union mines of West Virginia were seriously handicapped by the strike though judges issued injunctions of such drastically arbitrary nature. As soon as I knew of the injunction I declared that it was illegal because contrary to constitutional guarantees. I resented the unwarranted and unconstitutional invasion of citizens' rights to go upon the public highway and to address fellow-citizens in such places as would not interfere with traffic or private rights. The clash between the judiciary and the executive of the State of West Virginia made the miners' issue conspicuous. As I was in the West I stopped at Columbus to consult with Blatchford and offered to go into West Virginia to conduct the fight. In a short time Blatchford wrote, asking me to call a conference of representatives of national labor organizations in Wheeling to consider what labor ought to do.

I sent out a call for a conference in Wheeling on July 27 to which about twenty-four valiant fighters for the rights of the common people responded. That was one of the most inspiring, courageous conferences I have ever attended. It was a group of strong men,—among them: M. M. Garland, P. F. Sargent, Pat Morrisey, Val. Fitzpatrick, J. R. Sovereign, Gene Debs, W. D. Mahon, Robert Askew, J. F. Mulholland, G. W. Perkins, and several representatives of the miners and others. The spirit that fired Patrick Henry to demand "liberty or death" urged us on to our new phase of the world-old struggle of men. That conference carefully considered the situation and recommended that we inaugurate a special campaign of organization. I was charged with the task of assigning speakers for a free-speech campaign.

Sovereign, Blatchford, and I constituted a committee to confer with Governor Atkinson at Charleston, West Virginia, to present to him our demands for "free assemblage and free speech." The Governor promised to take the matter under consideration and to communicate to the committee later. Later, he declared he would uphold the Consti-

SNAPSHOT OF SAMUEL GOMPERS TAKEN BY A DETECTIVE
AT NEW RIVER, WEST VIRGINIA

tution. I had gone into West Virginia as an agitator pure
and simple, an agitator for constitutional and industrial
rights.

When Judge Jackson's order was issued, we had many
organizers in the field, a few of whom we paid salaries
and bore their immediate expenses. There was one of
them from Wisconsin. He left West Virginia and went
over to Kentucky and from there sent me a telegram
something as follows: "No doubt you know of the injunction issued by Judge Jackson forbidding organizers holding public meetings in West Virginia. I am here in Kentucky and want your further advice what I shall do." I
immediately dispatched the following answer: "We want
organizers in West Virginia. If you prefer remaining in
Kentucky I prefer that you return to Wisconsin."

Employers of the country watched to see what would
result from the practical test of the injunctions in West
Virginia. I went on my way over to the Kanawha and
New River Valleys and there I stayed working, planning,
holding conferences, talking to miners and workers wherever meetings were held. I worked as I had a right to do
and paid no more attention to injunctions than I did to
querulous commands of other persons who attempted to
interfere with my work. One meeting I remember very
distinctly. On a roadside in the mountains, all of the
miners from fifty miles around in the Kanawha Valley had
gathered. Some had started the day before in order to be
present on time. While our meeting was in progress and
I was speaking from a farmer's wagon, a United States
marshal arrived accompanied by two assistants, each with
satchels. These satchels were brimful of injunctions in
which, together with others, I was enjoined from speaking

in any connection with the miners' strike on the roads to or from the mines or in any place at or near the mines or in the district at all.

The marshal pressed forward until he was near the wagon in which I stood, and handed to me two separate and different injunctions. I glanced at both of them and saw the purport of them. The marshal and his assistants began serving these injunctions upon the miners. I asked the marshal whether he would not desist for a moment that he might hear what I had to say, and he consented. I said: "It may take you half an hour more to serve all these people with these injunctions. If everyone here will assent to the declaration that they have been served with these injunctions even though they are not actually served, will that be satisfactory to you?" He answered, "Yes." I said: "Pardon me then for a moment," and I called upon the great crowd to listen and I repeated to them in a loud tone of voice to reach them all the question that I had put to the United States marshal and I informed them of the essence of the contents of the injunctions, told them that by the injunction they were forbidden to participate in a gathering such as the one taking place; that if they continued to remain there they would be liable to be held and tried for contempt of court which might involve a monetary penalty and also a term of jail. I said: "Now you know the consequences of the thing that I am going to put to you. The marshal has said that if you acknowledge that you have been served with these injunctions it will be just as binding as if you were served with the papers. Now all who will agree that they have been served with copies of the injunction will please say 'aye.'" A shout all at once thundered the word, "Aye."

I then explained that that might not be satisfactory and therefore asked all who acknowledged that they had been served with the papers to raise their hands and the hands of everyone were raised. I asked, "Is there anyone who declines to acknowledge that he or she has been served? And all who decline to so acknowledge will please raise their hands." There was not one hand raised.

I turned to the marshal and said, "Are you satisfied that all of us here acknowledge that they have been served with these injunctions?" He said, "I am." "Now will you do us the kindness of leaving this group if you must, or staying if you care, and I shall proceed to continue to address this gathering." I went on to the end of my talk. The courts made no further attempt to molest me or to interfere with my work.

I have found that if, after mature consideration, you have your own course planned and are sure of the justice of your case, the enemy is less likely to regard you as insignificant and unworthy of their attention except for prosecution or persecution.

My course has been to know, to understand my guaranteed constitutional rights as a citizen, and to exercise those rights, regardless of the consequences. Neither any one nor all of labor's enemies are able to make me afraid, and I have said and repeat, guided by a right motive and purpose, within my constitutional rights, I propose to exercise the natural right of free speech, conscious that I may be held responsible for my utterances. Therefore, my utterances have been guarded. But I hold a jail more roomy in the expression of my judgment and convictions than would be the whole world if I were to submit to repression and be denied the right to express myself. As I sounded the keynote to resist reductions in wages, I so sounded the keynote to ignore injunctions in labor disputes. Upon these two basic principles my leadership in these fields rests.

Mahon was also in West Virginia. He contributed about two months of his time to the struggle and received not a cent in compensation, not even expenses. Mahon's attitude toward injunctions was the same as mine; he proposed to exercise his constitutional rights and he always did so without challenge. Our course was not without danger other than from that attaching to procedure, as incident will illustrate. I stopped in one West Virginia town where I thought I was unknown. Early in the morning I walked to the edge of the town where a bridge crossed the mountain stream, leading to the mining region. I walked along the bridge, stopped, lost in the beauty of the scene. When I had stood there gazing for some time, I became conscious of a man beside me. He was a giant in size. We talked a bit and then walked along together. After a while I thought he was making a sign to ask me if I was a Mason and I responded, indicating that I was. Then he told me that he was a guard in the employ of the neighboring mining company with instructions to watch me. He showed me his kodak with several snapshots of me and gave me pictures that had been taken of me previously, together with the negatives. One is reproduced in these pages. I have frequently found that my affiliation to the Masonic order has been a protection to me.

As a result of the tremendous effort put forth in their strike, the miners found they had mutual interests that required co-operation and mutual support. They rallied splendidly and finally the victory was won. It was the first successful strike of the United Mine Workers of

America. The coal operators declared for the principle of a uniform minimum rate. The following year the joint agreement was established in the central competitive field.

My most grilling experience with injunctions came in the Buck's Stove & Range Company case. The foundry employes, as well as the metal polishers, declined to submit to an increase in the hours of their labor and they were peremptorily dismissed by the company. Of course, the unions resented this action against their men and brought the subject to the attention of our succeeding convention and asked that the company's products be placed upon the "We Don't Patronize" list. Before so doing, as is the usual practice, the matter in dispute was referred to the Executive Council and in turn to me for investigation and an effort was made for an adjustment. Joseph Valentine was the president of the International Molders' Union as well as member of the Executive Council of the Federation and because the Buck's Stove & Range Company belonged to the Employers' Association of the industry which had in other molding establishments agreements with the Molders' International Union, Mr. Valentine was in a strategic position to try to adjust the situation. Despite all of his efforts, with much regret, he failed.

James Van Cleave, president of the company, was also president of the National Association of Manufacturers. The intensity of his bitterness was shown later by the arrangements he had with the Turner Detective Agency to secure strike breakers to act as agents of the company in the controversy. Finding all chances of an adjustment impossible, the Executive Council decided to publish the Buck's Stove & Range Company on the "We Don't Patronize" list in the *American Federationist*. It did not call upon any one to refrain from purchasing any product—it merely stated a fact—that the company in question had acted unfairly toward the workers involved in the dispute. However, the company secured an injunction from the court forbidding the publication of the statement in the *American Federationist* or elsewhere. It enjoined all reference to the dispute in circulars, letters, or the spoken or printed word. It enjoined even our attorneys from discussing the principles involved.

Of course, as president of the A. F. of L., I could not ignore the terms of the injunction. It was absolutely essential to report the history of the case, including the injunction, to the following convention of the Federation, and this report, as well as the other evidence, was used in the contempt proceedings showing the violation of the terms of the injunction. This I held was manifestly in violation of the constitutional guarantees involving the right of free speech and free press. The injunction process denied that right in advance, preventing expression of opinion by individual or group.

Abuse of the injunctive writ had grown in frequency, until it had become the paramount issue in labor problems. It was at my suggestion that the Federation determined to select a particularly flagrant injunctive abuse to make a test case. Soon after that course was determined, the Buck's Stove & Range Company instituted injunction proceedings against the A. F. of L. This case was selected as it contained practically every phase of the abuse we wished to remedy.

The injunction proceedings instituted by the Buck's Stove & Range Company, and the decision to make them a test case, were reported to the next convention and thereby to organized labor of the country.   That suit represented the unified opposition of forces hostile to labor.

In one form or another the National Association of Manufacturers schemed for the corruption, or disaffection of representative labor men and for a considerable time they concentrated their efforts upon me.

In September, 1907, I was in New York.   One day as I was leaving the Victoria Hotel a man greeted me and asked if I remembered him.   He told me that he was a newspaper man who had met me at the Immigration Conference the previous year.   His name was Brandenberg.   After we had talked a brief time, he said he was in the employ of the National Association of Manufacturers in their campaign against labor, and that he was in a position to help me get together with James Van Cleave, then president of the N. A. M., in order that we might come to a better understanding.   He offered to arrange an interview between Mr. Van Cleave and me.   I merely replied that we could discuss that matter later, and hurried on to my appointment.

When I returned to the hotel that evening, I found a note at the desk.   I found it to be an unsigned request for me to go to Brandenberg's room on a matter of importance. I had other engagements and paid no attention to the request.

On the following day I received another unsigned note in which Mr. Brandenberg referred to our unfinished conversation and stated that he was going to Edgefield, South Carolina, where he urged me to join him.   I wrote him, telling him that my engagements would not permit me to go and asked him whether it would not be possible for him to stop in Washington on his return trip.

In October I received a telegram from Salisbury, North

Carolina, saying that he would arrive in Washington and giving me the name of the Pullman car upon which I could find him. However, the telegram reached me too late for me to meet him and I wrote him, stating that fact and also telling him that I would be in New York shortly. In a few days a note came from him in which he expressed his regret and stated that "matters are most critical"; hence he urged me to see him as quickly as possible.

I went to New York City in October for a conference on the building trades with James Duncan, James O'Connell, William Huber, James Kirby, James Hannahan and William Spencer. I told my colleagues on the Building Trades Committee of the situation and asked their advice. They urged me to have a conference with Brandenberg for thereby I might get important information. Just as our Building Trades Conference had been completed, I was told that Brandenberg was in the lobby desirous of speaking to me. I arranged to meet him in the lobby that evening and had Duncan and Huber with me in order that they might identify him. I so arranged the situation that Brandenberg would have to address me before my colleagues. Then we went to my room for a private conference. He seemed deeply troubled in mind and ill at ease and walked up and down the room while he talked to me. He told me that he was in charge of a Bureau organized by the N. A. M. for the purpose of exposing the immorality and dishonesty of the leaders in the labor movement. With a face drawn as with intense feeling he began a melodramatic story which he had written as my thanatopsis as he called it. The outline of his story was that at the time when I was ill in Little Rock, Arkansas, in 1895, when I was expecting to die I made a statement which was a kind of confession. This statement, Brandenberg told me, he had written out for me and requested that I sign. Now as a matter of fact, I had been ill, not critically, one night in Little Rock in 1895, but I restrained my resentment and sought to lead him on further. Whereupon he told me that the N. A. M. did not want me removed from the presidency that fall, but wanted me to wait until a few months after the Norfolk election and then resign. He then showed me the typewritten document which he wished me to sign. That paper was as follows:

So by devious ways I have come in view of the end of the period. Not far away is the final cessation of something mortal, that I know, but that mystery of the suspension of other things immortal must yet be made clear. Soon I shall stand where I shall see with unblinded eyes, and to that point must come every one no matter by what path, and the realization of that fact palliates the bitterness with which I could contemplate my own course, were it not true.

For I have struggled with the humblest on a plane of equality, and I have walked and talked with the mighty ones of the earth and have lent them my power. The poor cigarmaker's apprentice has lived to become the master of a million minds, and lived a little longer to be what he is today, not even a master of himself.

There is nothing of the whine in this. Emptied, broken as I am, I have nothing to ask. Nothing I might achieve would matter in a little while, and this what I write is after all nothing more than my retrospective thoughts expressed through the accustomed medium of my pen. Wisdom is cumulated and out of my abundance I might endow posterity. Vengeance by the law of compensation overreaches the grave, and I might undo more men a score of times than will regret my passing. Justice is exquisitely elusive, and I might with a truth told here and there palliate many a grave miscarriage. But why? Why should I, having driven on to my own aims, leave my now disabled chariot to retrace the hippodrome?

Each man in his way, be it great or small, exists in an attitude toward the world at large, in a second attitude toward his immediate associates, and in a third and almost invariably different, very different attitude before his own inner consciousness. Stripped of the sophistry that served as a mental lubricant when in activity, I stand at halt contemplating my own ego.

I see lust of power that has triumphed again and again.

It was with difficulty that I restrained myself in order to keep this document within my possession and to get marks of identification on all of the papers connected with the Brandenberg proposal. I terminated the interview with the statement that I would see him again in a few days. I wanted to find out whether or not Brandenberg had any authorization from Mr. Van Cleave. In a few days Brandenberg offered to give me all manner of references. He told me that the N. A. M. was anxious to eliminate me, hoping that my removal would make it easy to get rid of the "smaller labor men." He assured me if I would only lend myself to the rôle he had created for me, that I would have a competence for the rest of my life.

The conference with Van Cleave was never brought about. I disclosed the whole episode to the Norfolk Convention which was printed in full in the official proceedings and used the story together with a statement of the purposes of the N. A. M. to arouse labor throughout the land to the danger of the situation.

After the injunction became operative, I gave orders to discontinue the publication of the "We Don't Patronize" list, but I refused even to consider suggestions that I should restrict my discussion of economic issues or place limits to my freedom of speech—written or spoken. When the injunction was made permanent, I continued to exercise the freedom which I knew was my right. Since the Federation had made this injunction a test case, upon me rested responsibility for leadership in this campaign. That implied making plain labor's grievances and suggested remedies. It was impossible for me to obey the injunction and perform my duties. It was impossible for me to be true to my ideals of American principles and those bulwarks of free institutions—freedom of press and speech—and recognize a judicial order subversive to them. I determined to maintain my rights as an American citizen and continued to discuss the principles involved in the controversy between labor and the Buck's Stove & Range Company and the principles involved in the misuse of the injunctive writ.

In 1908 remedial legislation to prevent abuse of the injunctive writs was the crucial issue for which labor launched an intensive national campaign. We urged organized intelligent use of wage-earners' ballots. We presented labor's cause to the platform committees of both parties and then to the voters of the United States. Elsewhere, I have told of the declaration of the Democratic National Convention of 1908 approving labor's request for the abolition of the injunctive abuses in labor disputes when no such injunctions would be issued under other conditions.

Following that campaign contempt proceedings were instituted against John Mitchell, Frank Morrison, and me in the court of Judge Wright. Mitchell's offense was that he presided over the convention of the United Mine Workers which adopted a resolution to boycott the Buck's Stove & Range Company; Frank Morrison was charged with the act of distributing copies of the *American Federationist* and the official proceedings of the convention in which the history of the case was reported and discussed.

It so happened that the *Washington Law Reporter* which printed the injunction issued by the court was printing the *American Federationist* and I republished in the *American Federationist* the injunction from the same type with which the original injunction was printed. In the trial my publication of the injunction—without a word of comment—was held as evidence of my violation of its terms. My arguments in the presidential and congressional campaign, urging my fellow-citizens to take into consideration in casting their votes for the candidates for the presidency and the members of Congress the principles involved in our injunction suits, were held to be in violation of the terms of the injunction.

Being a "martyr" for a cause is a bitter-sweet experience. There are moments of humiliation as well as periods of exaltation. The hour which I spent in Judge Wright's court listening to him read his opinion and pronounce sentence upon us was one which burned itself into my very soul. Judge Wright, in violent language and with vindictiveness of voice, excoriated us as dangerous promoters of disorder and lawlessness. I value my good name and I value institutions of freedom and justice. I have given years of personal sacrifice and privation for the cause of labor; I have worked, starved, and dreamed for others, sustained by an indomitable will to serve. Yet I had to listen to a judge thus characterize my conduct: "Utter, rampant, insolent defiance is heralded and proclaimed; unrefined insult, coarse affront, vulgar indignity measure the litigant's conception of the tribunal's due wherein his cause still pends." The judge's opinion was in reality a furious tongue lashing furiously delivered. We were called leaders of the "rabble" who would "unlaw" the land, "public enemies" whose intent was to bring "relentless blight" of a "hideous pestilence" and subordinate the "supremacy of the law" to "anarchy and riot."

Before pronouncing sentence the judge asked me if I had any reason to present why sentence should not be pronounced against me. My reply was:

Your Honor, I am not conscious at any time during my life of having violated any law of the country or of the District in which I live. I would not consciously violate a law now or at any time during my whole life. It is not possible that under the circumstances in which I am before Your Honor this morning, and after listening to the opinion you have rendered, to either calmly or appropriately express that which I have in mind to say. But, sir, I may be permitted to say this, that the freedom of speech and the freedom of the press have not been granted to the people in order that they may say the things which please, and which are based upon accepted thought, but the right to say the things which displease, the right to say the things which may convey the new and yet unexpected thoughts, the right to say things, even though they do a wrong, for one can not be guilty of giving utterance to any expression which may do a wrong if he is by an injunction enjoined from so saying. It then will devolve upon a judge upon the bench to determine in advance a man's right to express his opinion in speech and in print.

There is much that I would like to say. I feel that I can not say it now, but if Your Honor will permit me, I will say this.

Your Honor has, in the course of your opinion accepted the testimony adduced by the Buck's Stove & Range Company, accepted it as evidence, and laid much stress upon the fact that the evidence is not denied; and upon the failure to deny, I can readily understand it may be accepted as having been admitted. But Your Honor will see the situation. Suppose some citizen were brought before a court charged with a crime, aye, even murder, and if advised and believing that the judge sitting upon the bench would undertake to proceed with the trial of the defendant without submitting such a case to a jury, if the defendant were advised that the judge, in the exercise of that function, violated the fundamental constitutionally guaranteed rights of the citizen, hence that it was not requisite on his part to enter any defense, and that in the last analysis the higher courts would reverse the decision of the judge upon that ground, the citizen would therefore enter neither denial nor offer evidence in rebuttal to that presented by the prosecution.

It is true that the judge might hold that there being no denial of the testimony presented against him, therefore he would hold the charge as proved; yet, as a matter of fact, it may prove nothing of the kind, even though it may be before the court.

I may say, Your Honor, that this is a struggle of the working people of our country, a struggle for rights. The labor movement does not presume to be a higher tribunal than the courts or the other branches of the government of our country, and the language quoted by counsel for the Buck's Stove & Range Company, which

I am very glad to have the opportunity of explaining, the language accepted by Your Honor in your opinion in regard to the A. F. of L. Conventions being the highest tribunal in the realms of labor, was not, either in my mind, or in the mind of any man that heard that report read, to apply to anything in which the rights of others outside of the labor movement were concerned. It was that in the A. F. of L. convention some question as to jurisdiction, as to internal strife, and disputes, between these organizations, that in so far as these contests were concerned the decisions reached by the convention of the A. F. of L. should be received by all concerned as determining their contentions.

Yes, sir, it is a great struggle, it is a struggle of ages, a struggle of the men of labor to throw off some of the burdens which have been heaped upon them, to abolish some of the wrongs which they have too long borne, and to secure some of the rights too long denied.

If men must suffer because they dare speak for the masses of our country, if men must suffer because they have raised their voices to meet the bitter antagonism of sordid greed, which would even grind the children into the dust to coin dollars, and meeting with the same bitter antagonism that we do in every effort we make before the courts, before the Legislatures of our states, or before the Congress of our country, if men must urge this gradual rational development then they must bear the consequences.

That which Your Honor has quoted and criticized and denounced in us, in the exercise of our duties to our fellows in our own country is now the statute law of Great Britain, passed by the Parliament of that country less than two years ago. If in monarchical England these rights can be accorded to the working people, these subjects of the monarch, they ought not be denied to the theoretically at least, free citizens of a republic.

In this struggle men have suffered. Better men have suffered than I. It is true that I do not believe that there is a man alive who would chafe more under restraint of his liberty than I would, but if I can not discuss grave problems, great questions in which the people of our country are interested, if a speech made by me on the public rostrum during a political campaign after the close of the taking of testimony in this case, if the speeches in furtherance of great principle, of a great right are to be held against me, I shall not only have to but I shall be willing to bear the consequences.

I say this to you, Your Honor, I would not have you to believe me to be a man of defiant character, in disposition, in conduct. Those who know me, and know me best, know that that is not my make-up; but in the pursuit of honest convictions, conscious of having violated no law, and in furtherance of the common interests of my fellow-men, I shall not only have to, but be willing to, submit to whatever sentence Your Honor may impose.

The court then sentenced us to the following terms of imprisonment: Gompers one year, Mitchell, nine months, Morrison six months.

As I learned afterwards, advance information of the decision had been given to the press, for it appeared in New York papers practically simultaneously with the scene in court. From all parts of the country, letters and telegrams poured in, bringing suggestions, sympathy, and encouragement. In that crisis I was glad to know I had the good will of my fellows and the moral support of broad-minded citizens.

It was agreed between Mr. Mitchell, Mr. Morrison, and me that we would publish a joint statement in the *American Federationist* in regard to the opinion. I prepared an account of the decision and the scene in court in which I undertook to describe in a realistic manner the bitterness of attitude of Daniel Thew Wright, the trial judge, which I read to Mr. Mitchell and to which he apparently consented. Mr. Mitchell, however, did not care to have his name appended to that part of the article describing the scene in court. As I did not wish to place Mr. Mitchell and Mr. Morrison at variance with me upon any matter, I assumed personal responsibility for that first section of the statement and the review of the case was published under the name of the three of us.

The new year 1909 found us with two appeals pending in the District Court of Appeals—upon the validity of the original injunction and Justice Wright's decision with the punishment affixed. The higher court modified the Gould-

Claybaugh injunction.   The modification eliminated the most flagrant violations of free press and free speech, which forbade printing or discussing anything in relation to the Buck's Stove & Range Company boycott or even the injunction itself.   With that change, Justices Robb and Van Orsdel reaffirmed the injunction reaching a common conclusion by very different methods of reasoning.

In a dissenting opinion, Chief Justice Shepherd held that there was no authority to restrain publication and that the only remedy for libelous or injurious statements, if such there were, was through civil action for damages.   He therefore disagreed with the terms of the injunction even as modified.

The Court of Appeals opinion was made November 2, 1909; Justices Robb and Van Orsdel reaffirmed the sentences, holding that regardless of whether the injunction was valid it must be obeyed.   Chief Justice Shepherd dissented saying: "Convinced that the court was without authority to make the only order which Gompers and Morrison can be said to have disobeyed, I can have no other opinion than that the decrees should be reversed."

We wanted the United States Supreme Court to pass upon the fundamental principles involved and counsel for the A. F. of L. asked for a writ of certiorari to have the record of this case brought before the Supreme Court.   The request was granted.

When the Supreme Court rendered the decision in the Buck's Stove & Range Company case, May 15, 1911, it held that the petition was civil in nature and that criminal penalties could not properly be affixed.   The court reversed the judgment of the lower court and remanded the case to the Supreme Court of the District without prejudice to

the power and right of that court to punish by proper proceedings, contempt if any, committed against it.

On the very next morning, before the opinion of the
Supreme Court was printed and available for general use,
Justice Wright appointed a committee to investigate
whether there were sufficient grounds to consider Gompers,
Mitchell, and Morrison guilty of contempt. He appointed
to constitute that committee, Darlington, Davenport, and
Beck, who had been the attorneys for the Anti-Boycott
Association in pressing the first case. From this "impartial" group which had spent about three years in trying to
secure our convictions, it was not surprising that a report
was made that there was good reason to believe we were
guilty of contempt.

In concluding their report, the committee said that inasmuch as I asserted I had the right to do the various things
with which I was charged on the grounds that the injunction
was not binding, it might be that since the Supreme Court
had not upheld my contention I would be prepared to make
due acknowledgment, apology, and assurance of future submission to the law and thus satisfy the authority of the
court.

I indignantly rejected this offer as an insult to my integrity and an attempt to break my spirit.

Not without obvious reason our counsel sought to have
the case tried before another judge, but Justice Wright
would not relinquish jurisdiction but perfunctorily asked
some of his associates to sit with him. The Anti-Boycott
lawyers asked Judge Wright to allow testimony to be taken
before an examiner. As that course would allow much
irrelevant testimony to be inserted in the record, we urged
that the case be tried in open court with opportunity to

confront accusing witnesses. Judge Wright refused our request. The second trial then proceeded without an opportunity to meet witnesses face to face, and without the right of jury trial.

Justice Wright reaffirmed his original sentences of prison terms of twelve, nine, and six months for Gompers, Mitchell, and Morrison respectively. An appeal was immediately taken to the District Court of Appeals. Our counsel took the position that since the contempt proceedings were criminal in nature, the rule of criminal procedure and the Statute of Limitations should apply. On May 15, 1913, the opinion of the court was read. It was written by Justice Van Orsdel and concurred in by Justice Robb. The court sustained the judgment of Wright in holding us guilty of contempt but declared the sentences a violation of judicial discretion and changed them to thirty days for me and a fine of $500 each for Mitchell and Morrison.

Chief Justice Shepherd held that all particular charges specified in the case were barred by the Statute of Limitations except one involving John Mitchell, "which was too general to put the party under notice." He therefore believed the case should be dismissed.

Justice Wright filed a unique petition with the Supreme Court, charging that the Court of Appeals had exceeded its authority in mitigating the sentences. As labor had been pressing this case in order to secure a judicial ruling upon the fundamentals involved, counsel for the A. F. of L. was instructed to ask the Supreme Court for a writ of certiorari in order that the highest tribunal of the land should review the case.

The hearing before that court occurred in January, 1914. As one member of the court was absent, at the request of the court, the case was argued again before a ful bench in April.

On May 11, 1914, the decision of the Supreme Court was handed down. It considered the nature of contempt trials, and held that criminal contempts should be tried according to usual criminal procedure. Under this procedure the acts specified could not be presented after a lapse of three years. The court, therefore, reversed the judgments.

Before the second case came before the Supreme Court for decision, there was a change in management of the Buck's Stove & Range Company and an adjustment of the dispute was reached. The case was then regarded by the court as moot, but in the meantime our counsel made a proposition to us that we make a plea to the court that would remove the possibility of our being tried to serve the sentence imposed by Judge Wright on the ground that the appeal was moot. This I positively declined. I prepared a letter of refusal to which Mr. Morrison agreed and, reading the letter to Mr. Mitchell over long distance telephone from Washington to New York, received his full endorsement of it. The case then went from court to court until it again reached the Supreme Court where it was dismissed. We were not sent to jail and be it said that Judge Wright very shortly after that was no longer judge. An investigation by a committee of Congress into Judge Wright's conduct brought about his "voluntary" retirement.

The case had been doggedly contested through every stage up to the highest judicial authority. For seven long years we were either presenting briefs, or awaiting court decisions. The litigation was expensive and absorbed money, time, and energy that were needed for constructive work. In that period I was several times seriously ill. It was hard to reconcile myself to the thought that if the end should come a blot would rest upon my name which no amount of explanation could completely remove. The shadow of that prison sentence harassed my wife, my father, my children, for seven years.

When finally the U. S. Supreme Court came to pass upon our case, it evaded the fundamental issues and declared the case outlawed by the Statute of Limitations.

However, because of the discussion growing out of the case and because judicial perversion had solidified labor's forces in the political field, we were able to press for remedial legislation. The case disclosed the lines along which relief must be drawn and the basis for the labor sections of the Clayton Anti-Trust Law.

Some dispute, of which I now have little recollection, arose in the Joint Committee on Printing of the Senate and House, and a party in interest obtained a writ of injunction from Justice Wright of the Supreme Court of the District of Columbia (it occurred shortly after the injunction proceedings in the Buck's Stove & Range Company case against Morrison, Mitchell, and me) restraining the committee of both houses from exercising the functions assigned to it by both houses of Congress.

The Senate decided to ignore the injunction and refused to be represented before the court to answer. The House, under the leadership of Speaker Cannon, acknowledged the injunction and was represented before the court, thus consenting and recognizing the right of a judge sitting in equity to issue an injunction against the procedure of the legislative branch of the government. It was common

understanding at the time that the reason for the pusilla-
nimity of the House was the influence of the court procedure against my associates and me in refusing to comply
with the terms of the injunction issued against us.

I entered into this case with my eyes wide open. There
were two points of advantage in having the fundamental
questions brought before the court and the public. We
hoped to obtain a decision from the courts that would sustain labor's contention that the issuance of injunctions in
a dispute over labor relations was unwarranted and unconstitutional. We hoped that the issue would attract country-
wide interest and concentrate the thought of the people
upon the principles involved; that if we failed to gain a
favorable decision from the court, the subject would become
an issue of paramount importance in the political campaign,
and finally, as a cumulative result, we would obtain from
Congress the legislation establishing justice denied us by the
courts.

We called upon the men in the labor movement to
stand their ground and contend for the principles involved
in the abuse of the injunction and take the responsibility
of their action. An opportunity came to me and I felt that
it would be cowardice did I attempt to avoid it or evade it.
We had excellent and faithful counsel—Judge Alton B.
Parker, Jackson H. Ralston, and Frank L. Mulholland.
They defended us with great ability, but they would not
contend for the fundamental principles upon which we had
predicated our hope to test the constitutionality of the procedure. It is a fact that despite one invasion after another
which the judiciary has made upon the rights of the citizens, we find few if any of the members of the real prac-

ticing legal profession to challenge the jurisdiction of a court upon a fundamental constitutional law when the violation of rights affect workmen engaged in an industrial dispute with employers. The bench has constantly moved forward, and practicing attorneys have yielded ground and continuously conceded rights guaranteed by our constitution. Few lawyers have understood that the original term *Advocat* was the tribune who maintained the rights of the citizens of the humblest walks of life. The practice of law has become too much of a commercialized institution.

Even after the enactment of the provision of the Clayton Act intended to protect labor against an invasion of its rights by injunctions or anti-trust procedure, such cases continued. The two most conspicuous with which I have been concerned were the Anderson injunction against the Miners and the Wilkerson injunction against the striking Railroad Shopmen.

In neither of these cases did I yield one inch of the contentions I had urged against usurpation of power by the courts.

In these cases, as in all previous ones, I took the ground that the issuance of such injunctions was usurpation of power on the part of the courts, and therefore the injunctions ought to be ignored. When the lawyers conceded the use of injunctions to restrain illegal acts, I emphatically voiced my dissent. Where law made certain acts illegal, it also provided remedies; but there should be trial and punishment under the law for all proven offenses.

I believe that the price of liberty is resistance to encroachments upon rights. It was not a pleasant thing to stand up under the abuse and obloquy which the Administration and the press hurled at me, but it was much easier than sacrificing my personal integrity. Though we may not establish in law all that we desire at once, the uncompromising protest of labor is definitely influencing legal thought.

CHAPTER XXXIV

CAPITOL HILL

WHEN I first saw Washington about 1871, I, like all pilgrims to the nation's capital, went to the white building on Capitol Hill. The wings had only recently been added to the old building, making a structure which has been a never-failing source of inspiration. I little dreamed at the time how familiar the legislative chambers, the committee rooms, and even the domain of the Supreme Court were to become to me. There is hardly a committee room in which I have not appeared to plead the cause of labor.

Until Federation headquarters were moved to Washington in 1897, my trips were widely scattered. There were about seven years between my first and second trips. That time I went on Cigarmakers' business and in 1883 I went representing the Federation. I remained several weeks. Frank Foster was with me and we were impressed with advantages labor would gain by maintaining representatives through the sessions of Congress. After 1886 I was in Washington at least once a year. Usually, my trips were planned in advance so I could accomplish as much as possible.

Within my lifetime has occurred the development of present-day social legislation and laws dealing with industry and labor. My work has kept me in close touch with all phases of legislation from analysis of fundamental principles to mechanics of getting law enacted and enforced. My experiences with the tenement-house law taught me much and showed me the essential difference between economic matters and political. That distinction has been the foundation upon which my course has been developed.

I have persistently held that economic organizations ought to be free to operate as economic needs developed and that opportunity for initiative is essential to sustained progress. This was why I did not join in the hue and cry against industrial combinations that gained momentum in the late 'eighties.

I was in Washington when the Sherman Anti-Trust Bill [1] was under discussion. Though I had been watching with keen apprehension the growth of industrial trusts, I followed the making of that law with a feeling of even greater disquietude. Industrial happenings had convinced me the labor union should remain a voluntary organization in order to protect its usefulness and opportunities for development. Since in the legal vocabulary normal union activity and conspiracy were interchangeable terms, I was convinced that if trade unions were not specifically excluded from the provisions of the measure, the law would be applied to the organized effort of the workers. I talked this matter over with Senators George, Blair, and Hoar. Senator George discussed with Senator Sherman a proposal to exempt specifically wage-earners and farmers and Senator Sherman submitted such amendment. Though our amendment was accepted in the Senate as a committee of the whole, it afterwards disappeared in the Committee on Judi-

[1] I recorded this history in "The Charter of Industrial Freedom," in *American Federationist*, November, 1914.

ciary to which the bill was referred and which reported
the bill rewritten. Senator Hoar expressed the opinion that
the bill then was satisfactory to all elements and would
not apply to labor unions.

In the more than six decades, during which my work
brought me to Capitol Hill, I have known many in public
life including the majority of the Speakers of the House.
Schuyler Colfax was the Speaker of the House during
my first legislative work, and I met him at the time.
Thomas B. Reed was the first speaker whom I knew
personally. James G. Blaine I knew, but not when he was
Speaker. Samuel J. Randall, was a protectionist-Demo-
crat who gave us cigarmakers friendly consideration when
we presented any matter in which our industry was concerned. Joseph W. Keifer, who had been a labor candidate for Vice-President of the United States, was an active
member in the Independent Order of Odd Fellows where
I met him several times. He was an ardent advocate of a
single tax on land. D. B. Henderson I knew only
slightly.

Thomas B. Reed I first met in connection with legislation for the cigar industry. He was always willing to make
a sincere effort to get at the fundamentals of any proposition I put before him. He cordially urged me to bring to
him any matters that would help him to understand industrial problems. I often met him in his private office in the
Shoreham Hotel and thoroughly enjoyed our conversations.
Reed was as deep a student of economics, political and
social affairs as anyone I have ever known. His great
powers of mind and expression made a deep impression on
me. He was a very human sort of man, and as a fighter
in the House he was the match for any member. When

he became Speaker, he concentrated his great ability on promoting the business of the nation. The rules then in use in the House had been drafted when the membership was comparatively small and the Representatives were very loath to give up methods which they thought added to their prestige. The House had developed the practice of filibustering until it was not only a nuisance but a menace to legislative work. Important in this practice was the rule that in counting a quorum only such members as responded to the roll-call were counted. As a result, often no quorum was announced when sufficient members were plainly visible. This practice was abhorrent to Speaker Reed's common sense and instinct for efficiency. He mastered that legislative situation, but he did not try to manipulate legislative action. Though he was known as czar, there was a very wide difference between his methods and the boss-control set up by Joseph G. Cannon, a man of a very different caliber. That difference is illustrated by the following incident. During a colloquy in the House of Representatives with one of the House members, Cannon made use of an expression that shocked the public, and the New York *Sun* at that time took up the campaign for his defeat and published a cartoon depicting the lips of Mr. Cannon and had it headed as "Foul-Mouthed Joseph Cannon." He was defeated in the following election. I remember the utterance, probably not the exact words but nearly so. I had met Mr. Cannon before this.

When in the election of 1895 the Republicans gained control of the House, it was obvious that Reed, who was minority leader, was to be Speaker in the coming Congress. Labor was much concerned to have as a chairman of the House Committee on Labor someone who could give under-

standing sympathy to labor legislation. Reed was then in
Europe where I wrote him suggesting that Thomas W.
Phillips of Pennsylvania be made chairman of that committee. Phillips had been deeply interested in all phases of
the trust problem, especially as manifested in oil and steel.
He was of the opinion that there were new elements in
the industrial situation which made it necessary to survey
the whole field in order to determine national policies. In
the previous Congress Mr. Phillips introduced a bill for
the creation of a commission to make an investigation into
industrial conditions. While I was in Belgium in 1895,
I found that a similar commission had been making a study
of Belgian industries and I secured such information and as
many reports of the commission as were available. These
I gave to Congressman Phillips after Reed had appointed
him. Mr. Reed had replied to my letter, saying that if
elected Speaker he would undoubtedly appoint Mr. Phillips
chairman of the Committee on Labor. In the meantime
before the session was on, I aided Mr. Phillips in recon-
structing his bill which was finally enacted creating the
Industrial Commission consisting of five members of the
House, five of the Senate, and five representatives of the
public.

Before the headquarters of the Federation were moved
to Washington, it was my custom to arrange with the chairman of the House and the Senate Committee on Labor to
hold hearings upon labor measures at some time when I
could be in Washington. Usually, other members of the
Executive Council or official representatives of trades interested in special matters arranged to be present. The arrangement was far from satisfactory. The formulation of
legislation is a development and during the whole discussion

of measures affecting labor there was need for labor advisers to keep in touch with changing proposals.

So in 1895, Andrew Furuseth and Adolph Strasser were selected to serve as the legislative representatives of the Federation to remain in Washington during sessions of Congress. Furuseth served for several years until his organization was able to keep him in Washington to give full time to promoting Seamen's measures. The problem of the seamen involved the development of a philosophy of human freedom and progress. That philosophy also determined labor's position upon injunction and compulsory arbitration proposals. When the Supreme Court rendered its decision in the *Arago* case, upholding specific enforcement of contracts or compulsory labor, the need for a law establishing the rights of seamen became imperative. The demand for both the Seamen's Act and for the prohibition of the use of injunctions to regulate industrial disputes is predicated on the fact that the distinguishing characteristic of man is his power to create—a human quality—not property—but inseparable from the human being. The Seamen's Act was one that interested me deeply and our joint work strengthened the friendship between Furuseth and me.

We were not lawyers, but we had to meet lawyers on all committees. It was not an easy matter for us to think through constructive suggestions and to be ready to defend them against trained legal minds. But we had learned the principles of human freedom in a school that burned them into us and no one could shake our grasp of them. The law held seamen liable to imprisonment for violation of contract. Seamen quitting their ships in safe harbor were liable to arrest and return to their ships for desertion. The seamen demanded the right of all free men—the right to quit ships in safe harbor. They were bondmen—who could be hunted down like serfs of old. They were the only workmen compelled to perform the specific terms of a contract. The issuance of a writ of injunction to regulate personal relations is postulated in the same principle—that the worker is property and hence unfree. The parallelism between the injunction and seamen's problems continued in the interesting fact that desired legislative remedy for each became law within a few months of each other. The Seamen's Act was signed March 3, 1915, and the labor charter (contained in the Clayton Anti-Trust Act), October 15, 1914.

After headquarters of the Federation were moved to Washington, I kept regularly in touch with happenings in Congress. My opportunities for getting labor's contention before the Chief Executive in the White House and the legislators on Capitol Hill were greatly increased. McKinley was then in the White House and Reed was Speaker. They were fair-minded men to whom a reasonable appeal could be made.

The first conference between the Executive Council of the American Federation of Labor and an Administration responsible for legislation came in 1898. During a meeting of the Executive Council we decided to go as a group to make a personal appeal to President McKinley and to Speaker Reed, urging that remedial labor legislation be enacted during that term of Congress. Unemployment was serious. There were about three million without work.

There were about nineteen in our party. When we got to the White House, we found the President on the eve of departure to Philadelphia, so we journeyed down the avenue to the hill. The Speaker received us in his room and gave us a serious and sympathetic audience. P. J. McGuire, James Duncan, and I presented various phases of labor's plea. We asked for an amendment to the eight-hour law to make it effective, remodeling of immigration law, reform in national banking law to avert financial crises, and liberal appropriations for public works.

I told Mr. Reed that we didn't ask to have those laws enacted tomorrow or the next day, but we earnestly urged action during the current Congress. However, we didn't get what we asked. The patience of labor is one of the most remarkable features of the whole labor struggle. Our rational method made little impression on members of Congress. They recognized little else but votes. That was several years before the Federation began deliberately to mobilize its voting power.

Later, I had an interview with the President after he returned from Philadelphia. He asked me to submit to him suggestions upon labor matters I thought he ought to deal with in his message to Congress. That was a request with which I was glad to comply.

During 1897 the Committee on Labor of the House of Representatives under the chairmanship of Mr. Phillips introduced in the House what we believed would be an effective eight-hour bill. Eight-hour legislation had been the paramount labor demand for many years, for the first law proved ineffective. When that law was restricted by interpretations to a very limited field, labor at once undertook to secure adequate legislative remedy. The purpose of the Phillips bill was to extend the eight-hour law to contractors and sub-contractors to whom government works were let. We had many hearings before the committee. A few days before the termination of Congress, a meeting of the Committee on Labor was held. We desired that the committee report the bill favorably and if possible secure its passage in the House for the effect that accomplishment would have upon the next Congress. Congressman John J. Gardner of New Jersey for the first time attended a meeting of the committee. He criticized the phraseology and the legal principle of the bill, declaring that it was unconstitutional and unenforceable and would be so declared by the courts if enacted. Then he casually suggested as a principle upon which to frame an effective and constitutional bill: that the government in letting work out to contractors incorporate in its contracts the provision that eight hours shall be the maximum work-day. While I was indignant that Mr. Gardner had not concerned himself until the eleventh hour, I recognized that he had made a vitally important suggestion. Although a member of the Committee on Labor, he never attended a meeting during that entire term of Congress until that day. I expressed my deep regret that he had not attended the meetings and helped to formulate legislation while there was time for the committee and for the Congress to consider the proposal. However, the Phillips bill was favorably reported to the House and at least we had that much of moral influence.

As the term of Congressman Phillips expired with that Congress, we requested that Mr. Gardner be made chairman of the Committee on Labor and he was appointed. Together with the committee of the Federation, consisting of P. J. McGuire, James Duncan, and Andrew Furuseth, I had frequent conferences with him covering a period of months. An eight-hour bill was perfected and Mr. Gardner introduced it and did all he could. It was referred to his committee and hearings held lasting several months upon which big business with its lawyers and lobby were busy.

It was during those hearings that Mr. Cramp of the Cramp Ship Yards declared that the Russian government, having secured a loan from France, wanted to have warships built in France by the French ship-builders who were operating under the ten-hour day and that it would require five years to build ships which the Cramp yards, operating on a nine-hour day, could build in just half the time.

During that same hearing, Mr. Harrah, president of the Midvale Steel Company, made the observation that when he bought machines for his plants with contract stipulation that they would last five years, if those machines were not worn out in less than three he held the foremen responsible.

The bill was perfected in minor details and reported favorably, accompanied by an excellent presentation of the fundamental facts upon which the eight-hour day was based. Its passage was urgently commended, but the hearings had been prolonged to such length that action was impeded. The bill unanimously passed the House and went over to the Senate.

In the Senate we had a similar experience, only probably a bit more brazen, with Senator Kyle who came in the Senate as a reformer. Frank Morrison and I one evening went by appointment to see Senator Kyle at his Washington home on New Jersey Avenue and asked him whether he would not father and follow to its conclusion our eight-hour bill. After reading the bill carefully he said that he had always favored the eight-hour day and expressed his appreciation of our giving him the privilege of introducing the bill and stated that he would certainly do everything he possibly could to secure its passage. However, hearings on the bill were protracted and it was due to no consideration of Mr. Kyle that labor's representatives had opportunity to speak. The Committee on Education and Labor reported the bill with amendments and without recommendations. Senator Kyle submitted a minority report against it. When I went to see Senator Pettigrew, his colleague, and mentioned the name of Senator Kyle and was about to tell him the story of his colleague's action, he interrupted by asking: "Who's bought him now?"

At our solicitation, Senator Cullom was given charge of the bill on the floor. The bill was put upon the calendar for early consideration. We were assured by the Steering Committee of the Senate and by every Senator with whom we came in contact that the bill would pass. Nevertheless, there were persistent efforts to delay consideration in which Senator Kyle participated.

In the closing hours of the last of the session, Senator Cullom again moved our eight-hour bill be taken up. At that moment the naval appropriation bill, a preferred measure, displaced our eight-hour bill. Congress adjourned at 2 A. M. without acting on our bill. Two or three representative labor men were with me in the gallery of the Senate when that legislative tragedy was enacted. There have been many times in my life when I have definitely had to order discouragement from my mind and begin all over again. Never in my life have I been more disappointed than when just as I felt that victory was within our grasp, the work of years became as nothing. I was heart-sick over the disappointment. In the next session, largely through the efforts of Senator Kyle, the bill was defeated.

In the next Congress, Mr. Gardner was again appointed

chairman of the Labor Committee and he re-introduced the
eight-hour bill. Again the bill passed the House practically unanimously. It was introduced in the Senate by
Mr. Penrose, but never reported from the committee despite
all efforts by us and friends of the measure.

The same procedure recurred in the next Congress.
However, I noted that, although the National Association
of Manufacturers declared against our eight-hour bill, a
number of employers wrote us that they were not in accord
with that action.

In the next Congress, our bill was referred by the House
Committee to the Department of Labor for information
despite the fact it had been three times unanimously
adopted.

In the following Congress, Mr. Gardner again introduced the bill. The majority of the committee were extremely hostile to labor. After a while we observed Mr.
Gardner's lagging interest and his lack of effort to push
the bill and later on he went out of his way to invite persons and interests to appear in opposition to the passage
of the measure.

We were satisfied that there were enough members of
both the Senate and the House to pass our bill if it could
only be reported from committee. The organized opposition kept appealing for time to introduce new evidence and
as a last resort one of their attorneys, Judge Payson, read
the printed hearings before previous committees of three
or four Congresses on eight-hour bills. This reading continued for weeks simply for the purpose of killing time.
I was present at a meeting of the committee when a quorum
was present, when no further evidence or argument was
available and the committee was on the point of taking a

vote when a member of the committee ostentatiously got up and left the room, thus breaking the quorum. We sent out a couple of labor men to ask committee members to come to the meeting. Again a quorum was secured with the minority temporarily in control. The committee voted 4 to 3 to report the bill favorably. Chairman Gardner voting in the negative.

Of course, we found fault with Mr. Gardner for his conduct. I wrote to him again and again, but could get no answer. I remember going to him one day accompanied by Arthur Holder, legislative committeeman for the Federation. In that conference Mr. Gardner complained that he could get no support from his committee. Holder suggested to him, "Why don't you hold executive sessions?" Mr. Gardner sat still for a minute and I saw a great change in his face as though he were considering a very appealing suggestion. When we got out of the room, I remarked to Holder: "You have made an awful mistake in making that suggestion. Depend upon it, we will never get in that room again so long as Mr. Gardner is chairman." And we didn't. Whereas before he would invite us to meet him, he afterward evaded us, and the labor committee room which had been available to all parties for use when the committee was not in session, was now locked against labor men and, of course, the bill died in committee. When we succeeded in getting it reported out the next session, the bill passed the House by a ratio of ten to one.

In a meeting held in the Arlington Hotel during the 61st Congress, Mr. Nelson made the statement in the presence of about sixty other members of the House that Mr. Gardner boasted he was sitting on the lid and preventing labor measures from being reported to Congress.

Before we were able to discern the change in Mr. Gardner's course toward our bill, he told me that by seniority he was entitled, under the practice of the House, to appointment upon what are politically regarded as more important committees and that Speaker Cannon had upbraided him for his failure to prevent the eight-hour bill being reported and that therefore he was not advanced. Mr. Gardner also stated in one of the conferences I had with him that by his advocacy of the eight-hour bill he had lost the United States senatorship from New Jersey.

Yet Mr. Gardner took a sort of pride in the eight-hour law. On the day of the opening of Congress, Congressman Sulzer, who generally supported legislation for which we asked, introduced in his own name the eight-hour bill which had been perfected by Mr. Gardner and my associates and me. This irritated Mr. Gardner greatly. That Sulzer's attempt to steal Gardner's thunder was not fair to Gardner was quite manifest and he would not introduce the eight-hour bill unless Sulzer either asked for the withdrawal of his bill or made some explanation that he had introduced it without consulting either Chairman Gardner or the representatives of labor. At my request, Mr. Sulzer did make some such explanation and Mr. Gardner re-introduced the bill.

The bill was introduced regularly in each session of Congress and just as regularly was defeated at some state of legislative procedure. From 1902 when the National Association of Manufacturers joined the opposition forces, resistance to all labor measures became definite and regular. I knew the source of the influences brought to bear upon congressmen, but did not have proofs. They were afterwards produced before the Lobby Investigations Com-

mittee (Mulhall exposé).   In the meantime, labor inaugurated its non-partisan political campaign and our eight-hour
bill became law in 1912, after twenty years of work.

Our measures before the Committee on Judiciary fared
no better.   When Mr. Littlefield was elected to Congress,
he was regarded as a public-spirited tribune of the people.
We presented to him labor's amendment to the anti-trust
bill which he was then, with his committee, perfecting.   In
1902 the House Judiciary Committee had under consideration a bill to amend and make more drastic the provisions
of the Sherman Anti-Trust Law.   The bill was referred to
a subcommittee of which he was chairman.   The measure
seemed to us intended to rivet more firmly the portion of
the law which had been interpreted to apply to the normal
activities of the workers.

Mr. Littlefield apparently concerned himself solely to
handicap the organizations of wage-earners.   It proved
absolutely futile to try to move him from his purpose, but
with others I personally appeared, argued, and protested
against the provisions he sought to foist upon the working
people of the country.

We had prepared a section of the bill so that the normal
activities of workers in industry, agriculturists as well as
horticulturists, should be excluded from the provisions of
the bill and of the law to which the bill was intended to be
supplementary.   Without much ado, Mr. Littlefield declined to consider the subject further.   We approached
each member of the committee to present our amendment
and each in turn declined, and so the bill was reported to the
House and on the day when the bill was taken up and put
under discussion, I sent a request by one of the house messengers to Congressman Terry of Arkansas for a conference

in the lobby. We had a ten-minute discussion with him and when he re-entered the House, obtained recognition and presented our amendment to the bill. There was little discussion upon it and the House adopted it with but eight dissenting votes.

Littlefield immediately lost interest in the bill. His whole attitude changed. His legal ability was directed for the purpose of putting labor men in awkward or apparently untenable positions. He showed keen antagonism to the Seamen's Bill. His effrontery, if not his bulldozing of witnesses before him, was conspicuous. At one time in company with several of my associates I went to the Capitol where I met Mr. Littlefield and told him that we thoroughly understood that he was trying to put us in a false position before his associates of the committee. I charged him with unjustifiable antagonism. Mr. Littlefield could not defend himself and he turned me off abruptly. The bill was then passed by the House with the amendment and went to the Senate. No hearings were had upon it nor was any effort made to pass or even consider it. The promoters of the measure both in the House and Senate had lost all interest in the bill after our amendment was so emphatically incorporated within its provisions. The eight members who voted against the amendment were: William F. Aldrich, H. D. Allen, W. J. Bailey, W. A. Calderhead, Joseph G. Cannon, Robert R. Hitt, C. E. Littlefield, Chester I. Long.

I knew definitely that the strategic center to the opposition to labor was the Speaker of the House of Representatives. Mr. Cannon occupied that office and dominated legislation both through the power of his office and through his personal hostility. The committees of the House of

Representatives were appointed by the Speaker who both by rule and precedent was free to act upon his own best judgment. Mr. Cannon exercised this power primarily for the purpose of partisan advantage. As he continued in office for a number of years, he developed a system of discipline under which no one who showed a spirit of independence toward either party dictates or toward his orders was allowed to hold any committee position of importance. Mr. Cannon had determined that legislation in response to labor requests should not be enacted and on the other hand legislation desired by the interests should be facilitated.

Only one illustration of the opposition our bills encountered was the experience of Congressman Rucker of Missouri who asked Speaker Cannon to recognize him for the purpose of getting consideration of the eight-hour bill. Speaker Cannon replied in language more forcible than polite that he would not recognize him or any member of the House for the purpose of considering that measure.

In 1906 the situation was so serious for labor that I knew some new factor had to be brought to bear. Since the Homestead strike in 1892, organization in large-scale industries had been increasingly difficult. The use of professional strike breakers supplied by detective agencies injected a lawless element in strikes that caused me much concern. There had been a number of important strikes that had been waged with unusual ferocity.

In the legal field the use of the injunction had become a usual accompaniment of industrial disputes. Organized employers had three organizations, called the Anti-Boycott Association, the National Association of Manufacturers, and the National Council for Industrial Defense. That these organizations were practically one and the same and intended for use in the war on organized labor was evident from the fact that the same directing policies prevailed in each and the same agents were conspicuous in all three. Where the National Association of Manufacturers was active there were to be found James Emory, Judge Daniel Davenport, Walter Drew, and the rest of the coterie; where the Anti-Boycott Association functioned the same actors appeared; when the National Council of Industrial Defense was in order, the same cast of actors appeared. They were an able group, and were no mean antagonists. Mr. Emory was the Washington representative who sought friends on Capitol Hill and among the influential in Washington. He was a genial, facile conversationalist, who pleased the imagination by apt quotations from the classics and charm of diction. Judge Davenport was an able lawyer and student. Walter Drew was a bitter fighter. He was relentless in both matter and manner of presentation upon any subject in which labor was concerned. These three represented the employing interests in public meetings, in congressional hearings, and in all other capacities where representatives were needed.

In the courts, suit had been brought against the officers and members of the Hatters' Union under the Sherman Anti-Trust Act which threatened the very existence of organized labor.

It was of paramount importance that labor unions be specifically removed from the application of anti-trust law and that injunction use be defined and regulated. Such legislation would free us from harassing court litigation and enable us to fight out our economic problems in the economic field. To secure this result it was necessary to break the strangle-hold which enabled organized employers to control legislation.

In order to get action by Congress, I knew we had to make an appeal to congressmen and that no appeal would be stronger than a threat of action at the ballot box. I talked over the situation with Andrew Furuseth. Then I called together a group of local labor men to get the benefit of a frank discussion by them. As a result, I decided that we must make a special appeal to Congress for legislative relief. In order to give that appeal the proper authority and to focus attention upon our action, I sent a letter to the responsible executives of the various labor organizations, asking them to attend a conference in Washington late in March, 1906. Preparatory to that conference, a statement of labor's case was drafted. This I remember was done late one evening in my office on G Street. Andrew Furuseth was with me and we worked over section by section giving our best thought to a clear statement of fundamentals as well as an appealing presentation of the situation. It took Andy and me some time to decide upon the crux of the whole situation. It was not only the draft for the measure of relief that we had difficulty in framing, but the question as to how the matter should be more conspicuously impressed upon not only the representatives of the government with whom we had the engagement to meet but as to the declaration of our purpose as to the means that we would seek to employ for the purpose of securing the redress. We finally agreed upon drafting the following closing paragraph of the Bill of Grievances:

Labor now appeals to you and we trust that it may not be in vain. But, if perchance, you may not heed us, we shall appeal to the conscience and the support of our fellow-citizens.

The conference called was something altogether new in the annals of the Federation. From the beginning, the Federation had been committed to a policy of independent political action, but there had been no effort to develop organization discipline for the most effective use of the political power of labor. As a result, labor men were identified with political parties and guided by the same sense of loyalty to them that influenced so large a part of the American citizens. At that time, party regularity was the rule. It was an appreciation of party regularity which made the Federation's action seem audacious in the eyes of the ordinary politician. Nevertheless, our conference convened and the declaration known as "Labor's Bill of Grievances" was ratified and ordered submitted to responsible heads of the Administration. I then wrote to President Roosevelt, Speaker Cannon, and Acting-President Frey of the Senate asking for an appointment for myself and others to present to them labor's plea. Courteous responses were received. First of all we went to the White House where the President received us, listened intently to the reading of our bill of grievances, made an occasional note, and asked a few questions. His concern was evidently with that portion which charged the executive departments with negligence in enforcing the eight-hour law.

After leaving the executive offices, we went to the Capitol to the Speaker's room for our appointment with Mr. Cannon. Because of the size of our party and the report of our mission that had spread rapidly, a large crowd gathered around our group as I read the bill of grievances. The crowd was composed of newspaper men and members of the House. After I had finished reading, Mr. Cannon delivered us a rather patronizing lecture, asserting that the committees of the House were not selected for the purpose of defeating labor measures but were made up as fairly and liberally as such committees could be.

I called Mr. Cannon's attention to the fact that labor legislation was being suppressed and that the make-up of committees was not fair and impartial and suggested that the committees ought to be so constituted that legislation sought by the people could be given sympathetic consideration. Mr. Cannon replied to me: "You are not the whole thing. You are not the only pebble on the beach." I replied: "We are just a few pebbles whom you ought to consider and whether we are small or large, influential or impotent, at least our earnest requests ought to be given favorable consideration." Mr. Cannon replied, "I am only one man, only one representative of the House." And with rather lurid language he ended the interview.

On the following day I received a communication and visit from Dr. Charles P. Neill, then Commissioner of Labor Statistics, telling me that the President had authorized him to investigate the charges of violation of the eight-hour law. Dr. Neill was known as the close friend and adviser of President Roosevelt.

Ranking next to Speaker Cannon as an implacable and conspicuous foe of labor legislation, Chas. E. Littlefield of the Sixth District of Maine was in a strategic position to defeat our measures.

In the spring of 1906, I was in the state of Maine attending the convention of the Maine State Federation of Labor. During my address to the convention, I related the history of Mr. Littlefield's opposition to labor measures. A number of the men discussed the situation with me and suggested that a campaign be inaugurated to elect someone from Maine more fairly inclined toward labor. In a mass meeting held in the evening, a committee was appointed to confer with me and to inaugurate the campaign.

Preparatory to the Littlefield campaign I sent into Maine a group of the organizers of the Federation who were to make the arrangements. In August the campaign began actively. As conducted by labor, the campaign was entirely educational. We gave the voters of Maine the facts about Mr. Littlefield and his record in Washington. We addressed meetings and distributed information. Nothing else was necessary.

The Maine election has always been regarded as a political barometer. The Republican Party became exceedingly concerned as to the outcome in Maine. They sent into the state and district some of the most important party orators, including Secretary of War Taft, Senator Beveridge, Senator Lodge, Speaker Cannon, Representative James E. Watson, and Representative Hamilton of Michigan. These men made party speeches and did everything within their power to discredit labor's campaign. Speaker Cannon, particularly, was very abusive and some of his statements on the platform and in private conversation were practically vituperation. President Roosevelt himself sent a letter to Maine, stating that the defeat of Littlefield would be a national calamity. I noted at the time that strenuous efforts were made to organize labor opposition. A number of the type of "professional labor leaders" who organized paper associations and sought to simulate labor opposition to Mr. McGillicudy, the opponent of Mr. Littlefield, were in evidence. The Socialists were also active and seemed to have unusually large funds. Of course, I had

my suspicions, but I never positively knew the origin of
the opposition campaign until Mulhall made his disclosures
of the political activity of the National Association of
Manufacturers in 1913.

We did not defeat Mr. Littlefield in that campaign, but
we reduced his majority from 5,000 to 1,000. Mr. Littlefield gave out the statement that Mr. Gompers had helped
him in his campaign, but there were no other congressmen
of Littlefield's type requesting my "help."

Resentment against exercise of autocratic power as practiced by Speaker Cannon speedily increased. Soon after
Congress convened in the fall of 1906, Congressman Burleson of Texas tried to secure a conference with me. Owing
to absence from headquarters it was about two weeks before
that conference could be arranged. One morning I met
him at the Capitol and he went over with me the legislative
and parliamentary conditions prevailing in the House of
Representatives and particularly the nature of the autocratic power of the Speaker. He told me that there were
a number of Republicans who were chafing under the Cannon régime notwithstanding the fact that they themselves
had preferred committee positions and generally enjoyed
full privileges. Mr. Burleson further said there were
a number of congressmen who resented as keenly as he did
the autocracy exercised by Speaker Cannon and who though
not in entire accord with the demands of labor would welcome, in the revolt against Cannon, leadership of someone
who could speak for a considerable portion of the citizenship and who could put behind his words some degree of
authority. Mr. Burleson wanted to know how I felt in
regard to the subject of the change of the Cannon rules.
I expressed the opinion that the large body of American

workmen as well as the majority of the American people were opposed to autocratic power generally and particularly to Cannonism or the control developed and exercised by him. The Speaker, to my thinking, should be an impartial chairman and free from partisanship or partiality. I said that if any effort was to be made to change the rules to make the House self-governing I should be glad to help to the best of my ability. He called attention to the fact that if anything was done the effort would have to be made before the adjournment of the 59th Congress, for experience had shown that when new members came with the opening of a Congress they were full of expectancy and had no reason to think that all would not receive impartial treatment at the hands of the Speaker. Then these new members, together with the dominating group in the party caucus, would vote to adopt the rules of the last House for the Congress just opening, which, of course, automatically resulted in the perpetuation of the tremendous power the Speaker had organized. After that was done, Congress would be helpless during the remainder of the session. He called my attention to the fact that Mr. Littlefield was among those who had freely declared himself opposed to the irresponsible power placed in the hands of the Speaker, but who later showed himself unwilling to help to break that power.

Mr. Burleson asked me whether I would participate in a conference with several members of the House not more than six in number, for the purpose of inaugurating a movement to compel a change of the rules. The men he had in mind had pledged themselves to that purpose. There were about twenty-five Republican members of the House who could also be counted upon to co-operate in any effort of the Democrats. It was the thought of those pledged to this course that I could be materially helpful in creating confidence in the minds of many friendly to that purpose that there was sufficient public interest to justify them in undertaking the work.

The rules of the House had been adopted automatically since the 53d Congress. In the interim, a system had developed which was known as "Cannonism," under which the Speaker was supreme. He not only controlled the appointment of members on committees which involved promotions but also ruled arbitrarily upon recognition of representatives on the floor. Under the system there was no way to force committees to report upon bills referred to them. Thus there had been built up machinery that controlled legislation.

Opposition to Cannonism, both within and without the House, had been steadily growing. It was those "insurgents" who came to me at my office. After a number of conferences had been held, plans were developed for a general public conference which was held in the old Arlington Hotel. I attended this conference also. It was from these efforts that the progressive movement in the Republican Party was developed.

The resentment continued to spread. In 1908 the Executive Council and several other men participated in a conference at Washington and called upon the President of the United States, the acting Vice-president, and Speaker Cannon. In the course of the discussion in his room, the Speaker declared his innocence and inability to control the House. I charged him plainly with so packing the committees as to stifle legislation of a reformatory character, and to prevent even a fair consideration of labor measures. During the four hours' conference with Mr. Cannon the members of the House swarmed into the chamber and our protest helped to crystallize the sentiment for a revision of rules.

As I tell in the next chapter, I went into Cannon's District in 1908, where in a speech I referred to Mr. Cannon as the Mephistopheles of American politics. The appellation was made the subject of cartoons and editorials which clung to him rather unpleasantly for many a day. However, Mr. Cannon was elected.

Some time after the election I was traveling toward Denver to attend the 1908 Convention of our Federation. At Harrisburg I walked the platform and seeing Uncle Joe with Congressman McKinley of Illinois, I avoided them, only to find Mr. Cannon in the club car smoking a cigar, a pastime in which I was about to indulge myself. I took a seat two chairs from him. He leaned over to me and said, "Mr. Gompers, why the hell don't you come over here and sit beside me?" I moved to the chair next to his and then he indulged himself in one of his well-known monologues and finally said, "Of course, you could not defeat me, when John Walker and another whose name I cannot remember were split against me. At any rate, I could fight you back, but how the hell could I fight these sky pilots and these short-haired prudish women?" We had an interesting conversation for the balance of the evening and parted with a little better mutual good will.

I have spoken quite freely of the hostility which Mr. Cannon manifested in every way against not only the labor organizations but constructive, progressive legislation. There is not one word that I desire to retract from that statement or to modify in any degree. But there were never feelings of personal antagonism. Outside of his political activities, his arbitrary exercise of power, in his time he was a man of great ability and I had a personal kindly regard toward him as a man.

Our labor campaign was followed very closely both here and abroad. The report was that the Federation was going into partisan politics. Both the politicians and the intellectuals hoped we would. The former knew that it would be an easy way to dispose of the labor vote and the latter wanted us to become "progressive" like European labor. But I felt I understood American labor and knew something of American politics and I insisted upon a policy that would secure results and at the same time maintain the independence and dominant economic character of the wageworkers' movement of America. I have not regretted my course. As subsequent developments have demonstrated, our course has been correct, progressive, and constructive, and notwithstanding our political activities through that campaign and the campaigns which have followed, sometimes winning, sometimes failing, the movement has kept its cohesive existence and whatever the result of each campaign, the good name of the labor men and the labor movement has been kept clean.

When the 60th Congress came to an end, it was evident that a special session would be called to revise the tariff schedules. Those interested in the movement to overthrow the autocratic power of the Speaker arranged for a conference to be held in my office in which I was to participate. The changes were formally drawn up and agreed to. The insurgent Republicans signed their names to the document as a pledge of good faith. The document was left in my keeping. The following were in the group:

Charles R. Davis, Minnesota

Henry Allen Cooper, Wisconsin

Daniel R. Anthony, Jr., Kansas

Victor Murdock, Kansas

George William Norris, Nebraska

Elmer Addison Morse, Wisconsin

George A. Pearre, Maryland

Paul Howland, Ohio

Edwin W. Higgins, Connecticut

Andrew J. Volstead, Minnesota

Asle J. Gronna, North Dakota

Henry E. Stevens, Connecticut

Everis A. Hayes, California

Gustav Kustermann, Wisconsin

Frank W. Mondell, Wyoming

John H. Foster, Indiana

John M. Nelson, Wisconsin

Edgar D. Crumpacker, Indiana

William P. Hepburn, Iowa

Party caucus had disclosed that Mr. Cannon would be the next Speaker. The insurgents consulted me as to whether they should vote for Uncle Joe. I advised them strongly not to vote against Mr. Cannon, for that course would simply put them at a disadvantage in assignment to committee work where they could at least check some of the schemes which Uncle Joe and others might try to put through. They acted upon my advice.

The special session convened on March 15. Mr. Cannon was elected Speaker without expressed dissent by the Republican Party. An agreement had been reached between the Democrats and the insurgent Republicans that they would ask for amendments to the rules which would permit the speaker to appoint only committees necessary for the special business for which the session had been called—namely, tariff revision, and that the House should appoint a committee of fifteen to revise the rules of the House. This revision was to go forward while the House was engaged with the tariff measure and also during the recess. A resolution providing for this course was submitted by Champ Clark of Missouri. However, John J. Fitzgerald, a very shrewd Tammany politician, either through collusion or undue influence, offered amendments that defeated the real purpose of the rules reform. It was our purpose to make the Speaker an impartial chairman who should be relieved of duties which might in any way be interpreted as exercising coercive power. Whatever his purpose was, Fitzgerald blocked the reform movement and the rule of Speaker Cannon continued for two years longer.

However, public opinion had been roused and at the next election the Democrats came into control of the House and Champ Clark of Missouri was made Speaker. House rules were so changed that the House appointed a committee on committees and assumed greater control over its own destinies.

In the winter of 1911–1912, Representative McDermott of Illinois came to see me and said there was something important that he wanted to tell me. He asked me whether I remembered Colonel Mulhall. I replied I did: I remembered him five or six years before in Philadelphia and Baltimore, but the last time I recalled seeing him was at the Republican National Convention in the Committee on Resolutions. McDermott said: "Sam, I would like you to arrange to meet Mr. Mulhall. He is very anxious to see you. He has something very important to say." I replied that I did not care to meet Mulhall and that I could not imagine anything of importance that he could tell me. McDermott, however, urged that I see him and stated that Mulhall was suffering. "He is suffering from a revulsion of feeling and conscience against the work he has been doing all these years for the National Association of Manufacturers and he wants to make a clean breast of it." I was still indifferent, but McDermott was insistent. McDermott came to see me two or three times again before I finally consented to meet Mulhall. I suggested a conference at my office in the Ouray Building, but McDermott said that because of the spies and detectives of the National Association of Manufacturers the conference ought to take place in a less public spot. I made arrangements then to meet Mulhall at the office of my personal friend and physician, Dr. Allen, who lived about a block from my home which was then 2123 First Street Northwest. When I reached Dr. Allen's office, Mulhall and McDermott were both there. Mulhall proceeded to tell me what he had in mind. He said substantially that he knew he had betrayed labor and that he was sorry for it. One of the principal reasons for his change of heart was the fact that his wife had become acquainted with the character of his work and it had preyed upon her mind so that she had almost or entirely lost her reason. She was then in an asylum and Mulhall felt that his conduct was responsible for her condition. The explanation seemed reasonable to me, for I am naturally of a credulous disposition. Mulhall took from his pocket two or three packages of letters and read portions of them to me and said, "I would be willing, Mr. Gompers, to go anywhere you say, before any committee in Congress, wherever Mr. Emory or any other representative of the N. A. M. will appear and I will expose the whole gang, their corruptions, and methods. If they have any sense of feeling, they will not be able to stand before any committee of Congress in the face of the exposure I am able to make by the documents I have." I listened to him. He gave me his home address and telephone number in Baltimore and parted with the understanding that I would either call him over the telephone or go to see him to arrange another interview. I took the matter up with some of my colleagues who were less credulous than I and they advised against further conferences with Mr. Mulhall. Mr. McDermott came to see me again to urge the conferences to be renewed. Later, I arranged for our attorney Mr. Ralston to confer with Mr. Mulhall. I was advised not to go to Mr. Mulhall's home in view of the previous efforts of the N. A. M. to embroil me in difficulties. Acting upon the advice of my associates, I made no further step in the matter and we heard no more about the Mulhall letters until they were published in the New York *World* in the summer of 1913. Shortly after, Congress had instituted an inquiry into lobby activities following a message to them from President Wilson. Mr. Mulhall had kept records of his work over a number of years for the organized employers as well as records and copies of letters and original letters showing the extent and nature of legislative, political, and industrial work he had done for the organized employers hostile to the labor movement in addition to the usual economic warfare.

Among the papers disclosed were reports of operatives completely substantiating the story I had revealed to the Norfolk convention of the effort of the N. A. M. to bribe me and to discredit my work and character.

The schemes, the practices, the corruption are fully disclosed not only in the hearings but in the report made to Congress. The disclosures and the reports place a stigma upon the activities of the N. A. M. which it has not lived down even to the present day, and though that association may have modified these practices, their antagonism has not been modified and their practices have been substituted in the workings of their kindred and allied associations which I have already recorded.

CHAPTER XXXV

EARLY in 1908 the Supreme Court of the United States rendered its decision on the demurrer in the hatters' case, ruling that labor organizations came under the operation of the Sherman Anti-Trust Law, thus making them liable to dissolution or the affixing of three-fold damages. Knowing how incompatible the judicial point of view was with procedure involved in industry, no other conclusion was possible but that disaster awaited the hatters' union. Nor could we expect to avoid similar catastrophes in other organizations. That decision was conclusive proof that labor must become active and insistent in order to secure legislative relief. There was no longer any escape from the opinion that it was imperative to amend anti-trust law to prevent judges from outlawing labor unions as unlawful conspiracies and to define and limit the use of the injunction to its original field—protection of property. All over the country, labor men and labor organizations emphatically voiced protests against the ruling of the Supreme Court. In this case and in the test injunction case of the Federation then pending were involved issues fundamental not only to labor but to the citizenship in other walks of life, for the injunctions issued in labor disputes established a precedent in conflict with American concepts of equality of opportunity and justice. Nor were we willing to subscribe to the notion that unlawful acts should be restrained by the process of injunction. If acts are in themselves unlawful, then it follows that there is an existing law making the acts unlawful and if such laws do exist, as they do, then men charged with the unlawful acts should be tried upon charge and indictment by a jury of their peers and not by the process of injunction forbidding the performance of unlawful acts and enjoining the commission of acts which are in themselves normal and lawful.

The right to organize I found challenged by injunctions and by perversion of law against illegal conspiracies to apply to trade union activity. Despite this unwarranted attitude towards the organizations of the workers, I could not and did not join the hue and cry against combinations in industry. I had no quarrel with large-scale organization, but I contended for equal freedom for labor. The use of injunctions in industrial disputes by Federal courts increased at an alarming rate. A suit was brought against the hatters of Danbury seeking three-fold damages under the Sherman Anti-Trust Law for union activities prosecuting a boycott. Opposition to trade unions in the industrial field became acute. Professional strikebreakers were a customary agency for use in labor contests. Detectives were employed as labor spies. This war on labor assumed the appearance of a concerted program shortly after David Parry was elected president of the National Association of Manufacturers. Up to that time the association had not been anti-union. In his first report to the New Orleans Convention Mr. Parry made a virulent attack upon all organized labor. He did not read his report or submit it to the convention, but contented himself with publishing it and announcing that it was available. Whether concerted or not, the legislative and the legal situations were supplementing the union-destroying campaign of the National Association of Manufacturers.

Under Mr. Parry and his successor, James Van Cleave, the opposition to the work of the organized labor movement in the legislative and economic fields became more aggressive. The situation in Congress prevented our getting relief there.

I realized that the labor movement was indispensable for the protection of wage-earners and that it was equally necessary to any constructive plan for progress in production. In seeking a way out of these difficulties, I found myself concerned more and more with national problems, national determining forces, and national policies.

During the years we had patiently sought legislative relief, I found a number of congressmen who had some understanding of industrial conditions and who were willing to sponsor bills which labor approved. I got hearings, sympathy, and promises, but not labor laws. When Mr. Cannon was elected Speaker by his party in the 60th Congress, his followers jeered me by boasting of their course in spite of "Dictator" Gompers and declaring they would show "that man Gompers" what they cared for his protests. I responded with a complete record of Mr. Cannon's activity on labor bills. I used every publicity medium at my command and so effectively that editorials in the *American Federationist* became of first page political news importance.

In my public speeches and editorials I helped to focus public attention in such a way that the protest of labor was given serious consideration. I put squarely before Congress labor's understanding of the situation. Then I called a national labor conference and put before organized labor plain facts of the congressional situation. The conference submitted to Congress a protest against its treatment of labor legislation and asked specifically for amendments to the Sherman Anti-Trust Law excluding wage earners and farmers from its purview, the enactment of the Pearre bill to regulate and limit the use of the injunction, the employers' liability and eight-hour bills. We communicated to labor organizations throughout the country urging them to defeat their enemies, whether candidates for president, Congress or whatever office, and those organizations in turn wrote their respective Representatives and Senators warning them that they would be held responsible for failure to legislate upon labor matters. Congressmen became at once deeply concerned and the inner history of the Cannon rule came to light. Many Congressmen declared that it was impossible to get action on labor bills because of the iron grip with which he controlled the House.

Congressman Brumm of Pennsylvania among others wrote me: "There is no disguising the fact that Speaker Cannon intended to prevent legislation on these lines by diverting the President's message and other bills to the congressional crematory known as the Judiciary Committee." I at once wrote to Mr. Brumm a letter which I made public, pointing out that the members of Congress alone were responsible for the election of Mr. Cannon as Speaker. I again stated that the voters would hold the congressmen responsible for a vote to adjourn before action had been taken upon the legislation deemed necessary by labor. I ended with the statement that they would be held responsible for voting to adjourn before action was had on our measures equally as though they had voted against them. However, Congress adjourned without taking the action labor requested and Representative Sherman declared on the floor that the Republican Party gladly assumed responsibility for that action.

At once a feeling of apprehension began to pervade the minds of the Republicans, and the Democrats began to sense the political opportunity in the situation. Within a very short time W. D. Ryan, who had been secretary of the United Mine Workers of America but who had resigned to accept a governmental position in the state of Illinois, sent me word from Springfield, Illinois, that his relations with Speaker Cannon had been such that he thought he could be helpful in bringing about an opportunity for a conference between Cannon and me. As Mr. Ryan was familiar with labor affairs, I felt I could place confidence in any suggestion that he might make to me and so I replied to him that I would be willing to avail myself of his suggestion. Mr. Ryan came to Washington and arranged for the conference.

In order to protect myself I asked Frank Morrison to accompany me to the conference. We went to Mr. Cannon's house where we remained from ten o'clock in the evening until about three in the morning, but nothing was accomplished. Cannon was known to have presidential aspirations. It was pretty generally known that Mr. Roosevelt helped to control the nomination. The G. O. P. leaders hesitated in taking decisive action because of possible effects on the selection of the presidential candidate.

Later, Gus Karger, the Washington correspondent for the Cincinnati *Post*, the paper owned by Charles P. Taft, brother of Secretary of War William H. Taft, called at my office to see me as was his custom. Mr. Karger knew the labor movement and recognized its potentiality in shap-

ing developments. We were personal friends. Because of
Mr. Karger's business connection, he saw Secretary Taft
frequently. Karger had the utmost confidence in Mr.
Taft, and inasmuch as he felt sure that Taft in all
likelihood would be the next Republican candidate for
President, he suggested that I should talk over with him
the difficulties in which labor found itself. One Sunday
afternoon about six weeks before the Republican convention, I went to Mr. Taft's office in the War Department.
Again Mr. Morrison accompanied me. The conference
lasted about two hours. Because of Mr. Taft's standing
in the Republican Party and his influence with the leaders,
I thought that it was advisable to talk over with him very
thoroughly all that was involved in the anti-trust and injunction issues and to try in every way to get him to see
that labor was not a commodity and hence should not come
under the same treatment as property. The conference
brought no satisfactory result except that it was agreed
that Mr. Wade Ellis of Ohio, at one time Attorney-General
for that state, to whom had been delegated the task of
drafting tentative planks for the platform dealing with
labor matters, should have a conference with me. We had
several conferences. A number of tentative drafts upon
this subject were published in newspapers previous to the
convention. These drafts met with the hearty approval
of President Roosevelt.

The planks proposed by Mr. Ellis were entirely ignored
by the Committee on Platform without the slightest regard for the labor and the liberal proposals; the platform committee reported and the Republican Convention
adopted a platform in direct conflict with the fundamentals
as contained in the Ellis or labor proposals. The fact was

that Mr. Roosevelt's insistence upon and activity in securing the nomination of Mr. Taft seemed to cool his ardor
for progressive declarations in the platform.

It seemed President Roosevelt and his group were more
anxious to secure the nomination of Mr. Taft than they
were to make a determined fight for a progressive, enlightened platform. The standpatters in the Republican Party
foresaw that they could not prevent the nomination of Mr.
Taft, but they shaped the platform as they saw fit. Senator Lodge was permanent chairman of the convention and
Senator Cullom chairman of the Platform Committee.

The Republican Convention was to meet in Chicago in
June and the Democratic Convention in Denver in July.
The Executive Council of the A. F. of L. met in Chicago
just prior to the Republicn Convention, to prepare the
planks and platform which we would urge be inserted in
the convention's declarations. In that meeting we considered the report of our legislative committee. Additional
workers had been detailed to the legislative committee in
order that we might have the labor record of every member
of Congress and that there should be no misunderstanding
on the part of any members of Congress as to the gravity
which labor attached to its grievances and its demands for
remedial legislation. The report of this committee was a
recounting of the records compiled from votes on labor
measures, but in effect it was an indictment of those in
control of Federal legislation.

There were two members of our Executive Council who
were known as adherents to the Republican Party, James
Duncan and Daniel J. Keefe. Mr. Mitchell was generally
regarded as more closely allied with the Democratic Party,
but with a strong personal feeling for President Roosevelt.

James Duncan, Daniel J. Keefe, and I were selected to appear before the Committee on Platform. Mr. Keefe arranged for two interviews with Mr. Wade Ellis and we discussed labor planks. Mr. Ellis was fairly confident that he would be able to secure the adoption of Mr. Roosevelt's proposals on labor issues.

So relentless was Mr. Cannon in his hostility to labor that despite the fact that it was considered good form for candidates to stay away from conventions, he hastened to Chicago to add his personal activity against us. The committee refused to give us a hearing before the whole committee, but arranged for us to confer with a subcommittee. We were then told I could have ten minutes' time in which to present our position and I replied that that was not long enough in which to make a comprehensive statement. However, as the hearing proceeded the committeemen became so interested in my argument that my time was extended. In the room were James Emory, Martin Mulhall, and James Van Cleave. Labor demands were a pivotal factor. The progressive wing was strong, but not dominating. The reactionary wing would listen to no concessions to labor.

It was pretty general knowledge that the personal influence of President Roosevelt was very strong in that Chicago convention. Although Roosevelt was for progressive policies, he desired to maintain party leadership and that led to compromise with the reactionaries in the Republican Party. As stated above, the platform contained an evasion on labor's paramount issue and the convention nominated as its standard-bearer William Howard Taft known as the "injunction judge." James Van Cleave and the Republican reactionaries jeeringly told Labor to "Go to Denver." That was in accord with our program and our Execu-

tive Council proceeded to Denver and we presented the
identical propositions which we had presented to the Republican Platform Committee. There we were accorded a
hearing before the full Platform Committee of which Judge
Alton B. Parker was chairman.

We were subjected to considerable questioning and exchange of views, with the result that the committee did
include most of the requests that we presented. On the
following morning, coming from the convention hall to our
meeting room, I met Lincoln Steffens on the street. He
stopped me and said: "I have a piece of information which,
with regret, I feel I ought to deliver to you. The Committee on Platform has agreed to include labor's declarations and I am very sorry." I asked him the reason of
his regret. He said, "Well, you know I am a Socialist and
this will simply mean the taking away of a large number
of votes of the Socialist Party." I answered, "Don't you
realize that the inclusion of these proposals in the platform
is in the interests of the masses of the people and will make
for freedom and justice?" He said, "Well, I am less interested in that."

During the day I had a lengthy conference with Mr.
Charles Murphy at the hotel where he was stopping. It
was the first time that I had met Mr. Murphy. I presented
the matter to him and asked for his support. I had an
opportunity of meeting Judge Alton B. Parker. I received
from them assurances of the best assistance they could give.

Planks were incorporated in the Democratic Platform
which were substantially identical with our principal demands. While sitting in the balcony of the convention hall
and listening intently to the reading of the Committee on
Platform's report, I was touched upon the shoulder. I

turned around to see sitting in a seat behind me Mr. Champ Clark who, after greeting me, handed me a newspaper on the margin of which he had written in pencil, "Isn't that report all right?" I grasped his hand and told him that it was and thanked him for his support.

Rumor persisted that the desire of a large number of the delegates to the convention to nominate John Mitchell, vice-president of the A. F. of L., as a candidate for the Vice-Presidency on the Democratic ticket with William Jennings Bryan had gained great popularity. His deeply sentimental nature had caught the fancy of a large number of people. He had emerged from the successful leadership not only of the bituminous but of the anthracite miners' strike. I am sure that Mr. Mitchell did nothing either to encourage or discourage the movement and, of course, my associates and I and the other members of the Executive Council could take no action to further his nomination.

I have fully explained Mr. Mitchell's name was not mentioned in connection with the nomination in the convention, but it was rumored that because Mr. Mitchell was so great an admirer of President Roosevelt and under such obligations to him, he could not become known definitely as a member of or an adherent of the Democratic Party. However, for some reason that has never yet been explained, Mr. Mitchell's name was not presented to the convention.

The evening after the adoption of the Democratic platform, I received a long distance telephone call from Mr. Bryan who was at Fairview, Nebraska, asking me whether I was gratified at the platform declaration so far as labor was concerned and then inviting me with my associates to call upon him on our way East. Mr. Duncan, John Mitchell, Frank Morrison, and I filled the engagement and had a most interesting conference in Mr. Bryan's home.

After the party conventions began the real fight. As the campaign progressed, the opposition again attempted to discredit our activities with ridicule and perversion and declared that, "Gompers had promised to deliver the labor vote to the Democratic Party." I knew full well that I could not deliver the labor vote nor did I make any such promise or pretense. It was simply absurd for anyone to charge that I had in my mind either the desire or the will or the ability to deliver the labor vote. To meet that unjust criticism and attack, I frequently declared upon the public platform as well as in conferences and writings that I had not the power to deliver the vote of any man. The only vote which I controlled was my own. I did try as a citizen and as a man to exercise my right with all citizens to persuade people to vote for the principles in which I so firmly believed. Members of organized labor were identified with political parties for reasons similar to those that determined political affiliations of all other voters. Many were working in industries in which tariff was a determining influence. Many were influenced by sectional forces and others were simply under the sway of habit. To mobilize the latent political power of labor, organize political discipline, and to create political standards and agencies for independent political action was a task very similar to that of mobilizing economic power in trade unions for sustained and intelligent use in furtherance of enlightened self-interest. This political discipline I knew could not be established in one campaign. We could only establish precedents. I knew I had to make the directing control in labor's political program stronger than the opposition interests that would seek to discredit or to dissipate labor's activity.

Since the Democratic Party had clearly declared for labor's contentions, I knew there would be no difficulties with men who had been affiliated with the Democratic Party activity or with those of them who were not fully identified with any political party, but it was a serious question whether those who had been identified with the Republican Party organization could be brought to see that their interests as workingmen made it necessary for them to vote against that party because of its attitude on labor's paramount economic interests. Of course, party politicians were not blind to this opportunity.

As the political campaign progressed, it was easily noticeable that Mr. Keefe had been alienated from our program and it was asserted in the public press that the condition of his support of Mr. Taft for the presidency was that he would be appointed U. S. Commissioner of Immigration. After Mr. Taft's election and before his inauguration President Roosevelt appointed Mr. Keefe as Commissioner of Immigration. At the convention of the American Federation of Labor, which occurred within a week after the election, Mr. Keefe declined to be a candidate for re-election as a member of the Executive Council.

When I brought the labor issue into the presidential campaign, I realized that the labor movement had entered a new sphere of activity and that henceforth its spokesman must state its policies in national terms. The 1906 campaign had involved only concentrated efforts in widely separated localities to defeat conspicuous enemies of labor. In the presidential election, we had to direct labor's opposition to a national party that had pronounced against measures necessary to the functioning of labor organizations.

While beyond question the interest was focused upon the election of President, there was another vital consideration which we dared not ignore: that was the election of members of Congress; for after all, the making of legislative decisions lay primarily in their hands.

The problem presented the difficulties arising from a firmly rooted two-party system with no traditions of independent voting. Party organizations had jealously guarded their jurisdiction against any tendency to non-partisanism. Because politicians realized the potential political power of the organized labor movement, they hailed my political communications with ridicule hoping to kill our independent action by refusing it serious consideration. I knew the tactics of men too well to be bluffed away from our undertaking. I had thought my way through and was sure that I was right and I was determined to make the fight along the lines of my own choosing and not be forced to play the game as labor's opponents chose.

It was no easy undertaking. It meant an educational campaign in enlightening working people as to their interests in politics. The Federation had appealed to political parties for legislative relief, but in vain. Organized employers maintained a lobby at the Capitol to defeat our bills. The bi-party system had a strong grip upon the American people, including wage-earners. Independent voting was practically unknown with the exception of the mugwumps.

Up to 1880 the American labor movement usually

sought expression in partisan political action. Independent
labor parties were organized, lasted a short time—a few
years at the most—then disappeared to be replaced by
others. An independent labor and progressive movement
was inaugurated by the National Labor Union and David
Davis of Illinois was nominated by it for the Presidency
in 1872. The National Labor Union never held another
convention. It had spent its force; it had nominated a
candidate for president. This was the history of American
labor until the formation of the American Federation of
Labor.

The Federation has maintained itself since 1881 as a
purely voluntary association and despite adverse conditions,
great diversity of nationalities and languages and extent
of the country, it has been able to maintain continuous
progress and to promote fraternity and solidarity. The
secret of this continuous progress has been understanding
of the nature and possibilities of economic power and concentration on mobilization of that power. The Federation
has maintained that economic organization is adequate to
deal with all of the problems of wage-earners. Its political
action is simply to utilize the functions of the trade union
in another field.

The Socialists contested this policy, for they regarded
it as trespassing upon their field. They looked upon the
political field as their domain and fiercely resented any difference in political tactics. They asserted that they had a
party devoted to the promotion of the interests of labor
and that organized labor ought to use the Socialist Party
as its political expression.

We have been and are still confronted with prodigious
obstacles in the path of the full activities of the trade unions

in our general federation and we felt and feel it our duty to disregard speculative philosophies to the greater need of concentrating our efforts in securing practical results. The Federation was facing an emergency which threatened its very existence. The Federal courts had been using injunction writs of such a drastic nature and such wide scope of application as to paralyze labor union activity. Anti-trust laws were invoked to serve the same purpose as the old conspiracy laws and to outlaw unions. The Socialist Party could not muster enough votes to give us needed relief. Experience with third parties in this country did not warrant our attempting that course.

When the labor offensive of 1906 was launched, it was my responsibility pure and simple. My leadership was on trial. Socialists came into Maine to campaign against the A. F. of L. Socialists in my own local union in New York challenged my judgment and leadership. They arranged a special meeting in which I was invited to give an account of my stewardship.

The discipline of the 1906 campaign made the 1908 campaign less difficult. Again the Socialists did their utmost to defeat our efforts. Socialist money and Socialist orators crowded into the arena against us. The Debs Red Special, financed by anti-labor interests, tried to split the labor vote.

I took an active part in the campaign of 1908. I made speeches in Pennsylvania, Michigan, Ohio, Indiana, Illinois, and New York. In Indiana, for ten days a campaign was conducted by labor and myself against James Watson for Governor. Practically one half of my time during August and September was given to this work. I welcomed the opportunity to go into Speaker Cannon's home town for a

Labor Day speech. I reached Danville late Sunday evening and as I am so accustomed to working late I could not retire early. As I had not eaten anything since breakfast, I went out to get a bite to eat and to walk around a bit and was shown the Cannon "bloc." On all sides my companion pointed out the Cannon interests, including the Cannon Brothers bank. When we walked outside of the business district, property was pointed out to me as owned by Cannon and the Soldiers' Home which it was said had been placed in the outskirts of Danville through the interests controlled by the Cannons. The street railroad was Cannon's and Cannon had mortgages on a number of different lines of business and property and land. It seemed to me that not only was Mr. Cannon the dominating figure in American politics but in his home district he had a practical monopoly on banks, business, and town buildings. I remember the following day, Labor Day, a dozen men, sandwich men, carried boards in front and back of them and on each of them was printed "Cannon's Whiskey, 8 Years Old." It prompted me in my Labor Day speech to paraphrase the Charge of the Light Brigade somewhat like this:

> Cannon in front of you,
> Cannon in back of you
> Volleyed and thundered;
> Yours not to reason why,
> Yours to vote for Cannon and die,
>   You foolish six hundred!

Mr. Bryan was speaking in Chicago on Labor Day. I made arrangements for a conference in Chicago in the evening.

Litigation against which labor protested intruded itself into my busy campaign. I left Chicago the next morning after the Bryan banquet and reached Washington on Wednesday morning just in time to go at once to the court for a hearing on the Buck's Stove & Range Company contempt case. The hearing continued for several days. In the course of these hearings the legal question arose as to whether I could be held answerable for materials which I published as editor of the *American Federationist*. It was decided by a definite understanding with my attorneys that legal phases would be left entirely to their judgment, but that upon editorial utterances in the *American Federationist* on matters which could be properly made a subject of inquiry, I intended to insist upon my rights as an American citizen guaranteed by the Constitution of the United States. I believed that the right of free press implied full expression of my views and I was willing to take the consequences that might result from that stand, to speak and publish freely upon any subject and that if my utterances were libelous or treasonable, I should be held accountable for the violation of my guaranteed rights. The chief issue concerned in the injunction for which I was willing to make the test case was freedom of speech and press. We had the co-operation of the farmers in this campaign. A representative of the Farmers' Union met with our special conference of labor officials in March, 1908. I attended their convention which met in Fort Worth in the previous September. Another representative of the Federation attended the convention of the American Society of Equity in Milwaukee in October. Our common interest was an amendment to the anti-trust law excluding our organizations.

President Roosevelt from the White House personally assumed charge of the Taft campaign. On October 21,

1908, the President made public a letter he had written Senator Knox. The letter was a sweeping attack on me and defense of the Republican platform declaration on injunctions. The Colonel in his usual vigorous language sought to make it appear that the Democratic Party pledges were a sham and that I was in collusion with Mr. Bryan to deceive labor. President Roosevelt's letter made plain that the attack was not so much upon Mr. Bryan as it was upon me and for the time being it made me the center of the campaign. Of course, it was necessary for me to reply.

In my reply to the President's attack, I recalled his note and showed how inconsistent he had been, agreeing with me upon fundamental principles and then publicly attacking me in the campaign for my defense of them. That letter served as an opportunity to state in detail labor's grounds for objecting to the use of the injunction in industrial disputes and a clear statement of what were considered necessary remedies. Every trick method conceivable was employed to make it appear that my political activity was partisan and not disinterested action in furtherance of labor's cause.

In October there was little time to rest as I swung around from Washington to Philadelphia, through Buffalo and across Ohio. A concentrated campaign was arranged for Indiana. John J. Keegan of the Machinists, John Moffatt of the Hatters, and Edgar Perkins of the Printers and other active men in the labor movement of the state made the arrangements and chartered a trolley car with a motorman to traverse several parts of the state. Congressman James E. Watson was candidate for Governor against Thomas Marshall. Watson had been the Republican Party whip and not only did he manifest every opposition to labor legislation in the House but, as the party whip, called a special caucus for the purpose of organized opposition to the labor issues. Therefore, I had special interest in helping to defeat Mr. Watson's aspirations.

Our trolley car stopped anywhere we wanted—that is, wherever a group of citizens was formed. They had advance information of our party's coming. In the larger cities, mass meetings in large halls or in the open air were held at which I made more formal addresses. It was some satisfaction to know that notwithstanding Indiana went Republican for Mr. Taft as President, it defeated Watson and elected Marshall.

Those in charge of the Republican campaign in Indiana blamed me for the defeat of Mr. Watson for Governor. Democrats and the liberal-minded voters gave me full credit for the accomplishment of that result.

On the Sunday night before the end of the campaign there was a mass meeting held in the Grand Central Palace in New York. Mr. Norman E. Mack, chairman of the National Democratic Committee, learning that I was in the city, asked me to come and see him, which I did, I think, at the Hoffman House. We had a chat about the political outlook. He complimented me upon what he called the best vote-getting speech he had ever heard, which I had delivered the night before, and said that I must have incurred considerable personal expense during the campaign and offered in part to reimburse me in the sum of $2500. I declined the offer and refused to accept any money or other compensation. He then said that I was the only one whom he knew in the campaign who had refused any offer of compensation. This story Mr. Norman E. Mack repeated to several persons of my acquaintance and on the train to the Denver Convention in 1921 he told the story to my wife.

Critics of the non-partisan political policy of the Federation were not lacking. There were many who thought it impossible for the Federation to make any headway unless a labor party were formed. The "intellectuals" of the country made our problem doubly difficult by flooding magazines with articles on the British Labor Party and exhorting American labor to go and do likewise.

When I was in England in 1909, the Labor members of Parliament tendered me a dinner in a room of the House of Commons. When it came time for me to speak, I referred to the fact that since the British labor movement had inaugurated its political activity and launched an independent labor party, progress in securing better wages, hours, and conditions of work had been retarded. At the conclusion of my remarks David J. Shackleton, then leader of the Labor Party and prominent in the Trades Union Congress said substantially: "Mr. Gompers is absolutely right. I know from my own knowledge of the textile trade that wherever textile workers have been most active in politics they have been the poorest organized with the poorest conditions." After the dinner Mr. Whitehorn, official reporter for the Parliamentary Committee, told me that Mr. Shackleton had asked him to make no mention of that portion of the above statement. It seemed that for political expediency economic truth had to be suppressed.

However, many of us had a very clear understanding of the pitfalls connected with party organization. I was regarded as its spokesman and personally responsible for the effectiveness of the aggressive non-partisan political action. The results were not conspicuous and were not readily appreciable by those not closely connected with political affairs. To those of us who had occasion frequently to go to Legislatures and among elected persons results were evident in the changed atmosphere and the increasing respect paid to labor legislation. One by one those who had been conspicuous enemies of labor met with political misfortunes.

Although the Republican Party won the election of 1908, confidence in the party was considerably shaken and in the congressional election of 1910 they met a decisive defeat. The story of the defeat of 1910 and the purging of the Capitol of reactionaries in 1912 I have told in the preceding chapter. The results of those campaigns demonstrated the practical efficiency of the political policy inaugurated in 1906. In 1912 the Republican Party, which had repeatedly ignored labor legislative demands, lost control of both the legislative and executive branches of the national government.

As the majority of our enemies were identified with the party responsible for inaction in Washington, we regarded the transfer of the majority from the Republican to the Democratic Party in 1910 as an opportunity to get a sympathetic hearing for labor's cause. Under the reorganization of the House, Champ Clark became Speaker, and a more intrepid friend of labor never occupied that position.

The achievements of the non-partisan policy thus far were not sufficient to put constructive legislation on the statute books. The situation was discussed in Executive Council sessions and although all members were convinced that the non-partisan policy was based upon sound fundamentals, several expressed the opinion that unless some achievements could be shown after the 1912 election we would be forced to modify our policy. When the session of Congress approached an end and the time of national conventions was at hand, I became very much concerned at the failure to secure any congressional action upon either our anti-trust or our injunction bill. Elihu Root was slated for chairman of the Republican Convention and our bills were slumbering before his committee. To all requests for information he replied that bills must be given exhaustive consideration and he was not limiting the hearings. He declined to consider the extensive House hearings which were already in print. I went up to the Capitol to see Senator Root, but he was not to be found. I consulted with Senator Martin of Virginia who suggested that we try to have the committee discharged from further consideration of the bill. However, it was not likely that such a procedure would be effective. I believed that if the national conventions were held before action was taken on the Clayton Injunction Bill, we might look to heaven for any relief from that Congress.

However, practical politicians by this time were fully convinced of the potentiality of the labor vote. There was no question but that President Taft would be re-nominated by his party. Roosevelt's strong personality and the confidence the American people had in him caused the Republican Party some uneasiness, but they thought Roosevelt's popularity would be more than counterbalanced by the "third term" tradition. Because of Roosevelt's course in the 1908 campaign, I knew that if a candidate favorable to labor was to be nominated that candidate must be expected from the Democratic Party. Long in advance of the time for nomination I began considering possibilities. The names which were most commonly associated with the nomination were: Governor Harmon of Ohio, Champ Clark of Missouri, Governor Wilson of New Jersey, and Joseph W. Folk, also of Missouri.

Governor Harmon was so intimately connected with the financial interests of the country that there was little choice between him and Mr. Taft if they were to be the opposing nominees.

Governor Wilson, as president of Princeton University, had attacked the trade union movement in a baccalaureate address, although it was understood that after he became Governor he experienced a change of mind toward labor through contact with the actualities of life. If he were nominated, I felt convinced that his previous statements would be used by his opponents in a way that would embarrass the organized labor movement.

Mr. Folk, a former Governor of Missouri, was an unknown quantity outside of his own state. He had been given an endorsement by the organization of his state as a favorite son.

Champ Clark, on the other hand, had always been favorably disposed toward labor measures and had aided whenever opportunity afforded. He was a simple, straightforward Democrat. There was a manifest feeling among a large number of people and particularly working people for the nomination of Mr. Clark. I felt confident that Governor Folk would have little chance for election if nominated. I had several conferences with Mr. Clark in his apartment in Washington. He was in a receptive mood, but declared that inasmuch as his state committee had declared for Governor Folk he could not permit his name to be used. Talking this situation over with a few of his friends, we concluded that it would be too delicate to ask

Governor Folk to withdraw his name from the candidacy
and the best course would be to seek conference with Mr.
Bryan, who it was known had great influence with Mr. Folk,
and see whether he could use his influence to bring about
that result.   Mr. Bryan was traveling over the country on
one of his lecturing tours.   After several days of telegraph-
ing, an appointment was made with him for me to meet
him at Worcester, Ohio, where he was to deliver a lecture
one evening before the college faculty and students.   I had
an engagement to go to Chicago a few days later, but by
telegraph I arranged to advance the date of the engagement
and on my way to Chicago I stopped over at Worcester.
There I met Mr. Bryan in his room and I talked the matter
over with him, and yet there was insufficient time.   Late in
the afternoon there was a luncheon at which Mr. Bryan
and the faculty invited me to be present.   Mr. Bryan spoke
at the luncheon and I also was called upon to make some
remarks.   The faculty asked me, and Mr. Bryan joined in
the request, to preside in the evening during his lecture.
I was really disinclined, but was persuaded and acted in
that capacity.   In introducing Mr. Bryan I made the remark
that though Mr. Bryan might never be President there could
be no doubt that several of the propositions which he advocated had already been enacted into law and that others
would be in the future.

Mr. Bryan and I agreed to meet after the lecture.   He
had to leave within an hour and I had to wait until two
o'clock in the morning for my train.   After the lecture we
met and I again laid the whole proposition before him
after which he said to me in effect, and I am merely quoting
his own words, "You are right, Mr. Gompers, and although
I cannot write or telegraph to Mr. Folk requesting him to

withdraw, I expect to see him in the course of a few weeks and I am confident that he will see the situation as we see it." In about three or four weeks after that, Governor Folk withdrew from the candidacy and thus gave a free field for Mr. Clark to enter the race. With a number of Mr. Bryan's friends we secured the election of a number of delegates from several states who were pledged to Clark. There was a large majority of the delegates to the Baltimore Convention who were pledged to vote for Mr. Clark as the nominee of the party.

I went to the Republican Convention in Chicago in 1912 where with my colleagues I again submitted labor's legislative demands to the Platform Committee. The Old Guard was in full control and Mr. Taft was renominated with practically no change in the labor planks over what had been pronounced in 1908.

When the progressive element in the Republican Party revolted against the arbitrary and reactionary policies of party leaders, they formed the nucleus around which many independent voters rallied. During his term as President, Mr. Roosevelt had rendered a tremendous service by stimulating an attitude of mind among all voters known as progressive. It was a fearless sort of attitude based upon the paramount importance of human welfare. Masses of voters were caught by the spectacular tactics of the Colonel and were convinced that he could accomplish anything. The Roosevelt personality and the growth of progressivism were twin forces that produced the Bull Moose Party.

On Saturday afternoon after the close of the Republican Convention I left on the Pennsylvania train. The train was filled with prominent persons who had been in Chicago attending the convention. There were newspaper correspondents, cartoonists, politicians, and Mr. Bryan and his family. I greeted Mr. Bryan in the station before the train left. He spoke very cordially and heartily. He stated that he hoped to have an opportunity to talk over with me several matters on the journey East. That evening he came into my car and we spent considerable time discussing the outcome of the Republican Convention and the prospects of the Democratic Convention which was to convene in Baltimore on the following Tuesday. One of the matters which we discussed at considerable length was Mr. Bryan's declared opposition to Judge Parker for temporary chairman of the convention. During that conversation and in others that followed the next day I emphatically called Mr. Bryan's attention to the injustice and inconsistency of his position. I pointed out that since Judge Parker had been the presidential candidate in 1904, he had in the 1908 Convention added to his prestige by the service he had rendered his party. In the 1908 convention Judge Parker was New York's representative on the Committee on Platform. With my labor colleagues I argued before the New York delegation on behalf of labor's planks and other progressive measures that we wished to see inserted in the platform. Judge Parker with two other members of the committee constituted the subcommittee which drafted the whole platform of 1908 and he had warmly advocated before the whole committee the adoption of constructive measures which labor felt were necessary to the continued welfare of wage-earners. I called to Mr. Bryan's attention that the platform of which Judge Parker was the recognized author was the platform upon which he (Mr. Bryan) was candidate for election to the presidency of the United States. After that political service, Judge Parker had given further and undisputable evidence of his broad understanding and championship of the fundamentals of human liberty by becoming the leading attorney for Mitchell, Morrison, and me, in the injunction cases against us in the Federal courts and also becoming the consulting counsel in the Hatters' case. I do not believe that Judge Parker ever gave more whole-hearted, unreserved service and for a more meager compensation than he rendered in those crucial labor cases. I did not see how Mr. Bryan could consistently oppose Judge Parker as allied with the interests in 1912 when he had graciously accepted his services in 1908. Although I had great admiration for Mr. Bryan and confidence in his sincerity at that time, I felt that he was wrong in his opposition to Judge Parker and that he was not consistent with his course in accepting the nomination and that his opposition to Judge Parker was unjustified and unwarranted.

With other representatives of labor I went to the Baltimore Convention to submit proposals upon labor planks in the platform. Those were given cordial consideration. I watched developments in the convention with growing apprehension as the rumor grew that Mr. Bryan would oppose the nomination of Champ Clark. As is well known, in spite of the fact that a majority of the votes of the delegates to the convention were cast for Mr. Clark, he did not receive the two-thirds vote which under the rule of the Democratic Party the candidate must have in order to receive the nomination, although the practice of the party up to then had been that the candidate who received a majority of the votes was nominated. I was puzzled at the situation because I knew that Mr. Clark would never have been a candidate for the nomination if

Mr. Bryan had not brought about Mr. Folk's withdrawal from the race. After many ballots were taken the nomination finally went to Woodrow Wilson. Of course, feeling ran very high at the convention and even visitor as I was, I was affected by it. Ballot after ballot showed Mr. Clark having the decided majority. During a lull between the ballots, one of the delegates from New Jersey, Woodrow Wilson's state, William Hughes, who headed the state delegation, received a telegram from Governor Wilson requesting him to withdraw his (Wilson's) name from the contest, thus affording a clear field for Mr. Clark. This telegram, I am informed, Mr. Hughes suppressed.

Whether Mr. Clark would have been elected President is, of course, problematical, but I have always felt that Mr. Bryan was responsible for his defeat. I returned to Washington after Woodrow Wilson was nominated. After I got back to Washington, Representative Hughes called me up by telephone and asked me if labor would have any objections to the nomination of Thomas R. Marshall for Vice-President. I assured him that I knew of no reason that would make him objectionable.

I confess I felt very much disheartened at the outcome of the political conventions in the summer of 1912. Experience in the previous presidential campaign after the attacks were made against my associates and particularly against me, indicated that I could best help in this campaign by counsel and assistance rather than conspicuous service that would focus attacks upon me. I therefore made few engagements for public speaking. The Federation's widely distributed connections had by this time become accustomed to look to Washington for information and advice in political work. It had been no easy undertaking to develop the habit of securing congressional records from Washington so that the facts as developed by the votes of the candidates might determine the attitude of the local organized labor movement, but in the course of time this method and practice became firmly fixed. To accomplish this it was necessary that records at headquarters be absolutely accurate and that all information be impartial. When local organizations found that they could depend upon information sent them, it was not difficult to get response. The campaign of 1912 was marked by intensive labor activity in the congressional elections. When the vote came in November, Woodrow Wilson was elected President and the Democratic Party carried both Houses of Congress. The verdict was clearly interpreted by members of Congress and in the short session of the 62d Congress labor measures received unprecedented attention.

CHAPTER XXXVI

WHEN Senator Sherman proposed to forbid by law the development of industrial combinations, I felt that his theory was fundamentally wrong. The greater efficiency that follows unification of control and management benefits society through increased production. Sustained progress of industry requires freedom from legislative prohibition, and non-social tendencies can best be curbed by intelligent regulation. However, there ought to be inhibitions against the unlawful activities of the industrial and trust combinations—that is, the brazenness with which these financial and business corporations control not only elections but the administration of affairs, the judicial interpretation, and congressional action. As I was in Washington when the Sherman Bill was under final consideration, I endeavored to have labor organizations specifically excluded from its provisions. The proviso for the protection of unions of wage-earners which I urged was:

> Provided that this act shall not be construed to apply to any arrangements, agreements, or combinations between laborers made with the view of lessening the number of hours of labor or increasing their wages; nor to any arrangements, agreements, or combinations among persons engaged in horticulture and agriculture made with a view to enhancing agricultural or horticultural products.

I felt confident the law could not and would not be enforced against the trusts and experience warned me that officials would seek to detract attention from that negligence by over-zealousness against less influential groups. Though there was a fundamental difference between trusts and trade unions seeking to better conditions of life and work for wage-earners, I felt premonitions that we would be the field to which the judiciary would turn for atonement for failure to curb trusts. My premonitions were justified when suit was brought against the New Orleans Central Body under the Sherman Anti-Trust Act (Feb. 11, 1891). That action would be justified only under a commodity theory of labor—the very thought of which is revolting. The humblest of human beings possesses the mystery of personality that infinitely transcends the material products of human skill.

In addressing a meeting at Logansport, Indiana, I said: "You cannot weigh a human soul on the same scales on which you weigh a piece of pork. You cannot weigh the heart and soul of a child with the same scales on which you would weigh any commodity." That was one of my earliest attempts to declare publicly the principle that labor is not a commodity or article of commerce. I was at the time fighting theories of speculative economists, not only to protect labor from the quagmire to which their theories surely led, but to help to develop constructive economic principles that would serve to guide in practical industrial problems.

I have often been amused by the declaration that the "law of supply and demand" was an "immutable, natural" law, that it not only controlled wages but prices. I have often pointed out the utter fallacy of such a theory in so far as both the workers and prices are concerned and called attention to the fact that business co-partnerships and trusts in controlling output interfere with the so-called inexorable operations of the law of supply and demand and that the trusts had cornered prices to such an extent as to obtain higher profits during periods of industrial depression. Furthermore, so far as workers are concerned, the organizations of labor in the movement to reduce the hours of labor, to deal with common problems collectively, and pay union benefits were an estoppel to profiteers in the attempt to depress wages below standards established by the workers, necessary to absorb increasing national wealth. As for prices during normal conditions, whenever there has been a great demand for many articles, new and improved machinery, new tools, new processes, and the application of greater power have met demand, and through such improvements the prices of articles were reduced. Of course, if there is a limited natural supply of raw material, prices are maintained or enhanced according to the demand; but in respect to all other factors, when human labor and ingenuity can be applied to an increased demand for products they develop new tools, machine processes, and power to meet the increased demand, and thus, despite higher wages, the cost of production is lessened. This briefly set forth is the reason for my conclusion that the law of supply and demand is not an immutable law, but that it is amenable to human thought and action to overcome its most injurious results to the people. Economic factors are variables that respond to human control.

Labor power is a human attribute. Control lies in the will of each individual. This principle is essential in drafting legislation as well as in developing production methods. It is a principle we have taught employers, publicists, lawmakers, and some judges, but the slowest to learn have been judges. In fact, judges have created some of our greatest difficulties. Their misunderstanding resulted in judicial perversion of the writ of injunction as well as anti-trust law. Both the injunction and the anti-trust law were intended to apply only to property. When the courts put human labor power and commodities in the same category, they laid the foundation for serious injustice.

As the years went by, the scope and frequency of injunctions issued in labor disputes increased until the practice became a grave handicap in the necessary work of trade unions. Then we undertook to secure legislation to define the use of injunctions.

The first measure to limit and define the use of injunctions which had our approval was introduced by General Grosvenour of Ohio. This bill passed the House. By the time that the opposition to labor legislation became concentrated, a clear-cut measure had been formulated which at our request was introduced by Representative Pearre of Maryland. We were very anxious to have this bill enacted. The Judiciary Committee had referred the bill to the committee of which Representative Jenkins of Wisconsin was chairman. After two months of time-killing hearings, the essential features of our bill were referred to a subcommittee of the Judiciary Committee. The subcommittee withheld its report until just before the adjournment of the 59th Congress. That report quoted exhaustively decisions and opinions rendered by judges and courts against which our complaints were lodged. I prepared a review of the committee report which I wished to file with the Judiciary Committee so that it might be printed with the report of the subcommittee. However, the chairman gave me no encouragement. I wrote to the members of the committee. A number of them agreed, but four refused. They were: Jenkins, Parker of New Jersey, Terrell of Massachusetts, and Littlefield of Maine. My letter brought about a special meeting of the committee to which Representative Pearre submitted the signatures of the eleven members of the committee to report the bill favorably. The feeling was intense. We accomplished little.

However, Pearre was penalized by Speaker Cannon who refused to reappoint him to the Judiciary Committee for which he was so eminently equipped. I had several conferences with President Roosevelt on the injunction issue. He was keenly sympathetic with labor's difficulties, but was influenced by his advisers, among whom was Taft, his Secretary of War. It was commonly known Roosevelt hoped to make Taft residuary legatee of his policies.

The Executive Council then authorized me to issue a circular to all organized labor, appealing to our fellow-unionists and friends to safeguard their interests by pledging candidates for public office to express themselves upon the subject of injunction abuse and their attitude toward labor's relief from this injustice.

My first thought was to secure freedom from anti-trust application by a revision of the entire anti-trust legislation.

The decision of the Supreme Court in which the court read into the law that the term "reasonable" really relieved corporations to a very considerable extent of the rigid interpretation of anti-trust law, and in conference I took the same position as I had before and since. What I contended for was, a more liberal and enlightened interpretation of anti-trust legislation so that this "reasonable" interpretation should be applied in the normal activities of the working people. I presented the thought that resentment among the people against the trusts was aroused against their discriminatory policies as between localities, and favored and unfavored persons and companies, and also their activities to control legislators, executives, and the judiciary.

The American labor movement did not organize its political power until we encountered political obstacles interjected into our economic activity. The Danbury Hatters' case and the Buck's Stove & Range Company injunction were typical of a general problem which labor encountered all down the line. Clear differentiation between things political and things economic has been a compass that has steered me in deciding many a difficult problem. The economic world is essentially scientific; politics is the field of contending forces. In order to rescue the labor movement from the field of force, I urged regulation and restriction of the use of the injunction in industrial disputes and removal of labor unions from the scope of anti-trust law.

Following the failure of the Pearre Bills, William B. Wilson, a union-card representative from Pennsylvania, formerly secretary-treasurer of the United Mine Workers, introduced both anti-injunction and anti-trust measures which were approved by labor. Defeat of those measures was the objective of the combined effort of manufacturers. There were repeated and extensive hearings before the Judiciary Committee, in which I always participated. That was no child's work, for I was pitted against some of the ablest lawyers of the country. The issue rested upon a philosophy that few lawyers had grasped. In fact, at that time there were comparatively few labor men who were able to present a statement of our contentions. Since the issue was forced into politics, it was necessary to explain it to the American electorate in an appeal for support in the election. For a number of years, therefore, the most important progress made was educational. My annual reports, addresses, editorials dealt with the fundamentals extensively.

Despite our activity none of our bills in Congress were passed. Our task was much more difficult than that of the British labor movement in dealing with similar issues. England accepted class distinctions and was willing to enact legislation giving wage-earners relief without concerning herself closely as to the underlying philosophy that justified the action. In the United States, our institutions are founded upon the basic principle of equality and American labor had to make plain that it did not request special privilege but equality of opportunity.

It takes fortitude to continue hammering away at a project year after year, even though there is no visible giving way of opposition under your hardest blows. It takes straight thinking to resist all proposals to accept modification that sacrifices principle. For a long time the only results from our efforts were academic discussions. Finally, there came an opportunity to secure a precedent that lent itself to political usefulness.

Fortunately, late in the closing hours of the 61st Congress, there developed a clear-cut issue upon which we secured a record vote which distinguished our friends from our enemies upon our fundamental issue. When the Sundry Civil Bill was under consideration in the House, our legislative committeeman saw a brilliant opportunity to secure a record which would serve as a test. He suggested to William Hughes of New Jersey that he introduce the following amendment to that section of the bill providing money for the Department of Justice to be used in the prosecution of anti-trust cases:

Provided, however, that no part of this money shall be expended in the prosecution of an organization or individual for entering into combination or agreement having in view the increasing of wages, shortening of hours, or bettering conditions of labor or for any act done in furtherance thereof, not in itself unlawful.

The amendment passed the House, but was defeated in the Senate. The bill went to conference, but because of the proviso or "rider" as it was called, the conferees were unable to agree and so reported to their respective houses. The House by a roll-call vote instructed its members to insist upon the Hughes proviso. The Senate rejected the proviso and the bill again went to conference. Speaker Cannon named House conferees whom he knew were opposed to the measure. The situation was fraught with such political possibilities that Republican leaders became apprehensive. After the second deadlock occurred, President Taft summoned the Republican Party leaders to the White House the next morning and plainly gave them orders. When the deadlock continued, he summoned other wavering Representatives to induce them to change their attitude. It was a personal triumph for President Taft when the House receded under the President's whip. However, responsibility for opposition to labor's fundamental demand was definitely fixed upon the Republican Party and its leading members. This was the issue which we carried into the congressional election of 1910. Millions of small pamphlets giving the history of the Hughes amendment and the record vote on it were distributed in that election. No other argument was necessary to indicate to labor voters which candidates were their friends and which were hostile to their interests. The Republican Party was defeated in that campaign and control in the House passed over to the Democrats.

That "rider," as our opponents termed it, attempted to establish in law the principle that human labor power is not a commodity or article of commerce. That "rider" haunted many a member of Congress until it became law in 1913, and has been re-enacted in each recurring appropriation measure.

When the Sundry Civil Appropriations Bill at the close of the 62d Congress was under consideration in the House of Representatives, labor's famous proviso was offered and adopted by the House. It passed the Senate and went to the President with the proviso still intact. President Taft's course was awaited with interest. The Sundry Civil Bill was the largest appropriation measure and provided for a number of important governmental agencies.

The bill to create a Department of Labor had been introduced by Representative Sulzer. When the bill was in the making, Sulzer conferred with me upon its specific provisions. Our purpose was to create a Department of Labor along broad constructive principles. The bill passed Congress in the last hours of the 62d Congress. On Sunday, March 2, I spent a good part of the day at the Capitol conferring with various congressmen, including William B. Wilson who was to be the first Secretary of Labor if the President signed the bill creating the Department of Labor.

As a result of my conferences, it was decided that I should seek a conference with President Taft the next morning. I met the President at the appointed time. As soon as I saw him he said, "I want you to do something for me, but I know you will not do it." I replied that I

did not know and I reminded him that I had been of some
service to him in helping with things that he wanted done.
President Taft then said, "If you will take that labor proviso
out of the Sundry Civil Bill I will sign the Department of
Labor Bill." I replied: "I can't do that, Mr. President.
I can't do it and I won't do it. Besides, I think it is
essential for that proviso to be where it is, particularly in
view of the fact that your Department of Justice has just
begun suit in Chicago against two unions. The proviso to
which you refer is intended to prevent such things in the
future." Taft replied, "Well, I suppose the situation is
such that I shall have to sign the Department of Labor Bill
anyway"—which he did. That signature insured the presence of William B. Wilson, a representative of wage-
earners, in President Wilson's cabinet which attended him
at his inaugural. This achievement represented efforts extending over a period of thirty years.

Although it was then the fourth of March and his action
meant serious difficulty for important government work,
President Taft vetoed the Sundry Civil Bill and stated that
his reason for failing to approve the measure was the labor
proviso. Friends of labor attempted to re-pass this bill
with the "rider" over the President's veto and Victor Berger
—only Socialist congressman—was among those who voted
to sustain the veto. Nor was this the only demonstration
of perfidy to the cause of labor by which Berger exploded
the Socialist Party's claim to consideration as a labor party.

Not once did Mr. Berger appear before the Committee
on Labor of the House in advocacy of any bill which our
Federation sponsored or favored and only once did he appear before the Committee of the Post Office and Post Roads
to say a word to relieve the government employes from the

Gag Rule imposed upon them by executive order. On our eight-hour bill he gave left-handed support which called for criticism of other members of the House who favored the measure.

The situation made it imperative that President Wilson call an extra session of Congress soon after he assumed office. The inauguration of Woodrow Wilson was accompanied by Democratic control of both houses. It was a situation fraught with great possibilities and there were many of us who confidently expected that the administration would inaugurate a national policy in which human welfare and social service would be the dominant purposes. Personally, I felt that the trade union movement and I as president of the Federation, had considerable at stake. If the Administration fulfilled its pledges in good faith, the political policies which I helped to inaugurate would have proved themselves. The Administration recognized that labor had been an effective agency in taking the political control out of the hands of reactionaries.

To my great regret I was suffering keenly from a physical disorder that finally resulted in the mastoid operation mentioned previously.

In the meanwhile, I felt that something must be done to explain the significance of the labor proviso in the Sundry Civil Bill to President Wilson. I did not feel at all sure that he was in accord with labor's position on that issue. All through my illness I was worrying because I was not in condition to see him personally and to present the matter to him. However, I prepared a letter, explaining the reasons why labor looked upon the proviso which Mr. Taft had vetoed as a paramount issue and sent the letter to President Wilson. I received from him a very cordial letter, stating that he was glad of my letter that helped him in thinking the problem through.

When the special session of Congress convened, a representative of the Federation requested the chairmen of the House and Senate appropriations committees to include the labor proviso with the anti-trust section in the bill which they were to report. Practically all of the discussion in both houses centered on the labor proviso and a similar proviso applying to farmers. These were included in the bill as reported which passed both houses intact and went to the President.

At that time I was in the hospital just recovering from the operation. However, I again sent a letter to President Wilson on this subject, stating even more fully the reasons why labor urged his approval of the bill. The National Association of Manufacturers and similar organizations hostile to organized labor besieged the President to veto the bill. Notwithstanding, he signed it. This achievement indicated that there was hope that Labor might secure legislation which we so much desired. In the regular session bills were introduced both to define and regulate the use of the injunction and to establish the legality of trade unions. It seemed very difficult to get legislation that would assert positively what had been conceded in principle by the labor proviso. When in 1914 Congress undertook the revision of anti-trust law, Arthur Holder, our legislative committeeman, suggested we attempt to have labor sections included in the law instead of attempting to have separate bills passed. The suggestion was adopted.

The anti-trust measure was sponsored in the House by Congressman Clayton of Alabama and we had a number of conferences with him. In the formulation of the labor provisions of the trust bill, the leading members of the Judiciary Committee had frequent conferences with the labor group in the House. This labor group was organized after the 1906 congressional election. All members of Congress who held cards in bona fide trade unions were asked to co-operate for the enactment of labor legislation. Thus the organized labor movement secured direct representation on the floor of Congress without regard for party affiliation. This union-card group numbered only six the first year, but grew steadily with each election. It was organized with a chairman and held regular and special meetings both at the Capitol and in the office of the Federation. I usually attended the meetings of the group which in turn kept constantly in touch with my office while this bill was in the making. Amendments were made to the bill from the floor of the House which made the measure more satisfactory than the text reported by the House Judiciary Committee. I had conferences with both Senator Culberson, chairman of the Senate Judiciary Committee, and Senator Cummins, who were interested in making the measure a genuinely constructive piece of legislation in order that industrial rights might be assured wage-earners.

In a conference that I had with Senator Cummins after the bill had been reported out and was about to come up for action in the Senate, I suggested to the Senator that the section definitely removing labor unions from the purview of trust legislation would be materially strengthened if there were a statement of the fundamental underlying principle. I suggested the incorporation of the words: "The labor of a human being is not a commodity or article of commerce." The Senator was very much impressed with the suggestion and from the floor of the Senate proposed the amendment.

On the day when the labor sections of the act were to come up for discussion in the Senate, I went to the Capitol early and took a seat in the gallery. Opposite me I saw Judge Davenport who had been fighting vigorously against our labor measures. I must confess that I felt a measure of sincere gratification as I realized that the justice of our cause was about to prevail despite the tireless opposition of vested interests. As I was sitting there reviewing the long struggle that has extended over more than twenty-five years, Senator Reed came and called me out to ask me about a clause and to secure data for arguments for the clause.

When the debate began, I sat tense through the long hours that followed. Senator Cummins looked very splendid to me as he proposed the sentence which epitomized an ideal foreshadowing a new order of human relations in industry. The debate was keen and illuminating. It was evident that each speaker realized the importance and significance of the matters under consideration. When the labor measures were finally adopted by the Senate, my emotion well-nigh overcame me. It was a great hour for labor, when there was enacted into the law of our republic a basic fundamental declaration upon which humanitarian endeavor could be based.

The law contained this section from which we hoped to secure protection from perversion of anti-trust law:

That the labor of a human being is not a commodity or article of commerce. Nothing contained in the anti-trust laws shall be construed to forbid the existence and operation of labor, agricultural, or horticultural organizations, instituted for the purposes of mutual help and not having capital stock or conducted for profit, or to forbid or restrain individual members of such organizations from lawfully carrying out the legitimate objects thereof, nor shall such organizations or the members thereof be held or construed to be illegal combinations or conspiracies in restraint of trade under the anti-trust laws.

The Clayton Anti-Trust Law was signed by President Wilson, October 15, 1914. On the following day I received the pen with which the President signed the law. That pen was framed and placed with a collection of other pens with which other historic measures have been signed. A day later President Wilson, in a letter to Representative Underwood, said:

Incidentally, justice has been done to the laborer. His labor is no longer to be regarded as if it were merely an inanimate object of commerce disconnected with the fortunes and happiness of a living human being to be dealt with as an object of sale and barter.

But that, great as it is, is hardly more than the natural and inevitable corollary of a law whose object is individual freedom and initiative as against any kind of private domination.

Of course, I was not such a novice as to imagine that these labor sections constituted the end of our difficulties with the judiciary. Section 20 of the act, which deals with regulation and limitation of the use of injunctions in industrial disputes, was not the clear-cut formulation of policy that labor sought under the old Pearre bill. However, it was the best obtainable at the time and was intended, so the congressmen stated, to correct the abuse of the injunction writ in application to industrial relations. In view of the legislative intent of Congress, I felt justified in accepting the section as a frank response to labor's need and so interpreted the law in my editorial and public utterances. Of course, I, as everyone else, knew the effectiveness of the measure depended upon judicial action and interpretation. What the courts would do only time could tell. In the meanwhile, it was my duty to help educate public thought as to the intent of Congress. The purpose of Congress was plain. Sections 6 and 20 were intended as a guarantee of industrial rights to working men engaged in a conflict to establish better conditions of work. They constitute the charter of industrial freedom or, as I called it, "Labor's Magna Charta." The intent of Congress is important to courts which are to apply law. By making clear the intent of Congress in passing the law, labor could crystallize and establish interpretations from which judges must depart if they insist upon old legal theories.

In his address at the dedication of the A. F. of L. office building, July 4, 1916, President Wilson made a statement to which my mind often recurs with gratification. The statement was:

Mr. Gompers was referring just now to the sixth section of the Clayton Anti-Trust Law, the section in which the obvious is stated —namely, that a man's labor is not a commodity but a part of his life, and that, therefore, the courts must not treat it as if it were a commodity, but must treat it as if it were a part of his life. I am sorry that there were any judges in the United States who had to be told that. It is so obvious that it seems to me that that section of the Clayton Act were a return to the primer of human liberty; but if the judges have to have the primer opened before them, I am willing to open it.

Despite all that judges have done to weaken Labor's Magna Charta, the concept that labor is not a commodity or article of commerce has had opportunity to become a part of the making of national mind in a way that works an advance to a higher level of human justice.

BOOK V

CHAPTER XXXVII

PAN-AMERICAN LABOR

WHEN I was working at Stachelberg's in 1883, there were three Mexican cigarmakers working in the shop. One of them had a smattering of English and with what I knew of Spanish acquired in contacts with Cubans we managed to get pretty well acquainted. These Mexicans told me of the dissatisfaction in Mexico with the Diaz régime and gave me a pretty fair picture of industrial and political conditions within that country. They introduced me to a number of Mexicans who were interested in the movement to secure relief from the tyranny and corruption of the Diaz régime.

In the course of the years we were shopmates, many of the Mexican revolutionaries came to New York so that I was pretty well informed as to Mexican revolutionary thought and activity.

After the 1886 Convention of the Federation took me out of the shop, I saw but little of my three Mexican friends. However, they were constantly in communication with friends in Mexico. A number with whom they communicated and had commended to me came to my office. These occasional meetings helped me to follow developments. I was always ready to listen and glad to assist in

whatever way my counsel could be effective. Mexican
laborers, the class least able to defend themselves against
tyranny, were desperately poor both in spirit and in material possessions. Their misfortunes made a strong appeal
to my sympathy. I helped to bring them in touch with
the American movement.

On the other hand, American labor was not long in
recognizing an identity of interest in helping Mexican workers to establish standards that would not undermine standards across the border. But the vested interests at that
time had such undisputed control over American governmental institutions that our government was used to help
Mexico hunt down and punish political refugees. It was
the American labor movement that took the initiative in
calling national attention to the right of asylum for political refugees.

Under Diaz, Mexico was a republic in name only. The
liberal constitution established under Juarez was a cloak
under which President Diaz built up despotic control. By
use of his prestige and influence he controlled the election
of Governors in the federated states and attached them to
his personal machine. The workers of Mexico were practically peons. It was not possible to develop a labor movement. Here and there unions were organized, but election
to union office was always followed quickly by imprisonment and jail sentence. Opposition to the Diaz régime
entailed danger of imprisonment and death.

Repeatedly, the Mexicans came to me when there were
public manifestations for the overthrow of Diaz in order
to have my advice as to their plans. After 1897 when
the offices of the Federation were moved to Washington,
conferences with Mexican revolutionists became more fre-

quent. I met representatives of many groups, each organized in a junta. When the movement for freedom in Mexico took on more serious proportions, I was more frequently visited and consulted. Letters and telegrams from Mexico were frequent.

The Mexican Liberal Party established its headquarters in Los Angeles, and carried on its propaganda. Some of the most powerful financial organizations in the United States had investments in Mexico. The Standard Oil, the Copper Trust, the Sugar Trust, the Rubber Trust had millions of dollars invested. The Southern Pacific Railway, which owned the Wells-Fargo Express Company, had secured a monopoly of the express-carrying business in that country. The Diaz régime meant to them cheap labor. Foreign capital had obtained concessions and was eager to control public service institutions and all other sources of profit. These vested interests stood against reform in the Mexican government.

To Los Angeles naturally drifted political refugees and Mexican laborers seeking employment, so that the city became the seat of the Mexican revolutionary junta. It became the center of the Mexican population of the United States. On the other hand, California was the stronghold of a number of the powerful influences that had investments in Mexico and reaped big profits through the then existing régime. These interests financed occasional border expeditions for the purpose of maintaining the impression in Mexico that the United States was unfriendly to that country. That was not a difficult task. Mexicans had been taught in their schools and in their homes that in 1848 the United States government had despoiled Mexico of a large part of her territory; that American corporations had gone into Mexico and exploited the workers, tyrannizing over them to such a degree that their conditions were worse than under Mexican employers.   The border raids were used by the United States press to demonstrate the need of a strong-arm policy toward Mexico. These same interests financed uprisings against the Mexican government to strengthen the idea of its instability.   I felt that the fight for democracy in the United States involved lending a helping hand to Mexico in her serious need.

For a number of years I had been in touch with the leaders of the Liberal Party in Los Angeles, the two Magon brothers, Ricardo and Enrique, Lazaro Gutierrez de Lara, Antonio I. Villarreal, Librado Rivera.   In August, 1907, these men were arrested upon the demand of the Mexican government and a desperate effort was made to extradite them.

De Lara was a Mexican lawyer.   For years he traveled up and down Mexico making speeches wherever he could secure an audience, urging the Mexicans to make a fight to re-establish their constitution and to secure guarantees of free speech, free press, and the right to vote.   He had no connection with labor organizations until he saw the possibilities of their effectiveness in the struggle for freeing Mexico.   He was in and out of Mexico as he saw opportunity to serve.   His headquarters in the United States were in Los Angeles, but he kept moving along the borderline and up to St. Louis and to Washington as he thought he could best advance the cause of free Mexico.   A good part of the time he was under arrest or in prison under numerous charges brought by Mexican agents, which were promptly dismissed when brought before a court, but they served to put him in jail.

De Lara, Rivera, and the two Magon brothers took turns in editing the Los Angeles paper which they made the medium of their propaganda. They were generally successful in keeping at least one of their group out of jail so as to provide the paper with continuous editorial service.

From that time on, Mexico increased her effort to build up machinery for pursuing Mexican liberals and political refugees. Either group included Mexican labor organizers. Under that machinery Mexico suborned local police, detectives, and immigration authorities so that these men were receiving pay both from the American and Mexican governments and were taking orders from Mexico to arrest and return political refugees. These refugees were harassed by all manner of efforts to arrest and imprison them on illegal grounds and not a few of them were kidnapped and taken across the border. In most cases, when the charges could be brought before a court, it was easy to show that the evidence submitted against them was manufactured.

It happened that this situation became increasingly obnoxious at the time that the Russian Imperial Government was making demands upon the United States to return to Russia such political offenders as had sought asylum in our country. A number of leading liberal citizens of the United States formed in Chicago the Political Refugee Defense League. The league hoped to protect political refugees of all countries. John Murray had a leading part in its organization. His travels through Mexico and his contacts in Los Angeles gave him very wide information of the situation.

The league was at first particularly concerned over the cases of Rudowitz and Jan Pouren. As president of the

Federation, I was actively concerned both in the Russian case and on behalf of the Mexicans. Under authority of the Denver Convention, I placed the whole situation most emphatically and plainly before President Roosevelt and asked for the protection of both the Mexicans and the Russians. President Roosevelt was deeply interested and did what he could to prevent American agents from being used by Mexican autocrats.

Three times under President Taft's Administration, American troops were sent to police the boundary. In September, 1909, President Taft and President Diaz met on the International Bridge. Just prior to that conference everyone along the border-line who could even be suspected of sympathy with the Mexican liberal movement was put in jail or under surveillance and kept there until after the event was "safely over." Among this number were John Murray, José Rangel, and Thomas Sarabia.

Murray, who was arrested without warrant and denied counsel, came to Washington to try to get the truth about Mexico before the Administration and the American people. He was then identified with the Socialist Party and was suspicious of me because he knew my attitude toward the Socialist Party. So Murray carried his case to Congressman William B. Wilson. The Miners early became interested in the organization of Mexican miners as the boundary-line was no factor in the mining industry. Americans and Mexicans were working in the same mines both in Mexico and the United States, and Mexicans were not infrequently imported to this country. The copper mines in Cananae owned by Americans were the scene of many a movement which combined an effort to organize miners with propaganda for constitutional government in Mexico. The big strike of

1906 directed by Magon and Valliera was regarded by the Mexican government as an international riot and an attack on its sovereignty. I was in close touch with Mr. Wilson who introduced a resolution for the creation of a joint committee to investigate alleged persecution of Mexican citizens by our government. Hearings on this resolution were had by the House Committee on Rules. These hearings were put into the record—a vivid story of the persecution of Mexican liberals. John Murray, De Lara, and John K. Turner were given an opportunity to present information. As a result of this educational work, the Taft Administration became more circumspect in its Mexican policy.

From that time, John Murray took as his life-work the task of promoting freedom in Mexico and better relations between the United States and Mexico. His work earned for him the confidence of the people of all ranks of Mexico. When, later, he came to know me and my work better, he came to me and offered his information and services for developing channels of intercourse between the workers of both countries. It is not in any way an exaggeration to say that the American labor movement was the most potent single agency in inducing President Roosevelt and President Taft to refuse to permit the United States government to hunt Mexican refugees.

With the beginning of the Madero revolution in Mexico in 1910 began the danger of our government's being forced into a position where intervention in Mexico would become necessary. The big interests and a large part of the press of the United States were endeavoring to protect American investments in Mexico. The labor movement of the United States was endeavoring to establish guarantees for political

justice and freedom as well as opportunities of freedom
which were necessary for the development of a Mexican
labor movement. This situation was understood, not only
by the workers of the United States, but by those of Mexico
where the workers and the Liberal Party appreciated the
service the American labor movement rendered. American
labor had neither desire nor interest in the exploitation of
Mexico or the Mexican people.

My contribution to the cause of freedom in Mexico has
consisted chiefly in keeping both that country and this
country informed as to the facts of concrete situations.
That was no easy task for the Hearst papers and General
Otis' *Los Angeles Times* were leaders in the effort to spread
rumors and misunderstandings that would inevitably precipitate conflict. At one time the Hearst papers printed
at the top of their editorial page an American flag with this
slogan: "Plant it in Mexico and never take it down."
When the last revolt against Diaz in 1910 was in the making, I received a letter from De Lara, telling me of plans
for immediate action, to which I replied that if the movement should permit a man of the type of Diaz to be placed
in the presidency I would have nothing to do with it. A
prompt reply was received, giving me the assurance that
a man of high type, standing for freedom and justice for
all would be chosen to direct the new government. A
further assurance was given that the land would be justly
distributed and freedom accorded to all. In 1911 Diaz
resigned and Madero became president. I looked eagerly
forward to his government as an opportunity for great
progress in Mexico. Madero granted to wage-earners the
right to organize and took steps to establish institutions of
justice and freedom. Soon after he announced his policy

toward unions, Frank Hays and Mother Jones consulted him upon the organization of Mexican miners.

The Madero régime was contested by the counter-revolution under Huerta who in 1912 overthrew Madero, had him killed, and made himself dictator. After the assassination, it looked as though the counter-revolution would destroy the hopes of labor. This was the situation during the last weeks of the Taft Administration. President Taft felt that he ought to leave decision upon Mexican policy in this crisis to the incoming Administration and suspended action, keeping the army on the boundary-line to prevent disorder until his term should end and President Wilson should have time to determine his Mexican policy. President Wilson refused to have anything to do with the Huerta government, but the election of Carranza to the presidency removed his objections to recognizing the government. However, influences that were determined to embroil this country in trouble with Mexico remained at work. It was due to the extreme self-control and wisdom of the President in dealing with Vera Cruz and Tampico that general bloodshed was avoided.

Soon after the Carranza government was established, I discussed with my colleagues on the Executive Council the advisability of sending a letter to the representatives of the constitutionalist government who had headquarters in Washington. That course was authorized, and late one afternoon I carried over to the Mexican headquarters a letter which I presented to Señor R. Zubaran the *chargé d'affaires*.

In our letter we urged the Carranza government to declare a policy of generous treatment to political opponents and abandonment of the old Mexican idea of retribu-

tion. After the new government had established itself over
the followers of Huerta, Villa turned against Carranza.
This crisis again brought danger of intervention by the
United States. At this time, John Murray again came to
my office to lay before me the entire situation together with
its implications. He had recently been in Mexico. He
put before me documentary evidence that the Carranza
government had re-established the Madero policy of liberal
treatment of labor.

Carranza, through his representative, Rafael Zubaran
Campany, entered into a contract with La Casa del Obrero
Mundial, pledging his support to organized labor in return
for assistance against Huerta and his followers. Under
the agreement, labor organizations were given use of large
public buildings in important localities where they carried
on their activities and their labor and liberal papers. Transportation and other assistance was given to enable them to
organize trades in the industrial sections of the country.
In return, trade unions organized regiments under Carranza to fight against Huerta.

Murray brought me word from this Mexican organization that representatives had been elected to come to Washington to confer with me but found themselves unable to
finance the undertaking. Shortly afterwards, a personal
representative of the working people, Colonel Edmundo
Martinez, came to Washington to give me confidential information. Martinez was a Mason and under the protection of that fraternal relationship gave me invaluable
information.

Colonel Martinez had been closely associated with
General Aguilar and came of a family that had been influential in Mexican history. All of the direct and confidential

information that came to me on Mexico I laid before President Wilson, part in writing and that of a more confidential
nature, by personal communication.   On behalf of labor I
urged upon him recognition of the Mexican government.
After some time, to the surprise of not a few, President
Wilson followed that course.

When the pressure for intervention in Mexico was at
its height, I wrote to the organized workers of Mexico City
suggesting a conference of labor men in El Paso, Texas.
To my surprise, instead of waiting to make definite arrangements for a conference, the Mexican workers simply elected
delegates, sent them to Eagle Pass, there to wait the coming
of our delegation.   Information of this action reached me
in St. Louis where with other representatives of the Federation I had gone to submit labor demands to the Platform Committee of the Democratic Party.   As the Executive Council of the Federation was soon to meet, it was
arranged that the Mexican delegation should send two
representatives to Washington where representatives of the
Mexican workers might confer with us.   One of the representatives from Mexico City was Luis N. Morones, who
became an influential leader in developing a national Mexican organization of workers.   Martinez, representing the
Confederacion de Sindicator Obreros, was present at that
conference as were also two representatives of the workers
of Yucatan.   The state of Yucatan, under the administration of Governor Alvarado, had inaugurated many interesting reforms, including an attempt to establish good
schools for all.   Alvarado had sent two men to report to me
the conditions and undertakings in that state and to get
whatever advice and information could be secured through
the Federation.   All Mexican delegates brought creden-

tials showing them to be bona fide representatives of labor organizations. These five Mexicans met with the Executive Council of the American Federation of Labor and frankly stated conditions affecting labor and made satisfactory replies to searching questions. While our conferences were in progress, as a result of the clash between the American troops and the Mexican army, several American soldiers had been killed and others imprisoned and held in jail.

President Wilson issued an ultimatum to the Mexican government demanding the immediate release of the American soldiers. No reply came from Carranza. Our conference became extremely anxious as we feared that the catastrophe we were seeking to avert had become inevitable. Not all the members of the Executive Council were in complete sympathy with my efforts to help bring about better relations between the United States and Mexico. Therefore, on my own responsibility, I sent a telegram to Carranza appealing to him to release the American soldiers. On the following day I received a telegram from Carranza stating that his government had ordered the "liberty" of the American soldiers and concluding with an affectionate "salute."

As Carranza had vouchsafed no communication to the Administration at Washington and the telegram to me was his first direct communication with any one in the United States in this crisis, our conference looked upon it as a declaration of confidence in the sincerity and the representative capacity of our labor movement. I proposed that the Executive Council send a telegram to Carranza expressing appreciation of his action. This telegram was authorized. Between the Executive Council and the Mexican delegates a declaration was formulated and signed which we hoped would be helpful in promoting lasting understanding between our movements and as a contribution to the peace of our two countries.

It was agreed by the Mexican and the United States governments to submit their difficulties to a joint commission consisting of three representatives of Mexico and three of the United States. Labor welcomed that method as an opportunity for reaching some mutually satisfactory agreement which would help to bring under control the influences that constituted a perpetual danger to peace and good will between the two countries. The United States members were Franklin K. Lane, Judge George Gray, and Dr. John R. Mott. I went to Atlantic City where I had a conference with them as well as the three members of the Mexican commission, Señors Rojo, Pani, and Cabrera and also with the Mexican Ambassador, Bonillas. I was also in close touch with Judge Douglas, who was the legal adviser of the Constitutionalist Government upon its affairs in the United States. Judge Douglas is a very fine type of American citizen who rendered an invaluable service to his own country as well as to Mexico in his handling of affairs during this period.

While the commission was still sitting, the convention of the American Federation of Labor met in Baltimore. Before the convention had acted upon my report upon Pan-American affairs, press reports came from Mexico that Carranza had issued a proclamation declaring that anyone who advocated a strike or participated in meetings where a strike was discussed should be executed. Because of this action, it seemed questionable whether American trade unionists would have sufficient patience with the difficulties of

Mexico, while at the same time from Atlantic City came rumors that all was not well with the deliberations of the commission. I was expecting information from Mexico, so I telegraphed to Secretary Lane, putting the situation before him and asking him if he would not have patience for a few days. I shall never forget the characteristic reply I received, "Sure." I had known Secretary Lane for about thirty years. First I met him in San Francisco at the home of my friend Hermann Gudstadt.

In addition to being a man of great vision, he had deep sympathy with earnest aspirations of labor and wanted to know my attitude upon the alleged injunction abuse. He was a member of a group to which belonged John Barry, editor of the *San Francisco Star* who, together with a number of other progressive Californians, had been able to wrest that state from the control of the corrupt railroad domination.

As soon as my other duties permitted, I sought and obtained a conference with the Mexican representatives in Atlantic City and entered a protest against the Carranza edict making strikes criminal and subject to the penalty of death. I declared that Mexican labor had given invaluable assistance to the movement for the disposition of Diaz and later for the overthrow of Huerta, and that it was a piece of folly as well as ingratitude on the part of Carranza who was brought into power upon a program of freedom and justice to turn upon the workers of his country and to make their perfectly normal activities a crime. I added that if that attitude of Carranza was maintained the assistance and co-operation which American labor gave and was willing to give would be withdrawn, that our feeling was not against Diaz or Huerta as to their personality but because of their corruption and tyranny and when such practices were to obtain under the Carranza government the name Carranza meant nothing to us. My statement left a deep impression upon the Mexican commission and the proclamation of Carranza soon followed revoking the order against which I protested.

While waiting at the hotel desk to send up my card to the Mexican commission, a man came to the desk, gave his name, and asked the clerk to communicate his presence over the phone to Señor Pani. He spoke with a decided Teutonic accent, and when he got into touch with one of the commissioners over the phone, he told him who he was, said that he was a representative of the German government, and that he desired to have further conversation. When later I had a conversation with Secretary Lane, I gave to him not only an outline of the discussion I had with the Mexican commissioners but also this incident. So that we might have more privacy, the conversation with Secretary Lane occurred in a rolling chair on the board walk in Atlantic City.

In time the troubles of the commission were adjusted, a constructive agreement reached, and good faith was maintained between labor of Mexico and the United States.

As a result of the Washington conferences, it was arranged that the two delegates from Yucatan should make a tour of Pan-American countries to arouse interest in a Pan-American Labor organization. Subsequent conferences developed interest in forming a Pan-American Federation of Labor. In 1918 I sent an American labor commission consisting of James Lord, Santiago Iglesias, and John Murray into Mexico. That commission did good work. A plan that I had had in mind for months was to utilize all the friendly contacts developed so as to call a conference to organize a Pan-American Federation of Labor. A conference committee at my office did the preparatory work. Most of the labor movements in these countries were either Socialist or anarchistic. There was little understanding of the trade union movement as we know it. Most of their literature came from Europe and was prejudiced against the American Federation of Labor. Despite this handicap the idealism and effectiveness of the American labor movement had been practically demonstrated in Mexican affairs and a number of countries sent delegates to the initial meeting which resulted in a Pan-American Federation of Labor, in Laredo, Texas, in November, 1918.

The labor movements of the United States, Mexico, Central and South American states were represented by a total of seventy-two delegates. Hon. W. B. Wilson, Secretary of Labor, attended the conference as the representative of President Wilson. General Pablo de la Garza was present as the personal representative of Carranza. Governor Hunt of Arizona addressed the conference.

On the morning of the opening of the congress, the English-speaking delegates were in Laredo and the Spanish-speaking delegates across the border in Nuevo Laredo. In two great columns the delegates advanced simultaneously from the borders of our adjoining republics. The city officials of Laredo, Texas, heading our group, and those of Nuevo Laredo, Mexico, heading the Spanish-speaking column, advanced until we met at the center of International Bridge which crosses the Rio Grande. There speeches were made by Secretary Wilson and General Garza on behalf of the American and Mexican governments; by Luis N. Morones on behalf of Mexican labor, and by me on behalf of American labor. After the speaking, the two columns merged and returned to the Plaza in Laredo where the conference was opened. The conference of the Pan-American Federation of Labor represented a movement by the people to express the will of the people for peace and mutual advantage in international relations. The following year a second conference was held in New York.

In 1920 when our annual meeting was held in Mexico City, we were most royally entertained by the Mexican government. The American representatives in this congress were Thomas A. Rickert, Daniel J. Tobin, Matthew Woll, John P. Frey, and me. General Obregon was President. I had met him in my Washington office two years before when he came to the United States to arrange for marketing facilities for the produce of Sonora. He then extended the courtesy of letters which facilitated the work of the Pan-American Federation of Labor. During my stay in Mexico City I had several extended conferences with him. General Calles, General Villarreal, and former President de la Huerta participated in these conferences and extended to us many social courtesies. However, de la Huerta manifested an attitude of supercilious superiority. When he tendered invitations for a reception to our delegation I declined to attend, and I had made known to him the reason. All others manifested such frank appreciation of my various efforts to be helpful that I felt that these international friendships would be the basis for permanent policies of mutual honesty and good will.

We were to have met in Guatemala City in 1921, but due to a *coup d'état* overthrowing the government and the great unemployment in the United States, the regular conference was postponed.

On my return trip from the Pacific Coast after the

Portland convention of the A. F. of L. (1923), a conference was arranged with representatives of Mexican labor in El Paso. That meeting developed conclusively that the Mexican labor movement was directing its development upon an understanding of economic problems and principles similar to that of the A. F. of L. In our discussion I expressed my interest in the pending presidential election in Mexico and commented upon the significance to Mexican and Pan-American labor in the contest between General Calles and General de la Huerta. Calles I knew to be a lover of liberty and humanity. My experience with de la Huerta I have related—such a man would impede constructive development. An insignificant body of adherents of de la Huerta protested in the public press against my frank expression in favor of Calles and declared they would enter protest. That protest never reached me. I have no desire to interfere in internal affairs of Mexico. If I had in this instance, protest did not come with good grace from those who earnestly solicited "my interference" during the dark days of struggle.

I have served the Pan-American Federation continuously as president and it is my hope to make our activity a permanent agency not only for labor progress but for the maintenance of peace in the western hemisphere. Our labor movement has never been associated with any effort to secure economic concessions or struggle for world-markets; hence, we are not handicapped by having to explain or defend our motives. It is accepted that our motive is always to advance human welfare and what better principle is there upon which to square international policies?

The purposes for which the Pan-American Federation of Labor is founded are the establishment and maintenance of best possible relations between governments of the United States and Pan-American countries; the establishment and maintenance of best possible relations between the peoples of the United States and Pan-American countries; and further, to establish and maintain best possible relations between organized wage-earners of the United States and Pan-American countries.

CHAPTER XXXVIII

I ABANDON PACIFISM

WHEN on July 28, 1914, there flashed across the Atlantic the message that war had been declared in Central Europe, I could hardly bring myself to realize it was true. Though for years there had been speculation as to the possibility of war between leading countries of Europe, though we had seen yearly progress in armament and the production of munitions of war, though the specter of war had been always in the background of international relations, I did not believe it was possible for civilized nations deliberately to undertake to settle differences through force of arms and to enter into the destructive horrors of war made possible by human inventions and our increased knowledge of science. A war of aggression was abhorrent to the spirit of America. The American wars which had occurred during my lifetime were wars for a great principle. The Civil War, which freed thousands of human beings from bondage, thrilled me even though a mere boy in a way that has remained permanently a part of my intellectual life.

From early boyhood, vanquishment of war was an ultimate dream which I earnestly expected. I was a member of practically every peace society in which membership was open to me and participated in many conferences to promote peace between nations. I was a member of the New

York Peace Society, organized in 1815, the first peace society in the world. When William Randall Cremer, a pioneer advocate of international arbitration, came to the United States in 1887, I welcomed an opportunity to do practical service. I arranged that Cremer, a union man and a stone-cutter by trade, might have opportunity to address our Federation convention which met in Baltimore, and participate in public meetings held in New York on behalf of the cause of peace. Through his connection with the International Workingmen's Association, Cremer had first seen the potentiality of labor for peace between the nations. When that organization dissolved, he initiated a workingmen's movement to promote plans, especially arbitration, to adjust difficulties between nations, and to advance the ideals of peace. Cremer was elected to Parliament and there aroused interest among fellow-members on arbitration treaties. An organization to promote international peace was formed which became the Interparliamentary Union— a group of French members of Parliament being the first to affiliate. Later, a strong American contingent became identified with the movement. Cremer made several trips to this country in support of proposed arbitration treaties. I was also active in support of the proposal.

Like all men not personally familiar with the details of the problems of foreign relations, I had some very idealistic notions. So far as my attitude on foreign relations was concerned, I was a pronounced pacifist. When in 1897 the movement had progressed so successfully that the President submitted to the Senate an arbitration treaty negotiated between the United States and Great Britain, I was one of the hearty supporters of that treaty. At that time it was the custom for the Senate to consider treaties in executive session. In this we were following Old World customs which considered secrecy as indispensable in dealing with matters in the field of international relations. That field was deemed too intricate for the understanding of any except diplomats. However, while the treaty was under consideration the New York *World* took a poll of public opinion.

The *World* published the following statement of mine:

In all countries it has always been and is today that workers are required to bear the brunt of battle and to sacrifice their lives upon the field. It therefore is more essential to them than to all others that international disputes should be settled by arbitration instead of by force of arms; their lives and the interests of those dependent upon them are sacrificed by wars; the burdens of war are borne by the worker, the evils growing out of the passions excited by war all have the trend to oppress the laborers.

All humanity cries aloud and demands that the treaty be ratified and that the two English-speaking peoples should set an example to the world not only that the pen is mightier than the sword "but that good will is more potent to attain the higher degree of success and civilization than all the havoc and thunder of the cannon's roar."

Through a number of representative avenues an expression of general opinion in favor of the treaty was made so emphatically and so convincingly that even the Senate took notice of the extraordinary poll. The great change that took place in our thought on international relations between this period and the signing of the Peace Treaty of Versailles is extraordinarily convincing that the progressive establishment of democratic control makes for higher idealism and greater justice in this field.

When the United States declared war on Spain in behalf of Cuba, I felt again that our country was rendering necessary service as the champion of freedom and the protector of a weak and struggling people. I knew intimately the ceaseless efforts of Cubans to free themselves from the arrogance and tyranny of Spanish rule. I had helped revolutionary juntas that operated from New York, but I also realized the temptations that would arise when once our country had entered upon a foreign war. There were other Spanish colonies just as sorely pressed as was Cuba. If our republic should wrest all of these colonies from Spanish tyranny, what course would our government pursue in order to avoid a policy of territorial aggression and what disposition should finally be made of the Spanish colonies?

The war with Spain was comparatively a minor engagement. We were not opposed by a nation strong either politically or industrially. It was not the sort of war in which the industrial basis was conspicuously obvious; hence, there was no great need for a large-scale mobilization of industries in support of the American flag. The whole engagement occurred in the interim of conventions; hence, there were no decisive pronouncements of organized labor upon the war. However, in my capacity as a private citizen and as a representative of what I knew to be the spirit of the American labor movement, even before our troops reached Spanish soil, I joined with a large representative group of liberal American citizens in a memorial to the Senate protesting against any policy of imperialism. When the Hawaiian issue was telescoped into the situation by the annexation of Hawaii, I wrote to Speaker Reed, vehemently protesting.

After the fighting came to an end and arrangements were under way for the appointment of commissioners to negotiate a peace, I joined with a number of others in a conference held in Saratoga Springs, New York, to consider the future foreign policy of the United States. It was made up chiefly of men of distinction and achievement. There were college presidents, lawyers, men of industrial importance, bankers, attorneys, members of the Supreme Court, judges of the lower courts, newspaper men, and representatives of the clergy. There were representatives from practically every state in the Union. John Phillips, Henry White, and I represented labor. The conference for three days discussed national problems growing out of the war and our future foreign policy. There was an instinctive feeling that our nation had become a world-power. It was evident that we could no longer cling to the policy of isolation. The group of American citizens who met in Saratoga were anxious that our future foreign policy should be based upon a new ideal of relations between nations. However, within the scope of international action we hoped to avoid the practices of secret diplomacy and territorial and industrial aggrandizement that dominated Europe.

In speaking in the conference, I opposed retention of conquered territory and pointed out that the whole moral effect of the acquisition of the Philippine Islands with their semi-savage population would undo what had been accomplished by organization and education upon the line of social, economic, political, and moral reform, particularly in raising the standard of living for the wage-earners of the United States.

A committee of about fifty representative men was appointed by the Saratoga Conference to prepare a memorial for presentation to President McKinley. The conference adopted resolutions urging that the former Spanish islands be treated as temporary wards of our nation and that while the territories were under our protection, proper measures should be taken to enable the citizens to enjoy the privileges of self-development. We heartily approved the principle of arbitration and urged its largest practicable application through foreign treaties. I was one of the committee to present the document to President McKinley.

On August 20, 1898, I addressed the Foreign Policy Congress by invitation, in opposition to the retention of conquered territory. Anti-expansion addresses were made also by Robert Treat Paine and Moorefield Storey. The expansionists spoke through William Dudley Foulke of Indiana, and James T. Hooker of the Cincinnati Board of Trade.

After the troops had been brought home, a national peace jubilee was arranged for Chicago. It was held on October 18 and 19. The meeting was intended to afford not only an opportunity for rejoicing at the close of the war but to serve as a national forum for expression of opinion upon policies to be followed in dealing with national problems created by the war. The plan was to hold the jubilee in the auditorium, but even that immense building proved inadequate. Among the speakers were President McKinley, George R. Peck, Mayor Harrison, Archbishop Ireland, Mayor Speer, General Miles, the Secretary of Agriculture, and I. In my address I pointed out that we had intervened in Cuba on request of the people of Cuba, but that we had invaded Porto Rico as a military necessity and that our flag was waving in Hawaii and the Philippines over a people subjugated by our superior force.

However, the peace that was signed between Spain and the United States left us in possession of the colonies that had cost Spain so much turmoil with the exception of Cuba which was given its independence with certain guarantees to the United States under the Platt amendment.

The American labor movement then set itself to the

task of establishing higher standards of life and work in these new American possessions. We realized that in order to protect our standards within the states we must help the Island workers to develop their higher political, social, and industrial problems. The only possible agency through which this could be accomplished was an organized labor movement within the territories. I set myself about this work. The work brought me into new contacts with Federal administrative departments. It meant a new aggressive demand made upon Congress in behalf of political rights for these people, particularly Porto Rico.

In January, 1904, a conference composed of distinguished American citizens interested in promoting international peace was held in furtherance of an Anglo-American arbitration treaty. Though not an invited speaker, my interest was so compelling that after the day's work was done I went to the evening session. When John W. Foster, who was presiding, saw me, he insisted that I address the meeting, which I did.

The United States has had no more earnest worker for world-peace than Andrew Carnegie who gave time and money to the cause. He was the directing spirit of the National Peace Congresses held in 1907 and 1909 in New York and Chicago respectively. I was a vice-president of both these congresses and took part in the program. Representatives of our government and foreign nations participated in both and gave them the atmosphere of genuine purpose. When in Paris in 1909, I participated in an international peace meeting held in connection with the international labor meeting—a most impressive demonstration of labor's attitude upon war.

As I had seen in our practice of exchanging fraternal

delegates with the British Trades' Union Congress the creation of labor's ambassadors of peace, so I saw in the international labor movement a potential influence for world-
peace.

After the labor party conference and while I was in
The Hague, I was given the privilege of seeing the building given by Carnegie for the Peace Palace—even such
parts as are usually closed to the general public. I was
particularly interested in the gate given by Wilhelm II.
From the inception of the movement to establish it, I
heartily welcomed the tribunal and did what I could to
advance it.

At that time the American labor movement was not
affiliated with the international movement and it was arranged with the none too gracious acquiescence of the
Austrian delegate, Hueber, that I should participate in
debate but without the right to vote. To be sure, I did not
find myself in accord with all of the leaders upon labor
policies. The French group at that meeting was dominated
by the Syndicalists who taught revolutionary doctrines
which to me plainly promoted strife and conflict rather
than progress. Still, I felt that a federated world labor
movement would be the most effective way of voicing the
opinions and the interests of the largest number of people
of all countries. Upon my return to the United States, I
recommended that our Federation affiliate and action was
taken accordingly.

When in 1913 Winston Churchill recommended a naval
holiday providing that within a prescribed period no additions should be made to navies, I hailed the suggestion as
an opportunity to secure the endorsement of a policy that
would diminish the dangers of war. I secured a mandate

from the American labor movement to submit to the International Secretariat a proposal that the labor movements of our various countries urge upon our governments approval of the naval-holiday plan. Carl Legien, president of the International organization, who was also head of the German labor movement, replied that under the laws of Germany he could not forward such a document to the officers of the other national trade union centers. German law carefully distinguished between political and economic organizations and the action contemplated by my communication fell under political classification. Legien also expressed the opinion that it would be inexpedient to circulate the manifesto through the medium of the International Secretariat. I was anxious to have our Congress adopt a declaration on the naval holiday and with our legislative committee induced the House of Representatives to pass the declaration. The Senate, however, never gave it consideration.

Thus the strictures that the German government placed upon economic organizations were one reason why labor there had no constructive plan for dealing with the war situation. The significance of this German limitation developed in the International Miners' Congress which was held in Stuttgart in 1912. There had been introduced in the convention of the United Mine Workers of America a resolution sponsored by Adolf Germer who proposed that in the event of war the miners should refuse to mine coal. The United Mine Workers thought it would serve no purpose for their organization to adopt the proposal unless they could secure the co-operation of the miners of all countries. The resolution was therefore referred by the miners of America to the International meeting to which Adolf Germer was elected delegate. When Germer introduced his resolution, the German delegates stated that they could not remain in the congress if the proposal was to be considered, much less discuss or vote upon it. The resolution was therefore withdrawn.

Such was my experience in the field of international policy. Like so many of today, I was a doctrinaire pacifist. I had thought much of world-peace and had dreamed of an international parliament of man. Just how all that was going to come about mattered little to me. There was plenty of sentiment against war, but no organization or technique for peace. I had written quite a bit for international peace. Just before the World War broke upon us in 1914, the Carnegie Peace Foundation had requested me to furnish them with copies of all my articles and addresses on international peace to be published as one of their series. I was glad to comply with that request, hoping that the document would be of service. In July, 1914, I received an invitation from Plattsburg, New York, to deliver an address as part of the hundred years' anniversary of the signing of the Treaty of Ghent. Into that address, one of the few prepared addresses that I have made, I put my bewilderment that our years of progress and civilization had not been able to avert the cataclysm that had befallen Europe. When I learned my hopes and dreams for world-peace were ruthlessly destroyed, I hastened to the Carnegie Peace Foundation and withdrew the manuscript I had given them authority to publish. I was no longer a pacifist.

The propaganda carried on by Austrian and German representatives in this country, even in high official places, convinced those who were accustomed to watch the forming of public opinion that our government could not remain neutral.   There were a number of us who felt keenly that there was much that ought to be done before the coming of the overt act which we knew was the German plan to have happen sooner or later and which would precipitate a formal declaration of war.   The American people were anti-military, so much so that we had not maintained a policy of adequate defense in proportion to our country's increased participation in world-affairs.   The basis for our international policies was radically different from that of Europe.   This was both a reason and a result for our policy of aloofness.

Our people did not want to be drawn into the affairs of Europe because we did not wish to incur consequent possibilities of war together with the necessity of maintaining an army and navy commensurate with the scale maintained by European nations; but now that war was inevitable, we felt that the American mind must begin its education in preparedness.

In order to focus public thought on this problem, we arranged that the annual meeting of the Civic Federation held in New York in January, 1916, should present various aspects of the problem of national preparedness.   A number of our most influential citizens were invited to participate in that conference and accepted.   Among them were Theodore Roosevelt, William Howard Taft, Henry Stimson, and General Leonard Wood.

I made my first public preparedness speech.   In view of the uncertainty which the public felt as to the attitude of labor in the approaching war, that speech of mine was important news and was carried in great length by the metropolitan press.   In this speech, as in my letter to the Carnegie Hall meeting of the Friends of Peace, I was speaking directly to the wage-earners of the country. I did not anticipate great difficulties in mobilizing labor opinion in defense of the issue I saw involved in the European War —the defense of democratic institutions.

The response that came to that speech of mine was very gratifying to me, though I think it was rather a surprise to many.

CHAPTER XXXIX

AVOIDING THE PITFALLS OF PACIFISM

IN the next few months I was to learn that the world was a unit so far as industrial organization was concerned and that political organization, which had lagged so far behind industrial progress, would shortly involve the whole world in one struggling mass of contestants. With the world aflame for military conquest, it was not possible for any important world-power to remain neutral. I was convinced that Germany was the real aggressor. I had many German friends whom I loved dearly. Notwithstanding my great admiration for German science and technology, I also had a pretty comprehensive idea of the influence of Wilhelm II. and the dominating militarist party of Germany. I understood to what an extent autocratic regimentation of the German people had extended so that their conditions of life and work, daily intercourse and even the information taught in schools and disseminated by publications were directed by a system of "Verboten." The German Ambassador to the United States, Baron von Sternburg, I had known very well as I had Baron von Speck. He was followed by Count von Bernstorff with whom also I was acquainted. On two occasions von Bernstorff asked me to go to the embassy and we discussed labor conditions in the United States and the situation of the labor men here. I belonged to German societies and clubs and found the members companionable.

334

Millions of American citizens were of German origin. They were good citizens, industrious, thrifty, and progressive. That the Germans were pronounced in their fealty to their "fatherland," even though they were good American citizens, was fostered by the "Turnvereins" and "Saengerbunds" and German-American leagues. I had for years been a member of the Washington Saengerbund—a relationship which terminated with the War.

As it became obvious that the United States could not escape becoming involved in the European War, I began to consider the possibilities of German-American societies being utilized for German propaganda. I also was conscious that there were thousands of Germans and German-Americans in the American Federation of Labor. Some few organizations and certain local units were practically made up of Teutonic members.

Because of the readjustments following so closely upon the British declaration of war upon Germany, for the first time since 1894 the British Trade Union Congress did not send delegates to the Philadelphia convention of the A. F. of L., though there were two British labor men present, James Seddon and Albert Bellamy. They met the representatives of American labor at the convention and, of course, all were eager to get first-hand information of happenings in Europe.

They were not at our convention with any standing at all as delegates. They were on the same footing as any other visitor to the sessions which are open to the public. I did not know of their coming, nor am I aware of any other person who expected them. They did not address the convention, nor was any official notice taken of their presence.

Seddon and Bellamy made a coast-to-coast tour of the country, going up into Canada, and they came back with a pretty accurate knowledge of the sentiment among the American workers. I was glad to get the benefit of their observations and to learn the attitude of the British labor movement.

I had known Seddon for years as it happened that I was with him frequently during my stay in London in 1909, and he had been fraternal delegate to our 1912 Convention. From him I got a line on the nature and the methods of German propaganda in England. All this was valuable preparation for me in the difficult job that lay ahead in the year of 1915. In that year German propaganda began to make its influence felt in this country. I was convinced that the real issues of the War concerned those who believed in democratic institutions and that the time had come when the world could not longer exist part democratic and part autocratic. It was an issue upon which there could be no real neutrality, and therefore propaganda for neutrality was propaganda to maintain autocracy. Those not actively for democracy were in effect against it. Germany planned to control American public opinion and to get us committed to policies helpful to them before we awoke to the fact that we were involved in the War. I felt that even though we were technically neutral we could not permit German propaganda to intrench itself and prejudice our decisions. This propaganda made its appearance in the labor movement among the longshoremen of New York. It came first in the guise of I. W. W. preaching the doctrine of sabotage. They urged strikes that would tie up shipping, taking care that the ships to be involved were for British or French ports carrying munitions of war.

Mysterious fires made their appearance on such vessels shortly after leaving port. There were "accidents" in munition factories and in industries producing basic articles from which war munitions and foodstuffs were to be made.

Gradually, this propaganda became more open and the subject of neutrality was injected. German propagandists sought to make it appear that selling munitions to one or the other contesting armies in the War was a breach of neutrality. I held that American workmen were not concerned with the destination of the products they made, but that they were concerned only with the processes of production for which they were paid.

I cited the fact that during previous wars Germany as well as other countries had sent materials whether munitions of war of clothing or foodstuffs to any one or all of the belligerents; that the United States was selling its products to any person who wished to buy them; that their destination was not the concern of the United States; that if Germany cared to buy munitions, clothing, foodstuffs, her agents could do so. The reason why Germany did not make these purchases was because she had not the means to carry them to her shores.

Both the longshoremen and the seamen had especially difficult tasks during 1915 because they were regarded as the key to the problem of preventing England and France from buying in our markets. Repeatedly, I was given authoritative information of attempts to use German money to induce strikes among these workers, but American workingmen showed themselves generally to be superior to bribes.

I was in New York a great deal and I was kept informed of the longshoremen situation through T. V. O'Connor, Dick

Butler, and Paul Vaccarelli who were doing valiant service to drive the I. W. W. out of the longshoremen and to defeat German propaganda. Andrew Furuseth told the seamen that it was their duty to work and thus carry out the actual and full neutrality of the United States, for to refuse to work in their regular trades and callings would be a violation of neutrality.

It was in January, 1915, when I went to New York to testify before the Federal Commission on Industrial Relations that I was first approached on behalf of a peace movement. Mrs. Sargent Cram came to me with the request that I should speak at a peace society meeting which she arranged under the auspices of the Central Federated Union. The meeting was to stage a demand for immediate peace which was to be enforced through a universal strike. I emphatically declined. Upon investigation I found that certain persons of more or less influence in the New York labor movement had consciously or unconsciously allowed themselves to be drawn into a movement which was intended to mobilize public opinion against the United States allowing herself to become involved in the War. Sometime later, I received a letter from Ernest Bohm asking me to address a meeting to be held in Carnegie Hall.

In my reply I endeavored to state some of the reasons why I had been jarred out of the complacency of pacifism. I had learned that any plan for organizing international relations must be based upon an understanding of human nature and national affairs.

I gave copies of my reply to the press, and it was published in all the papers. Thus this pacifist meeting afforded me an opportunity to issue a rallying call to American labor. Many were groping, undecided as to what course they ought to follow. My letter was accepted as the key-note of labor's war policy—we did not propose to be used in the interests of any individual country, but were concerned about principles of international justice.

A more subtle form of propaganda made its appearance early in 1915. This again was an appeal to the workmen .who constitute the major proportion of our population. It was largely in the form of pacifist movements and therefore subtly dangerous, for the labor movement had for years been committed to anti-militarist ideals. Certain influential men in various groups were interested in movements to promote pacifism. One of these efforts known as the Friends of Peace was inaugurated with the prestige of a number of well-meaning prominent citizens including William Jennings Bryan who as Secretary of State made a record in negotiating arbitration treaties. This group constituted an index to a very considerable number of American citizens who could not at that time see in the War anything except the results of European secret diplomacy and hence felt that the United States was not concerned.

Soon another endeavor was under way. Labor men throughout the country were deluged with invitations to form labor peace councils. There is in practically every community a fringe to the labor movement consisting of those who are "professional" labor men. This fringe can readily be converted to new causes and movements if sufficient financial incentives are offered. In New York and in Washington a few were induced to assume leadership. Labor Peace Councils were formed in Chicago, in Washington, and in Baltimore. I was much concerned to find that a number of valuable labor men had been caught in this net. Among them was Milton Snellings, a stationary

engineer.   German propagandists were making a special
effort to get control of the stationary engineers, seeing in
them a key to control of industrial production. Snellings
came to me in my office some days later and stated that
at a meeting of the executives of the Washington branch,
a New Jersey labor man by the name of Jacob Taylor had
declared that if shipping could be tied up for a few weeks
Germany would win the War. Snelling asked my advice
as to what his course should be. Without further ado, he
wrote his resignation from the organization and Lorch and
others followed the same course.

I went personally to a number of other engineers and
explained to them what was involved in the situation and
induced practically all of them to sever relations with these
peace councils. The president of the Engineers was offered
large sums of money to inaugurate strikes among the engineers in Bridgeport, Connecticut, but the offer was refused.

Frank Buchanan, former president of the Bridge and
Structural Iron Workers and member of the House of Representatives, was president of the Chicago Council.   In
August I had an engagement with the executive committee
of the Building Trades Department of our Federation to
insist upon compliance with a decision of the Federation.
The meeting was held at Atlantic City. On my arrival
at the meeting I read in the New York *Sun* an interview given by Mr. Buchanan, attacking me for casting aspersions upon the motives of the Labor Peace
Council, with the admonition that he was coming to
Atlantic City, in order that he might administer a rebuke
to me in person. I attended the meeting of the Building
Trades executive board, delivered my message and my

recommendation upon it, and was then informed that Frank Buchanan was in the vicinity of the hotel. I asked Thos. F. Tracy, one of my most trusted friends who was indisposed and in Atlantic City for recuperation for a few days, to join me in my room. I then got in touch with Buchanan and invited him to my room and "fell upon him." Tracy came and joined us and in an hour there was some hot talk which can not be well described. Suffice it to say that Buchanan took great care not to attack me or my motives in public. I could not be brought to believe that Buchanan had been corrupted; that he was at least misled I was sure. In the House of Representatives he was a stanch defender of the rights and interests of the working people. As a member of the tariff committee of the House, he strongly urged that all munitions should be manufactured exclusively by our government, and whether as a logical consequence of that attitude he voluntarily entered into the movement with which he was connected or advantage was taken of him by German interests to lure him so near to the precipice of danger, I am not ready to assert. He continued to hold his office, but the activity of the Labor Peace Council diminished.

In the meanwhile, these Labor Peace Councils and a number of other national organizations such as the American Truth Society, American Independence Union, American Women of German Descent, German-American Alliance, United Irish Societies, Austrian and Hungarian Societies called a national conference to be held in Chicago in September. From all over the country I got letters from labor men asking me for an expression of opinion as to whether they ought to participate in such conferences. I also received information from many that they had been told all expenses would be paid, that there was "plenty of money." John Brisbane Walker, who suddenly became editor and publisher of a weekly newspaper bearing his name, was chairman of the convention committee; Alexander P. Moore of Pittsburgh was secretary of the publicity committee. Henry Weissmann, a leader of the German-American alliance, was one of its foremost advocates and spokesmen. A later meeting was held in Washington. Some of the labor men, who had not seen me for years, came to my office and told me they were stopping at the Willard, informed me that they had been given railroad tickets at Chicago and others had been telegraphed to come to Chicago where they were furnished with railroad tickets and money and taken on board the train, registered at the New Willard Hotel and had their return tickets given them and some money furnished them in addition to this expense. Some informed me that at meetings of the unions invitations or telegrams had been received which some ambitious persons urged their organizations to approve. Practically all were without credentials. Others had come upon their own volition. Those who visited me looked upon the whole project as a chance to come to Washington "in fine style" and have all their expenses paid. When informed of the real purpose behind it all, they never again showed themselves to the projectors of the movement. There were a number caught in the movement simply because they were totally unaware of the implications or the possible consequences. Americans were unaccustomed to the subtleties of international propaganda or secret service work and we had to learn much before we could protect ourselves from the penalties of ignorance. I used every agency at my disposal to send the warning through the ranks of labor.

The following is typical of some of my experiences. It was in August that I received a number of very interesting letters from a man who signed himself V. O. de Gaigne. De Gaigne came to me with a proposition to organize the men of the Bethlehem Steel Company, the Baldwin Locomotive Works, and establishments manufacturing war munitions. As a part of his plan, we were to issue weekly a paper printed in the Hungarian language. The paper was not to advocate openly organization of working people, but was to demand the eight-hour day and higher wages. He wanted the Federation to back him financially in undertaking the paper and he was to appoint subagents to work under his direction. The object of the paper was to create a discontented state of mind among munition workers, which could be utilized in an organizing campaign. He told me that he was a lieutenant in the Austro-Hungarian Army, was a draftsman and an engineer, and had worked for the Bethlehem Steel Company. He was in Europe when the War broke out and had returned to the United States in March, 1915. I saw how cleverly he had planned to establish an agency to control munition workers and I led him on from one suggestion to another, meanwhile finding out about him all that I could but leaving him up in the air.

It was in this period that the United States began to appreciate the price of permitting our immigration policies to be written in the interests of industries that wanted to maintain a surplus of cheap labor. That policy was a gamble with fate, and many an anxious hour it caused me in war-time. The labor movement had done what it could to Americanize this "cheap labor," but it was a struggle against powerful trusts. The corporations tried to restrict immigrant workers by language barriers and by foreign language papers which were subsidized by the Hamburg-American and German-American Steamship lines as well as by the corporations themselves. Through these papers the most bitter attacks were made against the American labor movement and its leaders, and any sort of anti-Americanism might be promulgated and their home country institutions idealized. Anything was resorted to to keep the men from organizing upon purely American trade union lines, because they feared the labor movement would educate their "cheap laborers" to American standards of life and work. With war-time appreciation of national unity came an epidemic of Americanization work. It went the way of all spasmodic endeavors used as substitutes for sustained activity based upon an intelligent program. Shortly before war was declared, an immigration restriction law was passed over the second veto of President Wilson. That measure will be, I hope, the beginning of immigration policy based upon intelligent regard for national welfare. America's destiny depends upon her conserving her virility.

It was in August there occurred the first big strike of munition workers in Bridgeport, Connecticut. The telegraphic news reached me in my office. I knew that the Germans had found some labor representatives who were not as honest and as loyal as the longshoremen of New York. I at once called into conference W. H. Johnston, president of the Machinists and representative labor officials then in Washington. It was unanimously decided to take immediate steps to adjust the strike in order to protect the good name and safety of the labor movement. Johnston and I went to Bridgeport. There were serious reasons for questioning the integrity of at least two labor men. While

we were in conference in Bridgeport, one of the men involved and under question was called by long distance
telephone from New York. Part of the conversation which
was audible did not heighten my respect for him or for his
honesty. He returned to the conference room and roared
at once that the visit of Johnston and me had spoiled a
most advantageous transaction. I was never more calm or
more determined in my purpose to see the thing through
and prevent what I had reason to suspect was anything but
a fair transaction and a neutral act.

I had many agencies of private information which I
cannot disclose at this time. I had a pretty accurate knowledge of the strength of opinion favorable to Germany and
her allies and the danger of that strength when our government should finally enter the contest. I was informed
of the organization of German reservists in this country
and the location of one hundred thousand guns with twenty
rounds of ammunition for each gun. I learned of the offices
from which orders were sent and in which intelligence as to
affairs within this country was centralized. I knew a number of their meeting places in New York City and I knew
when the headquarters of the "Kriegerbund" were moved
from New York to St. Louis to the office of a certain German consul and of frequent conferences held by German
representatives—high and low—in a certain hotel in Washington. Intelligence agencies which had been operating
through German-American life insurance companies and
banks had pretty accurate knowledge of German man-power
and resources in this country. In the case of the longshoremen's strike in New York, I learned that Captain
Boy-Ed and von Rintelen had offered to place in the hands
of Captain O'Connor and his lieutenants a fund of two

million dollars with which to conduct a strike on the Atlantic Coast.   Their proposal was to maintain a strike for
eight weeks, a period of time which Germany calculated
was long enough to enable her to demolish the Allies if
American markets were cut off.   It is due to the credit of
Captain O'Connor, Paul Vaccarelli, and Dick Butler that
the effort was frustrated.   They could have taken the
money, used it or not as they wished, and the German
agents would not have dared to call them to an accounting.
The honesty of these labor leaders and their loyalty to the
government can be paralleled by many similar instances.

In the fall of 1915, the Grand Jury of New York began
investigating so-called sedition cases—various attempts that
had been made to violate neutrality and put our government in the position of supporting or aiding one of the
groups of contestants in the European War.   The grand
jury began to inquire into the activities of the Friends of
Peace and the Labor National Peace Council and also the
origin of certain strikes in New York harbor and in munition factories.   I had foreseen before others in the labor
movement that the United States had entered a period
when all activity, whether individual or group, would be
interpreted in the light of its effect upon the one great
world-issue, the struggle between the European nations led
by Germany, and the group which represented more liberal
conceptions of government and personal relations.   The
German Empire I felt had inaugurated a titantic struggle
by which it hoped to establish German regimentation and
German domination throughout the world.   The ultimate
purpose I felt was so to organize economic conditions of
the world that all resources would contribute to German

aggrandizement under the domination of autocracy, militarism, and Kaiserism.

Upon an issue of this character I did not see how the United States could long remain neutral. American citizens I knew even then were not neutral in their sympathy. I thought that I knew conditions better than the majority of wage-earners—I had felt keenly my responsibility in helping to direct the labor movement and to protect individuals. We all had to shift from the freedom of action, thought, and speech that belongs only to peace over to the circumspection and control made imperative by war dangers. I had been able to direct a number of labor men who had not realized that things that can be done safely in time of peace arouse suspicion and condemnation in time of war. Because of my intimate knowledge of what was taking place in the economic world, I was subpoenaed to appear before the grand jury. Later, I was subpoenaed as a witness in the trials of Buchanan, von Rintelen, the Wolf of Wall Street, Schulteis, and others.

There were only a few of the labor men that I had not been able to convince that the so-called peace and neutrality movements were for the purpose of aiding the Central Powers. These men found themselves in the most uncomfortable position of having their loyalty to our government under suspicion.

The investigation disclosed the ramifications of German efforts to control public opinion through our press. Dr. Rumely, who was connected with this endeavor, I knew before the exposé and I had high respect and appreciation of his splendid work in making the tractor available

for practical service in agriculture. Later, I learned he had
taken over the New York *Evening Mail*. Then his pro-
German articles and editorials in the *Mail* were so glaring
that they aroused my resentment. On one occasion he met
me and engaged me in conversation. He manifested his
usual amiability toward me, but I called him sharply to
account for his un-neutral and particularly anti-Allies, pro-
German propaganda. It was a considerable time before that
interview that I told him I had a great admiration, as he
knew, for his work and that I did not lack in appreciation,
but so far as my attitude toward him was concerned it was
one of deep regret and resentment and that he would have to
live down this un-American activity if he was ever to come
into the good opinion of men who appreciated his contribution to agricultural progress. He answered, "I hope to
regain your good opinion, Mr. Gompers." My answer was:
"You will have to earn it. Good-bye." And by the way,
those who know me understand that when I say "good-bye"
to anyone it is a matter of indifference to me whether I shall
ever see him again.

In the course of the investigation inaugurated in New
York, the activities of Captain Boy-Ed, Paul Koenig, and
Captain von Papen were disclosed as the men higher up in
efforts to blow up munition plants, set ships on fire, and
call strikes. In the papers and evidence that were produced,
very frequently, Rintelen referred to me as "the $12,500
man" and stated that I had been offered that sum to help
in their purposes. It is true that early in 1915, when I
was in New York, a woman representing this group came
to me and offered me $50,000 for my support of such plans
as the Friends of Peace were promoting. My reply was so
emphatic that no similar offers were ever tendered.

Later, in the trial of Frank Buchanan I referred to the money classification under which Rintelen had characterized me.

After Rintelen had been in prison about a year, I received a letter from him, the contents of which surprised and pleased me. In the letter he said he felt it his duty to explain that he had used the phrase simply and solely because others in his group had used it in speaking of me, and he added, "I wish you to believe that I had no foundation whatever to attach any credit to such kind of gossip neither then nor now and I do not hesitate therefore to formally apologize to you for having adopted that gossip as a phrase in telegrams and to express my deep regret for having caused you in all probability a good deal of justified annoyance and righteous indignation." No matter what may be said against any of the other defendants, though Rintelen committed crimes against the laws and neutrality of the United States, the fact remains that he was acting in the interest of his own country and in accord with his conscience.

Among those early concerned for the interests of our Republic was John R. Rathom, editor of the *Providence Journal*. With his wireless station and knowledge of the enemy code, he had much valuable information. He reposed confidence in me and gave me much information.

CHAPTER XL

DURING 1916, the consequences of a German victory in the European War became increasingly obvious to Americans. The possibility of a German super-government was apparent to those who loved our personal freedom and democratic institutions. German domination was based upon a system of subordination of individual initiative to a central plan and purpose. I admire efficiency, but I do not wish it if established by force but rather coming as the product of individual development. There were many other Americans who had this same point of view. A few of these men were in a position to determine their own line of work and they took steps to collect information that would be essential to changing our industrial organization to a war basis. I knew of some of this work.

Among all the men who were aware of the crucial situation in which we were placed, none rendered service of more value than Mr. Howard Coffin. I was in touch with the survey of American business which Mr. Coffin made. It was early in 1916 that Mr. Easley introduced him to me in my office. He laid before me his proposition to have a survey made of the industrial plants of our country to learn what they could do in the making of munitions and would be willing to do in the event of the crisis occurring in the affairs of our country by which we might be compelled to enter the World War.

The project interested me. He prepared a questionnaire which we went over together, line by line, word for word. In its perfected form it was sent to manufacturing establishments all over the United States. The suggestion was: If the government were to submit plans, blueprints, specifications, etc., and place small trial orders with the concerns, would they file information whether they could and would be willing, if necessary, to convert their entire plants to the manufacture of war products. The responses were most gratifying. Although we were belated in nearly every respect, when we finally entered the War I am quite sure that not less than six months' time was saved the government by the survey. Though I, in a way, co-operated with Mr. Coffin in this undertaking, I deem it not unfitting to say that our government is under a great debt of obligation to him for his services.

While this work was under way, a bill providing for a Council of National Defense and an Advisory Commission was introduced in Congress. The bill provided a council consisting of Cabinet members—the Secretary of War, Secretary of Navy, Secretary of the Interior, Secretary of Agriculture, Secretary of Labor, and the Secretary of Commerce to be given authority to co-ordinate industries and resources for national security and welfare. An advisory commission to the council consisting of seven private citizens was to be appointed by the President.

While this bill was before Congress, the Secretary of Labor called me over the telephone and explained to me that the measure was an Administration proposal and that it was the President's intention to include in the Advisory Commission a representative of labor. The Secretary had urged the President to appoint me as that representative.

The President then commissioned him to find out whether or not I would accept such an appointment if offered. I told the Secretary that I would give him a definite answer shortly. It happened that the Executive Council was in session at the time and I asked their advice. The Council advised that I ought to accept the appointment. After considering the proposal over-night I decided that inasmuch as there was no salary attached to the position and that there was imperative need to have a spokesman for labor in the inner war council I would not be justified either as a citizen or as a labor man in declining the appointment. I informed Secretary Wilson that I would serve upon the Advisory Commission if the President desired to appoint me. After the bill became law, President Wilson appointed the following to serve on the commission: Daniel Willard, Julius Rosenwald, Howard E. Coffin, Bernard M. Baruch, Dr. Hollis Godfrey, Dr. Franklin Martin, and Samuel Gompers.

I received notification of my appointment in October. The Council of National Defense held its first meeting in December, but was not fully organized until March 3, 1917, although several meetings were held in the interim. We were deeply appreciative of the responsibilities which rested upon us. The world had never known anything like the European War which meant the complete mobilization of nations from the factories, mines, the farms, and transportation agencies to the battle-fronts on the European field. In the case of our own country, the necessity of transportation not only of troops but supplies over a distance of three thousand miles was an additionally serious problem made doubly perplexing by German submarines and mines and

SAMUEL GOMPERS AT 53

the Kaiser's policy of ruthlessness which was carried out in a thoroughly efficient fashion.

In January, 1917, I received a communication from Belgian labor, asking that I help in giving publicity to the hardships and terrible conditions under which they were living. I did not feel justified in acting upon the request without official substantiation so I wrote to the New York office of the Belgian Relief Association and asked for information. That office referred me to confidential information sent to this country by Herbert Hoover and shortly afterwards told me that he would be in this country within a few days. About the same time I received a cablegram from Mr. Hoover saying it would be helpful if I could find a way to speak for the relief work. Upon my invitation Mr. Hoover came to Washington to appear before the Executive Council of the American Federation of Labor. As his mission to this country was confidential, he requested that the information which he furnished be regarded as confidential for the time. I shall never forget the tremendous impression the man made on me as he told of the misery of devastated Belgium. He is not a man dominated by his emotions and yet his physical appearance and his whole demeanor indicated how his spirit was burdened by the need of Belgium. He gave us cold, hard facts of commercial and industrial conditions within Belgium and in that somewhat monotonous tone that is characteristic of his delivery described heart-rending conditions within the little country. The very bleakness of his presentation was convincing. That world-famous American engineer, who organized a relief expedition that thrilled the whole world, was a forerunner of the relief America was soon to bring to world-democracy. Hoover's personality, as I understood it through that conference, convinced me of his sincerity and dependability. Shortly afterwards, when the the problem of food administration was under consideration in the Advisory Commission of the Council of National Defense I proposed that we recall Hoover from Belgium by cable and entrust him with the job of feeding the American people.

Personally, I was seething with revolt against the atrocities and arrogance of the Kaiser's "ruthlessness." As the representative of American labor as well as an Americn citizen I felt intensely my responsibility in the War emergency. My desire to serve was a consuming passion and I was glad that opportunities for service were given me. There were three different capacities in which I tried to promote the cause for which I was willing to expend my all—as a spokesman for American labor, as official of the War government, and as a member of the international labor movement.

During the first months of 1917, we were almost daily expecting open rupture between the United States and Germany and a declaration of war. Yet I felt that I ought to make every effort possible in the way of an appeal to those who might have influence in averting a war that would take such a cruel toll of human life. American labor had maintained its affiliation to the International Federation of Trade Unions, but we had declined to send money to pay our financial obligations to Legien in Berlin. I had been in correspondence with him as well as other European labor leaders, which correspondence I published in full in our official magazine. My constant hope had been to promote mutual understanding.

On February 4, Sunday morning, I went to my office to attend to some important matters that could not be deferred until Monday. After these had been disposed of, I considered the crisis which had arisen between the United States and Germany and concluded that it might have some good effect if I were to send a cablegram to Carl Legien, president of the German Federation of Trade Unions. I then wrote the following cable:

February 4, 1917.

LEGIEN,
BERLIN.

Can't you prevail upon German government to avert break with United States and thereby prevent universal conflict?

GOMPERS.

After I had written the note, I called up the White House by telephone and talked with Mr. Tumulty and told him what I had in mind. I read him the cablegram which I had drafted and asked him to bring the matter to the attention of the President, telling him that I wished to send the cablegram but would be directed by his judgment. In the afternoon Mr. Foster called me up to say that the President had read the cablegram and said that he not only approved but thought it a splendid service. I sent the cablegram.

A week later I received the following wireless from Legien:

Berlin via Tuckerton, N. J.
Feb. 11, 1917.

GOMPERS, A. F. OF L.,
WASHINGTON, D. C.

German labor has striven for peace since war outbreak. Eighteen opposed to extension of conflict. Rejection of Germany's sincere offer immediate peace negotiations, continuation of cruel starvation war on our women, children and aged, enemies' frankly avowed aims at destruction of Germany provoked aggravation of war. No intervention with government on my part has any chance of success unless America prevails upon England to discontinue starvation war as being contrary to law of nations. I appeal to American labor not to allow themselves to be made catspaws of warmongers by sailing war zone and thus contribute extending conflict. International labor must unflinchingly work for immediate peace.

KARL LEGIEN.

To me, Legien's answer was an evasion of a duty. At least an attempt might have been made to prevent a break with the United States, and as for shipping, we had the right of a neutral nation. The hunger of the German people was due to the blockade which had the same effect as a siege upon land. I knew that when the United States entered in the struggle it would mean the mobilization of all the wealth and man-power in our Republic with attending sacrifices.

Meanwhile, I had received two anonymous letters, one with the post-mark of New York and the other, Oakland, California. It has always been my practice to read anonymous letters because there are those who can give me valuable information who are not always free to write over their signatures. Particularly was this true during the War. These letters both appealed to me strongly. One pointed out that the two hundred Germans about to return to Germany on the steamship *Frederick VII* might perhaps be made bearers of a peace message to the people of Germany. The writer suggested an address from the American people to the German people declaring our friendship for them to be unchanged though our hearts were heavy because of their wanton submarine warfare and urging them to exert their best effort to recall their government to the observance of the principles of international law.

The Oakland message urged that neutral nations might bring such pressure to bear upon the German government as would give them the necessary excuse for a change of front. I thought over these messages for a long time and finally determined to write a personal letter to the German Ambassador. Count von Bernstorff was then in Washington and would not leave for New York until the thirteenth as the government had not completed its arrangements for special train and safe passage. My letter to the German Ambassador was as follows:

Washington, D. C., Feb. 10, 1917.

COUNT JOHANN VON BERNSTORFF,
WASHINGTON, D. C.

SIR:

At the risk of being misunderstood and even rebuffed, I cannot restrain my intense desire to address this letter to you, and if possible through you to the German government and to the German people. The critical situation existing between the United States and Germany; the intense desire which I know is deeply set in the hearts and the minds of the people of the United States that there shall be avoided a conflict between our respective countries, that there may be avoided such actions and rupture as shall make an armed conflict inevitable is the fundamental force which impels me to submit this letter to you.

You may have seen through the American newspapers of Monday, February 5, 1917, that I forwarded a cablegram as follows:

Washington, D. C., Feb. 4, 1917.

LEGIEN,
BERLIN.

Can't you prevail upon German government to avert break with United States and thereby prevent universal conflict?

GOMPERS.

Beyond doubt you are aware that Mr. Carl Legien is a member of the German Reichstag, that he is president of the Generalkommission der Gewerkschaften Deutschlands (German Federation of Trade Unions); that his address is 15 Engel Ufer, Berlin.

It may be interesting, sir, for you to know that my colleagues of the Executive Council of the American Federation of Labor have formally and officially endorsed my action in sending the cablegram, and that in addition from many quarters in the ranks of labor and of the public generally there has been hearty commendation of the spirit which prompted the sending of the cablegram and the purpose it hoped to achieve.

I am as confident as anything else of which I have no positive proof that it is the intention and the purpose of President Wilson, of the American government and of the American people, and particularly the working people, that every honorable effort should be made to avoid war between Germany and the United States. And yet I am as fully convinced that the people of the United States are practically a unit behind the President in his insistence upon the rights and safety of neutral nations and peoples.

Should the calamity of a war come between Germany and the United States, upon the working people of both countries will fall its greatest burden in life, in treasure, in breaking the ties of long-continued friendships and fraternities.

The War has already engulfed many nations. Embroiling the United States in the conflict will inevitably make it practically universal. Emergence from it, the maintenance of civilization, the growth of centuries will be hazarded, and the final outcome none can foretell.

You are homeward bound and it is earnestly hoped that you may have a safe voyage. You are in full possession of existing sentiment, feeling, and judgment of the people of the United States; you can unquestionably be of great service in the cause of maintaining friendship between your country and ours.

It is my earnest hope that your good offices may be employed to remove the tension and the cause therefor now existing between Germany and the United States.

In the earnest hope that much may be accomplished for the good of international relations, I have the honor to subscribe myself,

> Yours very respectfully,
> SAMUEL GOMPERS
> President,
> American Federation of Labor

This letter I sent by a confidential messenger to the German Embassy. The message was received by Prince Hatzfeld, who stated that he thought my letter an excellent idea but he did not know whether the Ambassador would be permitted to take the letter to his country. The next

morning the German Embassy called me by phone and
stated that "Count von Bernstorff desires to acknowledge
the receipt of Mr. Gompers' very kind letter and to thank
him."

All during the pre-war period I had been turning over
in my mind how I could best perform my duty to the American wage-earners to lead them aright and to protect their
interests. England I knew had burdened herself with an
unnecessary handicap by not seeking the co-operation of
British labor at the beginning of the War. It was not until
Lloyd George as the head of the British War Cabinet
visited the Trades Union Congress and asked for their co-
operation to win the War that British labor dropped its
attitude of suspicion and its jealous guardianship of its
rights and concentrated on giving service in the War. As
America was entering the War late, it seemed doubly necessary that we profit by our allies' experiences. To remove
uncertainty as to labor's position and to protect wage-earners by providing them with a definite constructive program,
I sent out a special call for a conference of official representatives of American labor that we might confer and determine what should be the position of labor in the impending
crisis. We owed to our movement and to the government
to make our position known in advance. That conference
met in Washington on March 12, 1917, and after one day's
deliberations adopted a declaration expressing American
labor's position in peace or in war. The declaration was
a frank presentation of those fundamental principles which
must be the basis for co-operative action either upon
peace or wartime production. It was an offer of service by
labor and a statement of conditions which would make
possible fullest co-operation with war administration. Labor

felt that if we as a nation were going into a war in defense of democratic institutions it was important to insist that basic mobilization at home be firmly grounded upon principles of democracy and human justice, and tendered our services on such conditions with the following pledge:

We, the officers of the National and International Trade Unions of America in national conference assembled in the capital of our nation, hereby pledge ourselves in peace or in war, in stress or in storm, to stand unreservedly by the standards of liberty and the safety and preservation of the institutions and ideals of our Republic.

In this solemn hour of our nation's life, it is our earnest hope that our Republic may be safeguarded in its unswerving desire for peace; that our people may be spared the horrors and the burdens of war; that they may have the opportunity to cultivate and develop the arts of peace, human brotherhood, and a higher civilization.

But, despite all our endeavors and hopes, should our country be drawn into the maelstrom of the European conflict, we, with these ideals of liberty and justice herein declared, as the indispensable basis for national policies, offer our services to our country in every field of activity to defend, safeguard, and preserve the Republic of the United States of America against its enemies whomsoever they may be, and we call upon our fellow-workers and fellow-citizens in the holy name of Labor, Justice, Freedom, and Humanity to devotedly and patriotically give like service.

The mandate from the labor movement strengthened my position in the Advisory Commission and in the Council of National Defense. I never made the mistake of presuming to speak for American labor without possessing necessary authorization. This practice was of telling force in many a difficult situation. The Council of National Defense and the Advisory Commission were both new political agencies without precedent and were confronted by huge problems in inaugurating their work. The nature and scope of our work were essentially to be determined by us. Untrammeled by bureaucratic precedents, we established a going machine upon a basis of business efficiency.

Our commission had advisory power only and no executive or administrative responsibility. We commissioners were chosen because we represented groups essential to mobilization. We were to advise as to how the field which we represented could best be mobilized. It was agreed that each should constitute a committee and should organize as he thought best to do his particular piece of work. Our chairman, Mr. Willard, was to be responsible for transportation; Mr. Coffin for munitions and manufacturing and industrial relations; Mr. Baruch, raw materials, minerals, and metals; Mr. Rosenwald, supplies, including clothing, etc.; Dr. Martin, medicine and surgery, including general sanitation; Dr. Godfrey, engineering and education; and I, labor, including conservation of health and welfare of the workers.

In the beginning I was conscious that other members of these committees regarded me with suspicion or reservations, but after we had been working together for a while they all accepted me as genuinely eager to serve my country.

The work of the commission was fascinating to me. We were in reality getting reports on national resources in the basic fields. I was deeply interested in the immense possibilities for service in such mobilization of information.

There were two aspects to the problem of mobilizing labor in support of the War which were phases of the old problem of establishing good will. There were no new principles in the War labor problem. In fact, the problem was simplified by having practically but one employer and by the dominance of one all-pervading motive—to win the war. Mutuality of interests promoted good will. I am confident that the passage by Congress of the Seamen's Law and labor provisions of the Clayton Anti-Trust Act contributed much toward the crystallization of the patriotic spirit of labor. Labor, I knew, wanted to offer co-operation and efficient workmanship. Something must be done to assure reciprocal action by management, for labor alone could not guarantee continuity of war production. Major responsibility rested upon management. Working agreements must be determined on a basis of equity and mutual advantage. The first step in this direction I felt was some objective form of getting together in support of the common cause. I invited to assist me on the War Committee on Labor a group of representatives of organized labor, prominent employers, important financiers, publicists, and technicians. In this group were the members of the Executive Council of the A. F. of L., practically every International labor officer, John D. Rockefeller, Jr., V. Everett Macy, Theodore Roosevelt, Dr. Harry Pratt Judson, Rabbi Stephen S. Wise, J. G. Schmidlapp, Myron T. Herrick, Daniel Guggenheim, E. T. Stotesbury, Felix Frankfurter, John H. Patterson, Elisha Lee, Ralph M. Easley, Gertrude Beeks, Mrs. J. Borden Harriman, Dr. Alice Hamilton, and many others.

A meeting of those who accepted my invitation to serve on this committee was called for the headquarters of the A. F. of L. April 2, 1917. More than a hundred and fifty persons responded and we spent the entire day in expression of purpose and presentation of problems. There was a surprising unity of sentiment in that very diverse group which probably could never have been brought together for a common purpose under other than war emergency. Under the shadow of great national crises those things which separated groups of citizens became of minor importance.

I absented myself from the evening session sufficiently

long to go to the Capitol to hear President Wilson read his message to Congress on the European situation. It was the first of the wonderful utterances of President Wilson which better than any other declarations of that time interpreted the fundamentals involved in the War. The world had regarded the conflict as something more or less the result of secret diplomacy and the balance-of-power principle, but under the light of his incisive interpretative analysis the struggle was revealed as a contest which threatened all that men hold finest and noblest in life. In that speech President Wilson became the tribune of the world-desire and world-aspiration of humanity. Somehow I felt constrained on that momentous day to send the following message to Carl Legien:

> *Washington, D. C.,*
> *April 2, 1917.*

CARL LEGIEN,
ENGELUFER 15,
BERLIN.

This may be the last word the labor movements of our respective countries will have an opportunity to express before war conditions lasting perhaps for years may put an end to peaceful fraternal intercourse and communication. You know that the United States cannot influence another country with which it is at peace to prevent a siege or blockade of a city or a country with which that country is at war. The United States must however protect its citizens from unlawful and unwarranted destruction of their lives. We are all doing our level best to avert actual war and we have the right to insist that the men of labor of Germany exert their last ounce of effort to get your government to make an immediate and satisfactory avowal that shall save all from America's entrance into the universal conflict.

SAMUEL GOMPERS.

My Committee on Labor mapped out certain divisions of activity necessary to safeguard the life and health of wage-earners in war production. There were committees on wages and hours, mediation and conciliation, welfare work, industrial training, housing, women in industry. These were volunteer committees with no authority save desire to serve.

This committee felt that this country ought to have the benefit of the experience and advice of the allied labor movements on war problems. I therefore communicated with the British, Canadian, French, and Cuban governments, asking them to send to this country commissions authorized to speak authoritatively on war organization of labor in their countries. The British and the Canadian Prime Ministers responded cordially and sent delegations.

When the first British Labor Mission arrived in New York, I received the information through the Associated Press which has often extended similar courtesies to me. I at once called up the State Department and the British Embassy and informed them of the arrival of the delegation. I also advised Secretary Wilson who arranged to go with me to the station to meet them. The representatives of the State Department and the British Embassy met us at the station to join the reception committee which was composed of a number of labor officials and representative labor men from the District of Columbia and elsewhere. The British delegation consisted of C. W. Bowerman, James H. Thomas, Joseph Davies, H. W. Garrod. From the station the Mission came to labor headquarters where they were given a brief informal reception in the Executive Council room. Both Secretary Wilson and I made brief speeches of welcome to which responses were made by the four British delegates. They were entertained in Washington for several days and went to New York to attend a dinner given in their honor by the Mayor and the Mayor's Reception Committee at the Hotel Astor. They came back to Washington for the second meeting of the whole Committee on Labor which occurred May 15 to meet and confer with the representatives of foreign labor. In addition to the British group, G. D. Robertson and J. C. Waters represented Canadian labor and recounted their war labor experiences. It was a marvelously inspiring meeting.

We were told how British labor at the time of the beginning of the War with generous unwisdom agreed to waive all labor standards for war production. As a result, hours of labor were increased and there was a breaking down of all restrictions that conserved the vitality and the energy of the workers. Production had not proceeded many months on that basis before it was recognized that a serious mistake had been made and the recommendation of British scientists was to restore pre-war or better standards. They told us of British plans and practices for controlling and distributing labor power, its system of priorities, and all other agencies for war labor administration. It was arranged that under the auspices of our committee the representatives of British labor should visit practically all important industrial centers of our country and acquaint as large a number of people as possible with British war labor experiences. In addition to meeting with this representative group of citizens, I arranged for the British delegation to meet the Council of National Defense and the Advisory Commission, after which they left for a tour of industrial plants and conference engagements throughout the country. This Labor Mission was such an inspiration to us all that I cabled to Lloyd George, asking that a delegation of English women trade unionists, including Mary McArthur, be sent to the United States.

Only two full meetings of the Committee on Labor were called. The work of the committee proceeded under division committees and under direction of an executive committee which in the first months of the war met weekly. The executive committee consisted of representatives of organized labor and of management. Some of those representing management were groups that were not familiar with the organized labor movement and I felt that permanent constructive results could be accomplished by giving them opportunities to acquaint themselves with the work of organized labor. Several times I arranged to have distinguished foreign experts on labor meet our executive committee. Among those were Francesco Nitti, representing the Italian government, and René Viviani of the French High Commission. Perhaps the greatest purpose these committees furthered was to indicate the kind and nature of permanent labor administrative agencies that the government must establish for war-time production and despite all handicaps these early committees accomplished an enormous amount of work and made genuine contributions.

On a larger scale the same evolution was taking place in the work of the Council of National Defense and the whole Advisory Commission. The regular governmental departments became organized to assume executive war duties and additional war agencies were authorized. Among the organizations that resulted from the recommendations of the Advisory Commission of the Council of National Defense were the War Industries Board, Aircraft Production Board, the Food Administration, the Fuel Administration, the Munitions Board, the Emergency Fleet Corporation, the Railroad Administration. There was no man who gave greater service than Daniel Willard. It was his duty to secure co-operation and co-ordination of transportation and communication agencies of the country. His efforts reached an impasse when it was found that the Sherman Anti-Trust Law forbade the very thing that he had undertaken to accomplish. The railroad executives were willing to co-operate, but when they found that consolidating the service of parallel lines and pooling equipment, etc. was in plain violation of the provisions of the anti-trust law, they were not willing to place themselves and their liberty in jeopardy. The government, finding itself in that position, had no alternative but to take over railroad control and administration. Steps were taken accordingly and under government management Mr. Willard continued to render service.

The evolution of war labor administration came as a result of the suggestions contributed from many sources. My sub-committees of the Committee on Labor of the Council of National Defense had indicated the broad divisions of the labor field. Practical impetus to action came from government departments dealing with the problem, from the office of American labor, and from men who were special students of the field.

Through my committee there was developed the first plan for a national board of labor adjustment. This plan proposed a board of seven, three of whom should be representatives of organized labor and three representatives of employers, while the seventh was to represent the public. It was further proposed that the eight-hour day should be the standard for all war production work and that in cases of disputes concerning wages the standards should be those established by organized labor in the vicinity. This proposition I submitted to my colleagues on the Advisory Commission. There was considerable discussion and objection to the eight-hour day as well as to the acceptance of union conditions and scale of wages as of June 1, 1917. The proposal was taken to the Council of National Defense and discussed in joint conference. A committee was appointed consisting of Secretary Wilson, Secretary Redfield, Daniel Willard, and me. This committee had many meetings which did not result in unanimous findings. The other three members of the committee proposed a certain modification of the plan, changing the number of members from seven to nine, omitting reference to organized labor and union standards. In this form the measure was reported to a joint meeting of the council and commission. In the discussion I entered protest. However, the proposal was adopted but never put into effect.

One of the first declarations made by my committee was against the deterioration of working conditions established by economic organizations and the enforcement of labor legislation for the protection of life, health, and limb. It required vigilance on my part to forestall attacks on our labor laws, but we came through the War with our standards unlowered and the spirit of all citizenship buoyed to the highest pitch.

At no stage of our work was there time for indecision. Those of us who knew what had really been happening in both France and England appreciated the imperative need of putting an American army in the field with the least possible loss of time. Things happened very quickly in the war executive branch of the government and even Congress curtailed its deliberation. A political truce between parties and deference to the judgment of experts facilitated results. The first few months were a period of policy formation. Important decisions were reached quickly by those who had information and who were in responsible positions. When the world was aflame, men could not stand on ceremony or precedent. Those who knew what ought to be done owed it to civilization to see that machinery was set in motion. Many decisions were a complete reversal of prevailing thought and practice. Many of us who had been most resolute in advocacy of voluntary principles found it necessary to assume responsibility for initiating policies which placed control in the hands of the government. One of the first of such problems that developed was decision as to the basis for mobilization for military service. I knew that American thought was at variance with the draft principle. Organized labor had been distinctly anti-military and had opposed compulsory service, but labor's position I knew had been reached with consideration of a very different set of conditions from what faced us in the world-wide War. The war made it necessary for central authority to assume responsibility for defense of the principles of our Republic and to utilize national resources for that purpose. The most important national resources were the citizens of the country. The most essentially democratic method of mobilizing human resources was universal draft. Viewed in this light, I knew that this draft was in harmony with the principles of organized labor and that organized labor, after it had had the opportunity to consider the new situation would approve the policy.

I therefore assumed responsibility as representative of labor on the Advisory Commission of co-operating in the development of plans for the draft. I had secured from my various contacts and from the British delegation that had come to this country considerable information on British experiences. These indicated the importance of so organizing the draft that those necessary for industrial war work should not be put into military training or in the trenches. Profiting by this experience, our country avoided time-consuming mistakes in putting an army in the field. The crux of maintaining the draft on a democratic basis lay in the exemption boards. These boards would determine fitness or unfitness for military service and would necessarily have to do with determining as between military and industrial service. I therefore urged that on divisional exemption boards representatives of organized labor should have a place. It was gratifying to find General Crowder in full accord with the view I presented to him and his associates on the draft board, as to the manner in which discrimination might be avoided in determining the comparative importance of those drafted for military purposes and those to remain at home and give service in the field of production. I was requested by draft board authorities to name representatives of organized labor for local boards. I consulted by telegraph central bodies of organized workers throughout the country, asking their recommendation of loyal American citizens and intelligent labor men. The names of these men I submitted to the draft board which ordered an investigation as to the personnel. All were accepted but one, who was a native but son of a German who had declared himself against our entrance into the War. Such democratic principles contributed much toward maintaining general confidence in the administration of the Draft Law.

One of the first war problems which my Committee on Labor considered was that of assurance of adequate compensation for enlisted and drafted persons. We realized that taking out of productive pursuits the large numbers necessary for military purposes would work a great hardship upon those dependent upon them if compensation were not provided both for regular income and in case of death or disability. I secured the consent of Judge Julian W. Mack to act as chairman of a committee to draft legislation to be submitted to Congress. Judge Mack associated with him in the work the experts of the country.

The admonitions we had received from the war-tried countries of our allies, the appealing song from the British soldiers at the front to "Keep the Home Fires Burning" made a deep impression upon me. If wage-workers in the United States should maintain standards of work and compensation that would have its influence upon the souls of our American boys in the trenches over-seas, I felt need of going further to assuage discontent in the minds of our men abroad. It was my thought that the old-time method of rewarding veterans of previous wars by pensions with its aftermath of partisan political jugglery should be avoided and I presented to my associates that the principle of workmen's compensation should be employed as a substitute for the pension system.

Meanwhile, insurance companies had practically doubled premium rates for men in active service. That meant putting into the minds of our boys even a greater danger than the War involved. Thereupon a conference was called under the Treasury Department to consider drafting a bill to provide insurance for soldiers and sailors. Judge Mack and I agreed that the main thing was to assure our soldiers and sailors and their families financial compensation. We decided to place the work of our committee at the service of the war risk committee and Judge Mack sat in with the Treasury Committee and made available to that group the work of his group for my Committee on Labor. It was a matter of gratification to all of us that there resulted the enactment of a measure providing the most liberal compensation to American soldiers of all the countries engaged in the war. Regular monthly base pay was increased from $15 to $30 with additions in proportion to dependents. The government entered the insurance business to protect the men. War risk premiums were based on an actuarial basis, including only bare costs of administration.

The last big problem which our committee attacked was housing. Our tentative plans and undertakings were taken over by the Housing Corporation of the Department of Labor.

As far as American participation in the World War was concerned, American workers felt that the War was their war. The cause for which our government had declared war upon the Imperial German Government was one which we felt was righteous and wholly necessary. The issues of that War were stated by the spokesman of our Republic in a way that proclaimed to the world the spiritual reasons that made us willing to give our sons, our personal service, and our money to the War. So far as the duties of citizenship are concerned, American wage-earners have never felt that their identification with organized labor has built up any class lines that separate them from other groups of citizens. Organized labor realized that the most valuable service it could contribute to winning the War was to help maintain and raise production levels. So great were the destructive forces, that continuous lines of supply had to be maintained between the factories and the firing-line of battle. In the case of America, this meant building a bridge of ships to connect the two sides of the Atlantic, to transport our troops and keep them supplied with food and munitions and all other necessaries. It was an enormous undertaking even with the advantages of peace production. Organized labor was responsible for handling the tools with which the work was done. The same psychological conditions that promoted production under private agreements would in an intensified degree promote production of war projects. The problem was to establish collective agreements with the government covering war production.

The first big war contracts were for cantonment construction. The War Department plunged into this herculean job, mobilizing as rapidly as it could the necessary technical ability in administrative service. Secretary Baker was fortunately the type of man who attracted persons with such ability.

The first step was the letting of the contracts to construction companies which was placed in the hands of an able assistant who had volunteered for war work, Louis B. Wehle. It happened that, in addition to being a lawyer, Mr. Wehle had a broad sympathy with labor problems. He realized that one of the big problems for which the government had to provide was the adjustment of industrial relations. He came to my office where we discussed the problem and finally developed the following simple agreement to be signed by Mr. Baker and me:

For the adjustment and control of wages, hours, and conditions of labor in the construction of cantonments, there shall be created an adjustment commission of three persons, appointed by the Secretary of War; one to represent the Army, one the public, and one Labor; the last to be nominated by Samuel Gompers, member of the

Advisory Commission of the Council of National Defense, and President of the A. F. of L.

As basic standards with reference to each cantonment, such commission shall use the union scale of wages, hours, and conditions in force June 1, 1917, in the locality where such cantonment is situated. Consideration shall be given to special circumstances, if any, arising after said date which may require particular advances in wages or changes in other standards. Adjustments of wages, hours, or conditions, made by such boards are to be treated as binding by all parties.

NEWTON D. BAKER
SAMUEL GOMPERS

June 19, 1917

No one knew whether the War Department had authority to enter into collective agreements, but Newton D. Baker and I as individuals assumed responsibility for a course that we knew was indispensable. Shortly afterwards, additional memoranda were signed extending this agreement to all construction work done during the war-time by the War Department, the Navy Department, and the Emergency Fleet Corporation.

I shall always feel that Secretary Baker performed a very courageous and patriotic part in sharing responsibility for this initial project. Later agreements were made between various war agencies and the divisions of organized labor directly concerned with the specific undertakings. These agreements were modified in the light of experience under the Baker-Gompers agreement.

When it was finally determined that the Secretary of Labor was to be war labor administrator, Secretary Wilson asked me to appoint labor representatives to assist in the development of a war labor policy. I appointed such representatives who helped to draft the fundamental principles upon which the work of the War Labor Board was established.

When in 1918 the Secretary of Labor had been made War Labor Administrator and suitable war administrative agencies were established under the Department of Labor, I was free to attend to the newer problems of the War which had been demanding my attention.

The industrial side of the War was in itself a romance. Overnight big industries developed and existing plants were converted to new uses. In all cases the crux of the problem was the service of those who handled the tools and materials. War production levels are incontrovertible proof of labor's loyalty and industry. In no field were the difficulties greater than in shipbuilding, and that industry had developed at terrific pace. The speed with which ships were completed surpassed that of any period during the world's history. Ships of eight thousand tons were completed from the laying of the keel to their launching in twenty-seven days. At Hog Island outside of Philadelphia these vessels were turned out in rapid order. In recognition of labor's service, one of the ships was named *Afel*, the abbreviation of the name of the American Federation of Labor and cable code name. At its launching, I was its sponsor and Sara A. Conboy, secretary of the Textile Workers of America, broke the bottle over its bow. She was presented with a silver service and I with a mariner's clock by the employes engaged in this work.

The workers in the mines, factories, transportation, information transmission, and every relation of war work gave equally good accounts of their workmanship and their citizenship.

During my whole active life in the labor movement, I have found able, willing assistants who aided me greatly in my work and duties. This was never more true than during the World War. In addition to this, there came to me men and women far and wide, from every walk of life, big business men, multi-millionaires, high financiers, the bricklayer and baker and the candlestick maker and the ditch-digger. All responded with an energy and enthusiasm that surpassed even my fondest hopes and expectations.

CHAPTER XLI

FROM the time that our participation in the War was inevitable, there were serious misgivings in the minds of many as to what would be the attitude of foreign-born groups. America had let in foreigners without concern as to whether they had become really Americanized. We had no war cloud threatening us. We were working, conserving, and performing our duties as a people—as citizens. It is true that we had groups such as the German-American citizenship, the Irish-American citizenship, the "over-seas Americans," and these in turn frequently exercised a political power among nations, but in so far as our every-day lives were concerned there was a complacency, for there was no apprehension of any real division, or disunity of our people in an emergency which was then foreign to our state of mind. War brought troubled questions as to the allegiance of the foreign-born, the hyphenated citizens, as we came to call them. Not without reason, we wondered if America were really a nation or only an agglomeration of nationalities.

The military struggle itself was on such a gigantic scale that complete national co-operation for action was indispensable. The first problem of mobilization was to assure unity in the national mind. There were many groups that might have held aloof or given only half-hearted co-operation. This was in some aspects a labor problem. The great majority of the foreign born were wage-earners.

Perhaps the most important disrupting agency among them was the Socialist Party organization which was "international." It subordinated nationalism to international-ism, and as the Socialist Party largely emanated from Germany the sympathy of its devotees was with that country. I have no substantial authority for the statement, but I was and am convinced that the officers of our government deferred their action upon the acute relations between the United States and Germany by reason of their apprehension of the possible lack of national sentiment and unity among the diverse nationalities in our country. War experiences led me to wonder if Socialism, in addition to its philosophic and economic short-comings, had not been manipulated to further sinister purposes. Un-Americanized workers proved especially susceptible to Socialist propaganda. There were several hundred foreign-language publications within the United States, formulating and directing opinion among the foreign born. Whether these papers were aiding their readers to a better understanding of America was a matter to which little thought was given in pre-war time. There was a sort of complacent confidence that America was a melting pot in which all manner of diverse nationalities could be gathered and inevitably, without planning or con-sideration on our part, Americans would finally emerge. In the absence of constructive efforts on the part of the com-munity, the trade union movement had undertaken to teach foreign workers the economic bases of American standards of life, work, and ideals.

I held that if these foreign-born workmen, lured and

brought into our country by big business or with profit as the primary purpose, were good enough to be brought here for this purpose, they were good enough for us to try to organize them to make better citizens and make better men of them. New York was the index to the foreign-press situation, as it was headquarters for many of the racial groups and their organs. Large sections of the city are foreign countries in spirit and in language. Soon after war was declared, two long-time friends, L. E. Miller and Joe Barondess, came to me for the purpose of getting my help in bringing to the Jews of the country the understanding of all that war meant to them and all others who hoped to maintain their freedom. I considered carefully the information these friends gave me and then went to New York to get data on the foreign press generally. I was appalled to find how completely opinion-making in the foreign groups was under the control of the Central Powers. Somewhat later, the ramifications of Dumba's operations were revealed and the government undertook to serve the foreign press with authoritative news. I interested a number of men prominent in the New York Central Labor Union and the United Hebrew Trades in the problem.

As I knew East Side New York better than most people, I fully appreciated the influence it would wield against national solidarity in support of the War and therefore I planned so that these people might not have to grope blindly to find the pathway of service. I called conferences between representatives of the organized labor movement of New York and editors of the foreign press in New York City and we talked over plans for Americanizing the labor movement of greater New York.

In July, 1917, the Socialist Party met in regular convention in St. Louis in which they adopted declarations in support of internationalism and pacifism. Pacifism at that time was substantial aid to Germany and the Central Powers and therefore tantamount to avowed hostility to the cause of the Allies. From the time that policy was endorsed by the Socialists, it was no longer possible for loyal Americans to continue membership in the party. The declaration resulted virtually in the dissolution of the Socialist Party. This situation left thousands, and especially foreigners who had looked to that organization for leadership, without intellectual guidance. Not only was there need of establishing an agency for mobilizing sentiment among these foreign-language groups in support of national policies, but there was an opportunity to bridge over the more superficial differences that had separated groups within the labor movements.

I called into these conferences representatives of the National Labor Publicity Organization so that the work planned for New York could be extended wherever the foreign problem was acute. At these conferences we developed a plan for bringing together in one organization representatives of the American trade union movement and representatives of what were known as radical organizations. Members of this organization agreed to lay aside for the period of the War whatever differences they might have upon procedure and to rally in defense of the fundamental principles for which our government stood. This organization we called the American Alliance for Labor and Democracy. The Alliance was national in scale and under it were gathered the most influential Socialist leaders of the country, prominent trade unionists, and noted publicity persons.

As, of course, was necessary under war emergencies, I first submitted this proposition to the Advisory Commission and Council of National Defense and to George Creel who was chief of the Committee on Public Information. The plan was approved.

After our government formally declared war on Germany, the nature and method of German propaganda became more subtle and therefore much more dangerous. It assumed the form of ultra-internationalism and extreme "democracy." The war notes and messages of President Wilson, who had placed American concern in the War upon a very high plane, were purposely misconstrued to comprehend impractical methods.

In order to inject a dissenting wedge in public opinion, pro-German propaganda sought to carry international problems to lengths of democracy for which nations were not prepared either in agencies or technology. They sought to mobilize liberals of all countries in support of an international program which was a riot of democracy and idealistic fraternalism. Supported by immense sums from the government of Germany, this propaganda made rather surprising headway. In America the medium for disseminating this teaching was a People's Council in which there was a Workingmen's Division. It was about this division that I was chiefly concerned. The local branch in New York was called the Workingmen's Council which announced it would protect the interests of wage-earners during the War. This announcement was intended as a criticism and condemnation of my policy of seeking agreements in support of our national program for co-operation with the government. The council sought to alienate labor from the government's program and thus to interfere with production of supplies.

A few trade union organizations were beguiled by the Workingmen's Council and threw in their lot with it until they discovered its real nature. These rallied in support of the Workingmen's Council and they, together with the large foreign population of New York City, made the situation dangerous.

In the summer the People's Council announced that a National Conference would be held in St. Paul which would be "truly representative of labor and would reflect the real mind of labor." That was one way to refute that claim once and for all time, and I accepted the challenge. I called a national conference of the American Alliance for Labor and Democracy to be held at the same time in St. Paul. I had no official authority for my course in organizing the Alliance and serving as its president, but I had the intrinsic authority arising out of great national need and opportunity to serve.

However, the "city fathers" of St. Paul had little patience with the pretensions of the People's Council and refused to permit the conference to be held within their city. I heard of the action while attending the convention of the New York State Federation of Labor. I was chagrined because I wanted to meet them in the way they had chosen. I immediately sent a telegram protesting against the suppression. The council found refuge in Chicago. The contrast between its meeting and that of the Alliance in St. Paul was sufficient to show that the council did not represent American labor.

At the St. Paul Conference were substantial trade unionists, editors of the foreign and radical press, Socialists, liberals, interested in achieving national unity. There were: Lucien Sanial, John Spargo, William English Walling,

Frank P. Walsh, W. J. Ghent, Stitt Wilson, John Fitzpatrick, Matthew Woll, John P. Frey, Frank Morrison, William Edlin, J. G. Phelps Stokes, Mrs. Charlotte Perkins, Charles Edward Russell, Frank E. Wolf, and Chester M. Wright. These are names that indicate the many types united in the Alliance. There were about two hundred in all at that St. Paul meeting. The conference adopted a statement of purpose that was an inspiration for our future work and to all burdened with responsibility to maintain an understanding of war aims and duties. The publicity and speaker's bureaus organized under the Alliance were among the most dependable agencies supporting the policies of President Wilson. The pledge which each member signed was:

The undersigned hereby affirms that it is the duty of all the people of the United States, without regard to class, nationality, politics, or religion, faithfully and loyally to support the government of the United States in carrying on the present war for justice, freedom, and democracy to a triumphant conclusion and gives this pledge to uphold every honorable effort for the accomplishment of that purpose, and to support the A. F. of L. as well as the declaration of organized labor's representatives made March 12, 1917, at Washington, D. C., as to "Labor's Position in Peace or in War," and agrees that this pledge shall be his right to membership in this conference of the American Alliance for Labor and Democracy.

The American Alliance for Labor and Democracy became one of the unofficial agencies through which the National Committee on Public Information operated. It did splendid publicity work serving not only the radical press but all the labor press. Its speakers' bureau organized numbers of public meetings. After the Stockholm propaganda (which I shall discuss in the next chapter) started in Europe, the Alliance planned a country-wide labor loyalty program for the week in which February 22 fell. I cabled to George M. Barnes of the Labor Department of Great Britain to send over representatives of British labor to tour our country and begin their work with that loyalty week. Mr. Barnes sent over four able men, Messrs. Appleton, Butterworth, Mosses and Duncan, whose work was potent in cementing anew the spirit of co-operation between British and American labor.

By the fall of 1917 the mind of American labor had disclosed itself with reassuring definiteness. Even constant agitation from Stockholm made little impression. I felt that the one thing needful to assure our coalition till the end of the War was a personal message from President Wilson to the representatives of American trade unionism assembled in convention. I presented this thought to my colleagues in the Executive Council and when they approved, requested Secretary Wilson to convey the invitation to the President. The President accepted and declared he wanted to give his message in person. It was arranged for him to go to Buffalo for the opening day of the convention. Our honor was all the more distinctive from the fact that the President had not left Washington since the beginning of the War and had made no public addresses except his messages to Congress.

When he advanced upon the platform of our convention accompanied by his gracious and beautiful wife, I felt anew a thrill of pride in the manner of man who was our nation's chief in that critical period. His speech was a new revelation of the heart, culture, and incisive mind of the man who came to us in the spirit of common counsel. He spoke surrounded by the significance of a grim cordon of soldiers, but his words breathed the uplift of high human purpose at war with principles of unfreedom. A reference he made to me cheered me in some of the hard places where I had to contend against less appreciative understanding. With an appeal to the reader not to interpret my natural appreciation as vanity, I want to put in this record the following words of President Wilson:

While we are fighting for freedom, we must see among other things that labor is free, and that means a number of interesting things. It means not only that we must do what we have declared our purpose to do, see that the conditions of labor are not rendered more onerous by the war, but also that we shall see to it that the instrumentalities by which the conditions of labor are improved are not blocked or checked. That we must do. That has been the matter about which I have taken pleasure in conferring from time to time with your president, Mr. Gompers; and if I may be permitted to do so, I want to express my admiration of his patriotic courage, his large vision, and his statesman-like sense of what has to be done. I like to lay my mind alongside of a mind that knows how to pull in harness. The horses that kick over the traces will have to be put in a corral.

I look backward in bewilderment at the work I did. The work of the labor movement was unusually heavy. I felt it imperative to maintain personal contact with all regions. I had personal knowledge of the immense work which the American Alliance for Labor and Democracy was doing. Then I had my official work as Advisory Commissioner. By way of diversion, I gave many evenings to selling Liberty Bonds, on the street, in public gatherings, or special drives. I seemed to be always on a train or in a conference.

The world seemed very small in those days. We talked as intimately of experiences in Europe or Asia as we had formerly done of happenings in New York. We eagerly sought out any emissary reported to have definite information of how the struggle was faring in another country. Those who were not in the thick of the fight can hardly appreciate the tension and the anxious care with which we crowded into each twenty-four hours all the effective work we could accomplish.

I have no overweening conceit as to my service in connection with the World War, but I tried to do all that was possible for me to do. So I record in what may be regarded as too much detail some of the things I did for the information which it may give and because during the years of the world-struggle I was absorbed with the one object that it was labor's war as much as it was the war of any other group of our people; that labor had to make good in helping to win the War and to emerge from the War with freedom and democracy safeguarded and its honored name and high ideals maintained.

CHAPTER XLII

THE pacifism which we had effectively dissipated in the United States showed indications of gathering strength in the ranks of labor in the countries of our European allies. Pacifism and desire for peace between nations had been confused in declarations of international labor and labor generally. We were sure of the goal desired, but not at all sure of the way of reaching it. The basic idea was the brotherhood of man and a firm conviction that there was a stronger tie between the workingmen of all countries than that which united the workers of a single country to the other social groups which together constituted the nation. War weariness, which followed years of terrific fighting on the battle-fields on the Continent, prepared the way for alluring propaganda. That propaganda took the form of this proposal: Why fight, it means only the unnecessary loss of lives for the German military is invincible! Let labor show the world a new way. Let us confer with the workers of all countries and find the terms upon which peace can be based and end this fighting.

To understand the source and purport of this propaganda, it is necessary to know something of the international labor situation of the time. As I have said, international Socialism and trade unionism were largely under German control up to 1914. After the

Franco-Prussiah war in 1870, Bismarck, coming into control of the German Empire, found Socialism dangerous to his plans. He enacted his famous Anti-Association Law which made it illegal to print or circulate socialistic literature in Germany or to hold meetings at which Socialism was discussed. Like similar repressive legislation, it failed to accomplish its purpose. Socialist activity continued, although headquarters were for a time in London. Bismarck was too hard-headed and practical a statesman to continue on the statute books a law of his own making which produced results contrary to his expectations. Apparently at the same time he studied the problem of making this agency which he abhorred and hated, of practical use to the German Empire. The events of the War indicate that he anticipated the advantage to the German Empire through inculcating international Socialism among the citizens of all countries with which Germany might some day come in conflict, and accordingly he promoted internationalism among the peoples of other countries, but nationalism for Germany.

In the economic field there were two different types of international organizations, international trade federations and a federation of national trade union centers—the International Federation of Trade Unions with their headquarters in Germany. The majority of these international federations had their headquarters in Germany, the officers being in almost every instance Germans.

The frequent conventions of these international federations of labor in Europe for the ten or fifteen years preceding the War had brought about close personal contacts with all of the German and continental as well as British leaders, and this had resulted in the forming of many personal friendships. In the first months of the War we seriously thought that perhaps the international ties would prove stronger than the national. But the workingmen of country after country responded to the call to its colors. In Germany there was only a handful of Socialists that refused to vote war appropriations for the government.

During the war months of 1914, fraternal corespondence still continued between the representatives of the national centers. There were friendly letters between Legien, Appleton, and me which showed how each was endeavoring to maintain the international ideal. But as the military conflict grew more tense, it became evident that the lines between the enemy governments must comprehend the whole nation; so early in 1915 a group of trade union representatives of the Allied countries met in London and determined to take steps to neutralize the office of the International Federation of Trade Unions. As the United States was then not involved, Jouhaux and Appleton suggested that I take up with the various national centers the proposal for neutralization. I agreed to undertake the work and wrote to Legien, stating the purpose and plan. However, due to some misunderstanding perhaps caused by translation, Legien thought that I proposed moving the office to the United States. Before an understanding could be reached, the War had progressed so rapidly and become so menacing to the whole world that the hope of maintaining international labor contacts died. Although the office of the International Federation of Trade Unions was moved from Berlin to Amsterdam and the secretarial work taken over by Oudegeest of Holland, it was found impossible to maintain even a semblance of neutrality.

One of the most wholesome lessons that the War taught

labor was, that we must build our program upon facts and not theories. One of the most important principles that we learned was that although wage-earners are a distinct group in society they also are an integral part of the nation. The ties that bind workingmen to the national government are stronger and more intimate than those international ties that unite the workingmen of all countries. There was no international organization that could resist war expediency. This situation, I believe due to the fact that our attempts to organize political relations, had practically stopped with state boundaries. The field of international politics is still chaos, but I have faith in human intelligence and believe that some day this hope will be realized.

When the convention of the Federation met in Philadelphia in November, 1914, I prepared a resolution in which I presented a series of preambles deploring the waste of war and proposing that the Executive Council should hold itself in readiness to summon an International Labor Conference to meet at the same time and place that the Peace Congress should be assembled, to determine the treaty ending the War. In my first draft I included the suggestion that labor work for some form of international agency that could deal constructively and continuously with international problems and thereby minimize the probabilities of war. However, a number of my colleagues with whom I talked over my resolution objected to the proposal to organize international political agencies and I withdrew that phase of my suggestion until such time as there should be greater unity of thought. I did not then foresee that the United States would be involved in the War, so I thought to render service by mobilizing neutral power in support of constructive thinking.

Shortly after the War had begun, some of the German labor leaders began to spend much of their time in Switzerland where they were more or less in constant personal touch with leading representatives of the Socialist and trade union movements of Belgium, England, France, Italy. Through these conferences these men were able to carry out that part of the German war program which was designed to weaken the morale in the Allied countries. Presently, there began to issue from Switzerland suggestions of international conferences, then invitations, Zimmerwaldian proposals and vaguely disguised pacifist propaganda.

Labor never suspected any menace in the situation until the events of the War began to arouse misgivings. Those who had personal knowledge of the workings of the international Socialist movement told me after the War began that the Socialist propaganda committee received many large donations from individuals which could be traced to the German Imperial Treasury. I was shown records disclosing that the imperial government, through a private individual, had contributed five or six hundred thousand marks to one particular Socialist propaganda drive in Italy previous to the War. An article or speech by Bebel made open reference to this donation.

In contrast to the continental plan for international conferences was collective action by the labor movements in the countries opposing Germany. A conference of labor representatives of the Allied countries met in Leeds in 1915 and formulated a statement of minimum labor demands which they hoped to have incorporated in the treaty and which should specify the conditions of peace. To me the declaration was very unsatisfactory as it made no contribution to constructive planning for the better ordering of

world-affairs in the future.   I thought labor ought to be
thinking not only of its own problems but of the big problems of all society.

The conference and peace demands of Leeds were regarded by Legien as evidence of an attempt to establish
an international labor organization, dual to the International Federation of Trade Unions. Legien urged that the
establishment of international relations between Allied
nations would result in permanent lines which could not be
effaced after the War.   Just before our Baltimore Convention in 1916 I received a letter from him in which he
said that an international trade union conference was summoned for Berne, December 11, 1916.   That conference
was for the purpose of considering the continuation of the
International Federation of Trade Unions; publication of
the International News Letter; and miscellaneous proposals. Within a few days, however, I received a cablegram
from Legien stating that the conference had been indefi-
nitely postponed. No attempt to secure a meeting of the
International Federation of Trade Unions succeeded in
getting together a representative group. Such meetings as
were held were attended only by representatives of neutral
European nations and the Central Powers. It would not
have been possible for workingmen from France or Great
Britain to have attended these conferences even had they
so desired, for their governments would not have granted
passports.

This proposition of Legien raised the issue as to what
should be American labor's policy on international labor
matters during the War. I suggested to our Executive
Council that we ought to prepare a special report to the
convention making plain our position. This suggestion was

drafted and we submitted a statement in which we said that the American labor movement had approved moving the International Secretariat to a neutral country in order to protect the organization against the charge or appearance of partiality but it refused to consider or suggest any other international proposition concerned with labor matters during the War. This is the policy which we followed consistently. However, we ended our report with a rather comprehensive plan for an International League for Peace. Our plan did not suggest a super-government, but only wider application of the principle of voluntary mediation and arbitration in an international court, permanent mediation agencies to deal with economic difficulties and regular development of international law.

During 1915 and 1916 I had given much thought to developing plans by which as a neutral I hoped to be helpful in injecting constructive policies into the final determination of after-war relations. Each year the convention acts of the A. F. of L. contributed to the working out of a definite program. My thought was that a conference of representatives of the organized labor movements of all countries meeting at the same time and place as the Peace Congress, would constitute an organized channel through which the interests and the opinions of the masses of the population of all countries could be presented in such a way as to compel the consideration of the members of the Peace Congress. This thought I later modified on a basis of the co-operation which prevailed during the War and suggested that wage-earners ought to be members of the Peace Congress itself. The spirit of democracy made considerable progress during the War and my later suggestion found general approval.

After America entered the War with her enormous
material and human resources, there was no longer any
doubt but that Germany would be defeated on the battle-
field. Then there developed through various German international agencies an insidious propaganda designed to
weaken the morale of the discouraged and suffering.

When the Hindenburg line held its most advanced
position, the propaganda urged a negotiated peace—a peace
negotiated by the invaders with their military forces
intact. The argument used was that the German military machine was not only in the saddle in Germany
but irresistible in battle; that to destroy it was an
impossibility. During the three years of the War it had
shown itself able to win every drive it undertook. An
appeal to the heart was made by reference to the untold
hundreds of thousands of young Germans as well as young
men of the Allied countries who must die if the war continued. This idea emanated from the German Imperial
Government, carried to the Allied Socialist and labor leaders
through meetings with Mr. Legien and others in Switzerland, and took so strong a hold upon the Allied countries
that conferences were held for the purpose of putting the
program into effect.

After the United States had plunged into the depths
of war preparations and had completed our organization,
I became conscious of a new form of German propaganda which made a powerful appeal to sentiment
and humanitarianism. It argued that because of the
destruction and waste of the War, every possible agency
should be used to end fighting by securing agreement between peoples upon the issues involved in the War. It built
upon the foundations laid by international Socialism and

held that all peoples were the victims of their capitalistic governments. According to this interpretation, no one knew the causes of the War or which country was the real aggressor. All were equally responsible and therefore the quickest way to end the War was for the peoples of the warring countries to reach an agreement upon peace terms.

The propaganda varied from a bald statement of this nature to more refined phrases, such as international labor conferences to discuss war aims or peace terms. The whole proposal seemed to me not only impracticable but a pro-German invention. It was a proposal to make altruism and idealism consciously or unconsciously serve the cause of German autocracy.

On May 24, 1917, I received a cablegram from Oudegeest inviting the Federation to participate in an international congress of trade union centers to be held in Stockholm June 8, to determine a trade union program for peace negotiations.

It had been impossible to give a semblance of internationalism to conferences held in Switzerland. I discussed the Stockholm proposal with Frank Morrison and John Alpine, members of our Executive Council who were then in Washington and then I sent Oudegeest a cable stating that before the United States entered the War we had proposed an international labor congress to meet after the War and at the time and place where the representatives of each government were to meet in peace congress. Our proposal was rejected and we did not see how any good could come out of our participation in the Stockholm Conference during the War. Oudegeest and those he represented continued their efforts to induce our Federation to be represented at an international congress at Stockholm. From various sources of information I learned that the proposal to settle and end the War by negotiations was gaining favor. In England a group of advocates rallied under the leadership of Arthur Henderson who had been a member of the British Cabinet until his difference with Lloyd George over the Russian situation. In France the Socialist minority group was making serious trouble for the government and in Italy there was only a semblance of Socialist support for the government. Apparently, the rank and file of the workers— the trade unions—gave sustained loyal support manifest in war production.

A few days later I received a cablegram from Lindquist, the Swedish labor leader who was president of the Stockholm conference of neutrals and Central allies, telling me that the trade union centers represented in the Stockholm conference of trade unions would meet to discuss peace demands September 17 in Switzerland and inviting the United States to send representatives. As the Executive Council was meeting within a few days, I held this invitation for consultation with them.

The Executive Council decided that all such conferences as the one proposed were premature, untimely, and could lead to no good purpose. We were apprehensive lest such a conference would place obstacles in the way of democratizing institutions of the world and would hazard the opportunities for liberty and freedom of all people. I sent copies of this cablegram to Jouhaux, Appleton, and Oudegeest. For several months our Federation received frequent and urgent invitations to be represented at the International Congress at Stockholm, in all of which we declined to participate. A conference was held in which labor and the

Socialists of the Central Powers and of the central countries
were represented. As I have already said, even if British
and French labor desired to participate, they could not do
so by reason of the refusal of passports from their respective
governments. The whole project was one-sided and flat.

In the fall came the news of the Russian collapse. It
was a staggering blow to the Allies both for military and
sentimental reasons. The whole world had rejoiced in the
overthrow of czardom. In our country where there had
long been sympathy with Russian revolutionary movements
the news brought a feeling of great uplift. At the time we
were on the verge of war and were about to enter a period
of terrible sacrifices. There was cheer in the feeling that
the War had brought to that land of oppression a new and
wonderful opportunity. At this point I wish to relate
briefly my efforts to help the Russians with their problems.
I had been associated with so many labor endeavors in
Russia that I wanted to find some way of expressing my
sympathy and satisfaction. Through the editor of the
Novy Mir I secured the name of a labor representative in
the Russian Duma and cabled him:

The splendid proclamation of your provisional government declaring for free speech and press and the right of workers to organize and if necessary to strike for their rights guarantees to Russian
workers opportunity for freedom and progress and assures the new
Russia her future greater glory.

As I feared that cablegram was not received, I sent
through Ambassador Francis another message which I asked
him to make public. Again assuring them of our warm
sympathy in their achievement of freedom, I warned them
of something that I had learned in watching others who
had newly gained freedom—that it was impossible to

achieve the ideal state immediately and I pleaded with Russia's workers that they maintain what they had already achieved and seek to solve practically and rationally the problems of today and to safeguard the future against reactionary forces.

Our Executive Council sent an official cablegram conveying fraternal greetings and pledging the support of America's workers to Russia's efforts to secure freedom. In every message—and there were many of them—I urged them to build practically and constructively. I knew Russian workers and I knew the dangers of newly acquired rights and freedom.

Our government felt that as an older republic it owed a duty to Russia that had shaken off despotism in a period when its problems were made extreme by war difficulties. President Wilson sent a commission to Russia personally to assure the people of our sympathy and desire to help and to make arrangements to give them such practical assistance as they could. Our information was that pro-German propagandists were busy in Russia seeking to prevail upon the new government to withdraw from the Allies. Russia had suffered terribly during the War. Due to corruption under the Czar, her troops had been sent to the front with insufficient ammunition and supplies. The President, through Secretary Wilson, asked me to serve on that commission, but as I did not feel that I ought to leave America at that time I declined. The President requested that I suggest the name of a trustworthy labor man. I secured the consent of James Duncan, first vice-president of our Federation, and suggested his name. He was appointed.

The internal and economic problems of Russia alone

were sufficient to tax her resources and her ability, yet we felt that she owed a moral obligation to the Allies and to the cause of international democracy to continue the War.

When our Executive Council met in May, 1918, it was at the time of a grave crisis in the War's history. We were not ready to put an army in the field. The British and the French were not able to withstand the onslaughts of the German war machine. The morale of the Italian army and people was honeycombed with German and Austrian propaganda. News of the headway German propaganda was making in Russia was increasingly disquieting. For these reasons the Executive Council sent a cable to the Workmen's and Soldiers' Council and deputies at Petrograd, assuring them that the American people and America's workers were whole-heartedly behind our government in the War and urging them to withstand the propaganda of the Kaiser's agents. We appealed to them to make common cause with us to abolish all forms of autocracy and absolutism.

Ambassador Francis replied to the State Department that my cable had been delivered to Tscheidze and Dr. Miliukoff and given to the press and that he thought it would have a good effect. Dr. Miliukoff I had met in 1905 during his visit to Washington. He called upon me at the Federation office and informed me of the reform movements then in progress in Russia. We then discussed Russian affairs in general terms. Although there had been no meeting in the meantime, a friendly feeling existed between us, and on the occasion of his visit to Washington in 1922 he again called upon me. But all our efforts to prevent the second Russian revolution failed.

The Russian nation had made stupendous sacrifices in the War only to find that hundreds of thousands of her young men had been needlessly killed because of the dishonesty of officials responsible for munitions and supplies. The revolutionists had made promises to fulfill which would necessitate an economic revolution. When the Kerensky régime hesitated to precipitate the second revolution while at the same time maintaining an army in the field in cooperation with the Allies, the Bolsheviki seized control. These pirates ran up the black flag over helpless Russia and declared war upon the established order about which the fabric of civilized life had been woven and Russia was transformed from an Ally into a menace.

The coming of Communism in Russia gave world-wide revolutionary propaganda an impetus—an incalculable menace to war production. Realizing that labor's clear thinking was the key to the war, I lost no opportunity to get first-hand information of Russian matters—official or unofficial. I met practically every group of Russian representatives that came to this country as well as Americans who returned. It was no great surprise to me when the Bolshevik dictatorship was established on the ruins of the Russian revolution. I had years before predicted to William English Walling what would happen if there should be an attempt to establish a Socialist commonwealth. Since there was in Russia no middle class, no working class movement as such, when the storm broke it would not bring progressive, upward steps, but tyranny would be followed by unbridled license. I made this prediction to Walling when he returned from Russia where he was admitted to the inner circles of the "underground" movement—that was, the Nihilist movement for the overthrow of the Czar's dynasty.

He had been trapped by the Czar's officials, arrested, placed in jail, and sentenced to death or a long term of imprisonment or transportation to Siberia. I had known Walling for several years and although not agreeing with his philosophy I had respect for him as a man, so that when the information came to us of his imminent danger, I went to the State Department and urged that our government intercede for him. He was released and almost immediately thereafter made his way to the United States.

The Communist propaganda of Lenine reinforced German propaganda for a negotiated peace. Both railed against "capitalist" governments and urged the "people" to take matters into their own hands. There followed a world-wide Socialist offensive to control public opinion. Should labor be lured by the Russian will-o'-the-wisp, the gains of years would be lost. No one knew the tactics of Socialists better than I and I had no choice but to assume leadership to protect American labor and American institutions. I found on a pretty broad scale the truth of what Ferdinand Laurrell had said years before, "It is not a pleasant task to destroy men's dreams." I redoubled my efforts to prevent our being lured to Stockholm.

There is something alluring in the hypothesis that in the midst of the passions of war and the strife of the battlefield men can come together and decide their difficulties by appeal to reason.

At no time in my life did I have to work harder to prevent the labor movement from chasing a rainbow than when the international Socialists began sending invitations for war-time conferences of the working men of all countries. That was the time, they argued, for wage-earners to assume leadership in international relations and by simple conversations to vanquish capitalism in all countries. There is no more demoralizing theory than that which imputes all human evils to capitalism or any other single agency. That kind of thinking slurs over individual responsibility and moral issues.

I believed that the German government, finding itself defeated in its military objective, was seeking to mobilize forces that would enable the Central Allies to make the best possible terms of peace. There was war-weariness in both France and England, for there comes a time when human flesh revolts against such destruction of life as was taking place on the battle-fields. For four years these two countries had been pouring out their national and human treasure. There had developed in both countries groups of defeatists who would have been glad to have ended the destruction of human life on almost any terms. There were others who, while they believed the War was necessary to establish certain principles, still honestly believed that the declarations of some international conference would break the morale of the German nation and army. Despite the demonstrations of that World War, these theorists believed that it would be possible for a group within their own nations to act independently of their governments. They missed entirely the significance even of their own governments' acts in refusing passports to delegates wishing to attend the "international" conference. It was plain to all who wished to understand that no delegate to Stockholm from the Central Powers would be permitted to attend without the sanction and approval of the German government. Nor could any delegate whose acts were not pleasing to his government return home to spread propaganda in furtherance of his deed. Not only the personnel but the policies of their delegates would be dictated by Germany. The War was so universal in its effects that it would be impossible to discuss or decide peace aims without taking into consideration the forces that caused the War, and German delegates to that conference would be advised by the experts of the German government while other delegates would have to depend upon their own resources. Such an inequality in the discussion must inevitably affect conclusions. I believed that those who were advocating international labor conferences during the War were ignoring the facts of human nature.

But some of the leaders in the labor movements in the Allied countries finally succumbed to Stockholm and sought to commit their labor movements to its propaganda. The situation became serious indeed. On February 9, 1918, I received a letter from Arthur Henderson, dated January 16, asking on behalf of the Parliamentary Committee and the National Executive of the Labor Party that the A. F. of L. send representation to an inter-Allied conference to be held in London, February 20. Henderson was, as I have said, the leader of the English group of "negotiators." That conference was to consider war aims and arrangements for working class representation in connection with any official peace conference. Henderson stated that although they had had requests from American Socialists, the Federation was the only American body that was invited to the conference. The letter was received too late for delegates to make the trip from America to England, so I kept the letter for the consideration of the Executive Council which was to meet in a few days. The Executive Council authorized me to cable fraternal greetings to the inter-Allied conference and to assure the conference that we were pledged and would give our man-power and wealth in the struggle to secure world-justice, freedom, and democracy. In my cablegram I stated our Executive Council unanimously declared that we could not meet during the War with the representatives of those who were aligned against us in this struggle for freedom, but we hoped they would sweep away the barriers which they raised between us.

Somehow or other, the British press got my cable and there had been inserted in the text a sentence which made it appear that the Executive Council was seeking to imply that the inter-Allied conference had its origin in German influences. When this version of my cablegram was published, Henderson and Thomas gave out a correct copy and cabled me what they had done.

In the Allied labor conference of February, there was wide divergence of opinion. British labor was definitely split. The British Federation of Trade Unions, like us, was unwilling to meet with representatives of labor from enemy countries. The executives of the Labor Party and the British Trade Union Congress under the leadership of Henderson were advocating the Stockholm idea. As a result, the London conference adopted a proposal to send delegates to an "international" labor conference. When America with her vast resources entered the War, the balance was weighted against Germany so heavily she could not hope to win unless other factors could be brought into the situation. No more strategic advantage could have been secured for their side than to enlist working people of the Allied countries in support of a movement to negotiate a peace with Germany at a time when she would be likely to secure most favorable terms. Germany hoped to retrieve her military losses through diplomatic negotiations.

Since I gave unreserved approval to the Fourteen Points of President Wilson, I could find no good reason why I should attempt to mobilize a group within our nation to hold conversations with the enemies of our country. My conception of internationalism was altered by my war experiences—the alteration of one of addition, not subtraction. I learned that one had to be a nationalist before one could be an effective internationalist. It was characteristic of the individualism of America expressed in genuine absence of class stratification, that financiers, industrialists, farmers, wage-earners, and every group were solidly behind the President and that allegiance to the government took precedence over all other relationships. Each felt that his country was in danger and responded accordingly. We did not feel that we had to connive with wage-earners of other countries to forge a club against our own republic. We had determined with our own government our attitude as to the War and we saw no inspiration in the suggestion that we meet with those enemies who had cast their lot in support of the "junkerdum" of Prussia. The liberals and the practical trade unionists of all Allied countries had accepted President Wilson's leadership and to my mind only frank adoption of his war aims by enemy countries could be accepted as evidence of good faith and that position could be expressed only by suing for peace. German and Austrian labor must deal with their own political problems in order to earn the right to participate in discussion of terms of peace. I think I have had as much emotional idealism about internationalism as any living soul, but I held that the Germans must move back from Belgium and French territory as an evidence of good faith before conference was possible.

The news of British labor's "liberal" concept of international relations was given widest publicity by the intelligentsia in this country. As usual, they began a campaign to propagate the new thought. They were ably assisted by all German propaganda agencies.

The propaganda made little headway. We planned a Labor's Loyalty Week for the week which included Washington's birthday. As our guests for the event we had a mission of four British trade unionists. The chairman of the mission was W. A. Appleton, secretary of the British Federation of Trade Unions.

Paul Kellogg, one of the officious intelligentsia, ventured to challenge Appleton's right to represent the British —Appleton who had for years been an elected executive of a British trade union organization. At a public meeting in New York City, one of these self-constituted labor "experts" undertook to take American labor to task for its policies. How I riddled Kellogg's statement! He manifested no attempt to reply and the meeting was turned from passive thinking to a unanimous outburst of patriotic feeling. Shortly afterwards came the rumor that Henderson was sending a mission to convert me and American labor to his way of thinking. But I was denied the satisfaction of such a conference.

From that time on came many repeated requests for me to go to England and suggestions that it would be helpful to me to bring back to American labor a first-hand report of conditions our soldiers were meeting in the trenches. I knew that the rank and file of British labor did not follow Arthur Henderson's fantasies. That was evident in their war service, and I began to plan how best to get a manifestation of that real conviction. It seemed to me I was under obligation to go to Europe to bear a personal message from American labor.

The time had come for me to accept the many urgent invitations from governments and labor movements of Allied countries. The Ambassadors from England, France, Belgium, and Italy had transmitted many such requests.

CHAPTER XLIII

As the War continued to take its frightful tolls in human life, and the defeatists and pacifists spread the seeds of dissension and false hopes, the virile courage and clearcut declarations of American labor stood out in sharp contrast to the hesitant attitude of labor in other countries.

When the labor situation in our country was in a fairly satisfactory condition I was convinced that the service I could render by going to Europe was more than I then could do at home. I began to make my plans. Both from government and labor sources as well as individuals urgent requests tantamount to demands were made upon me which indicated a real opportunity to serve would be provided. The American government was anxious that representatives of American labor go to France for a visit to the American army. It was thought that a personal message from such a group bringing back an account of the hardships and dangers our soldiers were enduring in France would react upon ship-building. We were assured that all possible pains would be taken to enable the Labor Mission to actually get into the trenches and realize the lot of the soldiers in France. My purpose was in part to make a sort of personal inspection of our fighting-line extending from our factories, fields, and mines across the bridge of transport service between the New World and the Old to the armies in the field. I felt that there was something that ought to be done and I wanted to do it. The American Labor Mission which was sent abroad in the spring of 1918 brought back from British workers and British officials insistent invitations to me. The St. Paul convention, to which the American Labor Mission made report, authorized the Executive Council to arrange for my going. One of the men elected as fraternal delegate to the British Trade Union Congress found himself unable to go and the Executive Council directed me to go in his place. W. J. Bowen was the other delegate. The other members of the mission were John P. Frey, Charles L. Baine, Edgar Wallace. Guy H. Oyster was our secretary.

I cabled to Arthur Henderson that inasmuch as there had not been sufficient time to permit us to have representatives in the February Allied Labor Conference, if a conference were arranged while our delegates to the Derby Congress were in England we would be glad to participate. It was quickly agreed between Bowerman of the Parliamentary Committee, Henderson of the British Labor Party, Jouhaux of the French Federation of Labor, to call such a conference and our Federation was invited to send delegates. To me the whole situation was so simple that I wanted to state the case as I saw it to European labor. I knew that their oratory and their complicated philosophy would not rush me off my feet, but I could demand a hearing for plain speaking and the real things with which we had to deal.

Our preparations were rapidly made and we secured passage on the troop ship *Missanabie* sailing Aug. 16, 1918, from "an Atlantic to a British port." Leaving John Alpine on guard as acting president to assure the preservation of satisfactory conditions, I left for my new field of work. We were not told of the time of sailing but were notified to be in New York at a certain day. Thus began our experiences with actual war conditions. Ours was one of fourteen troop ships carrying forty thousand American soldiers. While our ships and convoy assembled, we anchored off quarantine for thirty-six hours. With all the portholes and doors closed, the intense heat of the August nights was most oppressive. This condition continued each evening and all night throughout the voyage. We were hermetically sealed. The first night out under heavy convoy we started an uncertain zigzag across the Atlantic. We were made to realize the seriousness of our undertaking by life-boat assignments, frequent life-boat drills, regulations requiring us to wear or carry life-preservers at all times, the order to "close all doors and portholes at night" as well as restricted use of lights. Even smoking on deck was prohibited at night.

Our ocean trip gave us time for conferences and discussion so that we were a unit when our work began on the other side. The members of our delegation met almost daily. On the trip over I made three addresses, two to the enlisted men and one to the officers and civilian passengers in the lounge or saloon. The trip was very pleasant during the day and lasted eleven days. When about a day and a half out from Liverpool the whole fourteen ships were stopped and British and American destroyers rushed in all directions. There was evidence that submarines were about. After laying to in Liverpool the *Missanabie* started on its return trip to the United States and eight hours out from Liverpool was sunk by a submarine with a loss of sixty-four lives, including many of the crew who had served us so well.

On August 28 we arrived in Liverpool. The reception committee waiting to receive us consisted of the Acting Lord Mayor of Liverpool, representatives of the British and American governments and several representatives of labor. The official of the War Department, who was in charge of the arrangements for our reception, enforced an order that none but authorized persons were to be allowed on the platform; thus the reporters were all kept at a distance. However, after I got into the army automobile and we had gone a little distance I saw the reporters all standing on the street and at a little distance. Recognizing some who were old friends I directed the chauffeur to stop and I got out and talked a bit with the boys and permitted them to take a few snapshots. I gave them the following for publication:

The American Labor Mission has come to Great Britain and expects to go to France and Italy to bring a message of good-will, co-operation, and determination to the workers of the three countries to aid in strengthening the bonds of unity that we may all stand behind our respective democratic governments to win the war for justice, freedom, and democracy.

The incident was typical of the whole trip. Everywhere I went, people knew me by name and they knew I had nothing personal to gain, but that in the War, as before, I had at heart only human welfare. In a way my trip was a Paul Revere mission to warn of danger and rally men in defense of that which makes life worth while. The American Embassy detailed W. H. Buckler to assist our mission. Captain Saunders was the British *liaison* officer to our delegation. Their fine sympathy and understanding made their assistance of highest value. Buckler went with us throughout the whole trip. We were received by the Mayor, after which we went to London.

George Barnes was at the station to receive us, together
with an under-secretary of the War Office and many labor
men and old friends. We made the Savoy Hotel our headquarters. Immediately following our arrival, a number of
men came to see me from the British government, the
American Embassy and many labor organizations. In addition, many personal friends came.

After a late luncheon, Mr. Barnes, Captain Saunders,
Charles W. Bowerman, and other labor men joined us. We
discussed general problems and also went over a tentative
arrangement for our itinerary for the next few days. Then
I went to my room to prepare to take a walk around the
Strand and the Thames Embankment, a neighborhood which
was familiar to me through my two previous visits to London. When I emerged from the hotel, however, and walked
to the corner of the Strand, the utter darkness of the streets
and all surroundings appalled me. To say there was darkness does not convey it at all—there actually was no light.
Once in a while there was a little bulb with a hood over it
which gave light for a radius of two or three feet on the
street. I saw outlines of taxicabs and other vehicles and
then figures passed to and fro which I knew to be human
beings though they were not otherwise recognizable. The
fact of the citizens of the towns of the Allied countries
living for four years with darkness in the streets and limitations on lighting in their homes and other rationing
regulations made its deep impression upon my mind and I
no longer wondered or even doubted how the people felt
toward the cause. I was not so familiar with the neighborhood as to warrant my groping in the darkness, and after
standing quietly and observing what I could, I returned to
the hotel and dictated to our secretary my first report to the

United States, recounting the trip to England and my impressions in brief.

On the first Saturday we were in London, about eleven o'clock in the evening, we were strolling, as best we could, about the streets where the theater crowds had just come into the busy thoroughfares. All of a sudden the skies were illuminated by hundreds of searchlights. Upon inquiry I learned that a German air-raid was anticipated and that the government agency had been signaled to that effect so that all anti-aircraft machines could be ready. It was the first air attack I had witnessed. The lights crisscrossed in the heavens and though momentarily bombing might be expected the lights were a relief to the people. Indeed, the people on the streets expressed their feelings by singing, whistling, and cheering.

Along the streets of London there were signs directing the people to places of safety in case of air-raids, such as underground and subway stations.

My first duty on reaching London was to visit the American Embassy. Because of ill health, our Ambassador, Mr. Walter Page, was then in Scotland, but I had the pleasure of meeting Mr. Thomas Nelson Page, our Ambassador to Italy. Mrs. Walter Page gave us a luncheon at the Embassy which was both interesting and charming. This was one of the many delightful social courtesies arranged for us, which served as opportunities to gather persons to hear the message of America's workers. On this whole trip I spoke wherever I had any kind of engagement. In the evening we went to the American Officers' Club which I addressed. Tentative plans were made with Admiral Sims for us to visit the American fleet. Next day I had conferences with the Belgian Minister, General Biddle, and

Admiral Sims to arrange our schedule. Everybody was anxious to help us to see as much of the war situation as could be crowded into our itinerary.

On Thursday morning as I had done on my two previous trips to England, I went down to see my old home in Spital-fields. I wanted to see the old house and dream again the boy's life that I had lived in that little two-story building. As I drove into the street it seemed absolutely unchanged except perhaps a few shades dingier. News travels rapidly on the East Side and it was not long before there was a crowd around the little house. There was one old woman in the crowd who claimed she recognized me and that she had known me when I was a boy. I also visited the school in Bell Lane where I received my four short years of school-ing and addressed the children there.

In accord with my wishes, it was arranged that one of my first trips in London should be to the Dartmouth Hospital which was the American base hospital near Lon-don for wounded American soldiers. They gave me a wonderful reception and of course I talked to them alto-gether after I had gone through several of the wards and shaken hands with the men, saying a word of cheer to each. It was wonderful to see their courage and to hear them hope soon to be fit again to re-enter the ranks. Afterwards I had an engagement with the Bishop of Oxford who was about to visit America.

Requests for conferences, public speeches, and other services as well as social courtesies were so numerous that it was not humanly possible to do all the things I was asked to do. My first care was to serve our common cause. I met with the officials of British labor in both official and private conferences to contribute to a real understanding of labor in the English-speaking countries. I was not concerned with the differences between the groups in British labor but with the welfare of all labor the world over.

There were a number of my relatives still in London. Many of them came to see me and others sent word that they were anxious to meet me. The first Sunday that I spent in London I made use of one of the government automobiles put at my disposal and I visited many members of my family, some of whom I had never met before. The members of the family located in England had drifted apart. The occasion of my visit to two of them brought about an arrangement by which we were all to meet about two weeks later, after my return from the Derby Trade Union Congress. It was my hope—and I was glad in its accomplishment—that all the members of the family should attend a family reunion, the first in twenty-five years. The oldest of the gathering of about forty was Clara Gompers Le Bosse, sister of my father. She was revered by all. Her husband was a Frenchman who had been employed in the London mint. Their son, Louis, with whom she lived, was a printer. As they lived among Frenchmen, most of whom were also employed in the mint, Aunt Clara spoke French as fluently as English. A most happy result of our family meeting was that Samuel von Flyman, finding that his Aunt Clara Le Bosse was dependent upon her son, Louis, who had a large family, there and then declared that he would give Aunt Clara a generous monthly allowance. He told Aunt Clara. She at once imparted the good news to me and I took occasion to announce it to all the assembled members of the family. They greeted it with manifestations of appreciation and gratitude. Samuel owned a wholesale china store. He was the son of Emanuel and Clara Gompers von Flyman. His mother's father, Emanuel Gompers, had been the first large diamond dealer in England. It is usual in any family gathering to take a photograph of the young and the old and the middle-aged, and a group photograph of the London Gompers family was taken in the backyard of the humble residence of Louis Le Bosse.

The first official engagement of the Labor Mission was August 30, a luncheon given by the British government at the Carlton Hotel. Among the distinguished persons present were George M. Barnes who presided, Mr. Lloyd George, Viscount Milner, Winston Churchill, Lord Robert Cecil, the Earl of Reading, Austin Chamberlain, General Jan Smuts, Stanley Baldwin, Sir Herbert Beerbohm Tree, H. H. Hyndman, Sir Leo Chiozza Money, Victor Fisher, Sir Stephenson Kent, Sir Johnson Forbes-Robertson, Sir David Shackleton, Sir Guy Calthrop, George C. Roberts, and J. R. Clynes. English labor men were among the guests. The luncheon was attended by representatives of all shades of opinion, governmental and private groups. I sat between Mr. Barnes and the Prime Minister. The occasion was a genuine tribute to labor.

In welcoming our mission officially and referring to me personally, Lloyd George said he was glad to present a man known internationally who was one of the very few people who approved of him before the War. He pointed out that I had devoted my life and purpose to democratic progress and was fighting the same battle now in the War as I was before the War. Turning to me he said, "Mr. Gompers, we were not always accepted as we are now, but we have never wavered from the ideals of justice, freedom, and humanity." There were other addresses made by

George Barnes, George F. Roberts, and the British Ambassador to Washington, Lord Reading. Of course, I was asked to speak and I did, making what I felt to be a telling war speech.

The following night a dinner was given us at the House of Parliament by George M. Barnes. Some of the foremost active men of England were present. It was a gratification to attend a labor dinner given in that historic place by labor's representative in the War Cabinet and to find Lord Bryce, Sir Arthur Balfour, Austin Chamberlain, in common counsel with Ben Tillett, J. R. Clynes, F. Hodge, and W. A. Appleton.

On the second Sunday of our stay in England we left London for Derby to attend the opening of the British Labor Congress. As very inadequate hotel provisions had been made for our party, the Mayor insisted that we be his guests until rooms could be placed at our disposal in the hotel which was labor headquarters. In the throngs of British labor men I met next morning were many old friends. In talking with them I found the sturdiness of fiber which reassured me that British labor would do its part. Further evidence I saw in the munitions and war production centers we visited. My firmly established policy to respect an organization's right to make its own decisions guided me safely through pitfalls set for me. I carefully confined my declarations to American labor and refrained from criticism or advice upon issues dividing British labor.

The jubilee meeting of the Trade Union Congress was held in Central Hall. There were about nine hundred delegates attending. J. W. Ogden was the presiding officer. Mayor E. J. Hulse presented the Congress a civic welcome in which he referred to the American delegation, which brought from the congress an enthusiastic ovation. The presiding officer's address was not a clear-cut declaration of policy, but was in part dangerously near pacifism.

In the opening session of the congress the Parliamentary Committee presented a resolution to be sent to Sir Douglas Haig, Sir David Beatty, and Lord Wier, congratulating the army and the navy and air-forces on their magnificent devotion and courage during the long struggle against Prussian militarism.

For midday luncheon we were the guests of the Merchant Seamen's League to meet M. W. Hughes, the Prime Minister of Australia, the chief speaker at the luncheon.

The second day of the congress was the time for receiving messages from fraternal delegates and others. Mr. Bowen spoke first and I followed him. After reminding the congress that this was the third time I had been privileged to address the body, I summarized the progress of human liberty in the new world within my experience, beginning with the Civil War which was in progress when I first came to the United States, pointing out the special significance to human liberty of the provisions of the Clayton Anti-Trust Act and the Seamen's Law. I then gave an interpretation of the World War as I saw it and said it was a war which held in the balance either the destruction of freedom or the destruction of autocracy. I told what we in America were doing for that War and I said that we would not prolong the War a single minute beyond what was necessary to assure the ideals for which we had been fighting, but I would be unwilling to shorten it one hour if it meant that the German military machine remained unbroken.

Arthur Henderson followed me, conveying the greetings of the Labor Party. There was little of pacifism or dangerous internationalism conspicuous in his speech. World-attention had been focused on that meeting which made it impossible to repeat things previously said in executive meetings.

During a lull in the affairs of the congress, I had the opportunity of a conference with Mr. Henderson in an ante-room and there I told him of the achievements of American labor in the past twenty-five years in our improved economic standards of life and in legislative achievements both in the Congress and state Legislatures. At the close of the conference I asked Mr. Henderson whether he could compare the achievements of labor of Great Britain, as to its political and economic movements, with what we had accomplished, and at last he very reluctantly admitted that we had surpassed them. I feel quite sure that the conference with Mr. Henderson had some influence upon him in the course which he pursued in the inter-Allied and Socialist and Labor Conference which began September 17.

My first real encounter with Henderson came after the congress. We were asked to attend a joint conference of the Parliamentary Committee and the Executive Committee of the Labor Party. That conference was held after the Trade Union Congress had adjourned. We met at a tea given by the two executive bodies. When we entered the conference room, tea was being served. We took our seats well in the middle of the hall. Mr. Henderson, Mr. McGirk, chairman of the Labor Party, and Mr. Stewart Bunning who had just been elected chairman of the Parliamentary Committee were well up in front. After Mr.

McGirk and Bunning had made introductory statements, Mr. Henderson arose and said substantially that the Allied Labor and Socialist Conference was called at the request of Mr. Gompers. He reported that there had been conferences between the executives of the Labor Party and the Parliamentary Committee and that they had been in communication with the French Federation of Labor and with the French Socialist majority and minority groups and that as a result a conference was to be held in London. The French bodies expressed regret that the Socialist Party of America had not been invited and stated that they would insist that either that party be invited or that the British Federation of Trade Unions, of which Mr. Appleton was executive, be eliminated. He reported that British labor had agreed upon a program which would be submitted to the conference in printed form and which he hoped would be approved. I had not intended to be the floor leader of our delegation, but Mr. Henderson's first remark made it necessary for me to arise, for I was the only man who had the accurate information with which to correct his statement.

I called attention to his misstatement and quoted from memory my cablegram, that if a conference of the bona fide labor movement bodies of the Allied countries was called the American Federation of Labor would be represented by delegates. I made the statement coolly and with an emphasis which stung him. He had the records with him and referred to them as though to read them, but hesitated. When he referred to having the records present, I insisted that he read from the record. He did so to his own discomfiture.

In reply to the protest of the French bodies, I replied

that there was no such thing as an American Socialist Party but a German adjunct in America of the German Socialist Party.

I declared that the American Federation of Labor yielded not an inch to any other organization to represent labor of America. We regretted the decision to deny representation to the British Federation of Trade Unions, but inasmuch as we held that determination of British representation lay with British labor, it was not within the power of the American delegates to impose or to attempt to impose our judgment upon labor of Great Britain. While we felt the decision was regrettable, we felt that we must accord to labor of Great Britain the rights upon which we insisted for ourselves.

On Saturday, September 7, the members of our delegation returned to London. Our delegation during the railway trip discussed the February conference and the tentative proposals as outlined to us by Mr. Henderson at Derby at the conclusion of which I asked my assistants' attention and our secretary to take stenographic notes and one by one I outlined the proposals which we, as an American delegation, would submit to the conference the week following. On Tuesday, September 10, we left for Scotland. This trip had been arranged by Admiral Sims.

The representatives of organized labor of Edinburgh, as well as the city officials, extended by telegraph an invitation for me to come to that city. It was impossible to give definite answer much in advance, for while our purpose was clear, our arrangements were always subject to change. As soon as we could decide I telegraphed to the president of the Edinburgh Trades Council and also to the Lord Provost (the Mayor) that I would be there the following evening and would be glad to deliver an address at any mass meetings arranged.

On the way to Edinburgh we stopped at Rosyth to visit the British and American fleets. Every arrangement had been made for our convenience. At the pier there was a launch in readiness to take us to Admiral Rodman's flagship, the *New York*. Admiral Rodman greeted us each in turn heartily and personally conducted us to every part of that wonderful ship. He invariably pointed to his men and mentioned their efficiency and gave them all credit. It was such generous and fine-spirited compliments which showed the high type of the man.

After we had been on board an hour, a messenger from Admiral Sir David Beatty came aboard and presented the compliments of Sir David and invited Admiral Rodman, another member of our party, and me to a luncheon on board the *Queen Elizabeth*, Admiral Beatty's flagship. Shortly afterwards John Frey and I got into the launch which took us to the *Queen Elizabeth* where Admiral Beatty welcomed us most heartily. He took me to his cabin where upon his desk he showed me the portrait of his American wife and their two children. He talked freely and spoke of hopes which had been revived although confidence had never been lost.

There were about twenty in the party to whom luncheon was served. Conversation became general, pleasant, and intensely interesting. The cordiality and camaraderie between Admiral Rodman and Admiral Beatty was especially noticeable. After luncheon we sat about for a while and then one of the swiftest launches in the British navy was assigned to us to visit all the American and British warships. There were seventy-five miles of these floating

fortresses and more than ever I felt assurance of the outcome of the world-struggle.   It was a curious sight to see
the great captive naval balloons being lowered to the decks
of the ships to which they were anchored as they passed
under the great Firth of Forth bridge.

After landing we went to Edinburgh to the hotel and
in the evening I addressed a tremendous mass meeting of
more than five thousand in Usher's Hall and I was later
informed that thousands of people were unable to gain
admittance.   The Lord Provost presided in all his regalia
and several members of the Common Council surrounded
him.   He introduced me to the audience in glowing terms
and mentioned the encouraging message which he was sure
I would bring.   At the conclusion of my speech the president of the Edinburgh Trades and Labor Council offered
a motion which was duly seconded and adopted expressing
to me the thanks of Edinburgh, of Scotland, and of the
Allied cause.

The following day we visited many places of interest
in the vicinity of Edinburgh.   It was my first visit to the
city and I was anxious to see some of the old castles.

From Edinburgh we went to Glasgow where we were
welcomed by the chairman of the western section of the
Scottish War Aims Committee and a number of others
including the American Consul and representative labor
men.   After visiting the City Chambers we motored to
the shipyard of John Brown & Company, Clydebank,
where we were received by Admiral Green and others including the directors of the company.   Notice of our visit
was too brief to permit arrangements for a public meeting,
but a luncheon was arranged by the War Aims Committee
at which prominent municipal officers and labor representa-

tives were present. As we were eating lunch we heard a
band in the street and the sound of marching troops. When
I learned that they were Americans, I rushed down to the
street, followed by practically all of the party, where we
stood to watch our boys go by. There were about four
thousand in all and many recognized me. It touched me
very deeply to have those soldier boys greet me by name
as fellow-workers.

Afterwards we visited the ship-building plants and witnessed the entrainment of two thousand American soldiers.
We left Glasgow to go to Blackpool. An invitation was
extended to me by the Mayor and the City Council to
participate in delivering an address at Blackpool, that body
having decided to give the freedom of the city to Lloyd
George. It was a roundabout train ride, but we reached
Blackpool Friday evening. An almost continuous down-
pour of rain had prevailed in England for several days,
and flags, bunting, and decorations at Blackpool looked a
sorry sight. We were met by a committee of representatives of the city and the labor movement and taken to the
reception room above the Mayor's office, where a body of
forty men of all walks of life were assembled. The Mayor
and his wife were doing the honors. There was an hour
of pleasant conversation and refreshments were served.
A message came that Lloyd George had taken cold at Manchester and had a high fever, making it impossible for him
to come to Blackpool. Of course, parades and all play-
time were abandoned.

I was escorted in the council chamber by the Mayor
who had me seated beside him on the dais. Upon the
Mayor's suggestion a motion was made and adopted that
Samuel Gompers be requested to speak to the gathering

formally extending the key of the city to Lloyd George. This I gladly did, expressing the thought that Lloyd George was giving service both to his country and the world, and I took advantage of the opportunity to urge all to perform their duty in individual capacities. From Blackpool our delegation returned to London where the Inter-Allied Conference was to be convened on the following Tuesday.

The Inter-Allied Labor Conference was held in Central Hall, Westminster, beginning September 17. On the opening day of the conference, credential cards were sent to our hotel for us to fill out. Across the top of the card was "Inter-Allied Socialist Conference." I had no intention of putting my name on any such credential card. I called my associates for consultation. They shared my indignation. We had not come to England to attend an inter-Allied Socialist conference and we were not going to attend one. We decided to refuse to sign the credentials. On the opening day of the conference we presented ourselves in good time at Central Hall.

We talked with a number of men and women who came to greet us. When the delegates were about to convene in the hall, we presented ourselves at the door. There was a woman guarding the door who refused to admit us unless we showed credentials on cards furnished for that purpose. We advised her that we had the credentials from the American Federation of Labor which were the only credentials that we would present as we would not use cards. "Well," the answer came, "you cannot be admitted." We replied: "It may be true that we cannot be admitted, but we will not sign any such card. We have our credentials from the A. F. of L. signed, and sealed, and will present them to any committee of the conference for scrutiny and recommendation, but we are not going to sign such a card."

Mr. Charles Bowerman, secretary of the Parliamentary Committee of the British Trade Union Congress, at that moment emerged from the door. He asked why we had not entered. I told him the situation and he directed that we be admitted. We entered the hall and presented our labor credentials. Mr. James Sexton, officer and representative of the Docker's Union of Liverpool, arose and called the attention of the conference to this situation, and declared that the American Federation of Labor delegates refused to sign any such document. He declared that it was not an Inter-Allied Socialist Conference, but an Inter-Allied Socialist and Labor Conference.

Mr. Arthur Henderson of the Labor Party made an explanation something to this effect: "It is really regrettable that such an error should have been made, but it has been made. It was due to the fact that the old card of credentials which had been used in former conferences was sent to the printer, no one paying any attention to it, and thinking it was all right." My comment was that politicians regarded labor as of so little consequence that the presence or absence of the name occurred to nobody.

We had determined to center our efforts on the following:

> First: Open sessions. In war-time men would restrain themselves from presentation of views which they would feel free to express in secret meetings.
>
> Second: American representation on the Committee on Resolutions and drafting.

> Third: Constructive declarations on peace aims,
> but unequivocal repudiation of conferences
> with labor of enemy countries.

European practices did not conform to our ideas of
justice or democratic deliberations. They were possible
largely because of the closed session rule. Minutes of proceedings were not published, but only such versions and
declarations as were prepared by a drafting committee
authorized to prepare publicity material. Much of the discussion and the secret declarations were of a very different
nature from what would have prevailed if the workers generally or the other groups of society had known what was
transpiring. In addition, the Drafting Committee was
chosen from those who were familiar with the secret activity
of the executives, and official declarations were made to
conform to secret purposes. Minutes of previous conferences had been written by Drafting Committees after adjournment.

To enter conference under such conditions was to concede defeat in advance, for irrespective of any agreement
reached declarations given to the public would conform to
those of the February conference. On the other hand, we
were in the right and could not help but win in open sessions.

All had expected me to take the lead. I believed it
was better to have the younger members of our group act
as a skirmish-line to draw the fire of the pacifists and pro-
Germans. For the first few days John Frey was our
floor leader and outside of asking a few questions, I
took no part in the discussion. The leaders of the
Stockholm Conference and "peace by negotiation" idea

reached the conclusion that I had "shot my bolt" and I was not going to mean anything in the conference. In the opening session John Frey presented our motion that the conference be open to the press and the public. In the discussion that followed we called attention to the fact that the labor movements of the Allied countries had consistently and with vehemence denounced secret diplomacy, that the A. F. of L. convention sessions were all open to the public to the fullest extent and capacity of the meeting halls; that we always saw to it that there was sufficient space in our halls to provide accommodations for the public and the press; that we could not consistently denounce secret diplomacy and at the same time hold secret sessions.

We were met with all kinds of practical arguments as to why the public should not be admitted, but with no substantial arguments for excluding the press. We therefore yielded one point, but refused to consent to the press being debarred. In making it possible for the press to report the proceedings, we knew that we had won our fight. In the first session our proposal for open sessions was adopted. Committee work was preliminary to floor discussions. The most important committee of all was the War Aims Committee. Mr. Frey was secretary and Sidney Webb was chairman. I advised Mr. Frey to fight in the committee. He did, and won. Mr. Webb imagined he was not only to write the committee's report but to read it. Frey came to me to talk over the situation. I said: "Mr. Frey, you are secretary. As such you are to write and to read the report. Stand by your guns." This experience is an indication of the methods by which not only some trade unions but the Socialist movements carried on the work—a parliamentary tactic which absolutely destroyed the functioning of democratic methods and placed the workers at the mercy of the "intellectuals" who had largely seized and dominated the movement. We dealt with the problem in our usual American fashion.

Frey and I were appointed on the Drafting Committee of which I was made either secretary or assistant-secretary. As we were constantly on the job, there was no chance to put anything into the record that was not accurate. The minutes of the September conference were never published during the War. However, we had galley proofs which we used and made public.

That procedure having been decided, speeches from a number of delegates were made which consumed nearly the entire first day and the following morning the business of the congress was begun. I sat and quietly observed, estimating the opinions and forces. There were eighty-one delegates present, representing over eleven and one-half millions of people. The report of the Credentials Committee made no recommendation upon voting systems. In view of the difficulties of agreeing upon a bloc system, a show of hands was to be had upon proposals. Then Jean Longuet, a French Socialist, displayed the usual Socialist animus in moving that the report be referred back because since the American Socialists were not represented the full quota of American votes ought not be given the A. F. of L. delegates. Vandervelde characterized Longuet's proposition as ridiculous and the French group was thrown into commotion.

I accepted the challenge and arose demanding the floor. I stood waiting for order to be restored and then I spared no force in telling Longuet we represented over three million wage-earners—and nothing but wage-earners. Longuet represented thirty thousand. I told him the conference could not override the right of the American labor movement to make its own decisions. That position was sustained by the conference.

On the second day of the conference I presented the war aims of the A. F. of L. I made no introductory speech because I wanted to focus attention upon the proposals. They were divided into two parts—basic principles and matters of vital interest to the wage-earners of all nations. There was no mistaking the clear terms in which the demand was made that war should be pursued to a successful conclusion as a necessary preliminary to the establishment of a just peace. The Parliamentary Committee submitted a document for British labor which was practically a repetition of the proposals adopted in February.

Proposals from individuals followed and became an avalanche when the chairman ruled that an individual might submit a resolution not approved by his delegation. As was anticipated, the pacifist section made the most of the opportunity to ventilate their views which led to a lively scene. Pages of resolutions were submitted by individual members and the controversial nature of many of them led to much wrangling. "The British delegates," as Mr. Gosling lamented, "came there as a united force, but no sooner had they got to work than the independent labor party wing proceeded to split their ranks by ridiculous resolutions." These resolutions were read by the speaker. After a number of most wildly impractical resolutions were submitted by pacifists and read by the presiding officer, James Sexton solemnly introduced the following by way of comment:

That this conference recognizing that the Kaiser and his associates were initially responsible for the present World War, the
devastations, ruthless murders, infamous inhumanities practiced by
Germany, insists that there shall be no peace until the Kaiser and
his associates and all who agreed with him are hung on lamp-posts
without judge or jury.

Discussion of the Austrian peace notes to the Allied
governments and a declaration on Russia brought out in
strong relief the difference in the attitude of American labor
toward their government and that of the Socialists toward
what they termed their "capitalistic governments." They
were fundamentally at war with their governments and
had no confidence in them, while we had confidence in
President Wilson and that which he represented and gave
him whole-hearted support.

In one of my arguments at the conference I said:
"Socialism holds nothing but unhappiness for the human
race. It destroys personal initiative, wipes out national
pride—the hearthstone of a people's culture—and finally
it plays into the hands of the autocrats. One has only to
watch its ravages on the human soul—the soul without a
country—to know that Socialism is the fad of fanatics, the
sophistry of so-called intelligentsia, and it has no place in
the hearts of those who would secure and fight for freedom
and preserve democracy."

When on the third day it was time for me to assume
leadership of my delegation, I did so with precision and
force. That our work was effective was evident when
during the noon-time intermission Arthur Henderson went
to John Frey and begged him to intercede with me not to
make his humiliation too great. The afternoon of the third
day was devoted to Russia, first a Russian declaration and
then a long address by Kerensky. During the whole after-

noon Socialism, the Socialist revolution, and similar conventional phrases completely eliminated such a robust word as labor. Just before the close of the session I remarked how strange it was not to hear the word "labor" used in such a conference and as a representative of labor I submitted that wage-earners should be called wage-earners and not Socialists.

On the last day of the conference came the real issue that had brought me to England—the adoption of labor's war aims. The previous conference in February declared for an international labor conference at which delegates from the Central Powers were to be admitted and pledged themselves to "endeavor by mutual agreement to arrange a program of action for a speedy and democratic peace." Thus upon the vital question they were pledged to demand of their respective governments the beginning for a negotiated peace with the Central Powers.

The statement of war aims prepared by the committee was a lengthy document. It began by welcoming the American Federation of Labor and recognized that the War was a conflict between autocratic and democratic institutions. It declared the unqualified determination of the conference to do everything within its power to assist the Allied countries in marshaling their resources to drive the armed forces of the Central Powers from the soil they had invaded and declared that those armed forces should be opposed as long as they carried out the orders or responded to the control of their militant autocratic governments. It then went on to approve and include the text of President Wilson's Fourteen Points, asked for labor representation at the Peace Conference, and put in a formulation of industrial standards. It regretted the position of the German Socialist majority and pointed out that their attitude was an obstacle to any international conference.

The report of the committee on war aims embodied the proposals of the American delegation and was satisfactory to me except the proposal for a labor conference in which all belligerent countries would be represented and a criticism of governments withholding passports from persons wishing to attend such conferences. I stated my objections emphatically.

In the discussion that followed, realizing that they were losing, the French renewed their attack upon the practice of voting by show of hands. There were vigorous protests from the majority of the French delegates and several British delegates, including Mrs. Philip Snowden. Jouhaux said that it was only because the conference was held in London that the British delegates were able to vote the others down and Mistral declared that if this were repeated the French delegates would leave the conference. A bloc system was agreed upon, allowing twenty votes to France, England, and the United States and proportionate allotments to smaller countries.

The discussion of war aims was initiated by J. W. Kneeshaw, a communist and one of the "wild men" from Scotland. He was a typical Independent Labor Party man. Mr. Kneeshaw was opposed to the essential features which the American delegation proposed to the conference and which were incorporated in the committee's report. He made a speech typical of the peace-at-any-price men who railed against capitalist government and regarded Socialism as the cure-all for every ill of life. That Kneeshaw's speech was made before the press of the world stirred the British delegates, for they could not condone it, despite the fact it was a bold statement of negotiated peace. Sidney Webb, James H. Thomas, James Sexton repudiated the Kneeshaw speech.

Mr. Maxton of Scotland challenged me to go to his country to convince them that this was not a war between capitalists. Maxton's challenge brought me to my feet. I told him I had been to Scotland and had a unanimous vote from the audience I addressed. When Maxton attempted to interrupt me, I fairly thundered at him, "I did not interrupt you, sir, hold your tongue." And he held it. Then I told him that the president of the Edinburgh Trades Council and other officials had been on the platform at that meeting and had moved that I be given a vote of thanks for my presentation of the American position which was adopted by unanimous vote of the audience. As for Maxton and others like him, I exclaimed, "Oh, these ultra goody-goody men, I trust them not." When I referred to Kneeshaw and his friends as those who did not know what the war was about, Kneeshaw protested I was putting words into his mouth. With indignation I rejoined, "I would not put words into *your* mouth even if I had the power, for I know they would come out perverted." Socialists the world over are of the same mental caliber—there is only one way to deal with them—don't argue, just tell them.

The recommendation of the Inter-Allied Labor Conference declared that so long as the German majority did not accept the war aims submitted to them by this London Conference, they created an obstacle to the holding of an international conference. There was a motion to substitute "difficulty" for "obstacle," but that was defeated. Then I proposed the amendment, "That we will meet in conference with those of the Central Powers who are in open revolt against their autocratic governments." Of course, my amendment was lost, but I had put into the records and the minds of the delegates the real meaning of the recommendation we had adopted.

The report of the Committee on War Aims was adopted by an overwhelming vote. That Allied labor document was an unequivocal statement that offered no leniency for the foes of democracy. The countries represented and the personnel of delegates differed from the February Conference in only one striking exception—America was there!

The third day I was accused, after the American program had been adopted in every detail, of running the A. F. of L. steam-roller over the conference. To this I replied that if five Americans unacquainted with European parliamentary procedure could put their program through a meeting of over seventy-four delegates familiar with these tactics, call it what they might, we were entitled to the victory won.

As a result of this conference, labor and Socialist representatives were pledged to return to their homes and devote their entire efforts to assist their respective governments in winning the war until such time as the Central Powers occupied no foot of invaded territory and their military machine was no longer a menace. Three days after the conference of September 17-21, 1918, had adjourned, Ambassador Page told me while in the Embassy that he had received word that the printed proceedings of this conference which proved that the American trade union movement had completely broken down the German propaganda, had been delivered and placed on the desks in Berlin and in Vienna. Mr. Page also stated that it would be impossible to calculate the influence this would have upon the German government and people and he was convinced that the last hope of Germany for a negotiated peace had been destroyed by the declarations of the London Conference; that from his information when the military forces of Germany were halted and driven back, the hope of the German government was to destroy the morale of the great masses of the working people of the Allied countries.

The German press had convinced the German people that the American trade union movement would fall in line with the policy already adopted by the trade unionists and Socialists in the Allied countries at the Allied conference in February, and this was the principal source for maintaining German morale. When the printed records of the Labor and Socialist Conference of September 17 were placed in Berlin and Vienna, the last hope of weakening Allied morale was gone and it became evident that the policy of the American Federation of Labor had superseded that of the February Conference.

The day following this conference, September 21, we were given a public reception at the Savoy Hotel at which all different groups of British labor men were present. We were also received by Winston Churchill, Minister of Munitions, and given a luncheon in Whitehall Palace where we met the representatives of the world's press.

On the following day, Sunday, I attended the meeting of the London Trades Council and delivered an address on America and the War. It was in that meeting that a few men tried to heckle me. When the interruptions began in the form of questions or comment, the chairman tried to maintain order and some of my friends and the more fair-minded men wished to eject the interrupters. However, I assured the chairman and the audience that I was quite able to take care of myself and after a bit the disturbance subsided. In answer to one of the statements of the heckler who called attention to strikes in America, I referred to the strike of the policemen and the bus and tramway drivers then in progress in London. When I referred to the number of persons involved, a number of estimates were offered from different parts of the hall, each number larger than the preceding. Beginning with something like six or eight thousand, the number was rapidly increased until I put the whole dispute into the form of an auction and asked for the highest bidder. In the laugh that followed all desire for heckling disappeared.

On the following Monday, our full delegation was received by His Majesty, the King, at Buckingham Palace. We presented ourselves and I, as the chairman of the mission, was ushered into the large room where the King was waiting for me. We had a conference of thirty-five or forty minutes. Several matters were discussed and he emphasized the situation which was being presented regarding Australasian territories, formerly German possessions, and other unprotected small islands in the Pacific. He urged me to communicate these suggestions to President Wilson and that some form of trusteeship should be undertaken of these territories under the authority of the American government. On my return to the United States I sought and obtained conference with the President and conveyed to him the message. But to return to the visit to the King—at the end of our discussion Queen Mary was ushered in and I was presented to her. We had an interesting chat for about five minutes and then my associates of the delegation were presented to the King and Queen. A remark which I made caused both of them as well as my own delegation considerable laughter. In presenting them I gave them the positive assurance that His Majesty, King George, was one-hundred-per-cent British. We left London for Southampton on the following day, stopping at the American camp at Winchester where I addressed both officers and men.

CHAPTER XLIV

ON THE CONTINENT

From Southampton we went across to Havre and hence to Paris. On the Continent the nature of our mission assumed a somewhat different character, for there we were in the actual war zone. In that field everything was under military supervision, with General Pershing in command of American activity.

In Paris our commission was met by representatives of the French government, the American Embassy, the American marines, and the Franco-American Commission on War Affairs, Captain Flood, Captain Jackson, and representatives of French labor. My cousins, Louis Gompers and his wife Flore and their son Sylvan, were among the party in the Paris station.

Following a lifetime habit, my first move was to go to the headquarters of the organized labor movement. At the office of the Confédération Générale du Travail were my friend Keufer and other militant trade unionists. The French representatives in the Inter-Allied Conference were making to the Executive Board their reports on the work at London. We joined this group and the conference became general. French labor was sadly lacking in unity because cohesive forces that would have rallied all in support of a practical economic program were frittered away in doctrinaire discussions and ambitions to be "progressive" advocates of radical proposals. At the office I saw a number of women whom I recognized as strikers. Upon inquiry I was told that the midinettes of a famous Paris dress-making concern were on strike and were holding a mass meeting in the large assembly hall of C. G. T. headquarters. I went to the hall and addressed the strikers.

That evening I attended a fraternal dinner and reception given by the Executive Board of the C. G. T. where I presented greetings from American labor and told how we were conducting war production. In these meetings we met the leading men of the French labor movement, some of whom I had known for years.

On the following day the Minister of Foreign Affairs and the Foreign Office entertained us at luncheon. There were present M. Pichon, Foreign Minister; Ambassador William Short; Dubost, president of the Senate; Clemenceau, President of the War Cabinet; Colliard, Minister of Labor; Tardieu; Marquis de Chambrun; Keufer; Melville Stone; Captain Jackson, Commissioner of Labor of Pennsylvania; Arthur Fontaine, and others. At Clemenceau's request I visited his office the following day and also paid my respects to Marshal Joffre.

We also participated in a public meeting held by representatives of French labor. From the beginning of the war the French Socialist movement had been the football of minority leaders. With the first lure of fantasy emanating from the Zimmerwaldians, French Socialists lent themselves to each succeeding will-o'-the-wisp proposal that was designed to obscure real issues. It was a deplorable demonstration of the power of socialistic materialism to smother the spirit. It was these irresponsible groups that by presuming to speak for French labor prevented the world from appreciating the substantial group of militant French trade unionists which supported their government in the War. In France as in England the sturdy support of the masses of labor for the War was demonstrated by sustained war production. To hearten the great rank and file was my mission.

Several of the French Socialist Deputies were present, including a number of those who were not giving loyal support to the government. After I had spoken, some of them began to give expression to their unwholesome points of view, among them Merrheim, the executive officer of the metal trades. He was the worst of them all. He indulged in copious criticism of the Allied governments and no faint praise of the German government. To his credit it should be said that since the close of the War he has been an outstanding figure in constructive measures in the interests of labor and freedom. I listened to their fantastic and irrational proposals as long as I could endure them and then I tersely told them they were traitors to the cause of the people of France. This remark brought the meeting to an abrupt end, for such a verbal tumult followed that speeches were no longer possible.

I spoke to the American Luncheon Club at which gathering were practically all the Americans then in Paris in an official capacity. These luncheons and dinners, official and private, were not social entertainments, but were opportunities for busy people to get together with the least loss of time for an exchange of opinion. At all of them I was expected to deliver addresses, long or short. These functions were the means of bringing together very democratic groups. In speaking to French groups I had as interpreter a Frenchman who had been in the United States for several years as a newspaper man and later became secretary to Jouhaux.

On that day there had been published a reported statement from Germany that of all those fighting the Americans were the most bellicose. In my speech I referred to the comment and asked: "What the hell did they think we went into the War for? Did they expect to have a pink tea with us as invited guests?" The remark was so expressive of what all had in mind that it was heartily applauded. I brought very cheering news of the progress that was being made at home in war preparation and assured them that the country was united to fight the War to an end.

Walter Berry, who followed me, predicted that the War would end when we had a "Gompers' Peace" which would be inevitable. His term "Gompers' Peace" became almost a technical expression during the rest of my stay in France.

I had a strong desire to visit the Chamber of Deputies then in session. With my associates we quietly and unannounced took seats in the visitors' gallery. The presiding officer, the late President of the French Republic, Paul Deschanel, was in the chair. He recognized me, advised the Deputies that he had noticed distinguished visitors in the gallery, and felt that as a tribute to their presence the Chamber should be immediately adjourned to give an opportunity to the representatives to meet them. The Chamber was adjourned. M. Deschanel personally escorted us from the gallery to the lobby where he introduced us to the Deputies and after a most cordial reception insisted that I should deliver at least a brief address expressing my attitude toward the War. This I did.

The purposes of our mission to the Continent were two-fold: To carry the message of the spirit and purposes of war work in the United States, thereby bringing hope and encouragement to hearten the war-weary soldiers and civilians to further service, and to see what had been accomplished on the military fronts. It was a most positive acknowledgment of the essential service that labor was giving to war work that we were given opportunities to see everything that was being done. We saw every phase of military activity when the final campaign was gathering momentum.

While we were making travel plans, I stated that I wanted to visit the American front first. My request was based upon a purely sentimental feeling of the fitness of that procedure, notwithstanding the fact it meant retracing our steps and consequent loss of time.

On the morning of the day we left for the front André Tardieu took our commission to see the famous Citroen Munition works which were just outside Paris. There were about forty-five hundred munition workers, chiefly women, making shells. The management was thoroughly efficient and practical enough to know that efficiency is conditioned by understanding of human nature. There was a demonstration of the Citroen system under which all employed were paid within a ten-minute period. The canteen of the plant was brilliantly decorated with flags and the Citroen orchestra furnished inspiring music. We ate luncheon in the canteen with the munition workers and I made a brief talk, conveying greetings from the munition workers of America. During the luncheon André Tardieu stated that an official request for peace had been received from Bulgaria. The announcement brought enthusiastic cheers.

Then we started for the front where the fighting was on.

The Allies were steadily hammering the German line back. There was not a person or a motion in that area except under supervision and by direction. It is difficult to imagine the activity converging on the front. Over forty thousand Americans were being landed weekly. All roads were simply jammed with troops, supplies, lorries, etc.

We left Paris in army cars at 2:30 P. M. accompanied by an officer of the United States Intelligence Department, Lieutenant Lloyd Georgeson. The weather was beautiful, and the roads were magnificent. We moved swiftly to the southeastward through Fontainebleau, Vincennes, Troyes, 187 mils to Chaumont, American General Headquarters, where we spent the night. There Col. George T. Bowman received us and extended official hospitality.

Next day we motored northward to Neufchâteau; from thence to Domremy where we visited the home of Joan of Arc and the memorial chapel erected as her shrine; thence to Colombey-les-Belles, headquarters of General Foulois, chief of the United States Air Service, who showed the military map and told me he had been giving Metz "particular hell during the past few days." We saw a German plane that had been shot down that morning and the German-American aviators who had been captured. At Toul we had lunch and the news of the latest air record—our aviators had brought down two planes within four minutes after the alarm was sounded. When we entered Flirey, we found it in absolute ruins and were glad to accept from Red Cross workers doughnuts made in their camp kitchen by the road.

It was shortly after the attack on the St. Mihiel sector. We had left Neufchâteau to follow the trail of our victorious troops. As we left Flirey and reached the point on the plateau where the American troops had started their victorious march, my attention was attracted to a plot of ground where a number of small wooden crosses and mounds were located and I asked the American Colonel who was our escort what these mounds meant. He informed me that they covered the resting-places of American soldiers who had been living twenty-eight hours before. I felt that I could not go any farther until I had visited this spot, so our company walked over to the mounds and stood for a while, silent, with hats off. It seemed to me that no religious service could fully express our deep feelings and yet I could not leave the place without saying something and a speech would be inadequate. I had read that remarkable poem by Lieutenant-Colonel McCrae, "In Flanders' Fields" and the poetic response by the State Librarian of Ohio. Knowing that my friend, John Frey, had committed these poems to memory, I called upon him at these biers to recite them, which he did with great feeling. There were no tears shed, but the spirit of the poems and the sacred spot remained with us for some considerable time, and sadly, but spurred to duty, we moved forward.

We entered the valley, climbed the sides of Montsec, a point of land higher than the St. Mihiel plateau, the most important observation point of the German forces on the eastern side of the sector. The town of Montsec half-way up the mountain (held by the Germans for four years) had been so obliterated by shell-fire before the American attack that not only was it impossible to discover where the houses had stood but where the streets had been. Turning southward we passed through the newly captured territory, Pannes, Nonsard, Vigneulles, Heudicourt, Richecourt, Beaumont (all total ruins), debouching at a point which took us through Seicheprey where American troops had their first baptism of fire in the war. From Seicheprey we returned to Neufchâteau about nine o'clock in the evening. The Germans prepared for our entertainment by giving us an air-raid just as we sat down to our late evening repast.

Next morning we started again at ten o'clock visiting the sixth base hospital at Bazoilles. It consisted of Johns Hopkins' units, built within a year with capacity for thousands of beds. We were taken into the operating room where operations were being performed and a long row of wounded men on stretchers reached down a long corridor waiting their turn. It was horrible! We were taken to the gas ward where lay the blind and those gasping for breath.

Returning to Chaumont, we had dinner in the beautiful château which was General Pershing's home and I sent a telegram congratulating the General on the achievements of the American Expeditionary Forces. We returned to Paris by rail that afternoon and there I received a telegram from General Pershing in response to my greeting.

Next day we started to the other fronts. Again we were under military escort and followed orders so that we were able to see much in a limited time. We left Paris by train and arrived in Boulogne the following morning. We had breakfast at Hotel Folkstone where we were met by an officer from the Belgian G. H. Q. and were swiftly taken northward in automobiles through Calais to Dunkirk. In Dunkirk we were detained a few seconds by inspection of our military passes. We had not gone more than a quarter of a mile before we were looking back gratefully to that detention, for a shell from a Big Bertha landed in the middle of the narrow road, about fifty yards in front of us. It made a crater fully twenty feet in diameter and fully six feet deep. The explosion and the bricks and dirt killed Chinese workmen, two women, and some children. It was the first shell that had been shot into Dunkirk for thirty days. We stopped for lunch at Houchem, the Belgian General Headquarters, where we met the General Staff. Everything was thrown wide open to us and we were conducted to positions of greatest interest.

I was given an opportunity to talk to German prisoners. It was the first German I had spoken since the War began. Several thousand had been taken that day. I was astonished at their utter ignorance. They were convinced that only a few thousand Americans had joined the fighting ranks—nor could I dislodge that idea. The trip through that war-devastated area was depressing beyond the power of words to convey. There was wanton destruction—an industrial waste that in no way contributed to military gains.

The American *liaison* officer at the Belgian G. H. Q. was Captain Edward Cresson. When after the War we met at the Arms Conference in Washington, he asked me if I knew what a narrow escape I had when I was at the Belgian front. He told me of the order given by the German officers in command which, if carried out, would have made not only the Belgian soldiers but my associates and me prisoners of war. It happened that instead of the order being carried out, the German forces were made prisoners in large numbers.

After our trip to the Belgian front we returned to La Panne, the general headquarters of King Albert. There we went to the home of Captain Cresson to make ourselves presentable before being received by King Albert. His headquarters were by the North Sea. Following European custom I was received first and then the others of our commission. While we were being shown a map of recent Belgian advances, word was received that St. Quentin had fallen. It was not generally known that General Foch's general headquarters were in the next château to King Albert's. One of the Belgian officers pointed out the building to me, and though I felt a strong inclination to tell my associates, I kept the confidence and only told them after we were in the United States.

Captain Scott of the English army came with cars to take us to the British front. We moved down the military roads back of the line, many of which were almost deserted, and through towns like Hazebruck without population. The offensive against Cambrai was on and every road leading back was jammed with tanks, guns, munitions, troops, ambulances, etc. We reached the British General Headquarters, Tramcourt, in the evening, where we had dinner and slept.

Next day we saw a battle in progress—the industrial side as well as actual fighting.

Leaving the Château of Tramcourt, September 28, 1918, in our military machines, at 9 A.M., we mounted a slight elevation to pick up the old road constructed over two thousand years ago by the Romans which was the main highway between Paris and Dunkirk. To our right as we reached this road was an open level space including some two hundred acres and beyond this dense woods which, from the beginning, have been maintained as forests. It was upon this little piece of ground that one of the world's decisive battles was fought in which Henry V defeated the French forces, the battle of Agincourt.

At Arras we took the Cambrai road which was crowded with motor trucks, artillery, etc. Heavy loads were constantly tearing up the road so that gangs of repair men were busy all the time. In the fields on either side only stumps of trees were standing and the ground had been plowed by immense shells. Overhead were numerous aeroplanes at which the German aircraft guns were firing. We passed vast numbers of German prisoners being marched to the rear. When we reached Canadian headquarters on the Hindenburg line, General Curry took us out to see where they had broken that famous line with its barbed-wire entanglements forming circular traps, etc. Passing through the entire battle line gave me an opportunity of witnessing all of the activities connected with a modern battle, from the aeroplanes directing the fire of the battery and the observation balloons to the manual labor of rushing ammunition to the troops. I was strongly impressed with the industrial atmosphere of the undertaking.

Toward noon while about half a mile from No Man's Land, I came across an exceptionally large shell hole some sixty feet in diameter and twenty feet deep. As I reached the rim I found some forty or fifty soldiers, ranging from Scots in kilts to "artillerists," who seemed to wear overalls more than anything else. They were taking a few moments during the heat of the battle to eat. They were endeavoring to warm their canteens of coffee on fires they had built and the scene reminded me of a group of laborers gathered together during the noon-hour eating their lunch. Their jokes and conversation were not of war but quite the same as usually occurs among groups of workmen during the lunch-hour. When they saw me, they insisted that I should deliver a speech. Because of their appearance and the surroundings, I could do nothing but yield to my impulses and deliver a labor speech and, to my surprise as well as pleasure, I found that the majority of those present were, like myself, members of trade unions.

It was typical on this trip that in the camps, in the hospitals, in the boxing arenas, and elsewhere I was always spied and there were shouts for me to enter and to make a speech. It seemed that everywhere I went I was accepted. They believed and had faith in me that I was doing all that was physically and humanly possible to aid for victory and that I had their personal welfare at heart whether at the front or for the folks at home.

It had been arranged that I was to meet General Haig that day. The invitation was extended to an additional member of my party and Mr. Frey was to accompany me. One of the General's aides met us and took us to where the General was in the fields between Arras and Cambrai. The General was a wonderful man, a kindly gentleman; he impressed me as a soldier and a man. It was October 2, 1918, immediately after the battle of the Canal du Nord while General Haig was making a battle-field inspection with the object of assisting the several Engineering Corps in throwing bridges across the canal which would enable him to move his army with the necessary artillery to prepare for the final battle of Cambrai. He kept us with him several hours. The midday meal was an illustration of the General's delightful personality and democratic manner. At this point the battle-field was covered with dead horses, dead bodies, shattered trees. But one tree within miles had any branches and under this we had our lunch seated on the ground, Sir Douglas Haig placing his large hamper between his knees and examining its contents

in much the same manner as a customary picnicker, informing us as he went into the depths of the hamper of its
various items of food, which consisted of ham and tongue
sandwiches, hot coffee in a thermos bottle, etc. Coffee was
served in tin cups. After that he had a small cake of
chocolate which he broke into bits and handed a piece of
it to each of us. While we ate, the shells were screaming
over our heads and dropping in the fields about.

Sir Douglas Haig spoke with much feeling upon the
Italian-Austrian military situation, wishing that he could
get General Diaz to understand that the Austrian army
was in a much worse condition than the Italian. He said
that while it was true that Italy had very few in reserve,
yet they were better situated in respect to that than the
Austrians who had absolutely no reserves, either of arms,
munitions, food, or other supplies, and that they were practically incapable of withstanding any attack which the
Italians might make.

It made such an impression upon me that I felt that
inasmuch as General Haig had spoken so frankly and so
insistently upon this situation, I should interpret it as a message that he wanted to communicate to General Diaz.

While we were sitting upon the grass at our luncheon,
there flew over us numberless aeroplanes and some of them
bringing news of battles. About fifty feet from us a great
white tarpaulin about twenty-five feet square was spread
on the ground and this was the target at which the aviators,
observers, and messengers while flying would throw small
heavy cartons containing their written messages.

On two occasions during the luncheon, squads of cavalry
passed close by us, the first one coming from the battle-
field, covered with sweat, blood and wounds of strife, and

worn out. Seeing the squadron approach, Sir Douglas left us, met the head of the column, spoke to the officer in command, stood at salute while it passed, and spoke a few words to the officer in the rear. Sometime afterwards a squadron, moving toward the lines, passed near by and he again left us, spoke to the leading officer, stood at salute until the troop had passed. We could see his magic influence upon both columns.

Returning, he bade us adieu, mounted his horse and, attended by his aides, dashed away. He was as true a knight as ever lived in the days of chivalry.

From Canadian Headquarters we took cars for the Canal du Nord. The German dead were on all sides. We went through the town of Bourlon and over the military crest. We cheered the Camerons going into battle and they cheered back. We found a Canadian boy lying in a shell crater with his head blown off and went back to call the sanitary corps to bury him. In the distance Cambrai was in flames. General Bing was laying a barrage up the road to the right of Cambrai. We could see plainly less than six thousand yards. General McDonald told us we were witnessing the most wonderful piece of actual fighting he had seen, as the fighting had previously been on plains and flat country. The heavy artillery back of us was firing over our heads. We saw a British "sausage" balloon fall in flames, the victim of "lemon" bombs dropped by a German plane, the two pilots descending in parachutes. A hurried summons came for General McDonald who hastily bid us adieu. An advance had been ordered. Again we spent the night in Tramcourt.

Next morning we turned to the southward, through Doullens—the first place we had seen people living in their homes for some time—and on to Amiens. The Germans had been within seven miles of Amiens and the city was greatly damaged. The beautiful cathedral protected by sand-bags had on its altar the flags of the Allies including the Stars and Stripes. We ate lunch in the deserted plaza opposite the municipal circus. We left Amiens by rail and in about two hours reached Paris where we returned to the Grand Hotel. That evening I called on Secretary Baker who had been making an inspection tour in France and then attended and addressed a meeting of the minority Socialist group of the Chamber of Deputies over which Albert Thomas presided.

We had finished our work in France and had only time for a hasty dinner before rushing to the train. Invitations to me to visit Italy had been very insistent, for Italy had a serious labor problem, in that revolutionary Socialists and Communists were largely in control of the machinery of the labor movement. The various Italian war missions that had visited the United States had urged me to go to Italy to help strengthen the morale of the loyal workers. The Italian Ambassador to Washington had several conferences with me in which he urged a labor mission to Italy and particularly that I should accompany the mission. When I met our American Ambassador to Italy in London, during the conference I informed him that I contemplated visiting Italy and then he added his insistence.

After our arrival in Europe we received greetings, invitations, and communications from Italians of all walks of life, so that we felt there would be a genuine welcome for us as well as an opportunity to give service. We were given practically diplomatic privileges and were exempt from customs inspection and the time-consuming visé at Modane

on the border.   Our train was the first to pass during the
War from Paris to Turin without change.

We reached Turin, the munition center, at 6:15 P.M.
A large delegation gave us a hearty welcome to Italy.   We
had a meal at the station and with the assistance of the
delegation that welcomed us, during the few hours interval
between trains we saw a bit of the city.   It happened that
the great electrical engineer, Marconi, was in the station
dining-room.   He ate as we did, and I found him not only
personally an intensely stimulating man but deeply interested in the human struggle.   My visit with him was without formality and was occasioned by my interest in his
genius.

Turin was typical of the New Italy that had developed
out of the War.   On every hand were the visible presence
of Italian love of beauty and reminders of the historic and
prominent rôle that Italy had played in world affairs.   In
sharp contrast was the new industrial life, for the War
had forced Italy to develop a degree of industrial independence.   Munition factories, ship-building yards, air-
craft factories, indicated that industries had been developed in Italy that had previously been a dump-
ing-ground for the surplus of German products and
that had carelessly left her artisans to seek employment in
other lands.   I felt genuine pride in finding American machinery helping Italy to meet her industrial emergency.
Italy, at once old and young, was an inspiration.   Young
Italy was protecting her heritage of beauty handed down
by the centuries.

The story of the expansion of the Ansoldo and the Fiat
Company to supply Italy with munitions and transporta-

tion is an industrial romance. Our stop at Turin was short, for we planned to return.

We took the night train for Rome reaching there at 11:30 A.M. There we were met by representatives of the American Embassy, Signor Bissolati of the Cabinet and Italian officials and representatives of Italian labor.

The situation was most difficult. The government had hesitated before throwing in its lot with the Allies, and when it did act it found the delay had been costly in fostering division. The masses of the population of Italy were generally in sympathy with the cause of the Allies and had forced governmental action. The Socialists in control of the official Socialist party were opposed to the War and refused to support the government. A group of independents formed a reform Socialist group which was strongly pro-war and supported the government. They were represented in the Cabinet by one of the most important men in Italy at that time, Bissolati, who had formerly been editor of the *Avanti* but who had withdrawn from the Socialist Party.

There was also a group of extreme "radical" Socialists which rallied around the *Avanti* as their spokesman. In money-centers there was almost revolt against the War. So aggressive was this group that the secretary of our mission was directed to go by side-doors to railway offices when purchasing tickets so that our itinerary would not be generally known. German propaganda and pacifist internationalism had infected both the industrial workers and the enlisted men. There was extreme danger of the Italian military front giving way. *Avanti* was an anti-government, anti-Allies, pro-German paper. It was in bad

financial straits at the breaking out of the War. After
Italy entered the War, an edition of the *Avanti* was published in Rome, Turin, Genoa, Milan, Naples, and one or
two other places. The paper was industriously propagating
pacifism in the face of a circle of hostile guns that had
advanced from the Austrian frontier. So seriously was
Italian morale undermined that there had been danger that
the Italian defense would crumble.

Our first engagement in Rome was with the Italian
division of the American Committee on Public Information
of which Charles E. Merriam was in charge. The committee gave us an accurate summary of the Italian situation. Afterwards we attended a reception given us by the
Italian Minister of Commerce, a concert at the Auguesto
and later were guests of honor at a dinner given us by Mr.
Page at the Embassy. It was a brilliant dinner which gave
us an opportunity to meet personally those intrusted with
important Italian work.

News of the first German peace note reached Rome on
the same day that our mission arrived. I regarded it as part
of the pacifist propaganda of the German government and
I gave place in each of my talks to a warning to the Italians
not to trust the enemy military machine even when they
came calling *"Kamerad."* I reminded them of what happened before on the Italian front when they trusted this
cry and were slaughtered for their confidence.

We then called at the American Embassy where we
discussed plans for our Italian work. Ambassador Page
was anxious that the people of Italy should know how unreservedly American labor was doing its part in the War.
German propaganda had sought to create the impression

that we would not be able to put an army in the field or do our part industrially for months.

My first public address had been arranged by the labor unions of the city for the Auguesto—the largest auditorium in Rome. Posters announcing the meeting covered the walls of the city. The following morning we discovered that these posters had been covered over with placards issued by the anti-war Socialists and the Communists. These announced that I was unable to reach Rome and that the meeting would, therefore, be postponed.

We were greatly disturbed as was Ambassador Page. At noon a conference was held in the American Embassy to consider what was best to do under the circumstances. Ambassador Page had his secretary call upon all of the afternoon newspapers with instructions to place in them, at the expense of the American Embassy, an advertisement stating that I would positively be in attendance and that all Romans should hear and meet me.

When the afternoon papers reached the streets, it was discovered that not one carried this advertisement. Instead there were notices that the meeting had been postponed. An investigation disclosed the fact that in each instance the order of the meeting had been set up, proof-read, O. K'd and sent to the press room; that after it had been placed in the form, it had been removed and in its stead inserted the notices prepared by the Socialists and Communists, the fact being that practically every printer in Rome at that time was a member either of the anti-war Socialist or Communist group.

It appeared momentarily as though the meeting must be a failure, but I nevertheless decided to speak that night.

The meeting proved to be one of the most enthusiastic held in Rome during the War. This enthusiasm influenced the representatives of the international press who were present. The Socialist trick, instead of accomplishing its purpose, provided the opportunity which brought the opposite result.

It was the custom in the Auguesto to reserve the seats for more distinguished citizens and to require working people to stand in the rear. I refused to proceed with the program until these wage-earners—those to whom I primarily wished to speak—had been given the vacant seats in the orchestra. For the first time in their lives they occupied these seats.

The interpreter furnished me, Signor Serra, was so competent that I asked that he might go with me throughout the Italian trip. The government made the necessary arrangements. Signor Serra was an attorney who had been attached to the Italian Embassy in London but was then in the Italian army.

Ambassador Page gave us a splendid banquet and a large number of invited guests attended. Among the guests were a number of bona fide labor men and Socialists who had broken away from the party.

We were given a reception in the City Hall. The large square in front was so packed with people who clamored to see me that it was with the utmost difficulty that the gendarme made a passageway for us. I expected to deliver an address previous to the luncheon following the reception, but the cries from the square became so clamorous that it finally became necessary temporarily to cease all speaking in the building and to address the massed citizens in the square from one of the balconies. It was not until they had satisfied their desire to hear the story of our movement's purpose in this War that I was permitted to return and complete the program within the hall.

A public reception for our mission in the Theatre Auguesto was arranged by labor unions of Rome. The public was invited and all manner of humanitarian groups were represented. With evident purpose, announcements appeared in some newspapers giving the name of another theater than the one in which I was to speak. At the meeting there were present representatives of the government, important publicists, representatives of Italia Irredenta, of women's movements, men who had been followers of Mazzini, Garibaldi, and Battista.

The people of Italy were, with the exception of the Socialist-Communist group, ardently supporting the Allies in the fight for freedom. Temporary wavering had given place to new purpose and endurance. The whole fighting population was at the front.

The following morning we met with the Italian Commission on Emigration which submitted proposals for the unconditional readmittance to the United States of all Italians who had been recalled for military service. The suggestion was in plain terms an agreement for the emigration of invalid and disabled soldiers from Italy to the United States at the close of the War. The proposals were most unexpected and I had no official mandate to make a definite decision, but I told the group informally my own personal views and what I thought would be the attitude of American workingmen toward such a proposal. My frank statement I feel sure was effective in practically killing the proposals. In this conference I met many friends who had been active in the service for years.

That afternoon we were given a reception in the Capitol by the government. It was a splendid appreciation of our work. As at all such gatherings, I spoke.

In the evening we left for Padua and the members of the Cabinet came to the railway station to give their farewell in person. Gendarmes cleared the way, and after there had been handshaking all around and our party entered its railway coach, the members of the Cabinet stood outside the car talking with us until the train pulled out. We were informed by some newspaper men that this was an unusual manifestation of appreciation.

On the following morning we arrived in Padua where we were greeted by General Treat who took charge of our mission for the day, taking us to lunch at the officers' mess and then out to Montebella. Padua was our headquarters during our trips to the front. The hotel was bare—there were no baths. The landlady told us the bath-tubs had been taken to the front.

We were invited by King Victor Emanuel to dine with him on the evening of his arrival. We went to his headquarters—a beautiful château in the forest. The King first gave me a private conference. I found him, though affable, a very serious man. He spoke English fluently. I conveyed to him the information conveyed to me by Sir Douglas Haig. The King mentioned the fact that Italy had no reserves upon which to draw; that they had really drafted their last men, both young and old. I answered by saying that my information was that the Austrian troops were in a worse condition and that not only were they at the end of their tether with men but this was true also of ammunition and supplies. The information impressed the King and he was evidently a bit preoccupied by it during the dinner which followed. We met the members of his personal staff.

The following morning, by the King's order, I received a compilation of the existing resources of the Italian army. Later, he sent me a book of photographs taken by official photographers showing the wonderful engineering and military feats of the Italian army. It is a book I prize highly.

The following day in the rain we went to Monte Grappa. We went up the twenty-mile road leading to the top and trudged through the tiers of tunnels in the mountain which contained guns trained over Piave upon the Austrians, with men on guard and all the ammunition stored for immediate use. I was also given an opportunity to view the engineering work performed by the Italian troops aided by Americans. Italy's scientists and engineers competed with her poets, her princes, and her industrials in defense of a land that inspired devotion. The Austrian army concentrated its attacks on the northeastern border where the mountainous natural defenses of the country constituted a complex military problem. I have never seen a more thrilling engineering marvel than I beheld on Monte Grappa with its roadways, tunneling, and teleferica.

Probably one of the most adroit pieces of propaganda to undermine the morale of the Italian forces was that undertaken by the Austrian army officers in this region. They printed in Austria a series of editions of newspapers in the Italian language, the headings, the titles of the papers, the date-lines, and type all being exact duplicates of papers published in several parts of Italy. The dispatches purported to have been received from the Allies reported France as collapsing and stated that the Germans had captured Paris and that Hindenburg was on his way to

London.   Probably the most cruel and the most effective propaganda were published reports of famine in the homes of the soldiers and malicious falsehoods as to the unfaithfulness of their wives.   These spurious publications were dropped by aeroplanes over the Italian lines.   I was given one of these papers while on Monte Grappa and also several paper bills inscribed in German that had been printed in anticipation of the capture of several Italian cities and to be used as the money of the area occupied. The paper money was captured in an assault made by a portion of the Italian troops.

After our trip to the fighting front we were guests of General Diaz and General Bodilio at dinner and I repeated to General Diaz the information given me by Marshal Haig and he, too, was much impressed.   On both this occasion and at the dinner at the King's headquarters efforts were made to impress upon me the urgent necessity for the immediate presence of at least 250,000 American troops and, in fact, I was urged to send a cablegram to President Wilson informing him that being on the ground and seeing the desperate situation, I felt it my duty to inform him of the necessity of these troops being sent to Italy. In this military problem I felt I had no right to interfere.

Our next expedition was to the sector of the Piave held by American troops, passing through Magliano where we met the Duke d'Aorta and Colonel Wallace of our troops at Villa Angelica, American G. H. Q. Then we were taken into the front-line trenches overlooking the Piave and opposite the Austrian guns.   As we neared the front the steady roar of artillery indicated some major activity, but to my surprise when I reached the front-line trench, washed by the river's water, I noticed no particular excitement on the part of the officers and the troops we encountered and to my astonishment, I was requested to raise my head above the trenches to witness the effect of this bombardment on the Austrian lines. I was informed that the Italians had intended to attack that morning but owing to a changed condition, the Italian chief in command had deemed the time inadvisable. Our batteries, therefore, had opened full force against the Austrian army and the bombardment was so terrific that not a shot was heard from the Austrian side. Every Austrian was as deep in the earth as his dug-out permitted him to crawl. It was, therefore, perfectly safe to walk along the top of the ramparts and with field glasses watch the American shells as they exploded in the Austrian lines.

Many of the soldiers—both Italians and Americans—asked many questions about America. They were especially anxious to know the standing of the baseball teams. Colonel Wallace asked us to join him in reviewing his troops (the 332nd Infantry) and to address them, after which we returned to Padua where we had dinner with the press representatives.

Next morning we left for Venice, by army automobile to Fresnia and the rest of the way in motor boats. We were received by the public officials and after a lunch we were informed that Gabriel D'Annunzio desired that we should visit his aviation camp some distance away. I received an enthusiastic welcome and was introduced to the members of his corps. He insisted upon taking me to one of the hangars to show me the aeroplane in which he had personally commanded those raids over the Austrian front which had made him famous in the army. He seemed to know much about me and my work both before and during

the War, and as I was an admirer of both his poetry and
his dramatic powers, we found ourselves *en rapport*, particularly in the prosecution of the War. During our conference he referred with emphasis that as a result of the
War which was then believed to be absolutely successful
for the Allied cause, Trieste, Trient and Fiume should
become part of Italy. The same subject had been brought
up in my conferences with Italians in the various cities I
visited. There was altogether too much importance placed
upon what I could do in accomplishing this result at the
end of the War and I frankly told all that although firmly
convinced that Trient and Trieste should be restored to
Italy, I had grave doubts about the justice of the demand
for Fiume. In my public addresses and private conferences
from that time on I urged the claims of Italy for these two
provinces but studiously avoided any reference to Fiume.

General D'Annunzio staged a number of air-craft dis-
plays for our benefit and he insisted upon my getting into
his machine to be photographed with him. I have never
seen the picture. He furnished us with two military automobiles which carried us to the lake where we boarded a
propeller which took us into the heart of Venice. We left
D'Annunzio at his camp some fifteen miles from Venice.
Our high-powered motor boat went through a portion of
the Grand Canal and stopped in front of a small palace
in Venice, where to my astonishment, Gabriel D'Annunzio
opened the door to present me with some relics from the
Italian battle-front. In keeping with his dramatic temperament, he had flown from his camp so as to give me a
surprise welcome when our boat reached his residence in
Venice.

Milan was our next objective. Mr. Oyster was told

the authorities had information that an attack was to be made on me and he was directed to take every precaution. All theaters and halls had been closed because of the "flu." It was arranged that I should speak in an open gallery or arcade opposite the cathedral. They insisted that I be taken into the gallery by the side passage and that the stairway from which I spoke to the crowd below be carefully guarded. But even though hostile pacifists had easy access to that meeting, there was only a suggestion of hissing which lasted for a brief time and the crowd stood patiently for over an hour listening to my talk which, of course, had to be interpreted.

Before I had half finished my address and appealed to their responsibility in the struggle for freedom and justice, the crowd was with me to a man. I knew nothing of the anticipated danger beyond noticing that John Frey and Charles Baine stood on one side and William Bowen and Ed Wallace on the other side all the while I spoke. Mr. Oyster sat on the steps below me. The meeting ended peacefully.

The officials of the Socialist Party had requested a conference with our mission. I wired them to meet us in Turin at ten-thirty on the day after our arrival. I found awaiting me in Turin a communication brought by messenger in which they refused to keep the appointment upon the strange ground that the emigration discussion had been completed at the conference with the Immigration Commission. To my mind there were other important subjects that we could have profitably considered, but I could not force upon them a conference. In the communication, they gave their address and telephone number. This I interpreted to be a suggestion for further communication, but I knew they were not seeking light through conference and I had no time to waste.

The following day the American-Italian Chamber of Commerce invited me to address a luncheon gathering. In that address I said that the official Socialists were afraid to meet the American mission. I spoke of their tyrannical dictation under which the Mayor of Milan, the Confederazione Generale del Lavoro of Milan, and three labor representatives had been compelled to avoid all contact with our mission or be expelled from the party. Two of them brazened the threat. In reply to their statement that though we represented American workingmen we also represented millions of capitalistic dollars, I said that at any rate we represented no "German" dollars and added that I wondered if the editors and managers of the *Avanti* could make the same assertion. Of course, I repudiated their charge.

In Genoa we were met by a large welcoming delegation. After a luncheon which, of course, I addressed, we went to labor headquarters where a bust of Signor Pietro Iglesias (Peter Church), the first labor member to sit in the Italian Parliament, was presented to me.

At the large gathering held in the evening on the reception committee were six Garibaldian veterans in their red shirts and military medals, guarding the actual colors under which they had fought.

Next morning we returned to Turin where we were given a magnificent reception with military honors and crowds thronged the streets between the station and our hotel. It was almost impossible for us because of the enormous and enthusiastic crowds to walk through the streets to the hotel and for hours after we reached the hotel the large square before it remained packed with people cheer-

ing and singing. The crowds would not disperse until I
had shown myself from the balcony and addressed them.
Once or twice afterward when I made an attempt to walk
through the streets, shouting crowds followed me. John
Frey had told me of some beautiful jewelry he had found
in a store nearby. I desired to purchase a few trinkets for
my family and went to the jewelry store where, among other
articles, I selected one for my daughter, Sadie. I discovered
that I did not have sufficient money on my person to pay
for it and informed the jeweler that it would be necessary
for me to return to my hotel to replenish my pocketbook.
To my surprise the jeweler said: "I do not want you to do
that, Mr. Gompers. Take this and pay me when you get
ready." He recognized me from pictures he had seen of
me in the newspapers and movies.

My official work ended with a reception at the Muni-
cipio, and a mass meeting at night. My last speech in
Turin was to be the final service in rounding out the work
for which I had gone overseas. The results of the Inter-
Allied Labor and Socialist Conference of September 17
had absolutely broken the German propaganda in Allied
countries. I had succeeded in securing the adoption, without any modification, of the American trade union program
in connection with the War. After this I had gone to
Italy for the purpose of heartening the people and assisting
the wage-earners to better understand not only the
principles involved in the War but their duty to themselves
which could not be performed unless they gave their fullest
service and support to their government.

My work had been accomplished and with this came
a personal satisfaction and a lifting of the burdens which
had rested upon my shoulders. I was in a mental condition

which enabled me to express my sentiments more satisfactorily than ever before. It had been the request of those who were loyal to the winning of the War that I should deliver one more address at which the representatives of the international press would be present.

My speech seemed to make a very deep impression on my hearers. They were enthusiastic in their applause and manifestation of commendation. It was my desire to get away from the assemblage as soon as possible, but my friend and associate, John P. Frey, approached me and in a very emphatic tone said that it was essential that he see me at once at the hotel. I was under the impression that something had happened among my associates on the commission and was a bit perturbed about it, for I did not, at that moment, care to have my mind diverted to anything of such a nature, since I had known no relief night or day from heavy responsibility. I had held to my course despite threats, ridicule, or physical danger, and when all was through I declared I wasn't going to think of work for a while. I wanted complete relaxation. Human nerves have limitations. I was rebellious, for I thought I had earned a few hours' holiday. However, John insisted in such a manner that I could not resist, so in one of the cabs which were waiting, we left the hall and proceeded at once to the hotel. Upon our arrival John said, "Sam, you have just got to brace up to receive a piece of sad news that will go to your very soul." He then informed me that as we entered the banquet hall the American Consul had handed him a cablegram which had been received within the hour from Secretary of Labor, William B. Wilson, announcing that my only daughter had died from the "flu" in Washington on that morning. That took the joy of work or holiday out of my life for many a month. Somehow I felt it was hardly just compensation for the service I had tried to render.

I cannot describe the experience I passed through—I would not if I could.

Arrangements had been made to leave Turin immediately. When I left there was a manifestation of sympathy that I shall always remember gratefully. The news of the death of my daughter evidently reached the people, so that from the hotel to the railway station there was not a sound audible from anyone. Men stood with heads bared. When I reached Paris, there were awaiting me seven letters from my daughter all of them breathing hope, cheer, and encouragement of how sure she felt of the service I had rendered in helping to bring the War to a close with triumph for American and Allied peoples. She had been, with her wonderful voice, entertaining the boys in the camps, singing to them, doing work for them, knitting for them, and yet she deprecated the fact that she was able to do so little and said she felt because she could do no more that she was a slacker. With the news that she had passed away and after reading the beautiful letters which awaited me, one can better imagine than I can describe the feeling which overcame me.

I asked Frey to go and see my cousins, Louis and Florence Gompers in the Place Vendôme and ask them to come to see me. They did so and closed their jewelry establishment. They remained with me all day and evening and summoned their family physician to attend me. It seemed that all the blood in my veins was congealed. I was chilled. For two days I was seriously ill.

While in Paris, before going to Italy, President Poincaré

invited my associates and me to dine with him and Madame Raymond Poincaré at the Palais de l'Elysée. I had accepted the invitation about two weeks before I went to Italy. While in Paris *en route* to Brest, to take the first steamer home, though I had the time I did not have the inclination to sit down to such a function with the pall of death about me, so I felt constrained to ask to be excused. President Poincaré graciously but regretfully consented. I was glad when Sunday evening came and I was on my way to Brest where provision was made for me to take passage on the S. S. *Tenadores*. On arriving, Admiral Wilson, in person, with his aide greeted me and took me at once to his office and home and gave me a real American breakfast. His greeting, his manner, and his cordiality, without verbally expressing his sympathy, made his every action tell upon my whole being.

Arrangement had been made with Henderson and Jouhaux for an inter-Allied conference in Paris, October 26, for which John Frey and Charles Baine remained. However, Henderson was prevented from attending and the conference was not held.

After breakfast Admiral Wilson took us to a room in which he and but few others were ever admitted. It contained a map of the seas of the world in which the German submarines were operating. He showed me on the map how these "subs" were congregated in one large group and that the only deduction of that was that something of a potential character was about to eventuate. I asked the Admiral how he knew this. "Well," he said, "you see, these Germans will talk and we overhear their conversation."

We were taken with our baggage on the Admiral's launch to the *Tenadores* where we went on board. General Harries of the American army and his aide, Henry Cole of Washington, an old-time friend of mine, came on board to express their gratitude for the work I had performed and to express their condolence upon my great loss. My associates left the *Tenadores* for the city of Brest and remained several hours. While otherwise I should have been very much interested to see the quaint city, I had no heart then for any diversion. I remained on board. The *Tenadores* was due to leave the following morning. I was so nervously strung up that I could not retire to my room, so my secretary stayed up with me. About eleven o'clock I saw gliding toward us a vessel. A gang-plank was lowered and we soon discovered the boat was loaded with wounded men who were taken from that boat on to our ship. The men who could walk were few. Many with only one leg moved forward with assistance and were assigned to their berths. When about half of them had come upon our ship, I asked the privilege of going aboard the hospital transport. There I met Kate and Emma Lansing, sisters of Secretary Lansing, who were in charge of the wounded. They recognized me and greeted me heartily, and then on behalf of the Red Cross gave me packages of oranges, cigarettes, and tobacco so that I could hand them to each of the wounded men.

There followed seventy-six men so badly mutilated that they had to be carried on stretchers. To each one I spoke a word of encouragement and hope in addition to giving to him the gift of the Red Cross.

Every day on the passage from Brest to Hampton

Roads I visited our wounded men and talked with them, read to some of them, and read aloud the daily bulletins containing news received by radio.

In spite of the depression which possessed me by reason of my daughter's death, my fellow-passengers insisted upon my addressing them upon the activities of labor during the War and all that the War meant. I could not fail them. I think that the two or three addresses which I delivered on that voyage helped me in some measure to assuage the great grief which had fallen upon me.

From Hampton Roads I took the first train to New York. The remains of my daughter were brought there. Her body had been embalmed and though I was not permitted to kiss her lips or to place my hands upon her in any way I had the gratification of looking upon her beautiful countenance. We laid her to rest in Washington Cemetery with our other dear ones.

CHAPTER XLV

ALMOST immediately after my Sadie's funeral I went to Chicago. The engagement was one which could not be canceled, for a meeting had been arranged in my honor as a form of endorsement for the work I had been doing in Europe. American labor wished to emphasize to the world its determination to stand behind our government in the War. It was a wonderful meeting, held in the Auditorium. Labor men were there from all over the country. Though I never felt less like speaking in my life, as I kept on I forgot myself completely and thought only of the world's need and the necessity for bringing to a successful termination the War for world-democracy.

Immediately after the Chicago meeting I went to Laredo, Texas, for a conference to organize a federation of Pan-American labor. The members of our Executive Council and a number of representative labor men were in Laredo to take part in that conference. Secretary of Labor Wilson was there representing the United States government and General Pabla de la Garza as the personal representative of President Carranza. Several Central and South American countries also participated.

On the way we heard the premature report of the Armistice. On November 11 soon after my arrival in Laredo, city officials called upon me and invited me to participate at the presentation of the local pennant at noon-time in the public square. The demonstration was to celebrate that the people of that city had gone "over the top" in their purchase of Victory Bonds. I accepted the invitation. Shortly afterward, while taking a constitutional, I bought a small printed sheet issued as an extra of one of the local papers. It contained a dispatch from Washington stating that the Secretary of State early that morning had given out the official statement that the Armistice had been signed. I hastened back to my colleagues and gave them the information. We were all overjoyed.

At noon-time when I was on the platform in the Plaza just about to begin my address, the representative of the Associated Press gave me the "flimsy" containing the terms of the Armistice which I read during my address. It contained the official announcement that the cause of the War for which the Allies and the American government and the people had fought had triumphed. The joy of the throng was almost delirious.

Immediately following the Pan-American Congress, our Executive Council held a meeting in San Antonio. We discussed labor problems growing out of the truce. The Council anticipated that the Peace Congress would be called shortly and planned to put the Federation in a position to carry out our various declarations and to have a part in shaping the peace treaty. It had been our thought, even before the United States entered the War, that a labor congress ought to be called for the same time and place as the Peace Congress. It was obvious that if constructive leadership did not at once assume the responsibility, "radical" groups would take the initiative.

On October 28, I had received a cablegram from Oudegeest requesting the appointment of delegates to an International Conference of Trade Union Centers to be held at the same time and place as the peace deliberations. The purpose stated was the reorganization of the International Bureau. I presented this proposal to my colleagues of the Executive Council and it was decided that I should cable Oudegeest that the A. F. of L. had in several of its conventions instructed our Executive Council to issue invitations for an international labor conference which should determine labor's proposal for the peace treaty as well as organize a new international trade union federation.

I was fully aware of the difficulties of calling an international labor conference. The program which the Federation adopted at the beginning of the War was evolved without practical experience in the field of international relations. My experience during the War taught me that many things that were appealing from a sentimental point of view were impracticable. I felt that a labor conference should not be held any place except Paris if we wanted to protect our deliberations from a Bolshevik stampede. Had I been making the plan anew I should have provided for an inter-Allied conference to precede the international conference but I was absolutely unwilling to consider an international conference held anywhere else than the meeting place of the Peace Congress, where labor representatives of enemy countries would be upon the same footing in our deliberations as their diplomatic representatives would occupy in the Peace Congress.

The Council appointed a committee of five to represent the Federation in such a labor conference and to initiate whatever action seemed most practical. That committee consisted of James Duncan, William Green, John R. Alpine, Frank Duffy, and me.

Even with this official authorization the way to action was not yet clear. Before an international labor congress could be called it was necessary to ascertain whether delegates could get passports and whether France would permit them to meet in Paris. On the other hand, immediate action was imperative, for we must be busy if we would forestall both those whose ends were the maintenance of the old order and Bolshevik influence in international labor. Labor must urge its rights, its desire, and ability to serve. We had reached the crucial situation when the principles that heartened men to endure appalling physical hardships must either be made the foundations of a new order or there would be reversion to the old jugglery of politicians and scramble for places in the sun. A number of men in public life, particularly those active in the War as well as many representative labor men, urged—in some cases unions adopted such resolutions—that the President appoint me as one of the American Delegation for the Negotiation of Peace. The Executive Council then sent a telegram from San Antonio to President Wilson, urging that I be appointed. Later, I learned that among those who wrote President Wilson a letter urging my appointment on the Commission was Governor Alfred E. Smith of New York.

There was danger that revolutionary ideas and policies, which I had done my utmost to thwart during the War, might entrench themselves in the new international labor movement as the result of decisions reached in the treaty. I was anxious that American labor should be represented in the Peace Commission. The recognition was due because of the service labor had rendered in making peace possible. It was expedient because our representation would present labor interests as economic problems, whereas otherwise the emphasis would be upon political aspects only. In addition, the distinction would help us in our own struggle. There were two groups eager for reaction to overtake American labor—reactionary employers and the Bolsheviks and near-Bolsheviks of all lands. Predatory employers had already launched an "open shop" campaign with its proposed wage reductions. Throughout the War the American labor movement had been the tireless foe of propaganda that served autocracy under another guise. War had created favorable conditions for revolutionary propaganda in all countries. Organized labor saw no reason why our government should suddenly change its policy of recognizing the constructive representative character of the American labor movement.

Upon my return East, people with whom I came in contact from all walks of life assumed as a matter of course that I was to be named on the Peace Commission. This was also true of those from diplomatic circles and distinguished foreign representatives. The situation grew exceedingly embarrassing for me as the President seemed to be thinking apart from the rest of us. There were many rumors, but the announcement of the personnel of the Commission definitely ended labor's expectation.

The political or "Stockholm" group in Europe were revising their program to adapt it to the changed situation. Pacifist propaganda was still used for ulterior purposes. Arthur Henderson sought the leadership of that movement. He believed that the obstacles to a war-time international labor conference vanished with the truce.

It was urgent that definite plans be made for an international labor conference. I received several communica-

tions from Henderson transmitted through Ambassador
Davis. Quick action was expedient, but if I sent out a call
for a world-labor conference at the city where peace should
be made and delegates found themselves prohibited from
gathering, I would not be adding to labor's dignity or
influence.

I received authoritative information that Premier Clemenceau had told French labor that he would not express
an opinion as to whether an international labor conference
could be held at the same time and place as the Peace Congress, since the problem involved a guarantee of the safety
of labor delegates from enemy countries before peace terms
had been concluded with their governments and the French
government would not make those guarantees. Lloyd
George made a similar reply. Both of them held that the
matter would first have to be laid before the governments
of the Allied countries. I was in New York when I received
this information. As President Wilson was then making
preparations to go to Europe, I immediately sent a telegram
asking his opinion. He replied, expressing the view that
he did not see any objection to my issuing the invitation
for an international labor conference and that my presence
in Paris would be of real service.

A few days afterwards as I was entering the office of
Secretary Baker to confer with him about a strike at the
army base at Brooklyn, I met Acting Secretary of State
Polk. After my interview with Secretary Baker was concluded, I was informed that Mr. Polk desired to see me in
his office in the State Department. I immediately went over.
He inquired when I was going to France. I told him that
it was extremely problematical and informed him of the
situation. I told him that I could not place myself in the

embarrassing position of seeming to force service without
a request to render it, and that I could not be responsible
for calling the conference which might be prohibited from
convening. He saw my position very clearly, but said
that he had just been advised that Premier Clemenceau had
cabled to the French Embassy that if I could be in Paris
I ought to be there, for my presence would be a real international service. Mr. Polk stated that he would put before
the *Chargé d'Affaires* of the French Embassy the situation
as I had outlined it and that he hoped there would be a
definite and favorable reply from Clemenceau within a few
days. Shortly afterwards I had an interview with Count
De Chambrun at the French Embassy in which I explained
to him the international labor situation. A few days later
the Count, accompanied by M. DeBilly, came to my office
to submit to me a memorandum which he purposed to cable
to Paris. I also discussed the situation with the French
High Commissioner, André Tardieu.

Next I had an interview with Mr. Barkley, *Chargé
d'Affaires* of the British Embassy in the absence of Lord
Reading, and laid before him the whole problem—its international complications and the relations between the national labor movements. I pointed out that unless representatives of labor of Great Britain and France were permitted
to participate it would be useless to issue the invitation;
that the invitation to labor of Germany and Austria would
be given, though whether they would be permitted to attend
would be determined by their governments; that the labor
conference would not take place until the Peace Conference
should be held and not necessarily during the preliminary
conference of the Allied governments. Mr. Barkley stated
that he would communicate with his government by cable-

gram at once and let me know the answer. He too expressed the hope that I should go to Paris because of the services he thought I could render in the interest of justice.

Meanwhile, Henderson continued cabling me about an international Socialist and labor conference to be held in Lausanne and asked for authority to sign my name to the conference-call. Believing it would be better to talk plans over face to face, I sent no reply but cabled to Bowerman of the Parliamentary Committee, asking for a conference between his committee, the French Confédération Générale du Travail, and our committee upon our arrival. My thought was to permit the national labor movements to decide upon a policy program. Mr. Barkley received word that the British government had not altered its position. However, arrangements were made for my associates and me to go to Paris. As this trip was to be of indeterminate length, I arranged with Matthew Woll, who was in Washington as my assistant in the work of the Advisory Commission of the Council of National Defense, to perform certain necessary and immediate official duties for me. Our delegation left New York on January 8 on the steamer *Carmania*. The vessel was crowded. Among the passengers were the entire Japanese Peace Commission. Accompanying the mission were a number of Japanese newspaper men, magazine writers, students, and technical advisers. Many of them sought interviews with me and their questioning was close and pressing.

Our group held daily conferences in which we developed unity of opinion upon policies. The voyage over was very rough. We landed in Liverpool on the seventeenth. There were a number of representative men of Great Britain and the United States to meet us, among them the American Consul General at Liverpool who invited us to the Consulate where we had a conference.

After a most miserable rainy-day experience, we boarded the train which was without heat or water for washing or drinking purposes. It was a special train but without comfort, warmth or convenience. Every man kept on his heavy overcoat, but still shivered. The cold rain and sleet penetrated to the very marrow of our bones. We arrived in London that evening where we were met by representatives of the American Embassy and Charles Bowerman. Mr. Bowerman had made arrangements for a conference between our party and the Parliamentary Committee on the following Monday.

In the conference it was disclosed that the Lausanne or Berne Conference was fostered by political organizations and workers that rallied around Henderson. On the call for the conference were the names of Arthur Henderson, Albert Thomas, Emile Vandervelde, and Samuel Gompers. I had not given authority for the use of my name for the call and so declared. I later learned from Vandervelde in his office in Brussels and from Thomas that they had withheld their consent for the use of their names. Thus the conference was called on the sole authority of Henderson. Since previous conferences at Berne and Stockholm were made up of the same bodies and had declared for policies to which American labor was opposed, our commission could see no good result from our participation in this proposed conference. I therefore formally stated that the A. F. of L. would not attend the Switzerland conference and suggested that an early meeting of the labor organizations of the Allied governments would facilitate going before the General Peace Conference to present a united statement of labor's demands.

Our conferences with the Parliamentary Committee continued over two days. Mr. Bowerman was authorized to say for the Parliamentary Committee that they would welcome an invitation from our Federation to take part in the formation of a new international trade union movement and he pledged their support to that end. On behalf of the American delegation I pledged our co-operation. A committee of five was appointed by the Parliamentary Committee to meet with our delegation to arrange a plan to carry out this proposition.

From London we went to Folkestone, thence to Boulogne and from there to Paris where we were met by two representatives of the Amrican Mission to Negotiate Peace. My cousins also greeted me most kindly. On the following day we had a meeting with the Executive Board of the Confédération Générale du Travail. The French Federation had determined to attend the Berne Conference, but they were willing to participate in an inter-Allied conference held in Paris. However, their real allegiance lay with the political group and they regarded the proposed trade union conference as a "conversation."

Our French friends labored under the impression that by going to Berne they would go in the position of accusers of the Germans, and the responsibility for the War and the supporting of the War could in the conference be fastened upon the Germans. We called their attention to the fact that the Germans would not come into the conference handcuffed or as accused culprits, but that they would come there on an equal footing with the representatives of the Allied

countries; and that in all likelihood the Germans, with their
sympathizers from the so-called neutral countries, would
dominate the conference. Furthermore, although Switzerland was neutral, the influence of Germany and Austria
was strong in that territory.

We asked that there might be a conference of the representatives of the trade unions from the Allied countries
previous to the Berne Conference. This they declined, but
stated that they would meet with us for the discussion of
such a proposal after their return from Berne. I stated
that the Berne Conference had been called without authority and that my name had been unwarrantably attached
to the call and that neither the British nor the Belgians
were willing to attend an international conference at that
time. In my opinion it was premature to meet representatives of the labor movements from enemy countries prior
to the admission of representatives from those countries to
the Peace Congress.

In our second and third conferences Belgian representatives joined. The Belgians were anxious to hold an inter-
Allied labor conference in Paris, but the French continued
to oppose.

After several days, Mr. W. C. Bullitt and one or two
others in some official way representing the American commissioners were reported to have committed themselves and
our government to the Berne Conference. We had an
interview with President Wilson at his Paris home. After
a full discussion of the subject he expressed himself as fully
in accord with our position. He suggested that we have
a conference with the other American commissioners the
following day. This we did and presented our position
upon the entire situation. I plainly stated that even if

W. C. Bullitt or any other person correctly represented the view of American commissions upon the question of holding the Berne Conference or American labor's participation in it, that report was in opposition not only to our views but our entire course; that if these men represented American labor, there was no further use for our commission to remain in Paris.

Secretary Lansing, General Bliss, Colonel House, and Henry White assured us that Mr. Bullitt had no right either directly or indirectly to make any commitment for the American commissioners and that our position was entirely justified. During our conference with these four commissioners, President Wilson entered the room for a few moments.

When these labor conferences were in progress, I received an official announcement from Secretary Lansing that President Wilson had appointed Edward N. Hurley of the U. S. Shipping Board and me to represent the United States on the Commission on International Labor Legislation. The designation of this commission to assist the Peace Congress made it imperative for labor to be in a position to submit a unified program. I therefore renewed my request for agreement upon some definite line of action. The inter-Allied conference was not held. However, a separate conference between the American delegation and the Belgian labor organizations was arranged to take place at their headquarters in Brussels.

On January 28 we met President Wilson in his home, Murat Palace. In his first words of greeting he insisted that we take all the time necessary for presentation of whatever matters we had in mind. The discussion was thorough and conducted with a spirit of deep interest and desire for mutual and common helpfulness. At the conclusion of the conference, the President asked us to see him again in the near future. He expressed the hope that I would accept appointment to the commission.

Just before the opening of the Berne Conference our commission made public our reasons for not attending. The Paris papers announced that there was a break between the President and me because of our refusal to go to Berne. During our meeting with the President, he referred to the story and stated that there was absolutely no foundation for the statement that was attributed to him and that, on the contrary, he was in full accord with the action that we had taken. I gave him a copy of the statement we had given to the press which he promised to read. The President explained the exceedingly uncomfortable position in which he was placed by reason of some statements attributed to him which were without basis in fact, and that at that time the privilege was denied him of publication of corrections in the Paris press.

I had a conference with Vandervelde in his official office as Minister of the Department of Justice, when he told me he had by use of the long distance telephone positively forbidden Henderson to use his name on the call for the Berne Conference. The Belgian trade union executives declared that they were in accord with our position on international policies. The conference was most interesting.

Paris during the Peace Congress was not a city but a cosmopolitan caravansary. "Everybody of importance" was there and the many who hoped to achieve that distinction. There were thousands of those necessary to the machinery of treaty-making, thousands of onlookers and hangers-on. Nothing was normal—prices were appalling

—there were apparently no restraints in living. The tension of work and responsibility was so intense that relaxation was in proportion. At no time in my life have I ever worked harder or against such tremendous odds.

There was already a definite alignment of forces which it was practically impossible to break. America was the one Power at the peace table alien to the diplomatic practices of Europe. We had gone into the War with high-minded purposes and aims. We were not interested in territorial aggrandizement or balance of power. We were interested in opportunities for freedom and the arts of peace. In nearly all conferences concerned with the Versailles Treaty, America's representatives found themselves in the minority.

The hard grind of months of close discussion wore heavily upon our American chief. From the first I doubted the wisdom of his return to Europe. It caused genuine elation when President Wilson first decided to be in person at the peace table. The acclaim with which he was received by persons in all walks of life gave him great power and overwhelming responsibility—by everyone he was hailed the Messiah. He was regarded as the almost inspired spokesman of a new ideal. It was expected that he would lead the world out of chaos and confusion and work toward the establishment of the principles of peace and good will. When we again decided to return to Paris to participate in the discussions of the details of the treaty, I looked askance and with many misgivings upon that course. If he had returned to Washington after his address in the first plenary session, he could have dictated principles and decisions and remained aloof from the days and months of tedious discussion of every detail. Such isolation

would have maintained his power without any diminution
of the glamour and reverent respect which his enunciation
of principles aroused. Of course, I had neither the right
nor the temerity to express this opinion. Even if I had
it, doubtless it would have had no effect.

Upon my appointment as a representative of the United
States on the International Labor Commission I was assigned an office in official headquarters in the Hotel Crillon.
Major George L. Berry was assigned to me as liaison
officer. Major Berry had been in Paris some time connected with the staff of Colonel House and had of course
fallen in with their methods and purposes.

The Commission on International Labor Legislation
convened February 1. M. Colliard, French Minister of
Labor, opened the sitting. Mr. Barnes proposed the appointment of me as president which was seconded by all
delegations. Arthur Fontaine was made secretary-general
and Harold Butler assistant secretary-general.

As chairman of the commission, an office was provided
for me in the building of the French Ministry of Labor.

The Commission on International Labor Legislation
met Mondays, Wednesdays, Thursdays, and Fridays of
each week, and of course not only as a delegate but as
presiding officer it was necessary for me to be present at all
meetings.

The first week-end that was open our American labor
group went to Brussels for our promised conference. On
Friday morning early we left Paris in automobiles, traveling over rough roads—snow, ice, and sleet, through fog,
mist, and all sorts of weather except sunshine. We passed
through much of the devastated parts of France and Belgium. My associates saw this destruction for the first time

and they were awed by it, as I too was when I first saw the wanton devastation wrought by the German army. I shall not attempt a word-picture of the holocaust brought about by ruthless and wanton destruction. Others have given vivid pictures far better than I can paint.

We went through Amiens and saw the ruins there. We had made shorter expeditions to Rheims before and saw the desolation there, and also at Château-Thierry, Soissons, and Belleau Wood. The desolation gave an idea of the misery—the unnecessary misery—which was inflicted upon the people and their homes. For miles and miles around one could not see a house or a semblance of a house standing; there were wrecks of factories, workshops, business houses, mine shafts—ruins, destruction everywhere and not a tree standing, not a growing thing, the ground burrowed up by shot and shell as far as the eye oculd see. It was enough to make one grievously sad and resentful.

We reached Brussels after two o'clock Saturday morning. After a sandwich and a cup of coffee we retired, exhausted by the trip. A few hours in bed and we were up early and had conferences with labor men of nearly all groups. We had a letter from our American Ambassador at Brussels and later in the day a letter from King Albert's secretary stating that the King expressed great regret at being unable to meet us, as he was confined to his bed by orders of his physician.

We went to the Maison du Peuple (People's House), the headquarters of the co-operative store of labor and the Socialists of Belgium. The ground floor was in use as a restaurant.

Before the commission had been working very long it was necessary for Mr. Hurley to return to the United States,

and Henry M. Robinson, also of the Shipping Board, was
named to replace him. Mr. Robinson and I made a valiant
fight to get practical recommendations reported by our committee. His experience had been in the business world
and he was unaccustomed to the methods of diplomacy,
but he gave a splendid demonstration of the superior effectiveness of a clear mind and plain speaking.

The British delegation had prepared proposals which
had been circulated in both French and English before the
second meeting and these served as the basis for discussion.
In a perfectly obvious way that draft controlled the thinking of the conference and it certainly made my task more
difficult and unpleasant. At once and continuously there
was apparent the difference between the Old World and
the New. Our political, social, and economic philosophy
and methods are in sharp contrast as they have grown out of
different environments and national characteristics. New
World individualism and initiative have shaped our thinking and activity.

The Old World was accustomed to dealing with labor
problems through legislation and it was natural for Old
World representatives to think of international labor problems only in the terms of international legislation. They
had in mind the development of a super-government that
should develop standards for the workers everywhere.

In the New World, in addition to regarding labor problems as a part of the economic field in which methods are
essentially different from those of the political field, we
had the problems arising out of a written constitution and
our Federal form of government. It is very difficult for
the average person of continental Europe to understand the
spirit and the practical methods of America. The repre-

sentatives from France and Italy were frankly in favor of
a super-government and they could not understand that the
objections Mr. Robinson and I advanced were based upon
facts and concrete obstacles. They seemed to credit us with
willful perverseness instead of an honest desire to indicate
a real situation that had to be met.

The British did not oppose the principle of super-
government, but sought protection by establishing through
colonial representation a control within the agency that
would enable them to make satisfactory changes later.
Their plan provided for an international labor organization to be composed of delegates from countries signing
the Peace Treaty. Each national delegation was to be
made up of one representative of the government with two
votes and two representatives of industry, one to be designated by the employers' organizations and the other by
organizations of labor. These internal conferences were to
propose recommendations or conventions which the governments would be under obligation to make effective.
Knowing the situation that existed in the American Senate,
I had a very keen realization of the summary action that
would be taken in regard to such a proposed invasion of
the Senate's treaty-making power as well as the legislative
field of Congress, to say nothing of the protests that would
develop from individual states.

Both Mr. Robinson and I were very much concerned
as to the resultant situation. We feared that if the International Labor Commission recommended or approved the
proposals before it, our work would be used as an argument
against the League of Nations which President Wilson considered essential to carrying out his policies. As chairman
of the committee I was somewhat constrained from free

participation in discussion. Robinson and I outlined our
campaign after consultation with the American commissioners and he certainly was an able floor general.

The debate continued for a number of days in which
both Mr. Robinson and I registered objections to the British
proposal and suggested alterations without being able to
convince our colleagues that radical revision was necessary.
Finally, the situation became so serious that after consulting with the other American delegates it was decided that
we should make a definite issue. We then submitted to
the commission a motion that such parts of the British proposal as were at variance with our political customs and
policies and against which we had entered our reservations,
should be submitted to a subcommittee to determine if some
compromise could not be worked out. There was vehement
protest, but finally Mr. Robinson made this motion: That
the commission withhold action upon the proposals under
discussion until he should be prepared to submit a counter-
proposal that would meet the American difficulties. This
was agreed to and in the meanwhile the commission discussed other provisions of the draft.

I opposed with vigor and persistence that part of the
draft that proposed giving two votes to the government
delegate, on the ground that there are really only two
groups in society—the employed and the employing. I
believed that the make-up of an international conference
thus weighted against labor would militate against confidence in the new body. I proposed one delegate, one vote.
This I won, but the advantage was lost when the government was given two representatives. Having in mind the
effectiveness of the use of the advisory powers of governmental agencies, I was not in favor of giving an inter-

national labor bureau mandatory powers. My experience had convinced me that legislation cannot accomplish that which is contrary to the general will and that far better results can be secured by reaching unanimous agreement after having made a survey of the facts in a case. It was impossible to convince the advocates of super-government that they were planning to defeat their own purposes. Perhaps there is no one who is so intolerant as the theorist who wants to do good. Time and time again I felt that the situation within the International Labor Commission was impossible and that no constructive results could be secured, but, on the other hand, I felt constrained to stay by the work because my withdrawal would react to the detriment of the purposes of President Wilson.

It was on March 17 that Mr. Robinson and I submitted our counter-proposals for such provisions of the British plan as were in conflict with our legislative and constitutional situation. We proposed to grant Federal states the right to treat conventions as recommendations.

The British saw our real difficulty more appreciatively than other groups and Mr. Barnes of the British delegation helped in the development of proposals to which we could agree. We were out-voted most of the time. The Cuban delegate usually voted with us and the French and Italian delegations almost invariably voted together usually joining the British. Upon the most of the measures the Japanese refrained from voting, pending instructions from their government. Mr. Vandervelde of the Belgian delegation was open-minded and practical, but habits of years inclined him to the continental point of view. A text was finally agreed upon which met the difficulties of law-making in a Federal government.

The second big fight I made was for the principle that the International Labor Office or its annual assembly shall not propose to any country a law, convention, or treaty which contains lower standards than obtain in that country. After the acceptance of the American proposals safeguarding the rights of federated governments (such as ours), this proposal was the crux upon which our commission was about to split. I announced that unless that proposal was adopted by the commission Mr. Robinson and I would be forced to refrain from signing the report and we would submit a minority report to the Plenary Council. We proceeded to argue this question for days and in addition to conferring with my associate, Mr. Robinson, and with my A. F. of L. associates I also had a conference with Andrew Furuseth who aided us in framing this safeguard. He assured me that if our proposal was made part of the plan, he regarded the document as perfectly safe, sound, and of great benefit to labor of all countries, particularly of those countries which were more backward, while it would safeguard the working people of the United States from any attempt to lower the American standards of life and work. After the die had been cast by my statement to the commission, they adopted the principle by practically a unanimous vote, the Japanese delegation again refraining from voting.

In addition to the Draft Convention which provided for the organization and operation of an International Labor Bureau and conferences, there was drawn up a declaration of labor principles to be inserted in the Peace Treaty. These principles constituting a Bill of Rights for Labor were to write into the treaty an extraordinary recognition of certain common principles of relations between

men in the affairs of daily life. The basis for this charter
was the principles which the American Federation of Labor
submitted to the Inter-Allied Conference in London in September of 1918. In substance the principles to be approved
by the countries signing the treaty were:

In right and in fact the labor of a human being should not be
treated as merchandise or an article of commerce.

Employers and workers should be allowed the right of association
for all lawful purposes.

No child should be permitted to be employed in industry or commerce before the age of fourteen years.

Between the years of fourteen and eighteen gainful employment
permitted at work not physically harmful and on condition that technical or general education be continued.

Every worker has a right to a wage adequate to maintain a reasonable standard of life.

Equal pay should be given to women and to men for work of
equal value in quantity and quality.

A weekly rest, including Sunday, or its equivalent for all workers.

Limitation of the hours of work in industry on the basis of eight
hours a day or forty-eight hours a week.

The commission designated Washington as the place for
the first International Labor Commission to be held under
the treaty and adopted an agenda providing for an organizing committee. The last meeting was held on March 24.

As soon as the work of the commission was finished
our American Labor delegation went to London for a conference with a special committee of the Parliamentary Committee to reach an agreement upon time and place of an
international labor conference which had been proposed for
May and which we hoped 'to have postponed until some
later date, preferably October in Washington. The committee agreed to report our request favorably and we left
London for Plymouth, whence we sailed *via* Brest for New
York.

While I was in Paris, I received an invitation to attend a dinner at Hotel Lutetia. The dinner was to afford an opportunity to present to representative citizens the movement known as the "Comrades in Service." I was told that the movement had the support of General Pershing and his staff and that President Wilson had been present at the preliminary meeting of the movement and had expressed his sympathetic interest. The object of the organization as stated was to perpetuate in civil life the spirit of democracy and fellowship created by war conditions and to place it at the disposal of the nation. That movement resulted in the American Legion. I have attended and addressed practically all its annual conventions.

Shortly after my return from abroad, a street car in New York collided with the taxicab in which I was riding and the next two or three weeks I spent in bed.

When our international commission concluded its sessions, there was no intimation but that our work was final or that the commission would be called together again. I had to return to the United States. Mr. Robinson remained in Europe for a while making some investigations for the Shipping Board.

Returning to Paris, Mr. Robinson was suddenly called to come to a meeting of the Council of Ministers. At that meeting Mr. Barnes as vice-president of the commission presented a request that a plenary session of the Peace Conference be called for the submission of the report of the labor commission. He gave two reasons: first, the need of the highest publicity for the work done by the commission; second, a reinstatement of the commission with authority to consider amendments to the draft convention that might be made by labor organizations and others as a result of such publicity. Mr. Robinson protested most vigorously, stating that the commission had adjourned *sine die* and that it was known that some of the members had left Paris. The motion was not decided in the Council, but was passed up to the "Big Four." Mr. Robinson took the matter up with Secretary Lansing and submitted a memorandum. He then wrote to the President, stating that there had not been the least intimation that the work of the commission was not complete and that it would be reconvened. He stated that to permit the commission to again take up its work would be irregular, unfair, and of harmful consequence in view of the fact that all of the American labor leaders as well as the labor leaders of other countries had left. The commission was not reconvened. Mr. Barnes, who was a member of the British Peace Commission, submitted our draft convention to a plenary session of the Peace Commission. Our proposals were made a special order for a plenary session in which Sir Henry Borden moved that the conference authorize the Drafting Committee to make such amendments as might be necessary to have the convention conform to the covenant of the League of Nations in the character of its membership and the method of adherence. The amendment was adopted and it was agreed that the labor articles should be accepted in a form to be submitted by the Drafting Committee.

The Drafting Committee found the provision "that no contracting party together with its dominions and colonies whether self-governing or not should be entitled to nominate more than one member," out of harmony with the League of Nations provisions and suggested other changes. Sir Robert Borden requested Mr. Robinson to return to Paris. Mr. Robinson told Sir Robert that he was confident

that American labor would not agree to the changes made
by the Drafting Committee. Thereupon Sir Robert shifted
his argument and said that while Canada might sign, it
would withdraw at the end of two years. Mr. Robinson
was undisturbed by the arguments advanced by Sir Robert,
for he felt that the predominance of Great Britain in the
general conference was the limit that could be asked of
the United States. All of these matters were cabled to
me, but this information could not be given me until my
injuries began to mend.

The change about which I was most concerned was the
insertion of the word "merely" after "regarded" in the first
principle of Labor's Bill of Rights, "that the labor of a
human being could not be regarded merely as a commodity
or article of commerce." I protested in a cablegram to
President Wilson against the amended form of that declaration. The other change did not disturb me so much. As
a matter of fact, we were assured that so far as the British
colonies were concerned they would more readily vote with
the representatives of the United States than they would
with those of England.

After I was able to resume work and the facts of the
situation were all before me, I still had no information
from Paris as to final action upon the labor charter. It
was necessary to have definite information, as a report had
to be prepared for submission to the approaching convention of the American Federation of Labor. I cabled to
President Wilson for the necessary information which was
sent as soon as possible. In replying to me, President
Wilson stated that in his opinion the Labor Charter was
one of the most valuable contributions to the Peace Treaty.
Since my protests were of no avail at that time, I followed

my habit of trying to make the best of every situation and I accepted the statement of the intentions of the Council in regard to the change in the declaration, leaving it for the opponents of the treaty to minimize the declaration if they could.

Without attempting to give a further outline of the whole proposal of the International Commission for Labor Legislation, I think it fitting to quote here the preamble as it was accepted by the Plenary Council and is part of the Covenant of the League of Nations of the Treaty of Versailles:

The High Contracting Parties, recognizing that the well-being, physical, moral, and intellectual, of industrial wage-earners is of supreme international importance, have framed, in order to further this great end, the permanent machinery provided for in Section I and associated with that of the League of Nations.

They recognize that difference of climate, habits, and customs of economic opportunity and industrial tradition, make strict uniformity in the conditions of labor difficult of immediate attainment. But, holding as they do, that labor should not be regarded merely as an article of commerce, they think that there are methods and principles for regulating labor conditions which all industrial communities should endeavor to apply, so far as their special circumstances will permit.

Among these methods and principles, the following seem to the High Contracting Parties to be of special and urgent importance:

First—The guiding principle above enunciated that labor should not be regarded merely as a commodity or article of commerce.

Second—The right of association for all lawful purposes by the employed as well as by the employers.

Third—The payment to the employed of a wage adequate to maintain a reasonable standard of life as this is understood in their time and country.

Fourth—The adoption of an eight-hours day or a forty-eight hours week as the standard to be aimed at where it has not already been attained.

Fifth—The adoption of a weekly rest of at least twenty-four hours, which shall include Sunday wherever practicable.

Sixth—The abolition of child labor and the imposition of such limitations on the labor of young persons as shall permit the continuation of their education and assure their proper physical development.

Seventh—The principle that men and women should receive equal remuneration for work of equal value.

Eighth—The standard set by law in each country with respect to the conditions of labor should have due regard to the equitable economic treatment of all workers lawfully resident therein.

Ninth—Each state should make provision for a system of inspection in which women should take part, in order to ensure the enforcement of the laws and regulation for the protection of the employed.

Without claiming that these methods and principles are either complete or final, the High Contracting Parties are of opinion that they are well fitted to guide the policy of the League of Nations; and that, if adopted by the industrial communities that are members of the League, and safeguarded in practice by an adequate system of such inspection, they will confer lasting benefits upon the wage-earners of the world.

In my argument in the following Atlantic City Convention of the A. F. of L. when the subject was up for discussion as to whether our Federation should or should not endorse the ratification of the Peace Treaty including the labor charter, decision centered upon that changed phraseology. I argued that the treaty was not perfect, but it was far in advance of any other of similar character. In addition, for the first time in history, the rights, interests, and welfare of the workers received specific recognition in an international peace treaty. Labor's convention overwhelmingly agreed to advocate the ratification of the treaty

Opposition to the treaty was intense, bitter and well organized. Indeed, before the treaty had been perfected a number of Senators wrote a round-robin protest declaring in advance that they would not only vote but do everything in their power to prevent its ratification.

I spoke at public mass meetings, private conferences, and gatherings of all sorts. I wrote articles and editorials and prepared an article in pamphlet form for general distribution, urging the people of our country to prevail upon the Senate to ratify the treaty. After fully setting forth my views upon the subject, I used as the caption for the article, "Why the Peace Treaty Should be Ratified."

CHAPTER XLVI

To my mind, the only fitting termination for America's participation in the tangle of European affairs that forced trial by combat in the World War was acceptance of responsibility for maintaining justice in international relations and full participation in the League of Nations.

The months following the making of the Versailles Treaty witnessed the far swing of the pendulum to reaction. The War left nations physically exhausted and with nerves overstrained. Europe looked upon wars as inevitable, regarding them as differing only in nearness of time —the war before this, this war, the next probable war. The United States has an essentially different international point of view. For us war must have a moral justification. We do not conceive of our government as organized in opposition to the wishes of the people. America was sustained in the World War by the inspiration that we were fighting to establish relations between nations on a higher plane in which there would be substituted for war, agencies for adjusting differences between nations. The President of our Republic was regarded by all peoples as the leader in the effort to create international machinery to carry out this purpose. Our ideal was clear and steadfast, but our knowledge of the technology of accomplishing our purpose was inadequate.

I did what I could to secure ratification of the treaty by our government. But the reactionary group in Congress blocked all efforts and threw the treaty into a presidential campaign.

Both personally and officially I championed the cause during the presidential campaign of 1920 and did my level best to mobilize public sentiment in support of ratification of the treaty. The vote of that year really expressed no judgment as to the League of Nations, although it was so interpreted. As I said in a previous chapter, it was a vote of hate.

Though the election vote brought complications for the league, yet it seemed necessary to release pent-up feelings. It seemed to me a tragedy in that we broke faith with those who made the supreme sacrifice that democracy might come to the whole world. The tragedy was two-fold, since the man in whose mind the league was conceived was stricken down.

Meanwhile, the League of Nations moves haltingly, but the machinery is there which at some future time can develop into the power and proportions envisioned in the original plans. There will yet be a "world parliament of man."

The years since the Versailles Treaty have been crowded. At no time during my life have there been such inspiring possibilities and such depressing disappointments. During the War we had been thinking upon a higher plane than selfish partisan interests. Although it was disturbing to find the strength of those who wanted to withdraw to the lower levels, there was no reason for discouragement. I had a fairly accurate estimate of the depths of the opposition that had been submerged or controlled during the War, and my information was considerably augmented by my experiences in the Amsterdam conference called to reorganize the International Federation of Trade Unions. There is need of much educational work.

In conferences with representatives of British, French, and Belgian labor it had been decided to reorganize the international trade union organization. The time and place were definitely set for Amsterdam, August, 1919. Daniel Tobin, John Hynes, and I represented our Federation. As we went through London we witnessed the wonderful parade and the ceremony of the dedication of the monument at Whitehall to Britain's soldiers who gave their lives in the War. It was the sort of thing that brought out very vividly the spiritual meaning of the War and fixed definitely ideals which we dare not forget.

Amsterdam was the first international meeting of labor representatives after the War. I had looked forward to that meeting with mixed feelings. I hoped we could bridge the War chasm, but I realized that bridge must rest upon the solid foundation of mutual understanding. While our party was getting identification cards in Amsterdam police headquarters, I first saw the German delegates—Legien, Sassenbach, and Baumeister. I avoided a social meeting then because I wanted first to know whether they were going to play the game squarely. We first met to wind up the affairs of the old International and to dissolve it. As the Belgian delegation was under instructions from their labor movement to present publicly complaints and grievances against the German labor leaders, Cornielle Mertens made a scathing indictment of the leaders of German labor. He called particular attention to the following acts of omission and commission of Mr. Legien and his associates in their failure to take into consideration the obligations which they owed to the other labor movements of the world; in failing to exercise every effort to prevent the war being declared by Germany, and supporting the Imperial German Government in voting for the war budget without which war could not have begun or sustained; for failure to effectively protest against the invasion of Belgium; for failure of the German officers to protest against the deportation of Belgian workers into Germany and the enforcement of compulsory labor upon them; for failure to protest against the cruelties and atrocities which were committed by the Germans upon the Belgian civil population; for failure to protest against the taking out of Belgium the means by which industry could be conducted and the toilers continue in employment; and the taking away of machinery and raw materials and other essentials to industry and employment.

Mertens' charges precipitated much plain speaking. The Belgians demanded that the German delegation admit to the conference Germany's responsibility for bringing on the War. The Belgians made this demand a prerequisite to further participation in the conference. I seconded this demand and our delegation gave insistent support to the Belgian proposal. I also submitted a motion that the business of the conference should be open to the press of all shades of opinions. This was carried and effectually aided our fight. Sassenbach submitted a statement in which he admitted the culpability of Germany and stated that the policies of German labor had been wrongfully based upon misinformation and were the outgrowth of the struggle of the German people for very existence.

The statement was submitted to a committee of which I was a member.

Sassenbach came before our committee and stated that the declaration he had submitted had been criticized by the executive in Berlin and he therefore submitted an amended declaration. I proposed that the original Legien-Sassenbach declaration together with the amended proposal be submitted to the congress without recommendation. When this motion was lost, I proposed a declaration to be adopted by the congress in which it was specifically stated that the aggression of the German government was a matter of common knowledge in Germany as well as in other countries and that it was the duty and the obligation of the representatives of labor in Germany to have publicly protested in the most effective way against the declaration of war as well as the acts of barbarism committed by their war machine. Sassenbach protested that if the resolution were adopted the German delegation would have to withdraw. Edo Fimmen then made a strong appeal to the Germans to stand by their original declaration and he appealed to me to withdraw my resolution. I agreed to withdraw my motion, reserving the right to take any course that might seem proper depending upon the attitude of the German delegation. The committee reported to the conference. Jouhaux proposed that the original proposition of Sassenbach be adopted as the expression made by him on behalf of his delegation, of Germany's culpability. This was adopted. Sassenbach, on behalf of the German delegation, made a statement to the effect that the entire delegation from the German labor movement to the Amsterdam conference loyally confirmed the spirit of the Sassenbach declaration.   The committee's report was then accepted unanimously and the old International passed into history. We then decided details of organization and began consideration of future policies.

There was a very sharp division among the delegates, some belonging to those who look upon labor problems as something to be approached in a practical way achieving whatever of success is possible at the present and planning for successive advancements in the future.   There were others willing to accept nothing that did not correspond to their vision of a reorganized society.   This group made a sharp attack upon the labor charter incorporated in the Versailles Treaty.   I defended that instrument, not because it was perfect, but because it constituted the fairest statement of labor principles that had ever been incorporated in an international treaty and it was a foundation upon which more complete declarations could be builded.

In the course of the business of the conference, I protested against a declaration of the congress that when any question was adopted by a majority vote it was binding upon all national trade union centers and they were compelled to conform.   This was a departure from the principles of the old Federation where autonomy of each national center was granted.   I urged that when vital national interests were at stake, a nation or a group of nations, even though a minority, could not yield its national independence of thought and action.   Because I opposed this new compulsory formula Legien attacked me.   He had the temerity and the audacity to declare that any delegate who would vote against the proposals of the committee was in the pay of the capitalistic class.   That brought me to my feet at once.   I replied at length to his statement, showing

SAMUEL GOMPERS AT 68

the baselessness of his attack and declaring that so far as the representatives of the American labor movement were concerned, to declare them in the pay of any element outside of the labor movement, was a mean, contemptible lie and the man who uttered it untruthful.

I declared that the accusation came with bad grace from one who had been executive head of the trade union movement of the world and who was compelled to admit the culpability of his country in all the complaints made by Mertens, sustained by the unanimous vote of the conference. My reply to and counter-attack upon Legien I delivered in both English and German.

To my mind it was useless to reorganize the International except upon a basis of honesty and straight thinking. Sophistry is always a liability. It fell to my lot to lead the fight to secure a plan under which all could work. When W. A. Appleton of England was made president of the new International, I felt a bit reassured of the future.

However, the loose thinking and irresponsible activity in certain labor groups that had caused so much trouble during the War was destined to create further dissension. A resolution proposing universal strikes as a general policy, which was defeated in the conference, was a forerunner of future difficulties that forced the A. F. of L. to withdraw from the international organization. The group supporting the proposal was small, but it happened to be the group that got control of the administration machinery of the international bureau. These resident officials began issuing documents which in policy and in spirit were in complete variance with the trade union movement. Without consent or even consultation, names were affixed to those impossible communications. The international office undertook to promote a general strike for the socialization of industry and to establish as an international labor policy that a general strike should be declared in case of any war even of a defensive character. The trade union movement of the United States is not without idealism, but it recognizes it must function in the world as it is and that its development must be part of the evolutionary process in which many other factors are involved. There is nothing to be gained in taking an immovable stand for an impossible cause. The American Federation of Labor is intensely interested in the internationality of the labor movement and while the interests of all nationalities may not be identical, upon certain fundamentals there is no division. We recognize the difference in the history of the peoples of the various countries, the diversity of characteristics, of trends of thought as well as economic, political, and sociological environment.

I made known the dissent of the American labor movement from the Amsterdam administration. In the correspondence that followed, there was little desire to give any consideration to the American point of view. Appleton, in whose integrity I have implicit confidence and in whose mind I have found most gratifying congeniality, could spend but little time in Amsterdam and soon found it impossible to continue in a responsible capacity.

The major obstacle to adjusting the situation is the difficulty of getting terms that convey the same idea to labor of other countries as they do to American labor. American trade union statements were translated into terms and meanings wholly at variance with their real intent. But translation is only a part of this problem—the loose use of such terms as socialization, Socialism, and the habit of oratorial exaggeration often gives European labor an illusion of "radicalism" not verified by their practical operations. I have formed the habit of precision in use of words and my economic philosophy makes Socialist terminology destructive as a conveyance for my ideas. I have no quarrel with radicalism that is based upon truths. On the contrary, the application of a truth is far more radical than ill-founded propaganda. I have no quarrel with Socialists, but I have no use for their proposals. In the correspondence with Max S. Hayes carried on through the *American Federationist*, I held that the Socialists had stolen the vocabulary of the American trade union movement to set forth the evils resulting from our modern industrial system and then used these criticisms to build a false philosophy. The result was similar to what happens to a person suffering from some specific disease when a novice prescribes all sorts of quack medicines and nostrums.

In the correspondence with the International Federation of Trade Unions on our differences, none has been more fruitful of possible effort to bring about real understanding and common action of a progressive, constructive character than that I have had with Johann Sassenbach. Finding efforts at adjustment met no constructive response from the revolutionary Socialists who were in control of the executive machinery of the International Federation, the A. F. of L. withdrew for the following reasons:

First—That the new constitution completely abrogated the principle of complete autonomy for each national trade union federation.

Second—That through the issuance of appeals and proclamations the executive body of the international federation had committed the federation to a revolutionary principle, to which the American Federation of Labor is and always has been uncompromisingly opposed and to which no labor movement guided by democratic ideals could give approval.

Third—That a system of dues had been adopted which would place upon the American Federation of Labor a heavy and unbearable expense.

The storm of abuse that followed was directed against me personally. Thus I witnessed a second failure of attempts at international organization. This does not mean that the international purpose was wrong, but only that unwise methods were used. The future holds achievement if we profit by our mistakes.

The first International labor conference under the Versailles Treaty was held in Washington in October, 1919.

It had been agreed at the Amsterdam conference that the International Federation should have a meeting in Washington simultaneously. At the time this was arranged, it was confidently expected that our Senate would have ratified the Versailles Treaty and that the United States would be officially represented in the conference. The Senate refused to ratify, but the President designated as an unofficial representative of the United States, Secretary of Labor William B. Wilson. According to international parliamentary procedure, Secretary Wilson was made chairman of the conference. The conference by unanimous vote invited me to participate in their deliberations and discussions, but, of course, without the right to vote. I attended the opening sessions and after I had expressed myself fully upon the proposal for the adoption of a maximum eight-hour work day, I felt that there was little service I could render in such an artificial capacity.

The Executive Council of the American Federation of Labor proposed to the 1921 convention that labor call upon the American government to take the initiative or co-operate with any nation or group of nations for the promotion of both military and naval disarmament. Sometime afterward, President Harding convened a world-conference on limitation of armament. The issue was of secondary importance to the organizing of world-relations, but it was evidence that a great ideal had been planted inextricably in the minds of nations. I was appointed by President Harding to serve in advisory capacity to the American delegation in the conference. Because I did not anticipate the program of Secretary Hughes, I apprehended that there would be need for an agency through which the views of American citizens could be known to our American delegation. Accordingly, I invited several hundred men and women to constitute such a voluntary committee concerned that the conference should reach constructive decisions. The cordial response to my invitation was evidence of the sincerity of public conviction for world-peace. The commission organized in committees. I served on the Executive Committee and the committee dealing with the Pacific and Far Eastern questions. Secretary Hughes startled the world by an act of straight-forward American diplomacy in submitting to the conference a proposal for genuine reduction in armaments. The world was in such dire economic straits that even professional diplomats did not dare to juggle seriously with proposals that were essentially humanitarian and necessary. At the close of the conference I received from President Harding (as probably did all serving the American government) a letter expressing appreciation of my services.

There are some conditions in Europe that make it seemingly desirable for the United States to remain aloof from a world-league or international association, but such faint-hearted policy does not accord with a robust sense of duty.

The League of Nations falls short of the vision which heartened us to strive for it, but it is yet in its infancy. Though the fully developed structure lies in the heart of the future, I am confident there will be an international parliament, that shall maintain justice in the word.

I firmly believe in the Monroe Doctrine—not as an empty phrase but as a virile force maintaining an essentially American principle. The fundamental policy which I have pursued in the organizing of the Pan-American Federation of Labor is based upon the spirit of the Monroe Doctrine, to establish and maintain the most friendly relations between Pan-American countries, to create and maintain not only mutual good will among the working masses of the Pan-American republics but their respective governments. As I have already said, I have declared for the internationality of good will and good relations between the countries of the whole world, and therefore I have supported and will continue to support the entrance of the United States into the League of Nations. That organization may prove the instrumentality of avoiding the friction from rivalry, ambitions, and aggrandizement which lead to strife and war, but if, after all, that hope should fail and there develop evil designs upon all America—the United States and the Pan-American republics would be in a position through the Pan-American Union to make a stand against aggression and effort to over-awe the people of our western hemisphere. It is significant that in the Pan-American Union Conference room there is a chair for the Ambassador of every Pan-American country. There is one chair vacant. That chair is reserved for the time when it may be occupied by Canada's Ambassador.

CHAPTER XLVII

PROBLEMS AFTER ARMAGEDDON

To me the War had been a crusade inspired by concern
for the higher welfare of humanity and glorifying the spirit
of service. I had flung myself into the cause without reser-
vation, happy to find myself in harmony with so many.
All my life has been a fight and it has so often been my
duty to say that which but few wanted to hear. It was
a real comfort for once in my life to find my purposes
understood and appreciated. The Armistice had brought
a sudden reversal of forces. Again I found myself leading
against the current, for I would not change my directing
purpose nor bow my head to avoid popular criticism. If
I had retired from active participation in the struggles of
life, my reputation would have stood one hundred per cent
patriotic and humanitarian. No progress was possible except upon foundations of tried and proven principles and
it would have been a confession of weakness to seek to
avoid the unpleasant. One cannot force progress, but one
can point out mistakes and help to lead along the right
path. Often I have wished that men would benefit through
the experience of others, but the years have taught me
patience. So I am not discouraged when division and strife
in the affairs of men and nations come.

It had been my hope that the principles of co-operation
and co-ordination effective during the War would serve as

a foundation for industrial reorganization after the War. It was a hope that did credit to my optimism. Instead there have been big battles to maintain pre-war standards.

When I returned from Amsterdam in 1919, I found confronting the labor movement gigantic problems in steel and transportation. Steel, a basic industry, while consolidating under trust control had arbitrarily and ruthlessly opposed the organization of its workmen. It was the only big industry to which the War did not bring constructive progress in industrial justice. Even during the War, steel companies refused to deal with bona fide organizations of wage-earners and created company-owned unions. At its 1918 convention the A. F. of L. authorized a committee to organize steel workers. That committee selected as its secretary a man whom I had seen but once.

When sometime before I was attending a meeting of the Chicago Federation of Labor one of the delegates in the body of the hall made a strong speech, declaring that he was converted from the old ideals he had, that he supported in full the fundamental principles, the ideas, the methods, philosophy, and policy of the American Federation of Labor which at that meeting I had enunciated. I was much impressed. I did not know the man nor even his name. I had never seen him before. A few days after my return to Washington I wrote to John Fitzpatrick, president of the Chicago Federation of Labor, and asked the name of the man who made the talk in support of the A. F. of L. I was informed that it was William Z. Foster. It was my desire to give this man the opportunity to be helpful to the *bona fide* labor movement. He had declared himself to be so thoroughly changed.

Whether the reports which came to me were truthful

or otherwise, I knew that he had been working in the stock-
yards organization which resulted in much improvement in
the conditions of the workers in the industry.   Then when
the convention of the American Federation of Labor in
St. Paul in 1918 decided to undertake the campaign to
organize the workers in the steel industry I was made
chairman of the committee, and Foster secretary. I was
really pleased with his selection as secretary of the organizing committee. The committee was made up of the representatives of all unions within whose jurisdiction steel
workers came. This was a working plan that provided
unity of effort with flexibility necessary to retain trade
alignments.

After the Armistice, the strength of the steel unions
increased materially.   Agitation against the twelve-hour
day gained impetus. The resistance of U. S. Steel to labor
unions became more aggressive. In a number of steel
towns, free assemblage and free speech were denied as effectually as though no constitutional guarantees existed.
Acts of violence against our organizers followed. On behalf of our committee I wrote Judge Gary, asking for a
conference. Not even the courtesy of an acknowledgment
was received. This was in conformity with the United
States Steel Corporation policy of refusing to "recognize"
the union. Refusing to recognize the obvious leads to
complications.

Because my official duties had necessitated my absence
from the country I resigned as chairman of the committee
and Fitzpatrick had been selected for that position. When
I returned from Amsterdam, I learned that a strike vote
had been taken and strike authorized. The committee personally applied at Judge Gary's office for a conference.

Judge Gary though in his office refused to see the committee but asked them to submit their business in writing. This was done and the reply received was that United States Steel would not "recognize" representatives of organized labor.

After the situation had been considered by our Executive Council, it was decided that we appeal to President Wilson to use his good offices to secure an adjustment of the situation. Fitzpatrick, Davis, Foster, Hannan, and I laid the situation before President Wilson who manifested sincere interest and who endeavored to bring about a conference. However, he failed. He had just started to secure popular support in favor of the treaty ratification.

I then called a conference for the full organizing committee in my office (September 8). I told the men that according to confidential information at a meeting of the "open-shop" interests held in New York City, it had been decided that the U. S. Steel should make the fight against further organization of workers. The Corporation was prepared for the contest and welcomed an opportunity to force aggressive action upon labor. Both Foster and Fitzpatrick assured me that it was impossible to prevent the strike on the appointed day.

As a committee, we sent a telegram appealing to President Wilson. The President replied, urging in view of his inability to arrange satisfactory mediation at that time, that strike be postponed until after the industrial conference which he had called for October 6 to develop national agreement upon fundamental principles of industrial relations. The steel strike was set for a date just preceding the conference of September 22. If it were deferred, there was a possibility that differences could be adjusted upon the basis of agreements reached in the conference; if it took place according to schedule, the background of conflict would render very difficult that spirit of conciliation and deliberation necessary to make the President's Industrial Conference effective.

When I received the President's telegram, I communicated with Fitzpatrick at Pittsburgh urging compliance with the President's request. The organizing committee met to consider the situation. With the assistance of William Johnston, president of the Machinists' organization, I made an insistent struggle to postpone action. After a two days' session, the committee decided to abide by their strike program and sent a letter to President Wilson stating the reasons for that course. Though I knew that the strike would fail, the best I could do was to suggest and advise, for it must be understood that as president of the American Federation of Labor I had neither the right nor the power to call the strike or to countermand the strike order.

In these conferences, Foster had been so insistent that the strike should take place upon the day set that I began to doubt his sincerity and to believe, as I am now convinced, that his whole conciliatory policy toward the American Federation of Labor and the trade union movement was for no other reason than to gain some foothold by which he could undermine and destroy the bona fide labor movement of America and to try to reconstruct it upon the Soviet revolutionary basis.

When the Senate Committee on Education and Labor made its investigation as to the causes of the steel strike and the conditions under which the employes were required to work, among others Foster was a witness. He hesitated, hemmed and hawed, and endeavored to escape questioning upon his previous writings as well as the purpose of his activities in that strike. He took the most absurd position, saying that if the newspaper men were excluded from the room he would answer the committee's questions fully. The hearing was public, an official stenographer was taking notes which were to be transcribed and printed and so there could be nothing of an exclusive character in any testimony he or any other witness gave.

During one such instance, I was sitting at the table near Foster. Indignant at his failure to make his position clear-cut, I almost hissed at him. "Why don't you talk freely and openly? There is nothing which anyobdy or any newspaper can say about you that they have not already said." Despite my admonition, he continued evasive through the hearing and when confronted with some of his own utterances and writings in print he would answer, "Well, I would not say it that same way again," or some similar rejoinder.

Though I protected Foster in public and in the Senate hearing, in private labor sessions I gave him no reason to misunderstand my mind. I called a conference of representative labor men in the New Morrison Hotel, Chicago, April 11, 1922. In the conference I attacked Foster's so-called amalgamation proposition. He rose in reply and called upon me to testify to my confidence in his integrity and sincerity. I promptly replied that I did not believe that it was possible for him to be sincere or that he had any honest purpose in so far as the trade union movement or the American Federation of Labor was concerned.

I had no sympathy with the attitude of Judge Gary. On the contrary, if an effective movement could have been brought about to teach him a lesson in industrial history I was not unwilling that it should be administered to him, but for me to have interposed or to have declared publicly that in my judgment the strike should not take place would simply have brought about chaos among the men who had been organized to the number of over one hundred thousand, and the result would have been even more injurious than it turned out to be.

However, the years of educational work in furtherance of the eight-hour day of the A. F. of L. and intensive efforts to establish eight hours as the maximum work-day in many industries, had made conspicuous the brutality of the twelve-hour day and the seven-day week. There were many who deplored the two-shift system in steel. Under the leadership of Morris L. Cooke, the Philadelphia Engineers' Club initiated a study of the technique of changing from a twelve to an eight-hour shift in continuous industry. The study challenged interest and finally led to an engineering report on the twelve-hour day in industry by the Federated American Engineering Societies which was submitted to the heads of the United States Steel Corporation by President Harding. Public opinion was roused to the social problem by the Inter-Church Steel Report. At last the end of the twelve-hour day seemed at hand and the organization of the steel workers was again put under way.

The Industrial Conference called by President Wilson was peculiarly constituted. There were representatives of employers, labor, and the public. The group representing the employers was 100 per cent employers; the group representing labor was 100 per cent labor; the representatives of the public were fully 90 per cent employers and among them some of the largest employers in the country includ-

ing Judge Gary and Mr. Rockefeller. It seemed to my
associates and me that if the conference was to reach
constructive conclusions, the best means to test it was an
effort to have the conference recommend mediation for the
purpose of reaching some cordial entente between the Steel
Corporation and the workmen on strike. It was vice-president Thomas A. Rickert of the Federation's Executive
Council who made the original suggestion. Our proposal
was discussed for several days and opposed acrimoniously
by the employers' group and members of the group representing the public.

In the meantime, the public and labor groups met and
after prolonged discussions agreed upon a declaration of
fundamental principles. After this agreement had been
reached, I took a severe cold, high fever developed, and
my physician forbade my leaving my bed. On the evening
of that day I learned that during my absence a discussion
had arisen in the committee which vitiated all the work
on declaration of principles. Our resolution for mediation
came before the conference in its original form and was
rejected. Despite my physician's orders, I went to the conference, previously having a meeting of the representatives
of labor which included the Executive Council of our
Federation and the representatives of the railroad brotherhoods. We decided that if our resolution was rejected and
the conference refused to declare for collective agreements,
it would be a practical waste of time to attempt to urge
any beneficial conclusion. As I have stated, our proposal
was rejected. After a vote was called, I obtained recognition to address the conference and stated that my talk
would be my "swan song," for rejection of our proposals
on the steel strike and collective bargaining legislated us

out of the conference. We left the conference in a body. Indeed, it was a mistake to expect that a conference of that sort would lead to an agreement upon principles that could serve as a working basis. Such a conference would attempt to "legislate" for industry, whereas really constructive changes and methods are evolved out of the experience of industry by those handling its tools and in control.

I have participated in the two economic conferences called by President Harding—the Unemployment Conference and the Agricultural Conference. The first under the chairmanship of Secretary of Commerce Hoover confined itself to concrete situations and technical problems. It led to practical additions to the information of management and brought home to industries the responsibility of handling their own problems. The Agricultural Conference did not prove so successful—the real farmers were not there, only those who exploit farmers. My observations in that meeting enabled me to tell a conference of "dirt farmers" in Chicago two years later that their way forward lay in organizing and developing information upon which to base action.

The government can supply counsel and information on industrial problems, but industries and all elements concerned must finally work out the solution.

In transportation, the situation had been complicated by unwise propaganda. Organization of workers in the railway shops had progressed tremendously under the Federal railway administration. As the time to return the railroads to private operation drew near came the Plumb Plan episode. This plan, sponsored first by some of the Brotherhoods, was presented to the shop crafts and an attempt made to commit them to the plan.

The proposal which had the appearance of progressive thought concealed many fundamental weaknesses. My name had been printed among the sponsors of the plan. As the situation was critical for the shopmen, I did not want to embarrass them by asking for explanations, so I held my peace publicly.

In one whole day's discussion with Mr. Plumb in my office I pointed out to him many glaring difficulties, obstacles, and unworkable propositions. He admitted to me then that his entire plan required reconstruction. However, I have reason to believe that he did not take kindly to the fact that I had pointed out the egregious mistakes in the bill which had been framed by him.

In the meanwhile, a Railway Labor Board was established under Federal law, and the experiment of government control over personnel was under way. Before long the unions were forced into strike and there began the revulsion against government operation and in favor of private operation and collective bargaining. And so men learn.

Through the transitional War period and the industrial storms of the past years, the labor movement emerged intact, stronger than at our entrance into the War. The past years have been a revealing test, sharply distinguishing the permanent from the ephemeral. They have demonstrated again the dependability of voluntary institutions assuring individual initiative. They reveal that genuine growth and progress do not come from above or the outside. They do not come through formulas or declarations but from the educational self-imposed discipline of the life process and are manifest in self-revealing work.

Whether the situation was of my own choosing or not,

I have tried to be of service. I have my dreams as to what ought to exist in industry—a dream of co-ordination of all in production with unrestricted opportunity assured to all to devote mind and skill to production and distribution in the service of human needs. I yearn to have workers in industry know what a marvelously satisfying thing it is to feel that one is creating something. At one time I proposed to my colleagues on the Executive Council that we formally lay before other groups in production a proposal to co-operate in concentrating attention upon the creative aspects of production. When my suggestion was rejected, I withdrew it, not in discouragement, but with the conviction that the future would reverse the decision.

We American trade unionists want to work out our problems in the spirit of true Americanism—a spirit that embodies our broadest and highest ideals. If we do not succeed, it will be due to no fault of ours. We have been building the A. F. of L. in conformity with what we believe to be the original intent and purpose of America. I have an abiding faith that we will succeed and with that success are involved the progress and the welfare of the great mass of American citizenship.

I have no overwhelming conceit of the value or the importance of what I have recorded in this book, nor do I wish to underestimate it. From my observations and experience I have reached the conclusion that over-modesty is after all in itself a species of vanity. So I have in these pages written a faithful record of what I have seen and done with such comment as seemed necessary for clear understanding of the subjects and facts with which I have dealt.

Perhaps, what I have not included may be as important

or more so than what these pages contain. So much which exists in the archives of the labor movement and elsewhere for the time being baffles gathering and research. Perhaps if life, time, and opportunity afford, I may again attempt to devote myself to further presentation of facts of life and work. This I say without fear of dispute or refutation, that the World War changed me only in one respect. That is, when the War demonstrated that pacifism in which I believed and which I faithfully advocated was a vain hope I realized that the struggle in defense of right and freedom must ever be maintained at all hazard. In all other things, I have steadily held to the faith and struggled for the right of all humanity to freedom, justice, and democracy; for full enfranchisement of the wage-earners of our country and our time not only politically but industrially; and to secure individual and social justice for all and opportunity for spiritual development. Labor must have the opportunity of free and untrammeled self-development that the toilers may find their places with absolute equality with all the citizens of our country regardless of their situation. Before the War I ardently advocated these principles. During the War I fought for them; since the War and so long as life shall remain with me I expect to devote whatever ability and all of the energy that is within me to the establishment, maintenance and perpetuation of this ideal.

Thrice since Armistice Day I have looked death in the face very closely. But my seventy-third birthday and then the 42d anniversary of the A. F. of L. (Nov. 15, 1923) found me as usual at my desk, doing the work that I love best—work that is such a privilege to do that I sometimes feel selfish because of my opportunity to do so much. Frequently, there comes over me a feeling like liquid fire—it just courses through my veins—a yearning to work. The first thought that comes to my brain is a desire to do something, to do some work, to be of some service. I do not value the labor movement only for its ability to give higher wages, better clothes, and better homes—its ultimate goal is to be found in the progressively evolving life possibilities of those who work. There are such wonderful possiblities in the life of each man and woman! No human being is unimportant. My inspiration comes in opening opportunities that all alike may be free to live life to the fullest.

The work of the labor movement does not grow less, for it has its roots in vital needs. That gives it the same intrinsic power to interest that life holds, and to me the two are inseparable. I hope to keep on with my work until I go out into the silence.

APPENDIX

HIS LAST YEAR
An Epilogue

BY

FLORENCE CALVERT THORNE

HIS LAST YEAR

Less than a twelve-month after Mr. Gompers closed his autobiography with the wish that he might be permitted to continue at his work until he should "go out into the Silence," death came to him under conditions that were fulfillment of that wish and fitting completion of the epic of his life.

In December, 1923, after personally placing the manuscript of his autobiography in the hands of Mr. Macrae, the President of E. P. Dutton & Company, with ceremony which his great dramatic instinct required for the completion of an undertaking into which he had put so much of thought and feeling, he went to Panama to make an investigation into working conditions directed by the Portland Convention of the American Federation of Labor. To exacting work in a tropical climate he gave himself unreservedly so that he came home fatigued and depressed. He refused to go away for a rest or even reduce his working hours, and thus undermined his vitality to such an extent that aroused grave concern.

He had a philosophy of personal freedom that he followed in his personal life—no inhibitions, no restrictions, but to allow natural inclination to take its course. The results brought rich and varied experiences that enabled him to understand many different kinds of people, and to develop that universal quality of mind that distinguished his leadership. His was a nature in which strong primitive instincts and spiritual vision in turn served his purpose. His doctors vainly endeavored to make him see the need of diet and physical discipline. Not yet convinced his body had failed him, he stoutly maintained there was only one way he could work and live and proceeded accordingly.

Among outstanding undertakings which occupied his special interest during the year were relief of the German trade union movement, organization of the power industry, organization of women wage-earners, Labor's political policy, international labor relations. In each of these undertakings his work served in a remarkable degree to reveal his purposes to groups that had misunderstood or misjudged him so that he had the satisfaction of bringing about sympathetic understanding and a spirit of co-operation even where specific plans did not materialize. He had learned the value of mutual understanding, for he used and appreciated the educational method.

From a number of sources information came to him that the trade union movement of Germany was threatened by the inflation and economic uncertainty that had paralyzed German economic life. From confidential as well as official informants he learned that German trade union offices could no longer pay rents or salaries or buy fuel, office supplies or even stamps. He was appalled by the consequences of such a calamity not only to German labor but to international labor and world economic organization. He had a respect for a functioning order that only a constructive builder can know.

He was deeply troubled, for he knew that feeling against Germany rooted in the World War had not died in the hearts and minds of America's workers. Though he had a great love for the German people, and the friends of

Hirsch's shop had a place in his heart occupied by no successors, he had been one of the first to see in the World War a conflict in which institutions of democracy were at stake and he had denounced not only the German government but leaders of German labor for not standing up to be counted among those repudiating German autocratic militarism. Yet for him the War was over. He held no lingering resentment. But his colleagues and the rank and file of American labor—would they respond to an appeal to help German labor? Quietly he set about finding out the position of American labor. It was interesting to watch him following the same technique as in the early days of the War when he probed the feeling of our foreign-born citizens on the War, preparing to mobilize them in support of the War. A number of confidential conferences with key persons, many of them persons who helped in the war effort, group conferences, a general conference and then he was ready to submit to American labor a proposal to lend a helping hand to German labor in their dire need, confident that the response would be worthy of the idealism and fraternal spirit of American labor. The results fully justified his judgment. American labor responded liberally and by so doing demonstrated the constructive internationalism for which the Federation was contending. In this as in other matters on which he was occasionally said to exercise too much domination, he intuitively sensed in advance labor's mind and more quickly than others appreciated the results of a policy. Though he expedited action now and then, he never led labor along paths contrary to its desires. He knew human nature, and that tyrannical leadership would be at least a Pyrrhic victory. He had an extraordinary ability to register the feeling and convictions of others.

While watching him in the process of doing this, one frequently got the impression that through highly sensitized appreciation of rhythm he got the tempo of the thoughts of others and made use of some universal language of which he himself was probably unconscious. He would sit very quietly, apparently every sense-organ quivering in its eagerness for impressions, the air highly charged with magnetism. Suddenly there would be a withdrawing—he had reached his conclusion.

For years Mr. Gompers had done what he could to help in the special problems of women. They had his sympathy as did any group placed at a disadvantage by existing conventions. He realized that the problem of securing economic justice for women wage-earners was in a considerable degree bound up with the general woman problem. After suffrage was won for women and the courts had outlawed protective legislation for women, he thought economic organization of women must be promoted more aggressively. In his own organization he won a fifty-year effort to open to women in the trade, membership in the union equally with men. He proposed to the Executive Council to submit to the Portland Convention that special plans to organize women wage-earners be developed. When that proposal was authorized, he gave to the work of developing it his special attention. He participated in conferences and discussions, taxing his failing physical strength to the limit to further this purpose. Through these conferences women in industry found he was the friend upon whom they could depend for understanding and help. Though the work was very dear to him, when it was later laid aside he manifested no resentment. He was then so ill that he could not contend for his policy, but with that acuteness of vision that often comes as the spirit is freeing itself from the flesh, he had confidence that some other way would be found. He felt he could trust the undertaking to the future because of his faith in the destiny of the labor movement.

There was developing a gentle remoteness that shrank from the physical ordeal of contest. The spirit was willing but the flesh was weak. But never once was there even a gesture of rebellion. In this, as in the handicap that had darkened his life for the last six years, he merely accepted the situation and did the best he could. That was a life-long habit. With failing eyesight he was compelled to get practically all information through his ears. His hearing always acute became so trained that he recognized people instantly by their voices. Over and over again he came to the office with hands and pockets filled with clippings or articles or books he wanted read to him, only his keen eagerness revealing how hungry he was for information. One morning he told of his happiness the night before when he discovered his volumes of Elbert Hubbard printed in type so bold that with reading glass, "I could read for myself."

Among the big public questions of the year in which he was deeply interested was Power. Traveling through the Northwest over an electrified road and seeing in that section visible evidences of the White Revolution, the implications of co-ordination of power and its coming function in society gripped his imagination. He sought information from engineers in that field, and quickly grasped what the development of far-flung power undertakings through co-ordinated regulation would mean in industry, in commerce, in community life, on the farms and in the homes, and he yearned to project early in the planning of the industry principles of organization that would assure continuous progress in the industry, the best interests of all co-operating in the production and distribution of power and service at lowest rates to consumers. He felt a compelling urge to contribute of his experience and influence and he went about that work with a youthful vigor of imagination seldom found at seventy-four.

He felt there was a glorious opportunity to make amends for the mistakes that had been made in other industries if social and economic experience were brought to bear upon the problems of the industry through the trade organizations of various groups with adequate social regulation. He believed that a new technique of regulation was necessary—a technique based upon specialized thinking. Pondering over one of his statements of the fundamentals upon which industry must be organized, almost dreaming he said, "If only management would make it possible for us to give all our thought and energy to production, what miracles we could work!" In his thinking, labor was but one of the groups in industry and society, and its welfare involved no inherent conflict with other groups—but he was the spokesman and the champion of that particular group and at times appeared to speak for a special interest. As time more clearly reveals his purposes, such championship is seen as a means to constructive synthesis through the removal of wrongs and injustice. In his mind the labor movement had authority because it served the high cause of humanity. In the message entrusted to Mr. Duncan to deliver after his death he said:

Say to them that as I kept the faith I expect they will keep the faith. They must carry on. Say to them that a union man carrying a card cannot be a good citizen unless he upholds American institutions and he is a poor citizen if he upholds American institutions and forgets his obligations to his trade association.

What he meant by America he thus expressed in a war-time speech:

America is not merely a name. It is not merely a land. It is not merely a country, nor is it merely a sentiment. America is a symbol; it is an ideal. The hope of all the world can be expressed in the ideal —America.   )

He accepted Governor Pinchot's invitation to become a member of the Giant Power Commission of Pennsylvania and went almost from the hospital to participate in a meeting of a committee to study the industrial load curve of Pennsylvania. When he found that plans were under way to organize the power industries of the world, jealous that labor should have recognition in order that it might have opportunity to render service, in a most vigorous fashion he urged that labor of the United States and Great Britain should be represented in the First World Power Congress, to be held in London in July. The executive committees of both Great Britain and the United States participating in arrangements for the congress were so constituted as to ignore both public and labor interests in the development of power policies. He sought the co-operation of the British labor movement and the British Labor Party that had just come into office. In our country he urged his cause so effectively that he and several other labor officials whose organizations were concerned with the power industry were invited to accept membership on our national committee co-operating in the movement which was to establish a permanent organization concerned with world labor problems. That he himself was precluded from participation in the conference chafed his spirit, but he busied himself in the preparation of a paper setting forth labor's power program and embodying the fundamentals of his philosophy.

In the last few years he had been working out an articulated statement of the economic philosophy and purposes which the American labor movement seeks to promote. Those things which he had done instinctively because he felt they were right, often without putting in words why, he was attempting to set down to serve as a guide for others. One of the few times he participated in the discussions of the El Paso Convention was to emphasize a statement of labor's economic philosophy, submitted in the Executive Council's report.

No single undertaking received so much of Mr. Gompers' time and thought during the past year as the child labor amendment. For children he had a very special tenderness and he wanted for all of them opportunity to know the fullness of life. His resentment against the labor of children was as vehement at seventy-four as it was when he made a passionate speech against it in the 1881 convention of the Federation. As chairman of the Permanent Committee on the Abolition of Child Labor he had helped formulate the amendment which he urged Congress to adopt. From his sick-bed in the summer he wrote advising the wage-earners of Massachusetts to rally in support of the amendment in their state. One of the last appointments he had in his office was to hear a report on the Massachusetts child labor campaign. Upon labor he felt rested major responsibility for the abolition of child labor for "we are those immediately affected in our own bodies and hearts and those of our children."

In May there came a time when his body failed. He was spiritually broken, and for the first time the will to

live seemed to waver. Day by day important engagements
were canceled which he was unable to keep, yet each day
he forced himself to routine work, chiefly because he was
happier with his work than any other place. At the end
of May he could no longer keep up and went to New York,
to a friend he loved, seeking refuge and care. Within a
few days he was taken to Lenox Hill Hospital, ill unto
death—"Ten days—perhaps four," the doctors said. But
the doctors worked with the strength of love and skill of
the most highly trained physicians. Slowly but definitely
they gained over disease and built up anew. It was the
middle of July before he left the hospital.

But in the meanwhile his mind had been busy with the
presidential campaign and his was the directing mind. He
went from the hospital to present labor's case to the
Democratic Platform Committee.

Months preceding the campaign Mr. Gompers, in conference with the leaders of the Democratic Party, warned
them that unless that party could show more constructive
results, labor's support would not continue. Mr. Gompers
anticipated the force of the world-wide tide of reaction and
felt that labor's most telling course would be a protest
movement. Because of his confidence in Senator La Follette's integrity of purpose, he regarded him as the logical
leader of such a movement. In his hospital room he heard
the reading of the Democratic platform which ignored his
plea, and remarked, "It looks as if we are forced to turn
to La Follette." After the nomination of John W. Davis
as the Democratic candidate he declared, "There is no other
way." Unable to confer with the Senator personally, he
sent two colleagues as his confidential representatives to
talk over the situation with Senator La Follette. He

outlined the basis upon which the campaign was to be conducted and suggested to the Executive Council endorsement of La Follette as a protest against reaction and materialism in politics. From his sick-room he kept in touch with the activities of the campaign.

The doctors prescribed a most rigid diet and told him his life depended upon following orders. The diet prohibited those things in which Mr. Gompers had reveled for years—and to him every phase of life in turn brought joy. He used to say: "I didn't know there were so many different kinds of greens in the world. They are all right as side dishes but—well this is not a diet to nourish strong men."

Though he seemed to be getting better he would repeatedly say, "I am really not gaining." He knew literally nothing about his physical mechanism, but something elemental told him he had lost his grip on life and was not regaining it. To him those last months were an artificial life. He lived on, sustained by his will—he had not yet run his course. To the rest of us it was like having one brought back from the dead to be with us for a little longer. There was about him that indefinable winged quality that made us try to keep in the background all but the most constructive, spiritually satisfying work. Nor was this feeling confined to the confidential office staff. It dominated the El Paso Convention. Strong aggressive men to whom policies were of vital consequence voluntarily withheld contention for their positions because they did not want to open discussion that would force the "Old Man" to defend his policies. There was nothing more beautiful in the convention than the eyes of the Old Viking of the Seamen when he held his peace as the committee reported against his resolution to condemn the International Labor Bureau. The

men waited only for a sign or a word from their Chief.
They were men of good will, eager to show their reverence
for service.

Mr. Gompers reached El Paso worn and weary from
the overland trip. He was mentally depressed—burdened
by personal troubles. Those were anxious days, for we
feared the strain of the convention. Then as the veterans
of labor gathered and he met the long-time friends, he
seemed to draw upon hidden reserves and we had again
that genial, lovable, dominating Chief of the Federation,
keen and alert mentally, with occasional flashes of the old-
time repartee which the men loved. Calling the convention
together with the thought he could probably preside for
only limited periods, he held the gavel in his hand practically the full time until the convention finished its business. His voice daily grew stronger, now and then ringing
out with old resonant quality.

As he had looked forward to the work of the convention reflecting on some of the situations most likely to cause
trouble, there was uppermost in his mind the thought, "How
can I best press home fundamentals which must not be
forgotten?" And he began planning for a written message—a method so unusual for him that it carried its own
significance. With the greatest of care he prepared that
message, setting forth his trade union creed, and with equal
care he selected the colleague whom he asked to read it.
The spirit of the message and the circumstances attaching
to it at once gave to the convention a dramatic intensity
which was sustained in the series of extraordinary events
and tributes to Mr. Gompers' work.

The outstanding events of the convention were the
international demonstrations that roused a depth of feeling

seldom evoked in an American audience. These demonstrations were the culmination of undertakings Mr. Gompers had been carrying forward and for which his vision and foresight were the chief inspiration. For years he had been interested in Mexico. For him internationalism was a practical idea, and he had the courage to make it an effective agency even in defiance of conventions. In December, 1923, in Jaurez, he made the initial speech in General Calles' campaign for the presidency of Mexico. It was a rallying call that cleared the air and united Mexican labor. He rendered service despite charges that he was meddling in internal politics of Mexico that might have troubled a man less sure of his facts and purposes.

After Calles was elected President of Mexico, as he came through the United States en route to Europe, he went to Atlantic City to invite Mr. Gompers and the Executive Council to be present at his inauguration in Mexico City in December. The Mexican Federation of Labor later extended an invitation not only to the Executive Council but to delegates to the El Paso Convention to attend the inauguration as their guests. When President-Elect Calles returned to the United States in October he planned to visit Washington. The State Department of course detailed representatives to receive him at the station. Mr. Gompers also directed representatives of American labor to greet Calles. The State Department objected, protesting it shared its prerogatives with no private group. But Mr. Gompers, knowing that Calles and Mexico regarded the friendship of American labor as the most dependable surety of peace and good will between the two countries, stood his ground, and labor men joined with state officials to welcome the first constitutional successor to the Mexican presidency—a man elected by the votes of Mexican workers. The only unofficial visit that Calles made in Washington was to President Gompers in the office of the American Federation of Labor.

It had been arranged that the Mexican Federation of Labor should hold its annual convention in Jaurez just across the International Bridge from El Paso and that in addition to simultaneous sessions there should be joint meetings of the two national labor bodies.

Mr. Gompers planned the joint sessions and met with the representatives of Mexican labor. He, better than many of his colleagues, visualized how the meetings would stimulate and sustain the higher idealism that is the soul of the labor movement. To Mexican wage-earners the opportunity to see and greet Mr. Gompers was almost a religious rite. They remembered that in one of the darkest hours of Mexico Mr. Gompers brought help and hope, and almost in spite of difference of opinion on their part, helped to organize a Mexican trade union movement based upon constructive idealism which in six years had almost reached the two million mark. They had come to understand the idealism that guided Mr. Gompers' practical measures and in the minds of thousands of peons the name "Gompers" implies their great Emancipator. They had come to understand his vision of the Pan-American Federation with functions extending into a field infinitely larger than that narrowly connoted by Labor. In his mind was a vision of a continent, the doors of whose Temple of Janus should be always closed because human intercourse conformed to ideals of constructive democracy.

When at the appointed time, representatives of the American Federation of Labor met the advance guard of the Mexican Federation of Labor on the International Bridge and escorted them to the hall where the delegates to the Federation were seated, and to the stirring music of the national anthems of both countries, the Mexican workers joined fellow workers from across the international boundary. It was a strange group to the Americans. Barefoot and sandaled peons with simple cotton suits marched side by side with workers in clothing fashioned in the United States and followed by others in more or less distinctively Mexican dress. Yet the Mexican workers with their ardent temperament had a capacity for expressing their more fervid emotions which the Americans have not yet learned. But so spontaneous and contagious was the manifestation of international fraternity that the thrill broke the repression of the American delegates when the representatives of many nations on the platform grasped hands as symbolical of a continuous chain of good will to bind together many peoples. The scene was an international labor demonstration without parallel in the history of labor of the New World, and, as one of the British delegates remarked, without parallel in his experience.

Appreciating fully the emotional opportunity of the situation, Mr. Gompers drew upon his reserve forces to speak to the gathering with the old-time vigor of imagination and persuasiveness of voice. Dramatic ability was his most fundamental quality. It served him in timing speech and deed. It gave him a control of situations that explains much in his leadership. Never did it serve him better than in these meetings. Though each speaker carried the listeners to higher levels of thinking, he dominated the scene. The tributes paid him in that meeting and the following day when American labor returned the courtesy by visiting the Mexican Federation of Labor, touched Mr. Gompers very deeply as was manifest in the extraordinary modulation of his voice, always rich and vibrant. These two scenes stored rich memories in the minds of all present.

Because gratified with the achievements of international labor in the Americas, Mr. Gompers referred regretfully to circumstances which had brought about the withdrawal of the American Federation of Labor from the International Federation of Trade Unions. In the summer he had asked a friend, in whose ability and purpose he had implicit confidence, to discuss the situation with the resident officials in Amsterdam in the hope that better understanding might lead to such adjustment as would make possible American reaffiliation. The report that was brought back to him encouraged him to believe that a way forward could be found. When in October additional information came from the friend acting as intermediary, with a radiance in his face that came in great crises, he dictated his reply and while waiting for his letter to be transcribed, talked of his hope and said: "When I am gone I want someone to do me the justice to let the world know that I was never in entire accord with my colleagues upon withdrawal from the International Federation of Trade Unions. I know they were right in the objections they made against certain acts of the International. I have written as directed but believed we could have met our difficulties in another way—from within. I believed that our American labor movement owed the same obligation to other national centers, that other trade union organizations owed to our Federation—to help the less progressive to elevate their standards."

During the convention in El Paso and the Pan-American Congress in Mexico City, he kept in mind the interna-

tional labor problem, hoping that the fraternal delegates
from Europe might carry home a new understanding that
would facilitate an adjustment. He took particular satisfaction in the presence of the first fraternal delegate from
German trade unionists. He enjoyed speaking again the
German language for which he had real affection and hearing intimate news of German labor. When in emergencies
he acted as interpreter for the German delegate, the words
of Peter Grassman lost nothing in spirit and individuality
and the convention manifested its pride and appreciation.

In three unusual ways was special honor shown Mr.
Gompers in the convention. On behalf of the International
Ladies' Garment Workers he was presented with a marble
bust of striking artistic merit for which he had given sit-
tings under the impression the bust was to be the property
of the International Ladies' Garment Workers; the convention authorized the creation of the Samuel Gompers Fellowship to be awarded alternately to Mexican and American
trade unionists affording opportunity to study for a year
the labor movement of the other country; and lastly it made
the autobiography he had written the official record of his
life for the American labor movement. Each manifestation
of regard in turn moved Mr. Gompers beyond power of
expression, but his silent emotion was eloquent token of his
appreciation. The Fellowship proposal had a distinctive
appropriateness in that Mr. Gompers had been an early
sponsor of workers' education and had championed the
Federation's undertaking through the Workers' Education
Bureau. With unusual emphasis he commended both to
the El Paso Convention and the Pan-American Congress in
Mexico the work and the progress of this bureau. Repeatedly he referred with mingled pride and humility to

the Fellowship and, despite the many things pressing on his attention in Mexico City, arranged for conferences with the Mexican Federation for agreement on practical details.

Though meeting again the friends who for years had worked with him in the labor movement and the beautiful spirit of the convention stimulated the mind and heart of the man until he seemed physically stronger, none of us on his personal staff was willing to influence him to go to Mexico. We realized the gratification that would be his in participating in the inauguration of General Calles and in again presiding over the Pan-American Congress which was primarily his vision. Many years of terrific fighting for ideals had left deep scars and it seemed only fair that he might have opportunity to enjoy the appreciation of those he had served. By evasions he warded off words of caution. From his doctors in New York whom he loved as friends in addition to his gratitude for prolonging his life, came a message not to go to Mexico. When it was read to him he sat silently as was his custom when making an important decision. One felt the power with which he concentrated upon the problem, weighing all aspects. In a few days he announced his determination to go to Mexico.

The Mexican Federation of Labor proposed to furnish a special train to take the delegates to the El Paso Convention to Mexico City, to extend hospitality while in the city and to carry them back again to the boundary. The trip afforded an extraordinary opportunity for representatives of American labor to see Mexico with all of its problems and possibilities. As the train moved southward through the deserts of Mexico there were glimpses of the most primitive conditions of life; though poverty and illiteracy were apparent everywhere in the groups of natives that met the train

at each stop, offering things to sell, nothing was offered that
did not have the marks in some degree of artistic creation.
Their buildings had a harmony of line, a distinctive adapta-
tion to the country, a suggestiveness, in marked contrast to
the utilitarian standards so completely dominating our sky-
scraper communities. Thus Mr. Gompers carried his labor
colleagues with him into the heart of Mexico that they
might learn for themselves the contribution which Mexican
labor can make to Pan-American labor and western civilization. It was a vision he got from a few Mexican cigarmakers in the 'nineties, and before passing he shared it with
hundreds that the work might be carried forward. At many
of the stations delegations of working men came to offer
their greeting. At the city of Aguascalientes, the governor-
elect of the state of Aguascalientes, a labor candidate, came
to pay his respects.

From the time he reached Mexico, Sunday morning,
November 30, 1924, Mr. Gompers began to give himself
without stint. He went at a pace that would have wearied
a well man. From the station he went almost immediately
to the stadium where the inauguration was to take place in
the open air. By special act of the Mexican Parliament
that ceremony occurred at noontime and in the open. It
was a brilliant, colorful, symbolic ceremony. Delegations
from all parts of Mexico arrived at the stations and
marched to the stadium. Many were bare-footed, others
in sandals, and the majority in picturesque native dress
with serapes and blankets. There were bands and military
groups. Into the stadium they marched in groups; the
political organizations with banners; the colors and banners
of the Mexican Labor Party everywhere mingled with the
colors of the Mexican Republic; each new delegation was

heralded by the music of bands. The stadium holding fifty thousand gradually filled with sustained dramatic effect that came from a building up of climaxes. Just before twelve began official arrivals—the two houses of Parliament; ambassadors and labor representatives curiously mingled and equally acclaimed; then Gompers, then Morones, the new Secretary of Industry, Commerce, and Labor, and the dramatic meeting on the central stage between these two men who had recently narrowly escaped death; then a marshaling of the American delegates to the Pan-American Federation of Labor—James Duncan, Frank Morrison, Mathew Woll, Martin Ryan and John Frey. Lastly, the stalwart, benign Calles, easily holding the attention of the assembled throng by simple dignity—that indefinable, gentle courtesy of one who loves his fellow men. Overhead aeroplanes circled; the air was gayly colored by confetti of red, black and green, with warm tropical sun rays gleaming through; flags waved everywhere; balloons were released from all quarters; how the crowd radiated happiness and seemed in spirit to surge toward Calles as with exultant *vivas* they hailed the first constitutional successor to the presidency. The brief inaugural ceremony heightened the dramatic feeling—standing in God's clear sunlight with his right hand raised upward, the President took the oath of office. Then from every part of the stadium hundreds of doves were released to hover over the crowd— a pledge of an era of peace. Everyone was on his feet singing, cheering, shouting; bands played and above all boomed the military salute.

The guest of honor in such an event was Samuel Gompers. That to him more than to any other one individual was due this Mexican achievement, was recognized in the distinguished honor paid him. Mexican labor hailed him as the prophet who had told them the way. During the years when Mexico looked to southern Europe for inspiration, his had been the voice of one crying in the wilderness. But Gompers was too truly the apostle of the cause of labor to let rebuffs deter him. He had a passion for men and labor was his religion. Because he wanted to help men to higher levels of life and thought, he yearned over those economically and socially disadvantaged, striving to help them to lay the practical foundations upon which higher levels of democracy might be reared. His purpose was to conquer material things in order that the spirit might be freed. His was no material goal, but he sought through the breaking down of unequal opportunities realization of the higher implications of democracy and progress toward the brotherhood of men. The spiritual motives that controlled his leadership stand out conspicuously in his relations with Mexican labor. It was his instinctive response to Mexican temperament.

It is gratifying to be appraised and valued at your highest spiritual value, and like a benediction came such appreciation to Samuel Gompers in his closing days. To those who remember the grieved look that came into his eyes after the World War, with its high acclaim for his service, when the tide of reaction beat against him and vicious epithets were hurled, it is good to know that in his last days he had fitting honor, respect, and understanding.

That Sunday evening after he had retired, thinking to conserve his strength, came a message from President Calles urgently requesting him to come to the diplomatic reception to be held in the Salon de Recepciones de Embajadores by the Secretary of Foreign Affairs. Hesitating at first, then reflecting on the nature of the occasion, he arose and went. In that gathering of ambassadors, officials, and dignitaries stood the old labor chief, a veteran crusader for humanity—extending one hand to Calles and the other to Obregon, he himself typifying the force that created the constitutional bridge between the administrations of the two presidents. Silently he looked from one to the other with emotions too deep for words. Momentarily there fell that hush by which we recognize that we are in the presence of that which escapes our words. But even in such surroundings the urge of the cause was upon him—it was about immediate undertakings for labor's welfare that he sought the co-operation of an ambassador.

Then came the reception of American labor representatives by President Calles in the National Palace after which he escorted them to the Sunken Gardens where luncheon was served. In that beautiful spot, the Mexican Venice, were welded new ideals of international relations and honor was accorded service in proportion to its intrinsic value. After the governmental representatives had gone, a heart-gripping incident came at sunset. A group of bare-foot peons approached the Chief, fell on their knees and embraced him, blessing him for what he had done for them and their country.

The next day came the opening of the Pan-American Congress. It was a small representative body but deeply mindful of its big task and responsibility. The opening meeting had a wide atmosphere of internationalism through the participation of fraternal delegates from Great Britain, Germany, and Canada. There was a fine spirit of fraternal co-operation but a tendency to delay which the Chief broke through with characteristic vigor. Something impelled him

to haste and he was impatient of each delay. A sidelight
on the nature of the problems in building up a Pan-American labor movement was revealed in the coming of a secret
commission from a Central-American country whose members dared not let their names be known or appear publicly
in the sessions. But they sought help to initiate their work.

With exquisite appropriateness it happened that Mr.
Gompers' last public speech which followed the speech of
C. T. Cramp, of the British Trade Union Congress, summarized the basis upon which constructive international
relations must be established, and was made in the hope
that the message would be carried overseas. He spoke with
unusual earnestness and force, for he was deeply moved.
After he had finished he sat down with a sigh of physical
exhaustion and turning to me—because he gave me the
privilege of sharing his hopes and plans for the international movement—he said: "I didn't intend to say so much,
but somehow I was impelled. I hope it will help."

The third day, Saturday, December 6, was his last day
of public service. On Sunday he seemed physically and
mentally depressed, resting in his room until afternoon
when he drove through the stately Paseo de la Reforma and
the beautiful grounds of Chapultepec, before he went to
hear Verdi's "Rigoletto" which, according to Mexican custom, began at five in the afternoon. At first he sat stiffly
and seemed to appreciate the music mentally only. He
commented on a few imperfections, and as the harmony
grew more fully rounded he relaxed and gave himself
physically and spiritually. The difference was perceptible.
After the beautiful aria in the third act he turned and said,
"I feel better now."

That evening we all noticed his feebleness. It was the

last time he walked among us. In the morning he was too ill to rise, but arranged to have Frank Morrison open the congress for him.

The last two days of the congress he was unable to attend, but he selected a colleague, Matthew Woll, to carry his last message to the Pan-American Federation of Labor, which was delivered in a way that made his spirit seem very close. As in El Paso there was the feeling in the congress that the time was very short in which the Chief would be with them and they wanted to use the opportunity to express their appreciation. The compelling insistence of Mexican labor for a meeting of the Federation in Washington in 1925 instead of 1926 was born of the hope that Gompers might again preside over its sessions.

Meanwhile the Chief grew no better. Additional doctors were called, but there was disagreement as to whether he should be moved at once. Travel arrangements were quickly made and held subject to the final decision. On Wednesday the majority of the doctors said, "Go at once."

So we made ready. As he watched the packing, the Chief in protest demanded his shoes and clothes. Though he rebelled at the idea of a stretcher, when the time came physical weakness made him yield. There was none who followed him out of the hotel without a premonition of dread. The crowd at the station was silent with trouble. Hardly had we got him in bed before there loomed in the doorway the sturdy, vigorous form of President Calles followed by Morones and other labor leaders who with deeply troubled hearts came to bid him farewell. The warmth of their love and respect came as a call to service and again the spirit conquered physical weakness. A new radiant strength seemed for the time to ease the pain of a failing heart. With this encouragement began our anxious journey to a lower altitude and American soil. As we first climbed the mountain heights preparatory to regaining lower levels, with hesitation we sought reports from the sick-room. The first night he seemed to hold his own. On the second day as we passed through the marvelously deep purple shadows of the mountains, his breathing was distressingly painful. Friday morning we reached Laredo. Because we were on American soil, we again allowed ourselves hope. We knew what America was to him. Government officials and railway representatives rendered every courtesy and service, and we hastened to San Antonio intending there to wage the same sort of resistance with which Sam Houston defended the Alamo. Whatever the results of the vigil we knew there would be a new significance to the gavel presented to him at El Paso which had been fashioned out of wood of the spreading elm under which Sam Houston made his first treaty with the Indians. There were throngs of anxious people at the station to meet his train. This time he rose in rebellion against the stretcher and tried to walk out, but we dared not let him tax his heart. Other doctors were called, and in the evening came the consultation. All the doctors talked frankly, telling us how his heart had weakened. Then the doctor in charge prepared a bulletin which did not extend substantial encouragement. The comment of the chief consulting physician, "That is too optimistic," prepared us for the change of the early morning.

In order to relieve Mr. Gompers' nurse who had been on duty almost constantly for three days, another nurse was brought in and absolute quiet ordered, so that Mr. Gompers might sleep. About one-thirty I asked the nurse if he was asleep. "No, he keeps making speeches," she said, and continued preparations for a second injection of morphine which had been ordered in case the first one failed to bring sleep. About two-thirty I was awakened by the nurse, "Come, Mr. Gompers is very low."

Both nurses were with him and the breathing was very difficult. His friends and colleagues quickly responded to the call. The nurse gave them the paper on which she had written down his last words. The room was large so there was space for all. The doctors came and made ready to follow the course agreed upon—bleeding to relieve the heart. The blood seem to congeal almost as quickly as it trickled into the vessel. The breathing became less labored and peace came to his face. The doctors stepped back— their work was done—there was only a gentle sigh or two and the Chief had passed out into The Silence.

Then friends and colleagues temporarily put from their minds thought of the sorrow which was to be with them for many a to-morrow, to make the plans necessary to take home the body of him whom millions desired to honor. In death he belonged not to a few but to the movement and the nation he served. The American Federation of Labor asked and was given full charge of his funeral. The tender messages, the flowers, the offers of assistance that followed quickly were eloquent testimony of the scope of his interests and service. The Sam Houston Post offered military escort and caisson and asked the privilege of giving a flag for his coffin, "For he was the Army's friend in a time of deep need." The Federal Immigration Service, the local labor movement, railroad representatives, the Mexican Consul and individuals sought opportunities to help. President Calles, who had insistently demanded reports at each railway stop, sent messages and flowers. All that day there was a steady tide of pilgrims drawn by the still figure of him who symbolized a great cause for humanity.

Late in the evening as his friends and colleagues prepared to go with him to the train to begin the long journey eastward, the streets were lined with reverent crowds who bared their heads at the sound of the funeral dirge and stood silently until the caisson had passed with its flag-draped casket.

As the train sped eastward over plain and prairie, men along the way and in track gangs catching sight of the black-draped train with its flower-massed room in which the casket was placed, with bared heads stood in silent tribute. At every station where it was possible, the gathered crowds were permitted to pass through for a last look at the leader whose name was known wherever the problems of labor had developed. As they came bearing beautiful floral tributes, two labor men who stood as the guard of honor, saw many touching scenes before the casket. At stops where the Baltimore and Ohio railway shops were, the entire force was given time for the tribute they desired. Six governors, many city officials, and thousands of men, women and children came in the groups along the way. From Cincinnati on, labor officials began joining the funeral train.

Meanwhile back in Washington his confidential secretary who had served him for twenty-five years and who by force of circumstances had been prevented from being with the Chief in his last hours, joined with a group of labor officials in a last personal service—that of preparing to receive him in labor's building which had been his heart's home. Day and night they worked, co-ordinating into a perfect plan generous offers of assistance from all sides.

The President's room in the Washington station was opened to Samuel Gompers—private citizen and one-time immigrant lad. The War Department sent military escort. The District Commissioners and police offered every co-operation. Thus labor carried back to its own threshold the Chief it loved and revered and placed him among masses of flowers, with the American flag he had yearly taken to labor's convention and near the bust presented him at the El Paso Convention, to rest in the House of Labor for the last time. It was the building he loved and which was to him a symbol of labor's constructive achievement.

From Washington the mourning draped train moved on to New York—the city Samuel Gompers loved so well. Not since the days of Lincoln's last journey had there been such a continent-wide outpouring of human sympathy and love as followed Samuel Gompers on what grew to be a triumphal journey to the grave. His was a life of service and love for his fellow men. He cared nothing for what the world calls success, and ignoring office, wealth, preferment, he reached for that higher thing which in death was shown to be of eternal value.

In New York the casket was carried to the Elks' Lodge Room which had given him asylum in the dark days when blighting hands sought to wrench from him his good name. There for a day he lay surrounded by exquisite flowers— for a day to belong to the New York that he learned to love, when as an active black-haired boy he began testing its resources and found that which became his life work. Many came to pay last tribute of love and respect.

The simple funeral on the following day conducted by Rabbi Stephen S. Wise, to whose faith Mr. Gompers' forbears belonged, was a beautiful recognition of his high service and ideals immortalizing his last words, "God bless our American institutions. May they grow better day by day." After a brief statement by his life-long colleague, James Duncan, the Elks' ritual concluded the service. During the long ride to Sleepy Hollow cemetery, there came again that spontaneous sincere tribute from those lining the streets and roads through which his body was carried. With the masonic ritual the casket was lowered to its last resting place.

As his body was given back to earth, throughout this country and many foreign lands, industry and commerce were stopped for a period in silent homage to him whose name was known and honored the world around because he gave his life in service for others. The United States Senate turned from other matters to consider his work and life; the Mexican Parliament and that of the Philippines did likewise. Flags were ordered half-mast in many lands. An extraordinary personality had passed from this world's work.

But the soul of Samuel Gompers lives in its potent influence on national life and customs. It lives in the daily lives of millions of Americans, in the higher standards of life and work generally prevailing; in the higher concept of duty which man owes to those with whom he works and for whom he works; in our enriched understanding of human justice; in an understanding of the finer effects of democracy in daily life; in the realization that human brotherhood is after all a thoroughly practical ideal and the only lasting basis for human relations.

His permanent record is written in the Book of Life and his death disclosed the magnitude of his work. The quality of his long leadership appeared again and again in

his absolute banishment of personal concern in decisions
of policy. Neither friend nor self influenced these decisions,
and in death his thought was only for that through which
he realized his religion—the labor movement.

FLORENCE CALVERT THORNE.

WASHINGTON, D. C.
January, 8, 1925.

INDEX

Abbott, Lyman, member Advisory Board, Social Reform Club, i 434

Abolition, supported by English workers, i 21

Abolitionists, carry story of anti-slavery struggle to England, i 20

Abrahams, Henry, first president Massachusetts state body, i 286; i 337

Actors' Equity Association, strike, i 474-5

Adams, Charles Francis, member of public group, Division of Conciliation and Mediation, National Civic Federation, ii 118; Miners' strike 1902, ii 121

Adamson Eight-hour Law, approved, ii 144; ii 146

Addams, Jane, i 481; i 490

Adler, Felix, founder Ethical Culture Society, i 433; member Advisory Board, Social Reform Club, i 434; People's Institute, i 436

Administration, Board of; see Cigarmakers

Advisory Commission; see Council of National Defense

Afel, launching of, ii 375

Agreements, i 166

Agricultural Conference, G. appointed to, i 554; ii 521

Agricultural Laborers, conference on Italian emigration (Rome, 1909), ii 58

Agriculture, International Institute of, aided by G., i 449; work of David Lubin, i 450-51; i 453

Aladyn, Alexis, asks assistance for Russian workingmen, ii 47-48

Alarm, The, i 293

Albert, King (Belgium), receives American Labor Mission, ii 447-48; regrets inability to meet Labor Peace Mission, ii 488

Aldrich, Senator, uses influence to withhold proceedings Labor Investigating Committee, i 446

Aldrich, Representative, voted against Labor's amendment to Trust bill, ii 239

Alger, George W., author of *Moral Overstrain,* i 528

Allen, Dr. J. S., ii 253

Allen, Representative H. D., voted against Labor's amendment to Trust bill, ii 239

Allen, Henry J., ii 149

Allen, James, i 91

Allen, Jos., organizer of the United Garment Workers, i 102

Allen, Senator, ii 136

Allison, Senator, manifests interest in workingmen's side of tariff issue, i 185-6

Alpine, John R., G. talks over Stockholm proposal with, ii 395; representative of American labor at Paris Labor Conference, ii 475

Alvarado, Governor, sends two labor men to confer with G., ii 313

Alward, Thomas, tells G. story of Cuban Secret Service, ii 66-67

Amalgamated Trades and Labor Union, aids Cigarmakers' strike (1877), i 152; i 154; co-operates in tenement campaign, i 187; promotes new federation, i 231; i 243

American Alliance for Labor and Democracy, formation of, ii 380;

Hawkes, V. F., i 314

Hayes, Dennis A., G. becomes acquainted with, i 374

Hayes, Everis A., ii 251

Hayes, Max S., congratulates G. for stand against ship subsidy, ii 95; G.'s correspondence on Socialism with, ii 509

Hayes, J. W., i 267; compared with Schonfaber, i 283

Hayes, Rutherford B., G.'s meeting with, i 518–19

Hayes, Mrs. Rutherford B., i 518

Haymarket Square, i 293–94; bomb destroys eight-hour effort, ii 178–81

Hays, Frank, consults Madero upon organization of Mexican miners, ii 311

Haywood, William, i 424

Hazeltine, M. W., reviews in *New York Sun* read by G., i 80

Health Board, white-washing report on tenement cigar production, i 113

Health Department, New York, i 187

Healy, David, friend of tenement bill, i 193

Hearst, William Randolph, gives $1,000 for striking miners, ii 121; anti-Mexican propaganda, ii 310

Hebrew Trades, United, ii 378; *see* Jewish workers, also ii 153; ii 378; ii 379

Heine, i 189

Heltmann, William, i 189

Henderson, Arthur, difference with Lloyd George over Russian question, ii 396; advocates "negotiated peace," ii 396; asks Federation send representation Inter-Allied conference (1918), ii 403; gives corrected copy of G.'s cablegram to press, ii 404; advocate of Stockholm idea, ii 404; ii 407; arranges Allied Labor Conference, ii 409; ii 419–21; ii 426; begs John Frey to intercede for him with G., ii 431; ii 470; seeks international labor leadership, ii 477; cables G. on labor conference, ii 480–1; ii 485

Hennessey, P. J., i 94

Henry, Representative, i 541–2

Hepburn, Wm. P., ii 251

Herald, New York, i 320; i 517

Hermann, Paul, on committee to negotiate with Levy Brothers, i 247; with G. editor of the *Picket,* i 249; designs type for *Picket,* i 251

Herrman, Fatty, fellow employe at Hutchinson's, i 67–68

Herrick, Myron T., served on G.'s War Labor Committee, ii 362

Hewitt-George debate, letters published in press, i 315–16

Hewitt, Abram S., suggests tax on tenement-made goods, i 183–4; democratic candidate against George, i 315; G. campaigns against, i 316–17; G. warns, i 319; Republicans advised to vote for, i 319; associated, People's Institute, i 436; relation to Peter Cooper, i 444; chairman Labor Investigating Commission, i 444; commends Strasser on case before L. I. C., i 446

Higgins, Edwin W., ii 251

Higgins strike, i 245

Hill, David B., asked to pardon Theiss boycotters, i 314; rejected for temporary chairman of the 1896 Democratic Convention, ii 86; through assistance of G. lays information before Senate committee on bad practices, New York Bureau of Immigration, ii 158

Hill, J. J., member of New York Positivists, i 104

Hillman, Carl, author of *Emancipationswincke,* i 75

Hillquit, Morris, i 383

Hindenburg, ii 461

Hirsch Fund, Baron, G.'s co-operation with, ii 45

Hirsh, David, cigar manufacturer